Freud and t..
Question of Pseudoscience

Freud and the Question of Pseudoscience

FRANK CIOFFI

OPEN COURT
Chicago and La Salle, Illinois

**To order books from Open Court,
call toll-free 1-800-815-2280.**

Open Court Publishing Company is a division of Carus Publishing Company

Copyright © 1998 by Carus Publishing Company

First printing 1998

Printed and bound in the United States of America.

Library of Congress Cataloging-in-Publication Data

Cioffi, Frank.
    Freud and the question of pseudoscience / Frank Cioffi.
      p. cm.
    Includes bibliographical references and index.
    ISBN 0-8126-9385-X (pbk. : alk. paper)
    1. Psychoanalysis. 2. Freud, Sigmund, 1856–1939. I. Title.
BF 173.C495   1998
150.19'52'092—DC21   98-26764
                                             CIP

For Nalini

Contents

Preface   ix

1   Why Are We Still Arguing about Freud?   1

2   Wittgenstein's Freud   93

3   Freud and the Idea of a Pseudoscience   115

4   Wollheim on Freud   143

5   The Myth of Freud's Hostile Reception   161

6   Symptoms, Wishes, and Actions   182

7   Was Freud a Liar?   199

8   From Freud's 'Scientific Fairy Tale' to Masson's Politically
    Correct One   205

9   Psychoanalysis, Pseudoscience, and Testability   210

10 'Exegetical Myth-Making' in Grünbaum's Indictment of
    Popper and Exoneration of Freud   240

11 Explanation and Biography: A Conversation   265

12 Through the Psychoanalytoscope: Bouveresse on
    Wittgenstein's Freud   280

13 A Final Accounting   288

Index   301

Preface

The first paper in this book, 'Why Are We Still Arguing about Freud?', was written especially for it. The others first appeared in collections or journals. They have been lightly edited in the interests of clarity but except for the removal of a few exegetical errors they appear as they were published. The order in which they appear is that in which I wrote them, with the exception of 'From Freud's "Scientific Fairy Tale" to Masson's Politically Correct One' which I have placed immediately after 'Was Freud a Liar?' since both deal with Freud's seduction theory.

I should like to acknowledge the help and encouragement of Frederick Crews, Allen Esterson, David Ellis, Edward Greenwood, Nick Bunnin, Sagar Nair, Frank L. Cioffi, and 'Lord' Harry MacFarquhar. I want also to express my appreciation to the personnel of the Library Enquiries desk and the Documentation Delivery Office of the University of Kent at Canterbury.

1

Why Are We Still Arguing About Freud?[1]

Consider some of the damaging charges that have been brought against Freud in recent years: that he lied about his role in promoting the use of cocaine for morphine addiction; that he propagated false and demeaning stories about Breuer's grounds for aborting their collaboration; that he boasted in 1898 of 'innumerable' therapeutic successes which were nonexistent; that having concealed for eight years that his imputation of infantile molestations to his patients was a mistake, he then falsely boasted of having discovered how to distinguish the aftermath of genuine molestations from the aftermath of fancied ones; that he gave distorted and self-serving accounts of the procedure which led him to mistakenly impute molestations in the first place and that he did this to obscure the fact that it was the same procedure on which he based his 'discovery' of the Oedipus complex and infantile polymorphous perversity; that in order to undercut the objection that apparent clinical corroboration of his theories was due to his patient's compliance he falsely denied that he had formulated these theories before his patients corroborated them; that he claimed to have validated his theses concerning infantile sexuality 'in every detail' by independent investigations of infantile behaviour, which had in fact never been undertaken; that while publicly insisting that his grounds for the privileged etiological role of sexuality were purely empirical and forced on him by his clinical experience, he privately acknowledged that they were *a priori* assumptions that he was unwilling to dispense with; that a careful scrutiny of his texts

This essay appears for the first time in this volume.

1. The following abbreviations are used throughout this chapter: *CP, Collected Papers; IL, Introductory Lectures; NIL, New Introductory Lectures; S.E., Standard Edition of the Complete Psychological Works of Sigmund Freud; Life, Sigmund Freud: Life and Work* by Ernest Jones.

reveal inconsistencies so gross that they point to a profoundly opportunistic cast of mind.

Now, what has been the response of a vocal and influential segment of the intellectual and academic community to this barrage of accusations? 'Nobody's perfect.'

It is then not unusual for Freud's misbehaviours to be mitigated still further by claims that the criticisms raised, whether justified or not, are of little interest since Freud's positive legacy outweighs any reservations that a more critical scrutiny of his texts and conduct than has been customary, entails. The oddity of this trend in Freudian apologetic can be brought out by an analogy. It is as if someone were to say 'There are people who claim that Marilyn Monroe had a big wart on her nose. Well, maybe she did and maybe she didn't, but aren't they ashamed to be introducing such considerations into the discussion of a warm, lovely person like Marilyn?' Wouldn't you be utterly bewildered by such a response? Wouldn't your curiosity be directed to the question of whether Marilyn Monroe really did have a big wart on her nose and, if so, how this came to be overlooked and, if not, how the delusion that she did arose? Yet an insistence that this is of little interest is a quite common response to the disquieting revelations that careful examination of Freud's clinical methods, and disputatious practices in general, produces.

This genre of apologetic obscures the fact that the charge is not just that Freud rigged evidence but that he rigged it in full view, and so the connivance, perhaps even collusion, of his partisans must be allotted a major role in the idealisations and falsifications which triumphed and have held the field for almost a century. They cannot plausibly plead, as with the Gulags, say, that the Gulags were thousands of miles away and so ignorance of them could be extenuated—the case for doubting Freud's *bona fides* as a genuine truth-seeker has for long lain on our library shelves under his own name and was accessible to all.

A mischievous result of the tactic of conceding this and, nevertheless, deflecting attention to some sublime but latent subtext is that it has permitted the precise nature of the case against the traditional view to go unexamined and so put its cogency in question. One risk of deflecting attention from a manifestly tendentious text to a sublime subtext is that the text will then go marching on. And this is what has happened. The delusion, shared by Erik Erikson, Peter Gay, Janet Malcolm, Adolf Grünbaum, Frank Sulloway and many others, that Freud based his seduction theory on confessions made by his patients illustrates how much that is ostentatiously baseless still circulates. Though there is no harm in discussing the diplomatic achievements of Richard Nixon rather than the Watergate cover-up, since there is now no risk that the upshot of such discussions will be to leave it in doubt that Nixon was involved in the Watergate cover-up, this is not the case with the legends surrounding psychoanalysis where it is still usual for ostensibly authoritative commentators, like those mentioned above, to repeat views which an hour in a library would have shown to be unsustainable (see 'Was Freud a Liar?' and '"Exegetical Myth-Making"' in this volume).

However, there is a more robust defense of Freud which does not retreat to a sublime subtext and finds little in the text which requires extenuation. There was no wart. Let us begin by examining this more traditional mode of apologetic. How are we to account for the fact that after almost a century of discussion there are those who see in Freudian psychoanalysis the greatest contribution to human understanding of our time and others who see it as the 'most stupendous intellectual confidence trick of the twentieth century' (Peter Medawar)?

The most appealing solution to this century-old dispute as to the credibility of Freudian theory is the cross-purposes one. Freud was prolific of ideas and perhaps we are dealing with a phenomenon like that of the blind men and the elephant. Each has seized a distinct part of the creature and is characterising that which he holds correctly. This is no doubt sometimes the case but it cannot account for those occasions when presumably the same segment of the total oeuvre is in view as, for example, in the divergent estimates of Freud's case histories.

In the NYU Symposium of 1959 Jacob Arlow recommended Freud's case histories as the sovereign remedy for skeptical doubt. Two contemporary analysts hold Freud's case histories to be 'a record of the human mind in one of its most unparalleled works of scientific discovery.'[2] Kurt Eissler called Freud's five case histories the 'pillars on which psychoanalysis as an empirical science rests'.[3] Yet on their publication in English in 1925 a reviewer wrote that Freud's 'case histories show a persistence in the application of a few fixed ideas which is almost terrible . . . To support his interpretations he will seize upon details of an almost unbelievable triviality, and attach to them meanings so far fetched as to pass the bounds of sanity.'[4] Similar views have been expressed by others. Thomas Szasz felt justified in speaking of Freud's 'fake case histories.'[5] And this view has even penetrated the ranks of apologists. In 1983 Janet Malcolm, though stalwart in her defense of the pretensions of psychoanalysis, tells us that, '(Freud's) case histories have probably done more to discredit psychoanalysis than any other single aspect of the profession . . . Of all Freud's writings they are the most dated and quaint, the most vulnerable, the least instructive.'[6] (Who would

---

2. Mark Kanzer and Jules Glenn, eds., *Freud and His Patients* (New York: Jason Aronson, 1980), p. 43.

3. *Medical Orthodoxy and the Future of Psychoanalysis* (International Universities Press, 1965), p. 395.

4. *Times Literary Supplement* (10 September 1925).

5. T. Szasz, *Anti-Freud* (University of Syracuse, 1990), p. xii.

6. Janet Malcolm, 'Six Roses on Cirrhose?' *New Yorker* (24 January 1983), pp. 96–106.

ever have thought that when the wolves began gaining it would be Freud who would be thrown from the sled?)

The hope that the disputants might have different case histories in mind also turns out to be unsustainable. Geoffrey Gorer said of the Wolf Man case history that 'for most of his readers the evidence of this case proved the crucial importance of the sexual experiences and fantasies of early childhood for the development of the neurosis in childhood and in adult life.'[7] Kurt Eissler asked rhetorically how many, after sixty years, had been able to produce a reconstruction of childhood history that can rival Freud's case history of the Wolf Man, a view in which John Forrester concurs.[8] The Rat Man case also has its admirers, Clark Glymour writes, 'The Rat Man case is . . . largely cogent, free of obvious indoctrination of the patient and has rather few arbitrary conclusions within it . . .'[9] John Kerr describes the Rat Man case as 'a stunning demonstration of the method and a matchless psychological study in its own right.'[10] Marshall Edelson thinks that both the Rat Man and the Wolf Man are models of good explanation.[11] Yet it was the Rat Man case in particular to which the TLS reviewer was referring.

How are these divergent estimates of Freud's case histories, and Freudian case histories in general, to be accounted for? There is a straightforward but ultimately mistaken answer to this question. It is that Freud's case histories are condemned because the etiologies they are invoked in support of are untestable; and because they are untestable they are pseudoscientific. I will argue that though Freud's etiologies are often untestable they are not pseudoscientific on that account alone and that we must look elsewhere for adequate grounds on which they might be condemned. However, the untestability of Freud's theories, and his infantile etiology in particular, has been so often denied that it warrants separate consideration.

Is Freudian Theory Testable?

Adolf Grünbaum's answer to this question is a notoriously resounding 'Yes'. But there are good reasons for discounting it. Grünbaum seems to have two criteria for the interest of a problem, one is that it have been previously addressed by Karl Popper, and the other that it have been wrongly resolved by him. Only so can we account for the way he handles the question of the testability of Freudian theory and its bearing on the charge of pseudoscience. He construes the testability question as whether the 'Freudian cor-

7. Review of Muriel Gardiner, ed., *The Wolf-Man and Sigmund Freud. The Observer Review* (London, 30 January 1972).

8. *The Seductions of Psychoanalysis* (Cambridge University Press, 1990), p. 207.

9. *Theory and Evidence* (Princeton University Press, 1980), p. 265.

10. Cited by Crews in *The Memory Wars,* from *A Most Dangerous Method* (Alfred Knopf, 1993), p. 184.

11. *Psychoanalysis: A Theory in Crisis* (University of Chicago Press, 1990), p. 357.

pus' contains any statements with observable implications. He gives no independent account of how the issue of untestability is related to that of pseudoscience but takes over what he believes to be Popper's view, assuming, mistakenly, that Popper holds untestability to be a necessary condition of pseudoscience and so a demonstration that the theory is testable is all that is necessary to rebut the charge.[12] Moreover, when Grünbaum chooses an example with which to demonstrate the testability of Freudian theory he ignores those theses against which the charge has traditionally been lodged. Nowhere does he mention anyone other than Popper who has objected to the untestability of Freudian theory and his book must be unique in failing to include in its index the most common ground for this complaint—the libido concept.

There is a another, distinct, source of Grünbaum's conviction that Freudian theory is testable. It lies in what might be dubbed his Swiss bank vault conception of testability. He argues that the failure of critics to work out what would count against the theory is perfectly compatible with its testability since the advocates of the theory may, nevertheless, meet the challenge by belatedly producing statements which are observable implications of the theory, just as someone might ultimately vindicate a claim by extracting a legal document from a secret safe deposit box.[13] But this can't be the only source of the conclusion that Freudian theory is testable, because the Popperian, J.O. Wisdom, also maintains this.

Potential Non-Instantiation Confused with Potential Falsification

An argument for the testability of Freud's theory of errors is advanced by J.O. Wisdom, in his exposition of Popper's philosophy of science, but it depends on a confusion of falsification with non-instantiation.[14] J.O. Wisdom thinks he has demonstrated the falsifiability of Freud's theory of errors by citing a case of memory failure which, though it initially looked unaccountable in Freudian terms, nevertheless, turned out to yield an association which made the memory lapse intelligible. But what he is supposed to be showing is that the theory is capable of falsification and not just that what proved a positive instance need not have done so. Since the failure to

---

12. Popper himself is not entirely blameless in this. In his replies in the Schilpp volume, *The Philosophy of Karl Popper* (La Salle, Illinois: Open Court, 1974), he writes: 'My criticism of Freud's theory was simply that it did not have potential falsifiers.' (p. 983) Popper is mistaken. His criticism of Freud's theory was not 'simply that it did not have potential falsifiers.' (See 'Psychoanalysis, Pseudoscience, and Testability', chapter 9 in this volume).

13. 'I reject the hubristic expectation that, if high-level psychoanalytic hypotheses are testable at all, than almost any intellectually gifted academic ought to be able to devise potentially falsifying test designs for them.' *Foundations of Psychoanalysis* (University of California Press, 1984), p. 113.

14. *Foundations of Inference in Natural Science* (Methuen, 1952).

produce an explanatory association could not have shown the theory to be false but merely that the instance had disappointed the expectation or hope that it would prove a positive one the falsifiability of the theory had not been demonstrated. Wisdom's defective proof involves a mistake which is very general, that of confounding the disappointment of the expectation that an as yet unexamined instance will prove to be positive, with the falsification of the generalisation of which it may prove an instance. The expectation that an instance will turn out to be positive may be disappointed without it being the case that the generalisation of which it is an instance was capable of being falsified by it. There is an asymmetry between instantiation and falsi-fication. If an analyst suspects that a patient has repressed homo-erotic impulses, and the patient, at a later stage in the analysis, reports his first experience of intense sexual arousal at the thought of making love to men, this would support the analyst's suspicion in a way in which the failure of the patient to produce such an experience could not refute it.[15] The question how a patient must behave in order to warrant our assigning him an uncon-scious complex is more readily answered than the question how he must behave to rule out the possibility of his having that same complex.

One of the questions Grünbaum fails to address was raised well over half a century ago by Max Scheler: 'What we look for in vain in Freud is any pre-cise indication of the way in which a justifiable and necessary "control" of libido and the sexual instinct differs from that "repression" of the same, which he considers to be a primary source of mental illness; nor do we find any definite account of the differentiating conditions under which repression of libido is said in the one case to make for "sublimation", and in the other to result in "disease".'[16] Grünbaum is of course entitled to hope that once the Freudian safe deposit box is opened we will know how to resolve this issue but, in the meantime, the theory is untestable (though not on that account alone pseudoscientific).

The Inadequacy of Untestability as a Criterion of Pseudoscience

The untestability of a theory does not show that it is pseudoscientific and its testability does not show that it is not. If the issue of testability were decid-able by quotation-mongering, in the way Grünbaum's procedure suggests, then it can be decided against him by citing Freud's comment on dream interpretation in the *New Introductory Lectures,* 'All dreams are meaningful

---

15. Lewis Wolpert makes this asymmetry point in a discussion of Grünbaum's criticism of Popper in *The Unnatural Nature of Science* (Faber and Faber, 1992, pp. 131–32). It would be typical of Grünbaum to object that the patient's homo-erotic feelings were due to the analyst's suggestion but if sexual arousal could be suggested in this way it is a wonder neglected spouses do not resort to it more often.

16. *The Nature of Sympathy* (London: Routledge, 1954), p. 208.

though not all dreams can be interpreted,'[17] and in the *Outline*, 'it is often hard to detect the unconscious motive force and its wish-fulfillment but we may assume it is always there.'[18] 'The neuroses have no psychical content peculiar to them . . . neurotics fall ill of the same complexes against which we healthy people struggle as well. Whether that struggle ends in health or neurosis depends on quantitative considerations, on the relative strengths of the conflicting forces.'[19]

If these claims do not illustrate untestability—even in Grünbaum's unnaturally restricted sense—where is untestability to be found? Nevertheless, on my view of the nature of the issue this does not decide the question of pseudoscience against Freud since it need amount to no more than candid unfalsifiability and so, though it underdetermines expectation, it need not mislead it.

Underdetermining Expectation Distinguished from Misleading It

Critics sometimes conflate their objection to the unfalsifiability of Freudian theory with their objection to spurious claims that it has been confirmed. Is the unfalsifiability of a theory a sufficiently strong ground for considering the theory pseudoscientific? Isn't what is really objectionable the combination of *de facto* unfalsifiability with the implication that the theory has been tested and thus is worthy of credence? A believer in astrology who maintains that though, as astrology teaches, 'the fault is in our stars/that we are underlings,' it is not yet in a position to say *which* stars, although he is advancing an untestable thesis, ought not to be conflated with someone who casts horoscopes. The latter has passed from an astrology which underdetermines expectation to one which, because it *appears* determinate with respect to conditions of falsification, actively misleads it. It is to call attention to this feature of apparent but delusory falsifiability of a theory that the term pseudoscientific is often employed. Our attitude toward someone who admits from the start that, given the complexity of the conditions of neuroses, say, what might count against his theory is beyond our current powers of detection, is quite different from that we would take towards someone who behaved as though his theory were one which had been submitted to testing and survived, and only under the pressure of contradiction conceded that its state of development was such as to preclude falsification. In the latter case he has misled expectation and not merely underdetermined it.

---

17. Hogarth, 1949, p. 1.
18. *Outline of Psychoanalysis*, Hogarth, 1949, p. 33.
19. 'Five Lectures on Psychoanalysis' in *Two Short Accounts of Psychoanalysis* (Penguin, 1962), p. 82.

So, though misleading expectation is a graver offence than underdetermining it, the distinction is often obscured by the form of our complaints when we complain *tout court* of 'untestability'. To get a grasp of the relative gravity of these two defects—misleading expectation and underdetermining it—consider some notorious specimens of oracular prophecy: When Croesus consulted the oracle at Delphi as to whether he should attack the Egyptians he was told that if he did 'a mighty empire would be destroyed'. He attacked the Egyptians and the mighty empire that was destroyed proved to be his own. When Pyrrhus under analogous circumstances consulted his oracle it intoned 'Pyrrhus the Romans shall, I say, subdue.' The grammar of the sentence obscured the fact that it was compatible with the Romans subduing Pyrrhus which is what happened. Nero thought he had been told he would reign till he was 73 but instead he was deposed by the 73-year-old Galba. When all the Delphic oracle told Alexander was that 'The bull is garlanded for the sacrifice' he was annoyed at its obscurity. Now, which of these supplicants for counsel had the greatest grounds for complaint against the oracle? Pyrrhus and Croesus and Nero, whose expectations they misled or Alexander, whose expectations they merely underdetermined? An example of misled expectation is that of the religious cult leader who, when the Kingdom of Heaven failed to begin on the date he had predicted, declared that it had begun invisibly. The chagrin of his followers would have been much mitigated if he had declared at the outset that at the given date the Kingdom would be established, if not visibly then invisibly (though such candour would no doubt have diminished his following).

That the untestability complaint against Freud is that it misleads rather than merely underdetermines expectation can be shown by considering the difference it makes to our judgement whether we are dealing with one or the other. Those who took Freud's invocation of the pathogenic effects of repressed libido to be verbiage from the start have lesser ground for complaint than those who expected that reform of the sexual code and their own indulgent treatment of their children's burgeoning sexuality would influence the incidence of neurosis. The complaint which was repeatedly lodged against Freud's pronouncements on the role of sexuality in the neuroses was not that 'the Tarskian consequence class of the theory' was without observable conditions, as Grünbaum puts it,[20] but that it misled expectation.

To resolve charges of deception it would be necessary to determine whether the later statements of the theory, which deny that falsification reports bear on it, are elucidations of its prior content or emendations of this content and, if emendations, whether the purpose of the emendations is to evade the admission of error and its implications. But exploiting the ambiguity of its terms is only one way of creating the impression that a theory

---

20. *Foundations of Psychoanalysis* (University of California Press, 1984), p. 113.

had passed tests when it had not. There is also the ambiguity of the epistemic terms in which the theory is recommended—for example, 'confirmed'. This ambiguity leaves many who accept the theory with the impression that it has been investigated in a more rigorous manner than has really been the case. But here too the reply can be made that they have misunderstood the conventions of exposition which govern pronouncements on the status of the theory.

The genre of issue involved is illustrated by the complaint of the classical scholar, Hugh Lloyd Jones, that in reading Tacitus's account of the burning of Rome he came away with the impression that Tacitus lays the blame on Nero but that when he referred back to the text he could not find any explicit statement to this effect, though the impression lingered. Was Tacitus being cagey? In any case this 'Tacitus effect' is continuous with what has been described in testimony before a congressional committee in connection with the Iran-Contra affair as 'plausible deniability'—the deliberate use of language which will contrive to convey an impression which is not so strictly linked to the words used that it cannot be denied if the need arises.

In his introduction to his *Critical Dictionary of Psychoanalysis* Charles Rycroft gives an example of the Lloyd Jones/Tacitus effect which may or may not also be an example of 'plausible deniability': 'Psychoanalysts attempt to explain phenomena encountered during treatment by reference to presumed events in the patient's past . . . without, as a rule, reference to any documentary or hearsay extra-analytical evidence that may be available . . . The unwary reader who does not realise this may, as a result, be led astray, since it may not occur to him that a chapter entitled, say "The Emotional Development of the Child" may be expressing ideas derived from the psychoanalytical treatment of grown-ups and not from direct experience of children . . .'[21] But might not the capacity of Freud's etiology to mislead be due to a failure of understanding on the part of those misled? The question whether analysts were conveying a false impression of the adequacy of their evidence transcends the issue of the falsifiability of their claims. The pertinent question is not 'Are Freud's speculations as to the infantile sources of neuroses formally testable?—do they have *entertainable* falsifiers?—but 'Is the repeated claim that they have survived prolonged enquiry warranted?'—did they have *ascertainable* ones?

The major ground for impugning Freud's status as a *bona fide* enquirer is not just that we are often at a loss to imagine ways of determining the truth of what he says. For if we had a situation in which, though credence to unfalsifiable theses is solicited, no confirmations (failed attempts at falsification) are claimed on its behalf, would we still want to call it a

---

21. Charles Rycroft, *A Critical Dictionary of Psychoanalysis* (London: Nelson, 1968), pp. XII–XXIII.

pseudoscience? Why shouldn't some find the balefulness of frustrated sexuality *a priori* plausible before anyone had designed a procedure for testing it? In fact thousands have. Don't we want to mark the difference between the unwarranted claim that 'If there were exceptions they would have been discovered by now' and the candid admission, 'Though we have sound theoretical reasons for doubting that there are real exceptions, unfortunately, at the moment we have no way of showing this.'?

Why Falsifiability Need Not Exonerate

Can we argue that though Freud did produce both spurious instatiation reports and spurious test survival reports and that these were due to tendentiousness, this is not an adequate reason for considering his theory pseudoscientific since his claims are, nevertheless, falsifiable *'in principle'*? Not if we want to go to heaven.

Falsification-Evasion as a Criterion of Pseudoscience

If a theorist refuses to abandon a theory in the face of falsification reports shall we call him a pseudoscientist on this score alone? Better not. I will attempt to show that when falsification evasion is invoked, though the appeal may appear to be the violation of some determinate rule about when capitulation is called for, all that is really available is a hoped-for consensus among informed and disinterested observers. The paleontologist Stephen Jay Gould in a critique of nineteenth-century racist anthropologists, spoke of their 'fudging and finagling.' It is unlikely that there is an algorithm for this. In a discussion of whether states of mind can be unconscious William James described its advocates' response to objections as 'sapping and mining the region roundabout until it is a bog of logical liquefaction into the midst of which all definite conclusions of any sort can be rusted ere long to sink and disappear.'[22] It is categories akin to Gould's 'fudging and finagling' and James's creation of 'bogs of logical liquefaction' that seem to be the appropriate ones in dealing with Freudian accounts of why apparent falsifications are not really such.

Here are some familiar intuitively-convincing specimens of blatant falsification-evasion:

- An astrologer defended the failure of his horoscope-based predictions by explaining that the time of conception had to be taken into account as well as the time of birth but that it was difficult to know the time of conception with similar exactitude.

---

22. *Principles of Psychology* (Dover, 1950), Vol. 1, p. 163.

- The failure of a millenarian prediction that the kingdom of heaven was to begin on a certain date was accounted for by claiming that it had begun invisibly.

- A Christian Scientist accounted for the illness of believers by invoking the possibility that their faith was not strong enough or that their health was adversely affected by the materialistic convictions of those around them.

- A believer in paranormal phenomena extenuated the failure to produce these under experimental conditions by invoking a 'shyness effect': the very precautions which permitted of experimental demonstration precluded it by interfering with the paranormal powers of the subject.

- The Nazi Gauleiter of Vienna at the time of the Anschluss when presented with ocular testimony as to the thuggish behaviour of his supporters argued that those observed misbehaving must have been communists in Nazi uniforms.

What I want to stress is that in none of the above instances was any algorithm or general rule invoked to justify the judgement of falsification-evasion. The appeal was to our intuitive sense of reasonable or honourable epistemic behaviour and departures from it. I don't think things are any different when we pass to the more systematically organised expositions of psychoanalytic theorists. This lack of statable general rules is even more apparent if we examine instances of apparent falsification evasion which have failed to generate consensus. Consider the relation between the thesis of A.J.P. Taylor that Hitler 'sought neither war nor annexation of territory but merely to restore Germany's "natural" frontiers in Europe' and the Hossbach memorandum which records that at a meeting with his service chiefs in late 1937 Hitler announced expansionist war plans going beyond Germany's 'natural' frontiers. Does the content of the Hossbach memorandum refute the Taylor thesis? Hugh Trevor-Roper was sure that it did but Taylor dealt with it by maintaining that Hitler was in part rambling and in part talking for effect in order to get the service chiefs on his side. Taylor argued in further support that Hitler's speech was so inconsequential that it was not even normally minuted but only came to light accidentally. This is true, but on the other hand Taylor fails to mention that Hitler referred to it as his 'testament'. There are no rules which will enable us to weigh these conflicting considerations against each other or to determine who, in invoking them, is stonewalling.

Michael Martin, for example, objected to my falsification-evasion charge against Freudians that I had 'failed to show what the methodological difference are between reinterpreting the data in accord with a revolutionary theory' and 'obstructing the discovery of disconfirmatory states of affairs'.[23] Martin is right but is his expectation a reasonable one? In my reply to a similar objection from B.A. Farrell I argued that what is wanted is 'an assurance that the theory has been subjected to as much investigation as is practicable and as much clarification as the character of the subject permits and that its deficiencies in these respects is not due to a fear that repairing them might undermine its credibility. It is obvious that theses of this kind do not lend themselves to rigorous demonstration.'[24] For example, in 1912 Morton Prince was protesting against Freud's sexual emphasis that 'impulses . . . other than sexual are sufficient to induce psychical traumas . . . To hold otherwise is to substitute dogma for evidence of experience.'[25]

What strikes some as a vindication of Prince's view of the dogmatic character of the libido theory is the following response to reported refutations of it. Horace Frink, one of Freud's early American disciples wrote, 'I am well aware that certain individuals have published reports of cases in which, they assert, the sexual factor was absent, and that all symptoms were to be explained on other grounds. But there are no exceptions to Freud's rule. I do not hesitate to assert that sexual factor was present in these case but that the observer failed to see it.'[26] What kind of demonstration could there be that neither Frink nor anyone who thought his defense adequate (more or less all Freudians) had left themselves sufficient means of recognising counterinstances should they come across them? All a critic of the libido theory could reasonably hope for is agreement that the considerations Freud and his followers invoke, when dealing with ostensible refutations, make it reasonable to conclude that they had been 'fudging and finagling' or creating 'bogs of liquefaction' in which it was hoped that 'all definite conclusions of any sort could be trusted ere long to sink and disappear.' Where the altered perception is not forthcoming there seems no room for further ratiocinative endeavours.

Here is a case where my expectation that any disinterested person would agree that Freud's exculpatory elucidations of what he meant by 'sexual' had created 'a bog of logical liquefaction' was disappointed. Freud held one of the sources of homosexual behaviour to be the obstacles to heterosexual gratification imposed by society, using the simile of a dam to make his point. In the *Introductory Lectures* he wrote that due to the 'frustration of normal sexual satisfaction . . . a collateral damming up, must swell the force of the perverse impulses so that they become more powerful than they would have

23. Michael Martin, *Synthese*, 26 (1973), p. 336.

24. Robert Borger and Frank Cioffi, eds., *Explanation in the Behavioural Sciences* (Cambridge University Press, 1970), pp. 509–10.

25. Morton Prince, *Journal of Abnormal Psychology* (1912), p. 240.

26. Quoted from Roland Dalbiez, *Psychoanalytic Method and the Doctrine of Freud* (Longmans, 1941), p. 251.

been had no hindrance to normal satisfaction been present in reality.'[27] It thus comes as a shock to be told that the force of homosexual impulses can be intensified by heterosexual gratification and thus produce (in accord with his theory that delusional jealousy, like other forms of paranoia, had its source in repressed homosexual feeling) a false conviction that a spouse was being unfaithful. Freud employed this mechanism of sexually earmarked libido in the case of a patient who had outbreaks of delusional jealousy immediately after an act of conjugal intercourse 'gratifying to them both.' Freud explained that 'after every satiation of the heterosexual libido the homosexual component, likewise stimulated by the act, forced for itself an outlet.'[28] A philosopher, James Jupp, wrote in Freud's defense that 'though the hypothesis that delusional jealousy results from an excess of libidinal energy . . . seems to be in need of some qualification . . . no such qualification is necessary.' The most Jupp would concede is that 'the idea of heterosexuality stimulating homosexual impulses is unclear and in need of further explanation.'[29]

Is the concession that Freud's idea that heterosexual gratification could provoke an upsurge of homosexual desire 'is unclear and in need of further explanation' sufficient? Is it not like saying, 'The idea that the kingdom of heaven began invisibly is unclear and in need of further explanation?' There may be a rule which will enable us to determine whether the defense of Freud's theory of delusional jealousy by invoking an upsurge of homosexual libido in consequence of heterosexual intercourse is as much an example of stonewalling as the agreed specimens I have given, but I know of none.

My next example of stonewalling is from the same philosopher dealing with a passage in my 'Freud and the Idea of a Pseudoscience' (this volume, pp. xxx) where I pointed out what I had hoped were instructive discrepancies between Freud's account of a child's upbringing, given in a paper of 1908, and his account of the same child's upbringing given a year later, after he had succumbed to a phobia. The child was called 'Herbert' in the first paper and 'Hans' in the second. I used the contrast between Freud's description of two childhoods which turn out to have been the same childhood, one written before and one after the child in question had developed a phobia, to illustrate 'the use which Freud makes of the indefiniteness and multiplicity of his pathogenic influences and of the manner in which they enable him to render any outcome whatever an intelligible and apparently natural result of whatever circumstances preceded it . . . ' (this volume, pp. xxx). Jupp found this argument 'grossly unfair.' I had quoted in support

---

27. *IL* 20.
28. 'Neurotic Mechanisms in Jealousy, Paranoia and Homosexuality' *CP2*, p. 235.
29. 'Freud and Pseudo-science.' *Philosophy* 52 (1977), p. 451.

Freud's remark that Hans/Herbert's parents had used 'no more coercion than might be absolutely necessary for maintaining good behaviour' and that 'the experiment of letting him grow up and express himself without being intimidated went on satisfactorily' in hopes that the reader would agree that Freud had here given a tendentious account of parents who are later revealed to have threatened their child with castration and given him the conventional obfuscation in response to his straightforward questions as to where babies came from. But Jupp rejects this response and denies that 'the castration threat' and 'the lie about the stork' are in any was inconsistent with 'enlightened child rearing' since 'Freud was not, after all, claiming that this was *perfection* in child rearing . . .' (Jupp's italics)[30]

The question I wanted addressed was, if the fact that the idyllic childhood described in the paper of 1908, nevertheless, produced the neurosis described in the paper of 1909, did not constitute a falsification of Freud's infantile etiology what could? If an upbringing of which the worst that can be said is that it falls short of 'perfection' can still be pathogenic what is left of the testability of Freud's infantile etiology? But I nevertheless, feel that my charge of falsification-evasion though cogent, does not have—and ought not to be expected to have—a strictly logical coerciveness. Such judgements are a matter of gestalt perception and illustrate the irony that the critique of psychoanalysis has the same epistemic character as is often claimed for psychoanalysis itself.[31]

Does the Seduction Episode Show Freud to Have Been a Falsificationist?

Those who hold that Freud's abandonment of the thesis that a sexual molestation in infancy was a necessary condition of a neuroses in adulthood is proof that he was exemplary in his response to refractory experience have failed to ask the right question.[32] The question it is natural to pose in view of Freud's 18-fold experience of sexually molested patients is not, 'How did Freud respond to the evidence that there were after all, black swans?' but 'How did he deal with the implication that his momentous discovery of a long-distance bird-colour detector was premature?' The admission of error in rashly extrapolating from his original sample to all neurotics need have no

30. 'Freud and Pseudo-science', p. 451.

31. As it is put in the entry on pseudoscience in Ted Honderich, ed., *The Oxford Companion to Philosophy* (Oxford University Press, 1995), we might do well to abandon attempts at formal definition and to say of pseudoscience what Duke Ellington said of jazz: it is impossible to define because it is a matter of how it sounds.

32. A. Grünbaum, 'Is Freudian Psychoanalytic Theory Pseudo-scientific by Karl Popper's Criterion of Demarcation?' *American Philosophical Quarterly* 16 (1979); C. Glymour, 'Freud, Kepler, and the Clinical Evidence', in R. Wollheim and J. Hopkins, eds., *Freud* (New York: Anchor Books, 1984).

implications at all for this latter claim, unless it was felt that the regularity with which Freud failed to detect black swans could not be plausibly accounted for by there just having been none in his sample. We need not speculate about this since Freud finally decided that there were several counter-instances in his original sample. How then did he come to miss them? The most plausible answer to this question is 'through a fallacious reconstructive method'; and this, Freud, whom Grünbaum praises for his falsificationist outlook, was not prepared to consider.

More significant than Freud's abandonment of the seduction theory is what he replaced it with—an etiology which committed him to nothing which independent evidence could reveal not to have been the case. What the seduction theory committed him to could have been recorded by a camera but we have no idea what a recording of the traumas expounded in the paper of 1905 would be expected to show. And yet Grünbaum can cite this very paper as eloquent testimony to Freud's alertness to the need to keep his etiological speculations testable, though what Freud says in that paper is that 'a specific etiology in the form of particular infantile experiences is not forthcoming.'[33]

Can Untestability Be Determined by Inspection?

Is the right objection to raise against Freud's libido theory that his formulations of it have no observable implications? It is not this against which Freud is defending himself in his reply to the charge that, as he put it in the *Introductory Lectures* of 1916, 'the term sexual has suffered an unwarranted expansion of meaning at the hands of psychoanalysis, in order that its assertions regarding the sexual origins of the neuroses and the sexual significance of symptoms may be maintained.' The rebuttal of this charge is much more pertinent than the accusation that Freud had advanced a theory which was without potential falsifiers. The charge which Freudians had to meet was not only that of attenuating the content of the term libido until it was empty, but of a disingenuous alternation in the scope of the term, now employing it in its narrower and then in its unconscionably wider sense, as it suited them—the charge was that they systematically misled expectation and not that they merely underdetermined it.

What is generally overlooked by those who defend the legitimacy of Freud's wider extension of the term 'sexual' is that episodes like the enunciation of his 'bold' thesis, and his derisive reference to Jung and Adler as having succumbed to the 'need to free human society from the yoke of sexuality'[34] *succeeded* his own anti-carnal elucidation in which he invoked what

33. *CP1*, p. 281.
34. *The Question of Lay Analysis* (1926) in *Two Short Accounts of Psychoanalysis* (Penguin, 1962), p. 119.

Plato meant by 'Eros' and St. Paul by 'love' *(agapé)*.[35] It was thus not merely a question of permanent, if tendentious, extension of the term 'sexual' but of disingenuous tergiversation. One of our grounds for distrusting Freud's claim that the rejection of his account of the role of sexuality in the neuroses was based on a gross misunderstanding of what he meant by sexual, confining him to a carnal view, is the number of occasions, subsequent to his indignant repudiation of the carnal construal, on which it is precisely this gross sense on which he insists. Although in a letter of 1909 to his Swiss disciple, Oscar Pfister, he reassured him that in psychoanalysis the term 'sex' was not restricted to the 'crude pleasure of the senses' but encompassed 'what Christian pastors called "love"'[36] he was later complaining to Jung, concerning Adler's defection, 'He minimises the sexual drive and our opponents will be able to speak of an experienced analyst whose conclusions are radically different from ours.'[37] Was Freud expressing apprehension that what Adler would 'minimise' was 'what Christian pastors called love?' A few months earlier he had told Jung that 'due to their prudery' once the Americans became aware of 'the sexual core of our psychological theories they will drop us' (17 January 1909). Since prudery would find nothing to object to in 'what Christian pastors call love' we can see Freud's intermittent extensions of the term 'sexual' to encompass what St. Paul meant by 'love' in *Corinthians* as a sign of his own deviousness and/or faintheartedness.

Consider this remark of 1925: 'I always used to warn my pupils: "Our opponents have told us that we shall come upon cases in which the factor of sex plays no part. Let us be careful not to introduce it to our analyses and so spoil our chance of finding such a case. But so far none of us has had that good fortune."'[38] Can we introduce Freud's 'legitimately' expanded sense of sexuality into these remarks, thus: 'Our opponents have told us that we shall come upon cases in which the factor which St. Paul called "love" plays no part. Let us be careful not to introduce it into our analyses. . . ' or, 'The analyst never entices the patient on to the ground of love. He never says to him we shall be dealing with the intimacies of your philanthropic impulses.' If this argument does not convince the reader of Freud's bad faith, or blindness to his own tendentiousness, I do not now what could. And this self-protective obtuseness was not confined to Freud. On innumerable occasions Freud's expositors met objections to his insistence on the indispensability of

---

35. *Group Psychology and the Analysis of the Ego*, 1921 (Hogarth, 1948), pp. 38–39.

36. Heinrich Mend and Ernst L. Freud, *Psychoanalysis and Faith: The Letters of Sigmund Freud and Oskar Pfister* (Hogarth, 1963), p. 15.

37. W. Macquire, ed., *Freud/Jung Letters* (Hogarth, 1974), p. 376.

38. *The Question of Lay Analysis*, in *Two Short Accounts of Psychoanalysis* (Penguin, 1962), pp. 118–19.

sexual conflict in neuroses by reminding readers of his broadened Pauline/Platonic sense of love without asking why indulgence in love of this kind should entail castration or undergo repression.

Stonewalling: The Arbritrariness of Interpretation

No one has done more to abet Freudians in their delusion that what accounts for the refusal to accord them the status of *bona fide* empirical investigators is undue attachment to an inappropriately 'scientific' standard of evidence than Adolf Grünbaum. Freudian apologists welcome his objections as the Undead welcome nightfall. At Grünbaum's approach they smile, stir, and emerge from their coffins.[39] But it is not the assumption that there can be no rational grounds for a causal imputation other than controlled enquiry that indicts Freudian theory but the contingent fact, that after almost a century of practice, it has produced no clinical grounds whose persuasiveness is impersonally compelling, and many which fail to attain assent even among its own adherents. *This* is the stake through the heart.

In his life of Freud Ernest Jones reminisced concerning the emergence of dissident views, 'the general psychologists and others gladly seized on the opportunity to proclaim that since there were three "schools of psychoanalysis"—Freud, Adler and Jung—who could not agree among themselves over their own data there was no need for anyone else to take the subject seriously; it was compounded of uncertainties.'[40] Jones did not explain why this response was misconceived. Among those who drew the obvious moral from the situation described by Jones was the academic psychologist, R.S. Woodworth, who in a 1917 article criticising psychoanalysis objected that equally convincing grounds for rival etiologies could be advanced.[41] The argument put by Woodworth was a venerable one but had been largely

---

39. See his attempt to deal with the defense of psychoanalytic explanation provided by Thomas Nagel in *The New York Review of Books* (11 August 1984). Is it reasonable to suggest that if we want to know whether a good case has been made by Freud for invoking the influence of the primal scene on the Wolf Man's development we are to await the outcome of as yet unperformed epidemiological studies? Grünbaum's commitment to this response unmasks his argument as the sort of conventional scientism from which psychoanalysis has least to fear. It is not the lack of support from controlled studies but the indifference to the failure of consensus or the sophistical manner with which this is dealt that grounds rejection of Freudian claims. In fact Grünbaum is himself not able to maintain consistency on this issue. In his reply to peer group commentary on his book he makes the extraordinary concession that he finds 'some empirical plausibility in the psychoanalytic theory of defense mechanisms, e.g., denial and rationalisation, reaction-formation, projection, and identification.' What sense can Grünbaum, whose only acceptable ground for a causal imputation is controlled enquiry, give to the plausibility of clinical inferences since for him the notion of 'plausible clinical inference' ought to be oxymoronic?

40. Ernest Jones, *Life* (Hogarth, 1958), Vol. II, p. 171.

41. Robert Woodworth, 'Some Criticisms of Freudian Psychology' *Journal of Abnormal Psychology* (1917), pp. 174–194.

hypothetical when advanced by Aschaffenburg early in the century, or by Lyman Wells on the occasion of the translation of *The Interpretation of Dreams* in 1913.[42] But by 1917 the inevitable results of the subjectivity of the method had made themselves felt in the defections of Jung and Adler, and so Woodworth's argument was no longer merely hypothetical. Yet it was met by Samuel Tannenbaum with a simple denial that rival etiologies were as well supported as Freud's.[43] At this stage simple denial had become unpersuasive since the defections of Adler and Jung, and their invocation of clinical data in support of their own etiologies, was now widely known. Perhaps the implications of this had just not sunk in, since Tannenbaum's confidence in his reply to Woodworth's objections was short-lived, and a few years later he was himself denouncing Freudian psychoanalysis as 'a pseudo-science like palmistry, graphology and phrenology.'[44] In the 1920s Bernard Hart once again pointed out that 'while the pupils of Freud confirm by their clinical observations the findings of their master, the pupils of Jung . . . have no difficulty in finding ample clinical confirmation for the quite disparate tenets of Jung.'[45] A few pages later the point is generalised: 'the doubts we have expressed as to the scientific trustworthiness of the method of psycho-analysis cannot but be enhanced when we observe the remarkably discrepant results achieved by it in the hands of men who start with different precon-ceptions' (p. 87). At about the same time this very argument was addressed to a non-professional audience by Aldous Huxley as his main reason for scepticism as to the scientific status of psychoanalysis: 'while all psychoana-lysts agree in regarding dreams as being of first class importance, they differ profoundly in their method of interpretation. Freud finding suppressed sex-ual wishes . . . Rivers the solution of a mental conflict; Adler, the will to power; Jung a little bit of everything.'[46] The same argument had been advanced by Adolf Wohlgemuth: 'If a dream of mine were analysed by Freud he would doubtless unearth some sexual complex, whilst Jung, with

---

42. F.L. Wells, Review of *The Interpretation of Dreams, Journal of Philosophy*, Vol. 10 (1913), p. 555.

43. 'Some Current Misconceptions of Psychoanalysis.' *Journal of Abnormal Psychology*, Vol. 12, No. 6 (February 1918).

44. *New York Times* (Sunday, 19 March 1922), 'Turns Against Freud; Dr. Tannenbaum. Famous Specialist, Former disciple of Austrian Psychoanalyst, Points out Errors in his Teachings.' Tannenbaum's change of heart may have been overdetermined. Though a found-ing member of the New York Psychoanalytic Society, he was denied a promised place on the editorial board of the projected official psychoanalytic journal for 'associating with a rather questionable crowd,' including 'a Russian Jew of the Bolshevik type,' as well as for having no affiliations they could make use of. See letter 240 in *The Complete Correspondence of Sigmund Freud and Ernest Jones, 1908–1939* (London: Belknap, 1993).

45. Bernard Hart, *The Development of Psychopathology* (Cambridge University Press, 1928), p. 76.

46. 'Is Psychoanalysis a Science?' *The Forum* (1925), p. 317.

the same dream, would discover some "prospective and teleological function", and Adler would find the "will to power, the masculine protest." This I think is sufficient proof that the result is due to the psychoanalyst and that the dream-interpretation is the *via regia* to the *analyst's* unconscious.'[47]

The argument advanced by Lyman Wells, Woodworth, Wohlgemuth, Bernard Hart, *et al.* has lost none of its force or relevance. In his *Freud Evaluated*, Malcolm Macmillan asks: 'How was it that Ferenczi was able to confirm Rank's observations but Freud was not?'.[48] As we have seen, this was often met by stonewalling, but in time the favoured method became recycling and the issue was rarely raised spontaneously, and so Macmillan is able to write, 'We are never told that the so-called discoveries are dependent upon methods of enquiry and interpretation so defective that even practitioners trained in their use are unable to reach vaguely congruent conclusions about such things as the interpretation of a dream or symptom let alone the basic clinical characteristics of infantile or perverse sexuality or the reconstruction of the early stage of an individual's development . . .'[49]

Were the Changes in Freudian Theory Empirically Motivated?

Grünbaum, who answers this question affirmatively, overlooks that Freud's altering his views is as consistent with his behaving like a suborned witness who changes his testimony as like a *bona fide* investigator responding to the force of empirical fact. In *Freud Evaluated*, Macmillan illustrates how some of the most prominent cases of theory modification, including those put forward by Grünbaum, were made without any alteration in their evidential basis. What determined the development of psychoanalytic theory was not empirical evidence but social feedback from relevant others: this was Edward Glover's view of the Kleinian movement, Morris Eagle's of the Kohutian developments and Marshall Edelson's of certain unspecified departures from classical psychoanalysis. None of them shows why the same should not be said of classical psychoanalysis itself.

Were Freud's repeated modifications of his views as to the role of sexuality in the neuroses empirically motivated? There was no need for him to abandon carnal sexuality just because it was discovered that the precipitating changes in life circumstances did not encompass any change in sexual circumstances. Freud had already anticipated this possibility. Once he had introduced a pre-existing weakness of the sexual constitution to enable his thesis as to the sexual character of the neuroses to be maintained, even

---

47. Adolf Wohlgemuth, 'The Refutation of Psychoanalysis.' *Journal of Mental Science* (July 1924), p. 499.
48. *Freud Evaluated* (Amsterdam: North Holland, 1991), p. 572.
49. *Freud Evaluated*, p. 505.

though the precipitating frustrations did not involve the patient's sexual life, the only grounds left for doubting his sexual etiology was the failure to uncover repressed sexual ideation, and this is not easy to imagine, given the laxity or ingenuity of Freud's interpretative principles. Or, in my terminology, Freud's thesis as to the pathogenic role of sexuality was without ascertainable falsifiers and yet mysteriously abandoned because found falsified. This is the opposite of the fault, which Freudians also manifest, of declaring theses to have been confirmed—to have had their credibility enhanced by failed attempts at falsification—even though we are given no account of what these falsifying circumstances could have been.

Post-Modernist Versions of Stonewalling: What Is Truth?

There is an alternative way of dealing with revelations such as that Anna O. was not cured by her treatment—though Freud repeatedly maintained that she had been—and that is to redraw, or in some way obfuscate, the distinction between truth and falsity. This is the path chosen by Elisabeth Roudinesco, and Lisa Appignanesi and John Forrester.[50]

Here is how Forrester and Appignanesi deal with the revelation that the therapeutic success in the 'founding case' of psychoanalysis was a fabrication:

> 'In writing about this first psychoanalytic patient there are two stories to be told: first the story of Bertha Pappenheim—her early life, her illness, her treatment by Breuer, her recovery and her later career; and second, the story of Anna O., what Freud made of the story Breuer told him, and how her case became a founding myth of psychoanalysis . . . But myth here does not mean, as it often does when 'history' and 'myth' are contrasted, an illusion, a self-serving mask of a deliberately hidden truth. Rather myth here signifies the structure which permits the story of the origin, the birth of psychoanalysis, to be told.[51]

The same tack is taken by Elisabeth Roudinesco:

> this invention bears witness to a historical reality to which we cannot oppose the simplistic argument of a reality of facts . . . [The truth of the story lies in] . . . its legend and refers to the way in which the psychoanalytic movement tells itself the initial fantasies about its birth.[52]

An analogous device is deployed by Forrester and Appignanesi in their dealings with *A Young Girl's Diary*, a work which has long been treated as a demonstration of the preternatural accuracy of Freud's theory of female

50. See Mikkel Borch-Jacobsen on origin myths in *Remembering Anna O.* (Routledge, 1996), pp. 10–12.

51. John Forrester and Lisa Appignanesi, *Freud's Women* (London: Weidenfeld and Nicolson, 1992), p. 73.

52. Quoted from Borch-Jacobsen, *Remembering Anna O.*, p. 12.

development. They quote Helen Deutsch's reply to the suspicion that the diary was a fraud perpetrated by the analyst, Hermine Hug-Hellmuth, who purported to have merely discovered it: 'If this was indeed the case, Dr. Hug-Hellmuth had both psychological insight and literary talent . . . The book is so true psychologically that it has become a gem of psychoanalytic literature.'[53] Their bizarre comment on this contemptible rationalisation for deception and mendacity is that Deutsch's 'verdict is as good as any.'

In *The Rainbow* D.H. Lawrence vividly evokes the struggle between a character's critical sense and the comfort he derives from the familiar and much loved Sunday School stories: 'Very well it was not true, the water had not turned to wine. But for all that it would live in his soul as if the water had turned to wine. For truth of fact it had not. But for his soul, it had.' Substitute Freudian hagiographic and clinical legends for the Christian miracle stories and you have the secularised torments suffered by Freudianising intellectuals as their credulity weakens—torments for which post-modernist obfuscation provides the balm.

The Confusion of Falsification-Evasion with Spurious Confirmation

Sometimes, what we object to is not a theorist's rejection of falsification reports but his treating his ingenuity in fending off the force of apparent falsifiers as further confirmation of his theory. This, rather than just wanton tenacity, is what Popper accused Adler of when Adler explained away an apparent exception by invoking his 'thousand-fold experience'. Popper commented that Adler would no doubt now consider his experience 'a thousand-and-one fold.' With this rebuke Popper was going beyond falsification-evasion to the charge of spurious confirmation.

Let me try to make the distinction between the rejection of falsification reports and the declaration of spurious confirmations clearer. I once heard an anecdote about J. Edgar Hoover to the effect that when he had decided to bug the phone of someone suspected of subversion he would prepare two headings, one—'subversive'—for cases in which incriminating conversations were overheard and the other—'cunning subversive'—for cases in which they were not. The same practice has been imputed to Freud, but before we decide on its justice we must be clear as to what the moral of the Hoover anecdote is. It is not, as a crude falsificationist might think, that Hoover ought to have declared the subject under surveillance to be a non-subversive once no incriminating conversations were overheard. That question ought to remain *sub judice*. What Hoover did which is reprehensible was not

---

53. Forrester and Appignanesi, *Freud's Women,* p. 201.

that he failed to exonerate when there were no incriminating conversations but that he convicted in spite of their being none. The parallel in the Freudian case is the mistake of confounding objections to Freud's failure to capitulate to falsification with the really damaging charge of his treating his ingenuity in explaining away facts contradictory of his assertions, not as their making the issue *sub judice*, but as their having decided it in his favour. This is what happened in the case of the war neuroses, where the claim that the role of repressed sexuality in psychoneuroses had been refuted was initially met by the not unreasonable defense that no thorough analyses of war neurotics had been conducted, and later that the scope of the notion of sexual repression had been misconstrued since it encompassed narcissistic as well as object libido and, finally, by the claim that the instinct of self-preservation was libidinal in any case. At a certain stage these grounds for rejecting falsification reports became grounds for considering the theory confirmed.[54] Gellner, too, obliterates the distinction between the advocates of a theory rejecting a reported falsification by somehow reconciling it with the truth of the theory, and their treating their ability to ingeniously save the theory as further evidence in favour of it. He gives the resistance argument as an example of a 'falsification-evading device.' But what he then goes on to say shows that what he has in mind is more than the mere refusal to capitulate, for he says that those who deploy the resistance argument hold the view that a patient's rejection of an interpretation is evidence of its validity and this is more than mere tenacity—it is spurious confirmation.[55] (That he is right about what analysts think themselves justified in inferring from reported failures to disconfirm psychoanalytic theory is illustrated by the expositions of J.C Flugel in one generation and Charles Brenner in another).[56] Anthony Quinton also, in citing as an instance of the vast 'array of refutation-avoiding devices which permeate Freud's writings . . . the practice of treating the occurrence of the contrary of what the theory predicts as being as much a confirmation of the theory as its originally predicted opposite,' has described a practice distinct from and more pernicious than the mere evasion of falsification.[57]

Did Freud Issue Confirmation Reports?

He was content to be thought to have done so until the incredulity provoked by the claim reached a point when, with a little help from plausible

---

54. T.W. Mitchell, *Problems in Psychopathology* (Kegan Paul, 1927), p. 174; Robert Waelder, *Basic Theory of Psychoanalysis* (International Universities Press, 1960), p. 165.

55. E. Gellner, *The Psychoanalytic Movement* (Paladin, 1985), Chapters 8 and 9.

56. J.C. Flugel, *An Introduction to Psychoanalysis* (London: Gollancz, 1932), p. 48; Charles Brenner, 'Classical Psychoanalysis', *International Encyclopedia of the Social Sciences*.

57. A. Quinton, *Thoughts and Thinkers* (London: Duckworth, 1982), p. 248

deniability, it was speciously maintained that he was merely suggesting or anticipating the likely outcome of investigation. In fact there are texts so unequivocal as to confute this but, in general, the issue is not one to be settled by recourse to texts but by describing a culture. What a reviewer said of Freud in 1925 ('He writes as if he had, at the back of him, a great body of tested doctrine . . . as if the writer were a scientific man referring to something as well established as the atomic weights of the chemical elements')[58] was still being said of Freudians in general several decades later. And this is not the kind of issue which is to be resolved by the scrutiny of texts.

Given that there is agreement that psychoanalysis has not lived among us as a speculative system, or a batch of working hypotheses, what grounds are there for maintaining that its claims are not just unwarranted but spurious? The charge is that the thesis said to have been confirmed could not have been since it had no *ascertainable* falsifiers. Even if we countenance Grünbaum's resort to the Swiss safe deposit box conception of testability to justify conferring on the theory esoteric entertainable falsifiers this has no bearing on the claim that confirmation reports issued on its behalf were spurious. The only adequate reply to this charge must be that the method would have allowed negative instances to be recognised and not merely entertained.

Once Freud had both universalised his pathogenic agents and rendered their relation to the child's environment equivocal by placing the emphasis on a constitutional factor which could, in unspecified circumstances, replace external traumas he could not encounter evidence inconsistent with a sexual etiology (as he could in the case of the seduction etiology). And though this inability does not in itself warrant the deployment of derogatory epistemic epithets like 'pseudoscience', that such adverse characterisations, nevertheless, may be justified follows from the repeated claim, necessarily false, that the theory has survived all attempts at falsification, when the most it could be claimed is that cases which might have disappointed his hope that they were positive instances, nevertheless, proved to be such.

As for the libido theory, even those who refuse to indict Freud for falsification evasion must concede that his reconciliatory elucidations left the theory in a state where it was in no position to be submitted to tests and, thus, any claims that it had been must be spurious. An ironical implication of this argument is that, though it is common for critics of Freud to complain of the obstinacy with which he clung to the libido theory in the face of apparent falsifications, the appropriate and more damning objection is that given its complexity, even in its unextended carnal form, he could have no adequate empirical grounds for abandoning it, and so he exposed him-

---

58. *Times Literary Supplement* (10 September 1925).

self to the accusation of the Reichians that when he he did so it was from self-serving motives

Does it follow from the fact that my free associations to the image of my mother do not terminate in love scenes involving her that I do not nurse unconscious incestuous inclinations? Of course not. It is even doubtful that Freud wants to claim that all his patients did have such intimate first-hand revelations of their incestuous proclivities. What he seems to claim is that they became convinced of such inclinations through the force of evidence. But the failure of patients treated by analysts with rival etiologies, like Rank or Adler, to produce memories confirmatory of Freudian theory was not treated as falsifying since it was believed that their patients, too, had the same unconscious networks of associations and symbolic equivalencies Freud had discovered, and that under suitable conditions—analysis by a Freudian—they would reveal this. For some critics of Freud this reply is in itself sufficient to damn him as a pseudoscientist. But I would prefer to reserve this term for those who claim for their framework a status it cannot have—a status that could only accrue through failed attempts at falsification.

Revisionism: When Did Psychoanalysis Stop Being Freudian—and Why?

There are those of Freud's defenders who do not bother with mounting conceptual or empirical objections to the argument that Freud's infantile etiology, or the privileged role he allotted sexuality, involved him in violating normal canons of evidence, procedure, or intelligibility. While leaving it unclear how much of this charge they agree with, they argue that it leaves Freud's essential achievement untouched. There are grounds for suspecting that these apologists have failed to engage with the criticism of Freud's more distinctive contributions, not from genuine conviction as to its irrelevance, but from embarrassment at having to acknowledge their own connivance, if not collusion, in the maintenance and circulation of so many rationally indefensible claims. This accounts for the heavily revisionist account of Freud's achievement such that theses which, only a few years earlier, had been widely treated as certainties and whose rejection was held to be proof of unreasoning bigotry, were now held to apply to areas remote from those in which Freud's real achievement lay. There seems to be an analogy between this stratagem and the distorted reminiscences of post-Twentieth Congress fellow-travellers. Like these, Freud's more recent apologists provoke the question whether they are genuinely amnesic for the views they once endorsed, expounded, and propagated, or whether they were always aware of the true situation but were silent from motives of solidarity. Fellow-travellers resorted to either of two stratagems for coping with public exposure of the enormities of Communist rule. One was adopted by the English socialist, John Strachey, who obliterated from his memory that he had once vouched for the propriety of the Moscow trials and the guilt of the accused. Others adopted the tactic of one of their number who on being asked why he had minimised the existence of the Gulags claimed that it wasn't because he was obtuse to the force of evidence but because he did not wish to give comfort to cold warriors.[59]

Some Freudian revisionists may have stood to the major tenets of classical psychoanalysis as eighteenth-century Anglicans to the Thirty-Nine Articles. As Dr. Johnson put it, these were 'articles of peace' which, though they might be privately dissented from, were not to be preached against. But current revisionist apologetic is so convoluted that it is impossible to tell in which of these two relations—secret dissidence or intellectual torpor—those who now wish to repudiate certain traditional psychoanalytic dogmas once stood to them.

'Plausible Deniability' and the Ambiguity of Revisionism

To use a phrase made famous during the Iran-Contra affair to characterise utterances deliberately chosen for their ambiguity, the practice of 'plausible deniability' is endemic to psychoanalytic apologetic.

Here is a prime specimen of 'plausible deniability' from Harold Blum's reply to Frederick Crews's *New York Review* piece: 'Freud's initial propositions, first findings and landmark case reports are no longer vital for the validation of psychoanalytic formulations.'[60] Which 'psychoanalytic formulations' are being referred to? Only if they are specified can we determine whether Blum means that Freud's 'first findings,' such as the Oedipus complex, castration anxiety, the pathogenic paramountcy of repressed sexuality, and so forth, have been abandoned and replaced by more credible theses or whether, though these 'initial propositions and first findings' have been retained, the claim that Freud had provided adequate grounds for them in his case histories and elsewhere is now retracted and the evidence in their support comes from other, less dubious, sources. One reason for the tendency of apologists to distance themselves from Freud himself may be that though Freud is a prolific author, not easy to hold in one's head, he has the same finishing school status among the intelligentsia as speaking French or recognizing a fish knife once did among those aspiring to upward social mobility. It is thus understandable that many apologists were at a loss as to how to reply to criticism based on a closer study of Freud's texts than they were willing to undertake themselves, and this supplied them with an additional motive for denying the relevance of Freud's own writings to the status of psychoanalysis, since it would exempt them from the onerous task of

---

59. David Caute, *The Fellow Travellers* (London: Weidenfeld and Nicolson, 1973), pp. 164 and 103.

60. Frederick Crews, *The Memory Wars* (A New York Review Book, 1995), p. 104.

acquiring sufficient familiarity with his arguments to make detailed replies to those who have condemned them as tendentious and incoherent. It would also provide them with an additional polemical advantage in leaving it unspecified what arguments are to replace those of Freud. Christians are committed to the Apostle's Creed (or were when I last looked) but it has become impossible to say what Freudian revisionists are committed to.

One of the commonest forms of revisionism is the abandonment of Freud's sexual emphasis. The attempt to turn the force of criticism by distancing psychoanalysis from its sexual emphasis is almost as old as psychoanalysis itself. An early example of this manoeuvre is to be found in a novel of the 1920s by Rose Macaulay in which a character who asks how analysts 'cure all those things just by talking indecently about sex?' is met with the defense, 'You're so crude, darling. You've got hold of only one tiny part of it—the part practised by Austrian professors on Viennese degenerates . . .' It seems that Freud himself is now to be included among these 'Viennese degenerates' in the interests of the continued prestige and credibility of the psychoanalytic movement. Marcia Cavell, who wrote protesting at Crews's *New York Review of Books* essay, is one of several recent, 'pick' n' mix' Freudians who have insisted on distinguishing Freud from psychoanalysis to the discredit of the former. I think we are entitled to the suspicion that the accusation of anachronism made against critics of psychoanalysis is a predominantly rhetorical device and that they are fully aware that views as to the determinants of neurotic disorders, child development and the nature of the mind in general, which derive from Freud and are parasitic for their credibility on his prestige as an astute and scrupulous clinical observer, are still widely held. But even if it were the case that classical psychoanalysis is moribund it would still be necessary for revisionists to discuss the classical claims and the classical arguments in support of them and why they fail. Otherwise they expose themselves to the suspicion that their current reservations are as shallow as their former advocacy. Though fewer Freudian apologists are now willing to stand by the authenticity of many of Freud's distinctive discoveries none has been willing to address the question as to how it came about that phenomena they now hold not to occur were reported so consistently over many decades through the use of a method they are nevertheless unwilling to abjure.

Over three decades ago the sociologist, Peter Berger wrote:[61]

> The questioning of the existence of the unconscious in a gathering of college-educated Americans is likely to be as much a self-certification of derangement as would be the questioning of the germ theory of disease. College-educated Americans . . . know themselves to be acquainted with an unconscious as a sure

---

61. P. Berger, 'Towards a Sociological Understanding of Psychoanalysis.' *Social Research* (1965), p. 28.

fact of experience and, what is more, they also have quite specific notions as to how this appendage is furnished.

Though the unconscious in general is as unquestioned as when Berger wrote, its contents have undergone a certain degree of refurbishment. In what respects and why? It is not easy to say.

As an illustration of the manner in which their mode of exposition makes it difficult to know what the position of current apologists with respect to classical psychoanalysis is, consider Wollheim's light-hearted allusion to the 'implausibility' of Freud's account of female development, 'I shall for the sake of simplicity (perhaps of plausibility also) . . . confine myself to the male infant.'[62] Does 'implausibility' here mean 'inherently unlikely' or 'Though true, so apparently false and so wounding to feminine sensibilities as to promote undeserved scepticism if not gently led up to.' That is, does Wollheim believe in penis envy? It is impossible to say. Here is another example where the ground may have been laid for future plausible denial. This is from a reply to the psychiatrist Anthony Clare's criticism of psychoanalysis by the Medical Director of the Anna Freud Centre in London, 'Childhood sexuality can surely be observed in every nursery; if, for some reason, the observer cannot see what is in front of his eyes the fault may lie in him.'[63] This remark was, ostensibly, Yorke's reply to the doubts Clare had expressed about penis envy and the oedipus complex ('ostensibly' since Clare spoke explicitly of these and did not mention 'childhood sexuality' in general which Yorke's rebuttal is confined to). Yet Yorke substitutes the expression 'childhood sexuality' thus leaving it open to him to deny that he was maintaining that penis envy and castration anxiety 'can surely be observed in any nursery.'

When Did Women Stop Wanting Penises?

The account of the 'developments' in Freudian theory revisionists wish to convey is that the psychoanalytic 'method', the essential part of the legacy for which they are beholden to Freud, led them to replace or modify the theses it had originally suggested. But there is an alternative, more plausible if less charitable, account of how these drastic changes in psychoanalytic theory came about. This is most clearly illustrated by the fate of the notion of penis envy as the key to feminine psychology. None of Freud's theses was more repeatedly confirmed than penis envy. When Robert Waelder issued his challenge to Freud's critics to demonstrate the inadequacy of clinical data by examining a particular specimen from his own practice it was his demonstration of penis envy in a three-year-old which he put forward.[64] As

---

62. Richard Wollheim, *Freud* (Fontana, 1992), p. 119.
63. Clifford Yorke, *The Times* (London, 3 July 1985).
64. Robert Waelder, 'Psychoanalysis, Scientific Method, and Philosophy', *Journal of the American Psychoanalytic Association*, Vol. 10, 3 (July 1962), footnote to p. 622.

late as 1968 an introductory text on social psychology by several Ivy League academics informed its readers that one of the discoveries we owe to the genius of Freud was that every woman has a deep-seated need to be appendaged like a man, and that in favourable cases the transformation of this need terminated in reconciliation to her stunted state and the replacement of the original desire for a penis by one for a baby. This was said to explain why so many women want their first born to be male—because he brings a penis with him. Moreover analysts had regularly confirmed these findings.[65]

We hear much less of penis envy today. Why? Over three decades ago B.A. Farrell explained why the falsification of penis envy by extra-analytic enquiry had no influence on the psychoanalytic community. 'We have to remember that almost any negative finding can be countered by analysts claiming that it is necessary to postulate such girlish envy in order to account for the material thrown up in analysis. The strength of this reply can only be resolved, presumably, by settling the validity of psychoanalytic method.'[66] Why are we not to infer from the fact that the thesis of penis envy has been widely abandoned that the invalidity of psychoanalytic method has been as widely conceded? Orwell had a word for it.

On the Importance of Distinguishing Confirmation from Instantiation

There is a frequent ambiguity in the way the term 'confirmed' is used. In its strong sense it implies that a thesis capable of falsification has been tested and survived. In its weaker sense it means that a thesis capable of non-instantiation (where non-instantiation refers to the failure to exemplify) has, nevertheless, been instantiated. When the concept of sexual frustration was confined to lack of carnal gratification it was falsifiable; when it was extended to include what Plato meant by Eros and St. Paul by charity it ceased being falsifiable but remained instantiatable in those cases where interference with carnal gratification appear to induce neuroses. The instantiation criterion is implicit in Walter Kaufmann's remark that 'Counter-examples do not show that we are not dealing with a major contribution.'[67]

Though the charge as to the dogmatic character of psychoanalytic claims to knowledge sometimes focusses on its generalisations, what is as often maintained is that the singular instantiation reports are without adequate warrant. What is found troubling is not the difficulty of conceiving or identifying counter-instances to the oedipal accounts of neuroses, or the wish-

65. Irving Janis, ed., *Personality* (Harcourt Brace, 1969), pp. 257–260.
66. B.A. Farrell, 'Can Psychoanalysis Be Refuted?', *Inquiry*, Vol. IV (1961), p. 23.
67. *Discovering the Mind* (McGraw-Hill, 1980), Vol. III, p. 115

fulfilment account of dreams, and so forth, but the feebleness or tendentiousness of the paradigmatic narratives, or interpretations, held to instantiate these theories and which we are encouraged to apply to the resolution of explanatory problems.

Though much of Thomas Nagel's case for Freud consists of the usual edificatory blather,[68] he does have an argument which the advocates of the ubiquitous applicability of a natural science standard fail to meet, though this argument involves a degree of revisionism—what can be called epistemic revisionism—as when Robert Waelder disclaims possession of all-embracing laws.[69] Suppose we see Freud as a natural historian rather than as a scientist—someone whose merit it is to have discovered extraordinary phenomena rather than general laws—will it not then be inappropriate to make the support of controlled enquiry a *sine qua non* of acceptance? The question Nagel is raising, which the demand for controlled enquiry doesn't address, is whether Freud has provided us with credible instances of his mechanisms and etiologies and thus good reasons for framing hypotheses invoking infantile sexual life or unconscious mechanisms when confronted by behavioural conundrums.[70] David Sachs speaks of Freud's 'laboriously won comparisons yielding him large classes of instances of his views concerning unconscious mental processes and content in general.'[71] It is on the authenticity of these 'large classes of instances' that the discussion ought to be focused. There are those who deny their existence. How are they to be shown mistaken? The response to those who issued this challenge was for seventy years or so (if indeed it has a term) to refer them to Freud's case histories and other clinical writings. Here apologists seem to bifurcate, though the overuse of 'plausible deniability' makes it difficult to be sure. Which of Freud's explanations (or of Freudian explanations) do those who fall back on an ideographic rationale believe to be credible? (Thomas Nagel thinks Freud's case histories are too 'complicated' to use in discussion). What specific theses of Freud's does Nagel think there are genuine instantiations of? Conversion? Displacement upwards? After a century of psychoanalytic practice is there one indubitable instance of a neurotic who came to grief due to the pathogenic repression of infantile sexual

68. 'Freud's Permanent Revolution', *The New York Review of Books* (12 May 1994).

69. 'Observation, Historical Reconstruction, and Experiment', in Charles Hanly and Morris Lazerowitz, eds., *Psychoanalysis and Philosophy* (1970).

70. Surprisingly Grünbaum inconsistently concedes this. In his reply to his peer group commentators Grünbaum says that he finds 'some empirical plausibility in the psychoanalytic theory of defense mechanisms, e.g., denial and rationalisation, reaction-formation, projection and identification.' (*Behavioural and Brain Sciences*, July 1985) Nowhere does he address the central question of how plausibility is to be assessed in the absence of controlled enquiry.

71. 'In Fairness to Freud'. *Philosophical Review* (1989), p. 372.

impulses? And by indubitable I mean one which meets humanistic standards of narrative compellingness.

Unfalsifiability, Falsification-Evasion, Spurious Confirmation, and Spurious Instantiation

Let me clarify how I have been using the terms 'instantiate' and 'confirm' in their bearing on the pseudoscience issue. If someone reports that he has seen white swans he is claiming to have instantiated the claim that there are white swans. If he says that he has never seen a non-white swan, though he would certainly have if there were any, he is claiming to have confirmed that all swans are white

When someone warns that a particular claim to knowledge is pseudoscientific what must he show in justification? That it is unfalsifiable? No. That though it has been falsified those who advance it insisted on retaining it? No. That they treat their ability to reconcile its apparent falsification with its truth as further confirmation? Sometimes. But someone can be engaged in a pseudo-empirical enquiry even if he did not advance untestable claims, or abstained from general claims altogether, or modified them in the light of falsifying reports, since there is an objection that such restraint could not meet—that he regularly issued spurious reports of having encountered authentic instances of the phenomenon in question. Or, to depersonalise the issue, that the examples regularly put forward, from varied sources, as instantiations of the theory are spurious. It is this which Medawar, in spite of his nominal adherence to the testability criterion, attempts to document in his 'Further Remarks on Psychoanalysis'[72] rather than either the formal untestability of the theory, or the obstinacy of its advocates in clinging to it in the face of apparent falsification. Suppose that someone committed to the view that all swans are rainbow-coloured declares that swans which appear to be white may, nevertheless, be rainbow coloured while failing to specify the conditions under which he would concede that they really were not rainbow-coloured. Is not this of lesser moment than that he should have reported innumerable instances of rainbow-coloured swans, when he had no adequate grounds for doing so? Spurious instantiation reports are a much more pernicious feature of psychoanalytic discourse than untestability.

Harsh dismissals such as 'the greatest confidence trick of the twentieth century' (Medawar) and talk of Freud's claims being 'false and fraudulent' (Szasz) seem to require more than just obduracy in the face of apparent disconfirmation to justify them. On the other hand, the willingness to forego generality is no proof of *bona fide* empirical status. Would anyone say of Lombroso's physiognomics of criminality that since it was both falsifiable

---

72. Peter Medawar, *The Hope of Progress* (London: Wildwood House, 1972).

and qualified by Lombroso with respect to counter-instances it was wrong to stigmatise it as pseudoscientific? Since the statement that long arms are indicative of criminality is both falsifiable, and conceded by Lombroso to have notable exceptions, is the issue settled in his favour? Analogously, is it really sufficient to point to the admission that there are non-reactive depressions (endogenous repressions), as Grünbaum does, to exonerate Freud from Popper's accusation of dogmatism? If Lombroso had claimed that there were physical stigmata indicative of criminality, though he didn't yet know what they were, we would have an untestable theory but one which is much less objectionable than the testable one he claimed to have repeatedly instantiated.[73] It is not the *counterexamples,* and the manner in which they were addressed on which attention should be focused, but the *examples,* if we are to assess the empirical genuinness of the theory. These raise several questions. The most central is, 'Are the instantiation reports about which disagreement has raged for over half a century genuine or spurious?' What we need is a rationale for resolving disputes over the authenticity of instantiation reports. And, since the claims are ideographic and largely based on private clinical data, there can be few which do not depend on prior judgements as to the astuteness and probity of the reporter.

What Does the Demonstration that Instantiations Are Spurious Show?

How is the difference between the views expressed by Medawar and Thomas Nagel to be resolved? One insists on the prevalence of irresponsible and glib interpretations and the other concedes that there are such but denies their representativeness, or believes them more than compensated for by the puzzle-solving ability Freudian principles bestow.

I think that what lies behind Kaufmann's remark, and the feeling that the demonstration of spurious confirmation and/or instantiation reports may not resolve the issue, is that, when a discovery is sufficiently momentous, the spurious instantiations (as well as spurious confirmations, or the untestability or falsification evasion), are of little account. If it were established that there was communication from beyond the grave how much interest would we retain in the exposure of fraudulent mediums? I think this a good argument but it ought to be made explicit, and we must be told just what the momentous foible-exculpating discovery was and when and how it was validated.

---

73. Stephen Jay Gould writes: 'We do know that Lombroso's stigmata became important criteria for judgement in many criminal trials . . . we cannot know how many men were condemned unjustly because they were extensively tattooed, failed to blush, or had unusually large jaws and arms' (*The Mismeasure of Man* [Penguin, 1981], pp. 137–38)

Are There Freudian Phenomena?

Only if Freud's arguments can be taken to have established that there are; for there is no other evidence more cogent or more reliable

The demand for epidemiological evidence of a causal relation between the childhood vicissitudes and adult afflictions of people long dead is an absurdity of which those wedded to an epidemiological conception of what is at issue must be oblivious. On the other hand a careful reading of Webster, Esterson, Macmillan, or Crews would cast doubt on whether there are any good grounds in Freud, or elsewhere, for crediting that any neurotic patient has been shown to be suffering the aftermath of repressed infantile sexual vicissitudes. Good evidence, in this kind of case, is evidence of the sort that Dickens gives for believing that Miss Havisham's eccentricities and perversities—her always wearing one white shoe, all the clocks in her home stopped at twenty to nine, her raising a beautiful little girl to break men's hearts—were causally related to the traumatic occasion on which she was jilted on her wedding day—at twenty to nine, while wearing one white shoe, etc., etc. But showing that instantiation claims are unwarranted or spurious is not as straightforward as showing that confirmation claims are. There are reports of Freudian phenomena which are credible unless we are willing to impugn the reporter's capacity for disinterested observation or narration This problem is not like that of assessing the warrantability of a general claim. For example, '*All* seventh sons of seventh sons can levitate' does not depend on the credibility of witnesses in the way that 'Daniel Dunglas Home levitated' does.

Why do so many people believe that Freud was able to reconstruct from the Wolf Man's nightmare, aged four, in which he was stared at by wolves on a tree, an episode several years earlier in which he saw his parents copulating dog fashion. Is the circumstantial detail so convincing? Does it reach the Miss Havisham level? No. (And Freud himself does not seem to have thought so.) They believe it not because of the evidence Freud gives but because of the evidence he says he has. And this is not objectionable in itself but only when inconsistently accompanied by protests at the introduction into the discussion of Freud's astuteness and reliability as a reporter.

Why Psychoanalysis Is a Testimonial Science

In 1913 the physician-author of a paper on Freud wrote in connection with his own conviction as to the truth of his theory: 'To deny the evidence of these psycho-analytical findings with regard to infantile sexual phantasies is to deny the intellectual integrity of Freud and his followers.'[74] I believe this to have been, and to be still, the real as opposed to the apparent basis of the division between those who do and those who do not accept the Freudian accounts of the nature and influence of infantile sexual life (as well as others of Freud's more distinctive theses).

I have always been suspicious of those analysts and their apologists who assure us that their own disinterestedness or probity is a matter of utter irrelevance to the question of the warrantability of their assertions. They protest too much. Jacob Arlow, one of the analysts who participated in the NYU symposium, and issued assurances of the demonstrability of much that 'enlightened' revisionists now hold is without warrant, maintained, 'The validity of a scientific hypothesis is completely independent of the motivations of the person who promulgates it.'[75] And yet this is what he was telling the NYU symposiasts a year or so later:

> In the course of a detailed psychoanalytic investigation it could be predicted that a specific childhood experience regarding bowel training and interest in excrement would emerge . . . These are predictions that have been validated regularly, hundreds and hundreds of times . . . the trained and experienced psychoanalyst can hypothesise correctly concerning the genesis and development of certain mental characteristics.[76]

How is the validity of contested claims like those advanced by Arlow to be assessed without taking account of the motivations of those who claim to have corroborated them? Freud's law-like claims might, where they are testable, accumulate support not dependent on the trustworthiness of analytic testimony, but what of the particular claims which are the staple of analytic publications? Here is a brief, manageable specimen of the kind of claim which we must attempt to assess when dealing with the copious literature corroborating Freud's thesis as to the sexual expressiveness of neurotic symptoms. Freud says of one patient that 'her fear of an erection of the clitoris expressed itself by the imposition of a rule to remove all going clocks and watches.'[77] Why did Freud think this? Because the idea of a nocturnally throbbing clitoris was the terminus of her associations to her rule about removing the clocks? Because she said at some point, 'I see now—my rule about moving the clocks and watches is an expression of my fear of being awoken by my throbbing clitoris,' or because she said 'I feel less compulsion to remove the clocks and watches before going to bed now that you have explained its connection with my throbbing clitoris'? Or was it because her associations and behaviour generally displayed a pattern which in Freud's judgement required the assumption that she unconsciously associated her clitoris with clocks and watches? Whatever the answers to questions such as

74. Maurice Wright, 'The Psychology of Freud and its Relation to the Unconscious'. *The Medical Magazine* (1914), p. 145.

75. Jacob Arlow, 'Truth or Motivations', *The Saturday Review* (15 June 1958).

76. Jacob Arlow, 'Psychoanalysis as Scientific Method', in Hook, ed., *Psychoanalysis, Philosophy and Scientific Method* (Grove Press, 1959).

77. *IL* 17 (Penguin, 1991), p. 306.

these it is plain how much acceptance of them depends on a judgement as to the astuteness and disinterestedness of those who supply them. What was urged in 1913 as to the dependence of 'psychoanalytic findings' on the 'intellectual integrity of Freud and his followers' is correct and extends beyond infantile sexuality to the entire clinical corpus. It is the credibility of psychoanalysts and not the cogency of their arguments which is the ultimate source of the division between those who do and those who do not accept the distinctive claims of Freudian theory.

Evasion of the Appeal to Clinical Experience

As an example of how far commentators are willing to go to avoid the issue of the credibility of psychoanalytic informants consider how grossly Erwin and Grünbaum misrepresent the argument of Robert Waelder.[78]

Waelder's asserts that the evidence for Freudian psychodynamics is the experience, 'repeated countless times,' during the analysis and in the patient's later life that 'this particular set of interpretations and no other can dispel the symptoms when they reappear.'[79] This argument is reinforced by a remark which both Erwin and Grünbaum ignore: 'There are patients who at a late stage of their analysis or after its termination can make or unmake their symptoms at will.' Erwin's comment is the feeble objection that Waelder's claim is 'undermined because we now have strong reason to doubt that the analyst's interpretations are necessary for dispelling a patient's neurotic symptoms.'[80] But this assumption plays no role in Waelder's argument which is of the same order as that which Erwin countenances when allowing that among the exceptions to the rule, that 'it is not possible to confirm a clinical hypothesis by using clinical data', are cases like that in which use of shock to eliminate the self-injurious behaviour of an autistic child was held effective because 'the the effects were so large and so immediate.' If Waelder's argument is to be rejected, it is his testimony not his reasoning that must be impugned.

Waelder ventures no specific example of how the patients' symptoms come and go according as they accept or reject the analyst's interpretation of their latent content. The result is that he makes it sound as if the relationship were as straightforward and as observable as that between the lengthening of Pinocchio's nose and the lies that he told the blue fairy. If things really did generally happen this way then the case for clinical valida-

---

78. Adolf Grünbaum, *Foundations of Psychoanalysis* (University of California Press, 1984), p. 147; Edwin Erwin, 'The Truth About Psychoanalysis, *Journal of Philosophy* (1981), pp. 555–56.

79. Robert Waelder, *Journal of the American Psychoanalytic Association*, Vol. 10, #3, (July 1962), p. 269.

80. Erwin, p. 553.

tion of interpretations would be overwhelming. But without a much more circumstantial account than Waelder gives it is not possible to assess the weight of his argument. For one thing, its implications are bewildering since we don't see how a patient's belief or disbelief in the analyst's interpretation can be commanded at will, as Waelder implies.

The natural doubts that Waelder's claim provokes do not have their source in the possibility that the patient was suggestible, which Erwin mechanically appeals to, but in its implausibility when we once attempt to form a concrete picture of what Waelder is asking us to credit. Suppose we try to imagine a particular instance of the kind familiar to us from psychoanalytic discourse: Dora's cough, say. Are we being asked to imagine that the tickle in her throat would go away only so long as she acknowledged her desire to fellate her father, and would come back as soon as she expressed any doubt about this: 'I don't want to fellate my father,' followed by a spasm of coughing. 'Perhaps I do after all', followed by by their immediate cessation? This is certainly in a class with Pinocchio's nose, but are the symptoms of neuroses and the repressed ideation maintaining them generally so temporally circumscribed that we can relate them in so clear-cut a manner? These are the questions raised by Waelder's argument but, instead of addressing them, Erwin and Grünbaum mechanically resort to the highly unlikely possibility that the facts Waelder asserts could be due to the patient's suggestibility.

The same moral of the centrality of our confidence in the analyst's ability to report accurately is illustrated by the testimony of Aaron Green, the pseudonym of the paradigmatic analyst in Janet Malcolm's *New Yorker* articles on analysis: 'I began to see things Freud had described—to actually see for myself symptoms disappearing as the unconscious became conscious. That was an incredible thing. It was like looking through a telescope and realising that you are seeing what Galileo saw.'[81] Those of us who do not believe in the existence of the phenomena Malcolm's analyst claims to have seen must form some account of why he, nevertheless, felt entitled to say he had seen them.

The Sceptic's Dilemma: Must Freudians Be Either Right or Lying?

> I do not say that they deliberately speak studied falsehood, or have a settled purpose to deceive . . . They are not much accustomed to be interrogated by others; and seem never to have thought upon interrogating themselves. So that if they do not know what they tell to be true, they likewise do not distinctly perceive it to be false. (Samuel Johnson, *A Journey to the Western Islands*)

---

81. Janet Malcolm, *Psychoanalysis: The Impossible Profession* (London: Picador, 1982), p. 71.

The problem is this: why were phenomena now acknowledged to be without adequate warrant reported so often by previous generations of analysts? Many revisionist deny the existence of penis envy. What account can
they give of the fact that this phenomenon was, nevertheless, so regularly
reported? Though one of their number assures us that analysts 'have not
lacked practitioners of the lie',[82] the antithesis between credibility and
mendacity which apologists sometimes try to force on their critics is a tendentious one. John Forrester wants to tie critics down to the thesis that
'the data is untrustworthy because the analyst made it all up,' and argues
that this is 'inherently implausible.'[83] The sceptic does not require large-
scale lying on the part of analysts to account for the consistent reporting
of phenomena now conceded not to occur. This is the logician, William
De Morgan, testifying in support of the reality of levitation and other
mediumistic phenomena: 'I am perfectly convinced that I have both seen
and heard, in a manner that should make unbelief impossible, things called
spiritual, which cannot be taken by a rational being to be capable of explanation by imposture, coincidence, or mistake.'[84] Is it necessary to believe
that De Morgan was lying in order to conclude that his judgment was radically defective? I don't think so and thus can see no reason why we should
not ignore Forrester's fake antithesis and say the same thing about Freud
and his followers. This is not to deny that mendacity may have played a
role but it is not the only option.[85] In one of the most famous and influential experiments in social psychology, Solomon Asch, in the course of an
enquiry into social conformity, investigated the likelihood that an experimental subject, gulled into believing that all eleven of his fellow subjects
had judged two drawn lines which were blatantly unequal to be equal,
would endorse what he knew to be a false judgment. How many would go
along with the false but unanimous view of the other subjects? Quite a few.
Is this how we are to conceive of those analysts who regularly reported
phenomena now held not to occur? It is unlikely and there are other possibilities. In his book *Tolstoi: The Comprehensive Vision*[86] Edward
Greenwood discusses the varieties of self deception presented by Tolstoi in
War and Peace. The one which most closely approximates to the compli-

---

82. Leslie Farber, *Lying, Despair, Jealousy, Sex, Suicide, Drugs, and the Good Life* (New
York: Basic Books, 1976), p. 207.

83. John Forrester, *Dispatches from the Freud Wars* (Harvard University Press, 1996), p.
221.

84. William de Morgan, quoted in *Miracles and Modern Spiritualism* (London: Alfred
Russell Wallace, Nichols and Co., 1901), p. 83

85. I deal with the 'lying for truth' rationale in my contribution to 'The Freud
Controversy' in Michael Roth, ed., *Freud: Conflict and Culture* (Alfred Knopf, 1998).

86. Edward Greenwood, *Tolstoi: The Comprehensive Vision* (Methuen, 1975), p. 90.

antly mendacious subject in Asch's experiment is that of a young woman, Sonya, who, looking into a mirror on an occasion when, according to tradition, she is expected to have some clairvoyant vision sees nothing, but on being eagerly pressed as to what she saw muses: 'Why shouldn't I say I saw something? Others do see. Besides who can tell whether I saw anything or not?' There is a psychologically penetrating addendum to this episode much later in the book: 'what she had invented then seemed to her now as real as any recollection.' Similarly, the analyst's initial distortion of what happened during the analytic hour may be obliterated from his memory when he comes to write his paper, or to testify in polemics that he has confirmed Freud's results 'on countless occasions.' So that initial deception is succeeded by self-deception.[87] Another of Tolstoi's varieties of self deception noted by Greenwood may fit the misreporting analyst even better.

It is that of a defeated general immediately after a battle who gives a false self-justifying account of what had transpired and on whom Tolstoi charitably comments that he had so wished that things had fallen out as he related that 'it seemed to him as if it had really happened. Could one make out amid all that confusion, what did or did not happen?' The transactions of the analytic hour are notoriously ambiguous and it requires no uncommon degree of duplicity for an analyst to reduce this ambiguity 'that the scriptures might be fulfilled.' I suspect that the average analyst's unwarranted confirmation reports are more like the face-saving distortions of Tolstoi's General than like Sonya's straightforward lying as to what she saw in the mirror. Perhaps a mean between charity and timorousness can be achieved by adapting to the case of those analysts who 'on countless occasions' confirmed the existence of non-existent phenomena the summary judgement the historian Sir Charles Firth gave on Macaulay's more egregious errors: 'His impressions and his recollections were singularly vivid and concrete. They became as real to him as if they were palpable, external things. He did not remember that they were his own creatures.' This allows us to give an account at once more realistic and more charitable. It isn't that analysts saw perfectly well, as in Asch's experiment, the true relation of the lines but reported otherwise; it is that they expressed themselves in ways which conveyed that they were dealing with matters as straightforward as the length of lines when their experience was much more equivocal. Freud, for example, says of Adler's heretical account of the dynamics of infantile life, 'Adler exhibits the most serious departures from actual observation.'[88] When the psychotherapist,

---

87. See William James on the distinction between first and later tellings in *Principles of Psychology*, Vol. 1, pp. 373–74.

88. 'The Psychoanalytic Movement' *CP I* (Hogarth, 1924), p. 345.

Tom Williams, objected that analysts were claiming an authority for their theories to which they were not entitled, Ernest Jones replied that anyone could verify them since one could learn analysis as readily as one could learn Italian: 'Neither is very difficult.'[89]

The case of Robert Waelder is even more instructive. In 1936 he was maintaining that the facts of infantile life discovered by psychoanalysts could be recorded on film. (Joan Riviere dissented from this.) But a quarter of a century later he tells us that those of only normal perceptual abilities would have to trust the judgement of an elite of analytically trained specialists for their knowledge of these matters.[90] That the deception generally consisted in making matters which were open to interpretation sound as if they were matters of straightforward perception, rather than unequivocal deception, is suggested by the following episode. One of the most intemperate of Freud's early American advocates was Samuel Tannenbaum who handled Jung very roughly when he severed his connection with Freud. 'On a psychoanalyst Jung makes the impression of one who accepts the unconscious from a theoretical knowledge only, not of one who became convinced of the reality of the unconscious by experience.'[91] A few years later the author of this statement was asserting with equal vociferousness that the unconscious was a 'myth', a 'fabrication' and an 'unwarranted deduction.'[92] How could Tannenbaum imply that he knew the unconscious at first hand, not merely theoretically, and then maintain that it did not exist? We need not brand him a perjurer if we bear in mind the distinctions made above.

Recycling More Pertinent Than Stonewalling

There is a practice which has a closer bearing on the adverse judgement of Freudian theory than stonewalling—recycling. Stonewalling has at least the merit of acknowledging the objections whose force is denied. In recycling, arguments and theses are merely repeated without any acknowledgement of the objections and corrections they have provoked, or which would natu-

---

89. *Journal of Abnormal Psychology* (June–July 1911).

90. 1936: 'The final proof of the results arrived at by psychoanalytic interpretation lies outside analysis in the direct observation of children. . . . It would probably be quite right to say that the evidence of these infantile processes could be presented in a talking film' ('Infantile Conflict', *International Journal of Psychoanalysis*, p. 422). A quarter of a century later Waelder is looking forward to a time 'several generations hence' when a situation will obtain with regard to the propositions of psychoanalysis in which the 'people at large accept the judgement of experts as correct although they themselves cannot check on it' (*Basic Theory of Psychoanalysis* [London: International Universities Press, 1960], p. 31)

91. Samuel Tannenbaum 'Psychoanalysis Desexualised', *American Medicine* (December, 1915), p. 913.

92. 'There Is No Evidence to Prove the Reality of the Unconscious,' *New York Times* (Sunday, 19 March 1922).

rally arise. An area in which this is most apparent but whose bearing on the issue of pseudoscience has been denied or underappreciated is Freudian historiography.

Recycling and Hagiography

When we consider the kind of stories that still circulate about Freud the impression forces itself on us that for many university-educated people the legend of Freud's heroic search for truth replaced Kipling's 'If' as a major source of secular edification. It might be thought that Freud can hardly be blamed for this. But the majority of Freud legends were not due to our inveterate tendency to idealise. Freud spares us this trouble and does it for us. It is Freud, for example, who first called attention to his 'moral courage.'[93]

On October 20 1895 Freud reports to Fliess that he had put his views on the role of sexual repression in hysteria to an assembly of his colleagues and that they had 'liked it.'[94] Some months later he speaks of a subsequent lecture on hysteria meeting with with 'an icy reception'.[95] What had happened in the interim? The seduction theory. Yet Freud was disingenuous enough to invoke his rough welcome at this meeting as evidence of the unreasoning hostility of his Viennese colleagues to the mention of sexuality while withholding from the reader that the thesis which was greeted with such sceptical derision ('a scientific fairy tale') was not his introduction of sexual repression but of the seduction theory which Freud himself later described as a 'momentous error' which 'collapsed under the weight of its own improbability.'[96] Freud's misrepresentation soon became proverbial. This is G.S. Viereck recycling it in an intellectual monthly in 1925:

> When first he delivered a lecture before a group of students assembled under the auspices of Professor Krafft-Ebing, he noticed the chill that struck the assemblage. For the resistance implanted in our soul against the recognition of the demon within us is equally strong in all human beings. Freud found himself surrounded by emptiness. A negative wall seemed to rise between himself and his fellow men. For many years, he lived, as he says himself, on a desert island. Undismayed, this Robinson Crusoe of Science continued his solitary studies.[97]

Though this account may, have been a manifestation of Viereck's personal tendency to hero worship—since he was later to transfer his infatuation

---

93. 'History of the Psychoanalytic Movement', *CP 1*, (Hogarth, 1924), p. 304.
94. *The Complete Letters of Sigmund Freud to Wilhelm Fliess* J.M. Masson, ed., (London: Belknap Press, 1985).
95. *ibid.*, p. 184.
96. 'History of the Psychoanalytic Movement,' *CP 1*, p. 303.
97. G.S. Viereck 'Freud: The Columbus of the Unconscious'. *The Forum* (1925), p. 303.

to Hitler—no other commentator who speaks of Freud's period of 'splendid isolation'—Freud's own self-description—notices that this 'isolation' coincided with his espousal of the privately repudiated seduction theory. The conventional account of the hostile response to Freud's lecture on hysteria in males of almost a decade earlier is almost as baseless. The novelist, Anthony Burgess, in a review wrote, 'Freud's contemporaries laughed when he said that hysteria was a male disease. "Hustera", they pointed out, was Greek for womb and males, they reminded him, don't have wombs.'[98] Burgess, like several others who transmit the story, has inflated a single comment by a person who was not a neurologist in any case, but a surgeon, into a chorus. Another account runs: 'when he was a young man he tried to present to the Vienna Medical society a case of hysteria in a male patient. One of the old greybeards said: "obviously, the young doctor doesn't know his Greek: 'hysteria' means 'womb sickness.'" The other members of the society jeered and hooted Freud out of the room, thus preventing him from presenting his evidence.'[99]

A much earlier version runs: 'He read a paper to his medical colleagues upon his explorations with Charcot into the hidden reality of the mind through hysteria and hypnosis. When in the course of his report he spoke of cases of hysteria in men, the angry tension exploded in a guffaw. "Has a man a hystero—a womb?" they asked, and stalked out of the room.'[100] In one version it is Freud who leaves the room having been hooted and jeered at; in the other it is his indignant and derisive audience who 'stalked' out. Since we have the minutes of this meeting we know that neither happened. But why are such accounts, nevertheless, circulated by those with no direct interest in the matter? It is partly inertia but also a function of their superior 'tellability': they make good stories. But whatever the reason it does go some way towards resolving the question of why more substantive theses, like the Oedipus complex, castration anxiety, the libido theory, sexual symbolism, and so forth, managed to surmount the most cogent objections. The hagiographical tradition matters because it fed into the more impersonal, substantive expositions and permitted lacunae, and even absurdities, to go unnoticed which, had they emanated from anyone other than Freud, would surely have been remarked on.

This compulsion for appreciative comment, however fanciful, persists to this day and is illustrated by Edith Kurzweil, an editor of the *Partisan Review*. She speaks in her book of an occasion when 'Anna O., relieved of her illness, embraced Freud. As Freud listened to her story, he connected her symptoms to the relationship she had with Breuer . . . Freud did allow Anna

---

98. Anthony Burgess, *The Observer* (London, 29 May 1966), Review section.
99. Neal Miller, Chairman's Opening Remarks. *The Role of Learning in Psychotherapy*, Ruth Porter, ed., (J.A. Churchill Ltd., 1968), p. 2.
100. Edwin Embree, *Prospecting for Heaven* (New York: Viking, 1932).

O. to question him and to tell him what she chose to . . . this change in roles did remove her hysterical symptoms.'[101] None of the incidents mentioned by Kurzweil ever occurred. Freud never listened to Anna O.'s story as he was not involved in her treatment which was terminated by Breuer over a decade before Freud began practising psychoanalysis. In any case, we have known for almost fifty years that Anna O. was not 'relieved of her illness'. As to what really became of her symptoms Mikkel Borch-Jacobsen's illuminating account can be consulted.[102]

How Hagiography Influenced the Reception of Freud's Theories

The way in which this unthinking repetition of the Freudian version of events affects even substantive issues is illustrated in Nathan Hale's account of Freud's paper 'Wild Psychoanalysis':

> In 1910, aware that he was being misconstrued, Freud issued a warning against wild psychoanalysis—the prescription of sexual intercourse for the relief of neurosis. Freud insisted that he did not define sexuality in terms of 'coitus'. He was using sex in the same broad sense as the word 'love'. No amount of coitus or other sexual acts could cure neuroses. Sexual satisfaction, then, was in large proportion a psychological gratification.[103]

Hale does not ask how the 'broad sense' of the term love could have produced the tickle in Dora's throat, or the Wolf Man's constipation, etc., etc. But more important for my present purpose, is his conventional misreading of Freud's text, which is at the same time an example of the Lloyd Jones–Tacitus effect, since it asks to be misread. What Freud says about sexual intercourse, and Hale, understandably, overlooks is that the advice to seek sexual gratification 'often . . . led to good results in the end . . .' And Freud concludes that the physician whose carnal construal of sexuality he had spent the paper deploring, 'did force her attention to the real cause of her trouble.'[104]

Masturbation is another topic on which Freud is invariably assigned more enlightened views than those he actually held. In 1896 he referred to it as a 'pernicious form of sexual satisfaction.' In the 1912 discussions he refused to accept Stekel's view that any harm resulting from the practice was entirely due to its psychic, rather than its physiological consequences. And yet in James Strachey's *Standard Edition* preface to the 1898 paper,

---

101. Edith Kurzweil, *The Freudians: A Comparative Perspective* (Yale University Press, 1989), pp. 62–63. Peter Swales called this to my attention.
102. *Remembering Anna O.* (Routledge, 1997).
103. *Freud and the Americans* (New York: Oxford University Press, 1971), pp. 292–93
104. 'Wild Psychoanalysis', *CP 2* (Hogarth, 1924), p. 304.

'Sexuality in the Aetiology of the Neuroses', he illustrates Freud's 'animad-versions against the social conventions of civilisation . . .' with his 'outspoken criticism of the attitude of the medical profession to . . . masturbation.'[105] One would naturally take these words to mean that Freud was expressing enlightened objections to the prevalent scare-mongering as to the damaging consequences of masturbation. On the contrary, in the paper Strachey refers us to, Freud criticises physicians for taking masturbation too *lightly* and being too inclined to underestimate its pathogenic effects. It is not surpris-ing then that so few are aware that Freud shared the masturbation phobia of his less enlightened contemporaries and contributed to prolonging a view of its deleteriousness that had for over a century cast a pall over Europe which, even if it did not quite eclipse the gaiety of nations, did much to diminish the harmless stock of private pleasure.[106] Another example of the extent to which the less creditable episodes in Freud's history are painted over is provided by the delicious obsequiousness with which Richard Wollheim conveys to his readers that Freud delayed for eight years his pub-lic admission that he was wrong about the invariability of infantile seduction in the history of his neurotic patients. Wollheim informs them that Freud's change of mind was 'only slowly assimilated in the published work', as if Freud's determination to conceal his error was as independent of his will as his metabolism. The representativeness of these euphemising distortions produces an impression that were it discovered that Freud was a cannibal and that he considered fricasseed babies a particular delicacy we would be informed that 'Freud's well-known fondness for children has recently received additional confirmation'.

Further evidence of Freud's Teflon status is provided by Jean Schimek, a psychoanalyst, who wrote a remarkably belated account of certain discrep-ancies between the received view of the seduction episode and what can be gleaned from the papers themselves.[107] Since the received view derived from Freud's own retrospective accounts, some critical reflections on his reliabil-ity might be felt in order. But not for Schimek who writes:

> An examination of Freud's texts of 1896 suggests that the early sexual trauma was not based on the patient's recovered memories but was reconstructed by Freud, by interpreting a variety of data in the light of his theoretical assumptions. This is not a startling or damning conclusion, since a few years later Freud read-ily admitted that many of the crucial experiences of childhood were never directly

105. *S.E.*, Vol. 3, pp. 261–62.

106. E.H. Hare, 'Masturbational Insanity: The History of an Idea'. *Journal of Insanity*, Vol. 108 (1962), pp. 1-25.

107. Jean Schimek, 'Fact and Fantasy in the Seduction Theory'. *Journal of the American Psychoanalytic Association*, 35, No. 4, (1987).

remembered but only inferred and reconstructed by the analyst, through the interpretation of dreams, fantasies, transference, etc.[108]

Why should the fact that the hypothesised 'sexual traumas were not based on the patients recovered memories' not be both startling and damning since it contradicts every account of the seduction episode Freud later gave? And how does Freud's later admission, that 'the early sexual trauma was not based on the patients recovered memories' extenuate Freud's repeated, untruthful, assertion that the patients of the 1896 papers recollected and related false accounts of infantile molestations thus misleading him as to the source of their affliction? What does it take to startle Schimek?

The intimidatory power of the Freud legend is such that expositors are as oblivious of the anomalies in Freud's accounts as biblical fundamentalists to the fact that there are two inconsistent accounts of the Creation in Genesis, or the improbability of Moses's post-mortem account of his own death. Here, by contrast, is an example of Freud's obliquity which only came to light as a consequence of the publication of his letters, and so it is only those who have issued testimonials to Freud's unremitting candour in the last few decades or so who ought to be ashamed of themselves. It pertains to the untruthfulness of his repeated insistence that he had no theoretical grounds for his emphasis on the role of repressed sexual impulses, but that this was forced on him by his clinical observations. (Not even Wollheim believes this, and in his book on Freud lists several theoretical reasons for the privileged pathogenic role of sexuality, though he does not, of course, draw the inference that Freud was misrepresenting the matter.)

In 1894 Freud wrote, 'In all the cases I have analysed it was in the sexual life that a painful affect . . . had originated. On theoretical grounds it is not impossible that this affect may at times arise in other spheres: I have merely to state that hitherto I have not discovered any other origin of it.'[109] Two years later, in Draft K of January 1896 which he sent to Fliess, the theoretical grounds for the requirement that the pathogenic trauma be sexual are elaborately stated. His repudiation of a theoretical commitment to sexuality is repeated in a letter to Jung of October 1906: 'I have no theoretical objection to affording equal importance to the other basic drive, if only it would assert itself unmistakably in the psychoneuroses . . . I content myself

---

108. This remark is from Schimek's letter in Frederick Crews, *The Memory Wars* (A New York Review Book, 1995), p. 77. Crews's reply is on pp. 111–112. See also Han Israëls and Morton Schatzman, 'The Seduction Theory'. *History of Psychiatry*, Vol. 4 (1993); Allen Esterson 'Jeffrey Masson and Freud's Seduction Theory: a New Fable Based on Old Myths'. *History of the Human Sciences*, Vol. 11 (February 1998); Cioffi, 'From Freud's "Scientific Fairy Tale" to Masson's Politically Correct One', Chapter 8 of this volume.

109. 'The Defense Neuropsychoses', *CP 1*, p. 66.

with pointing out what is glaringly evident, that is, the role of sexuality.'[110] But in January 1907 the theoretical rationale is reinstated. In connection with a dream reported in Jung's book on dementia praecox, of which he had failed to give a sexual interpretation, Freud wrote 'the wish revealed in the dream must *for reasons of fundamental theory* be different from what you state' (My italics—FC). His theoretical commitment to the privileged role of sexuality is repeated in two subsequent letters to Jung. In August 1907 he writes, 'I regard (for the present) the role of sexual complexes in hysteria merely as a theoretical necessity and do not infer it from their frequency and intensity.' Once again, in 1908, Freud, in reply to a letter from Jung suggesting that the sexual etiology of the neuroses was valid 'only for some cases' (19 April 1908) writes, 'I feel a fundamental aversion towards your suggestion that my conclusions are correct, but only for certain cases (points of view instead of conclusions). That is not very well possible. Entirely or not at all. They are concerned with such fundamental matters that they could not be valid for one set of cases only. One would have the right to designate those cases otherwise in which they are absent.' And yet to the end of his life Freud *publicly* insisted that his grounds for imputing an overriding role to sexuality were purely clinical. His last statement on the subject is even quoted by Laplanche and Pontalis in *The Language of Psychoanalysis* where it is taken at face value: 'Theoretically there is no objection to supposing that any sort of instinctual demand whatever could occasion (pathogenic repression) but our observations show us . . . that the excitations that play this pathogenic part arise from sexual life.'[111]

Recycling: The Discovery of the Oedipus Complex

The most common of recycled legends is that of Freud's discovery of the Oedipus complex. This comes in two versions though they are sometimes combined. According to one version Freud came to realise that what at first appeared to be his patients' memories of molestation at the hands of their fathers were self-exonerating distortions of wish-fulfilling incestuous fantasies. Even if we waive the objection that the seducer was only identified as paternal in Freud's retrospective accounts and not in his contemporary ones, that still leaves the question as to why, in almost a century since the Oedipus complex was bestowed on the world, no one has asked how a theory about the pathogenic centrality of the boy's sexual desire for his mother was inspired by women's false memories of having been seduced by their fathers. Though six of Freud's eighteen, presumably seduced, patients were men,

110. William McGuire, ed., *The Freud/Jung Letters* (London: Hogarth Press and Routledge, 1974). p. 8.

111. *Outline* (Hogarth, 1949), p. 52.

nowhere did he suggest that they were suffering the aftermath of sexual abuse by their mothers, even less that they had memories of such maternal abuse.

This difficulty in deriving the Oedipus complex from the incestuous fantasies of female patients may be responsible for its replacement or supplementation by another story. According to this account the discovery of the Oedipus complex was occasioned by Freud's heroic self-analysis. But this account also has its elided incoherences. There are two features of Freud's self-analysis which render it an implausible explanation of why Freud decided that 'being in love' with the mother and jealousy of the father, as he put it when he announced his discovery to his friend Fliess, was 'a universal event in early childhood.'[112] The first problem this raises is how 'a universal event' could explain why only some people become neurotic, an objection which could not be lodged against the the seduction theory which it replaced. In addition to this general objection, which would not arise if Freud had confined the complex to neurotics (as several of Freud's critics were later to argue he should have done), there was another consideration that told against the legitimacy of extrapolating from his own self-analysis to all mankind. At the time when he imputed infantile incestuous feelings to himself he was a self-diagnosed hysteric. Might not that be a sufficient explanation of his infantile desire for his mother without the need to invoke a universal incestuous propensity? Moreover, the reconstructed infantile occasion which was his putative ground for assigning himself infantile sexual feelings for his mother—an occasion on which he was sexually aroused by the sight of her naked body—took place only after he had suffered sexual molestation at the hands of his 'nanny'. This ought to have led him to assign his maternally induced excitement to his precociously aroused sexuality rather than to an innate incestuous proclivity.

Another elided issue is why the desire was repressed. Castration threats are far from universal and when they are made they are not linked to the child's erotic feelings for his mother. So why does he make this connection? It might be answered that he makes it because he is aware of the fantasies that accompany the masturbatory activities at which the castration threat is aimed, but this, oddly enough, is not Freud's view. What Freud says is that the child represses his memory of autoerotic activities because he is ashamed of their objectless character and so raises them to 'a higher level' by retrospectively endowing them with an incestuous character. Why he should be more ashamed of autoerotic masturbations than of those accompanied by incestuous fantasies is not addressed by Freud or his expositors. Nor is the question why he should substitute the demoralising thought that he had

---

112. *Freud to Fliess*, 15 October 1897, p. 272

been abused by his mother for the comparatively innocuous one that he had desired her. I believe that only two commentators have noted the anachronism involved in imputing to an infant the incest horror which is a product of culture, Voloshinov and G.K. Chesterton.[113]

Recycling: The Nature of Neurotic Conflict—What Is a Penis For?

The impression that the critical reflections which would normally arise are forced out of their natural paths in response to Freud's rhetoric or the pressure of tradition, can be copiously documented, though its precise implications may be disputed. Consider one of the most familiar components of Freud's theory of the neuroses, one that he most insisted on and which was repeated over a period of forty years until his last pronouncement on the subject: A neurosis is the outcome of a conflict between a repressed sexual impulse and a reaction against it due to the fear that its indulgence would risk castration.

There is something puzzling and incoherent about this account of the role of sexuality in neurotic conflict even before Freud began equivocating as to what he meant by the term 'sexual'. The conflict is supposed to be between the sexual instinct in pursuit of whose gratification the organism is endangered, and the self-preservative instinct, in the service of which the organism forgoes the gratification in question. It ought to be surprising then that the self-preservative instinct manifests itself as a fear of castration, loss of the penis. No commentator has stopped to reflect on what a penis is for and why its removal would be viewed with distinctive apprehension independently of its sexual function. How does an organ, which has two claims to be considered eminently qualified to represent the sexual instinct in that it is both a means of propagating the race and the main source of sexual pleasure, become a manifestation of the ostensibly antagonistic self-preservative instinct? Why has this anomaly in one of Freud's most familiar theses passed without comment for almost a century? There is a correlative anomaly. There is nothing particularly species-preservative about the gratification of oral and anal instincts, and yet Freud placed them on the species preservative side of the equation. Why? More significant still, why is it that in raising questions like this we are made to feel as if we had disrupted a midnight Mass with a demand for proof that Jesus was born on the 25th of December?

---

113. V.N. Voloshinov, *A Critical Analysis of Freudianism* [1928] (New York: Academic Press, 1976), p. 81; G.K. Chesterton, 'The Game of Psychoanalysis'. *The Century*, CVI (1923), p. 40.

Recycling: Unasked Questions; Why Is What St. Paul Called 'Love' Repressed?

In the preface to the fourth (1920) edition of *Three Essays on Sexuality* we have another observation which has passed without remark. Freud admonishes those who object to the 'stretching' of the concept of sexuality 'necessitated by analyses of children and perverts' to remember how closely the enlarged sexuality of psychoanalysis coincides with 'the Eros of the divine Plato.'[114]

Why are 'instincts which seek to preserve and unite'—which is Freud's description of Plato's Eros—repressed? And how would their repression produce the characteristic symptomatology of hysteria which they were initially introduced to explain? How did the Eros of the divine Plato produce the tickle in Dora's throat? Or the Wolf Man's constipation? Or the virgin's hysterical migraine headaches? (And why does 'the stretching of the concept of sexuality necessitated' by the oral and anal desires of infants and perverts bring it closer to the 'Eros of the divine Plato' than the narrow genital conception of sexuality manifested in straightforwardly heterosexual love-making? Has Freud been listening to malicious gossip about 'the divine Plato'?)

Freud's later emendations of what was comprised under the heading of sexuality have never been clarified, and even commentators as reverential as Laplanche and Pontalis are compelled to acknowledge their inability to explain what Freud meant by libido. None of this deters Wollheim, Seaborn Jones, Marshall Edelson, Thomas Nagel, and others from believing that, as Wollheim puts it, Freud demonstrated the 'variety' and 'pervasiveness' of sexual motives.[115] Anyone with an appetite for profitless exertion may consult Wollheim's chapter on sexuality and attempt to work out what he means by this. He will find no account of how Freud's repeated extension of the term to encompass matters he had hitherto explicitly excluded was clinically justified. Just what is it which Wollheim believes Freud to have demonstrated the 'variety and pervasiveness' of? What is it which Freud called sexual which had not previously been called sexual but which Freud (or as Freud prefers to put it, 'psychoanalytic research') demonstrated to be so?

This is the earliest of Freud's enlargements: 'We have extended the meaning of the concept of "sexuality" only so far as to include the sexual life of perverted persons and also of children . . .' Does the application of the term 'sexual' to the non-reproductive activities of perverts represent an extension of its ordinary use? Wollheim (like others) does not notice (or chooses not to remark) that Freud is here crediting himself with the

---

114. *On Sexuality* (Penguin Books, 1977), p. 43.
115. Richard Wollheim, *Freud* (Fontana, 1992), p. 123.

discovery that fellatio and buggery are sexual activities.[116] How can the non-carnal activities and impulses which Freud later called sexual ('self-love, love for parents and children, friendship, love for humanity in general, devotion to concrete objects and abstract ideas')[117] be considered hidden and in need of uncovering, or their pervasiveness in need of demonstration? Isn't it because, Wollheim, like other expositors intent on celebration, forgets Freud's extension of the term sexual and reverts to its explicitly repudiated and readily understood 'popular' sense while at the same time forgetting that in that sense it is far from pervasive and not even very varied.

Here are some representative instances of Freud uncovering sexuality in its familiar sense, where its presence was previously unsuspected. We are told that the tickle in Dora's throat was due to her imagining performing fellatio on her father, the Wolf Man's constipation was due to his unconscious wish to be anally penetrated, fear of looking from windows is due to the repressed desire to beckon to men from them, and so on. In cases like these it is at least clear why the repressed impulses are called sexual and how they would account for the symptoms they are invoked to explain. But when it is a matter of devotion to 'abstract ideas', and similar instances of Freud's enlargement of sexuality, the thesis becomes less graspable since it is difficult to imagine what associations to proportional representation, the single tax, states rights, or the axiom of extensionality could warrant their being recognised as disguised manifestations of sexual impulses. The only intelligible political examples that spring to mind are Jones's claim that the return to the gold standard was rooted in anal eroticism, where we can imagine associations leading from the clandestinely to the overtly excremental; and his explanation of Irish republicanism, where we are asked to imagine that an Irish nationalist's free associations to the theme of Irish unification might terminate in the thought of an English soldier ravishing an Irish virgin (since, Jones tells us, to a nationalist, Ireland is a woman—and the six Protestant counties of Ulster an English penis, presumably). Wollheim's one example of the pervasiveness of sexuality—the savage's animistic belief in the omnipotence of thought which demonstrate his 'lovingly', as Wollheim puts it, *'lovingly'*, conferring magical powers on his own mental processes—is less easy to make sense of. How is 'lovingly' overestimating the influence of one's thoughts on the external world like providing oneself with sexual pleasure by 'lovingly' stroking one's genitals. Isn't the likeness exhausted in both

---

116. Freud credits himself with the same astonishing feat in the *Introductory Lectures* when he writes: 'What is called sexuality outside psychoanalysis applies only to the restricted sexual life that is subordinated to the reproductive function and is called normal,' and 'painstaking researches . . . have revealed that classes of human beings exist whose sexual life deviates from the usual one in the most striking manner.'

117. *Group Psychology* (Hogarth, 1922), p. 38.

activities being gratuitously described by Wollheim as performed 'lovingly'?

It is characteristic of expositions of Freud's view of the role of sexuality to attenuate its fancifulness by describing it equivocally. In one passage Wollheim speaks euphemistically of 'the boy's loving wish for his mother.' There is something suspiciously evasive about speaking of the Oedipus complex in terms of the conflict generated by the child's 'loving wish for its mother' in one sentence and then of castration as its natural penalty in another. What kind of love is it which entails penile amputation as an appropriate penalty? Wollheim forgets to say. The same weakness for self-protective cirmculocution leads him to describe the boy's relation to his father as 'the wish to be loved by him,' when what Freud means is the wish to be penetrated by his father's penis. On the next page we are told that one of the routes to homosexual 'love' is as a reaction to an original rivalrous hatred once felt by the homosexual towards his male siblings.[118] Once again the use of the term 'love' gives the thesis a spurious symmetry—'hatred' becomes 'love'—while discouraging the natural question of just how repudiation of the satisfaction taken in punching a brother's head transformed the propensity to erect at the prospect of making love to women into a propensity to erect at the prospect of making love to men.

Whether you agree that these specimens of recycling are deeply discrediting or not, I hope I have at least made it clear how inadequately the notion of either untestability or falsification-rejection captures the consideration which move us to pejorative epistemic characterisations of psychoanalytic discourse and practices. The features which inspire adverse appraisal, and require defending, are better characterised as verbal formulae being inertly recycled and the prevalence of thoughts not permitted to follow their natural course.

Recycling: 'Symptoms Are Actions'

We sometimes get a distinctive kind of recycling which, rather than ignore blatant counter-examples to the thesis asserted, deploys the traditional verbal formulae while depriving them of their content. In a review of the Wollheim compilation of tributes to Freud's genius, I asked of some reiterations of Freud's claim that symptoms were actions, what account those who produced it could give of the action-like character of depression or anxiety, the most common neurotic symptoms.[119] Wollheim's co-editor, James Hopkins, was indignant at what he felt was my misrepresentation of what Freud and his contributors were asserting, and argued that all that Freud meant is that if you entertain aggressive thoughts you will consequently feel

---

118. Richard Wollheim, *Freud* (Fontana, 1992), p. 122.
119. 'Psycho-apologetics', *London Review of Books*, Vol. 5, No. 10 (2–15 June 1983).

guilty and depressed, and thus you have—in a sense—brought about your guilty feelings.[120] But the relation of aggressive thoughts to the guilt feelings they induce is not the relation of an action to its rationale, and so Hopkins has failed to reply to the natural objection raised by the formula 'symptoms are actions.' In any case, even if his contributors were so confused as to mean what Hopkins says they meant, this is not what Freud meant, which is far from Hopkins's banality. Freud places affects under the control of our will. He tells us that in phobias the patient displaces his fear from an internal to an external object because 'he feels he can protect himself better that way.'[121] On several occasions Freud confers on a patient the ability to bring about, not merely mental states, but physiological ones as well. In an early paper he speaks of an hysteric's will 'evoking in her all the subjective symptoms which in a malingerer would be put forward as an excuse.' That is, whereas a malingerer only *pretends* that he feels such and such—nausea, vertigo, or pain—hysterics unconsciously induce these states in themselves in order that they can then truthfully say that they are suffering them. Freud then further extends the patient's will beyond subjective symptoms to physiological processes in a way which 'is not possible to conscious effort' but which 'produces a number of objective signs in the digestive tract which a malingerer would be unable to bring about.'[122] Nor did Freud outgrow this. In a 1917 letter to Ferenczi he spoke of 'the power unconscious ideas have over the body.' Ernest Jones tells us that this was an allusion to a collaborative enterprise whose 'essential content is that the omnipotence of thoughts—"which creates and modifies organs" and "of which we see the remains in hysteria" was once a reality.'[123] And Freud intermittently expresses kindred views throughout his career. Apologists like Hopkins seem to stand to Freud's voluntaristic conception of symptoms as Catholics of my generation to the dogma of transubstantiation. Just as we were happy to recite the words without bothering overmuch as to their precise meaning, and were quite content to profess a belief that during the mass the host becomes the body and blood of Christ without being able to give an account of it which wasn't either superstitious or heretical, so Hopkins wants to recycle the formula 'symptoms are actions' while giving an account of it which renders it plausible only at the cost of rendering it trite.

This tendency to empty Freud's assertions of their natural content is not an idiosyncrasy of Hopkins and his contributors and is not confined to Freud's ultravoluntarlsm. Anthony Storr says of Freud's thesis of the developmental centrality of the fact that children fear castration at the hands of

---

120. Letters, *London Review of Books* (7–20 June 1983).
121. *NIL* (Hogarth, 1949), p. 111.
122. 'A Case of Successful Treatment by Hypnotism', *CP V*, p. 40.
123. Ernest Jones, *Life*, Vol. III, p. 335.

their fathers that, though it 'sounds ridiculous when taken literally, if we were to phrase it differently and affirm that small boys are . . . easily made to feel humiliated or threatened by disparaging remarks about their size, weakness, incapacity and lack of experience, most people would concur.'[124] In other words, if we drop the idea of castration from Freud's theory of castration anxiety 'most people would concur.' This bowdlerising tactic, though not often carried to the extremes of Hopkins and Storr, is not uncommon in Freud commentaries. It is as if there was an indifference as to what views are imputed to Freud so long as he is revered for holding them.

Recycling: Sexual Symbolism

In his paper 'In Fairness to Freud' David Sachs criticises Grünbaum for his concentration on free association to the neglect of symbolism since symbolism 'often plays a crucial role in the interpretation of neurotic symptoms, parapraxes, literary works, etc.' Sachs writes: 'When Freud states how he came to know the meaning of the symbols he does not depend on clinical findings . . . rather the reverse.'[125] And Sachs then quotes Freud's account of 'where we learn of this symbolism'—from 'fairy tales and myths, buffoonery and jokes; from folklore and from poetic and colloquial usage.' These provide 'so many parallels to dream symbolism we cannot fail to be convinced of our interpretations.[126] This satisfies Sachs. He gives no instances where an unpersuasive interpretation was redeemed by invoking 'extra-clinical', 'fixed' symbolism. Why is Sachs so perfunctory in his exposition of an argument which he says is 'one of the foundations of psychoanalysis'? Is it because when spelled out it is embarrassing in its fatuity? We are asked to believe, for example, that the topic of blindness in a dream signifies castration, even when without personal castratory significance for the patient, because it signifies castration in the legend of Oedipus, say. But the grounds for crediting that it signifies castration in the Oedipus legend are just as doubtful as that it did so in the patient's dream. And, even if they were not, how would they warrant the inference to castration in any particular clinical interpretation? It was Freud himself who said that a cigar was sometimes only a cigar. How is it to be determined when blindness is only blindness? That, for example, phallic interpretations, unsupported by the patient's association, should have been thought redeemable by the reminder that elongated objects have been traditionally used to represent the phallus is indicative of the supra-rational appeal of Freudian hermeneutics.

But the notion of fixed symbolism is in an even worse state than these

124. Anthony Storr, *Freud* (Oxford University Press, 1989), p. 25
125. David Sachs, 'In Fairness to Freud: A Critical Notice of The Foundations of Psychoanalysis', *The Philosophical Review* Vol. XCCCCVIII, No. 3 (July 1989).
126. *S.E. XV*, pp. 158–59.

considerations imply. For Sachs has promoted to one of the foundations of psychoanalysis' and 'one of the evidential bases for (Freud's) mature practice of interpretation in general' (p. 364) a thesis about which Freud is so ambivalent that he twice denounced it, expressing a view hardly less dismissive than that of its more vehement critics. And these repudiations occurred both before and after his expressions of confidence. In 1922 he speaks of 'the surprising fact that certain objects, relations and arrangements are . . . used by the dreamer without his understanding them and to which as a rule he offers no associations'[127] In 1932 he reiterates: 'Since we know how to translate these symbols and the dreamer does not, in spite of having used them himself, it may happen that the sense of the dream may at once become clear to us as soon as we have heard the text of the dream even before we have made any attempts at interpreting it.'[128] These are probably the remarks that Sachs had in mind. Yet in 1925 we have, 'Dream interpretation without reference to the dreamer's associations would in the most favourable cases remain a piece of unscientific virtuosity of the most doubtful value,'[129] and in 1939: 'Dreams can be interpreted only with the assistance of the associations provide by the dreamer himself . . . any other procedure is arbitrary.'[130] Sachs's mistake was due to the generally held assumption that Freud would not have contradicted himself so blatantly as these quotations show him to have done. It is a natural assumption and one so deep-seated that it is even shared by *critics* of psychoanalysis, like Grünbaum and Erwin, whose Freudian exegesis it similarly disables.

Here is a representative specimen of the tenacity which characterised the practice of symbolism since it is by someone who had had its dubiousness forced on his attention some years earlier in an exchange with a critic of its pretensions.[131] Flugel was an academic psychologist as well as an analyst. Flugel's exposition uses Freud's own example of 'the symbolisation of coitus by means of climbing or walking upstairs' where, Flugel tells us, 'the essential common thoughts are those of rhythmic movement and the actual position adopted in the reproductive act . . .'[132] The idea that climbing stairs involves 'the actual position adopted in the reproductive act' is Flugel's own improvement on Freud's argument, but Flugel must have had a very odd conception of the 'reproductive act' if he thought it accomplished while assuming the attitude of someone climbing stairs. Not even those who have

---

127. 'Psychoanalysis', *CP V* (Hogarth, 1950), p. 116.
128. *NIL* (Hogarth, 1949), p. 23.
129. 'Limits to the Possibility of Dream Interpretation,' *CP V*, pp. 151–52.
130. *Outline of Psychoanalysis* (Hogarth, 1949), p. 31.
131. J.C. Flugel, 'Theories of Psychoanalysis', *The Outline of Modern Knowledge* (Gollancz, 1931), p. 362. The earlier exchange was with Adolf Wohlgemuth in the *British Journal of Medical Psychology* (1924).
132. *ibid.*, p. 362.

been compelled to have intercourse on staircases—*faute de mieux*—will have adopted the posture Flugel foists on them. But examples of symbolism as fatuous as Flugel's are being recycled to this day and in comparably institutional outlets. Consider the entry on Freud in a reference work on epistemology.[133] The entry relates the dream of a university teacher who believed a pupil had revealed a desire to suck his penis (you can get into serious trouble making assumptions like that). He dreams that a lamb comes to suck his finger which emits milk. 'It was clear to him that the milk represented his teaching, the lamb his pupil, and his finger the penis that the pupil wanted to suck . . . the dreamer can be seen as representing the fulfillment of a specific sexual wish.' Such fantasies are said to 'obscure reality'; but how can this be so if they were so readily understood by the dreamer ('it was clear to him')? And since the dreamer had contemplated the prospect of having his penis sucked by his pupil the very day of the dream, why was it disguised in the dream when the censor is supposed to be at its weakest? This is one of the most obvious and commonly made objections to this kind of dream symbolism. George Orwell, characteristically, raised it, 'Why do sex impulses which I am not frightened of thinking of when I am awake have to be dressed up as something different when I am asleep . . . what is the point of the disguise if it is always penetrable?'[134] When the question why dreams should disguise thoughts the dreamer had consciously entertained was put to Freud his response was 'It just happens.'[135]

The Nicomachean Solution to the Freud Controversy

Some defenders of Freud's epistemic pretensions have attempted to meet disparagement with a philosophically sophisticated defense which may be handily subsumed under the rubric 'Nicomachean'.

In the early pages of the *Nicomachean Ethics* Aristotle advises us to 'be content if we can attain so much precision in our statements as the subject before us admits of' and admonishes that 'the same degree of accuracy is no more to be expected in all kinds of reasoning than in all kinds of manufacture.' There is a similar remark in Book Gamma of the *Metaphysics*, 'For not to know of what things one should demand demonstration and of what one

---

133. *A Companion to Epistemology*, eds., Jonathan Dancy and Ernest Sosa (Oxford: Blackwell, 1992).

134. Bernard Crick, *Orwell* (Penguin, 1982), p. 574.

135. Joseph Wortis, *Fragments of an Analysis with Freud* (Charter Books, 1954), p. 83. There is a penetrating discussion of this issue in the chapter 'Dreams and Symptoms' in Richard Webster's *Why Freud Was Wrong* (Harper Collins, 1995). The entry in *A Companion to Epistemology* also gives signs of the political correctness which now so often qualifies Freudian expositions. The author speaks in connection with penis envy of men's 'projection of feelings of lack into women'. Why not the *discernment* of 'feelings of lack in women' as classical Freudians insist, rather than its projection there? Could it be because the bigger battalions have carried the day?

should not, argues want of education.' It is implied by several defenders of psychoanalysis that its critics have demonstrated this 'want of education.' Is this then the solution to the problem of the persistence of disagreement as to the merits of Freud's theory—its critics' inappropriate demand for demonstration? To anticipate my answer to this question: a Nicomachean perspective can fend off mechanical dismissal of the probative value of clinical data but it cannot extenuate claims that Freud's generalisations concerning neurotic affliction are credible because they have survived attempts at refutation. Nothing the Wolf Man or the Rat Man did or said could have shown Freud's infantile sexual etiology of the neuroses to be mistaken. The worst they could have done is to have failed to illustrate the theory. They could have failed to instantiate it but could not falsify it. Two distinct objections have been made to the dismissal of the probative value of the data of the analytic hour. One is that it erroneously dismisses the evidential value of data not the outcome of controlled enquiry. The other that it fails to recognize the legitimacy of a mode of validation that has no parallels in natural science—the 'ultimate' endorsement of the subject. I will consider these in turn.

When Can Reflection and Enhanced Anamnesis Explain without the Support of Controlled Enquiry?

Much of our ignorance of ourselves may be due to the fact that, as William James puts it, 'The mass of our thinking vanishes forever, beyond hope of recovery . . .'[136] Why should not recovery of this 'vanished thinking' resolve some of the characterological and behavioural puzzles that beset us? How could a comprehensive survey of the long-forgotten themes on which our mind played its variations throughout some phase of our life be without explanatory value? (And even if the themes themselves remain unexplained I may now, nevertheless, finally understand why I did what I did. I did what I did because I was the sort of person that my anamnestically reconstructed reveries reveal me to have been.) There are a plethora of putatively explanatory revelations in autobiographical literature like this of John Stuart Mill: 'I grew up in the absence of love and the presence of fear and many and indelible are the effects of this bringing up in the stunting of my moral growth.'; and this of Coleridge: 'the hauntings of regret have injured me more than the things to be regretted.' It would take a great deal of disentanglement of the multiple issues raised by remarks such as these to determine what would constitute epistemic authority with respect to them, and it is a chore for which neither Freudians nor their 'scientific' critics have shown much appetite.

---

136. William James, *Principles of Psychology*, Vol. 1 (Dover, 1950), p. 276.

On 6 August 1824 Charles Greville, the Victorian memorialist, wrote in his diary: 'Forever be this day accursed which has been to me the bitterest in my existence. The particulars will remain too deeply embedded in my memory to need being written down here.' There is an annotation to this entry dated some ten years later, 'The devil take me if I have any idea to what this alludes.' Greville's ignorance as to why that day was so accursed was a straightforward function of amnesia and provides an instance where a literal filling of the memory gap would have resolved his perplexity. But facts like these ought not to be mechanically invoked to justify a validating role for the analysand's say-so in the assessment of psychoanalytic etiological claims. There are crucial differences. Consider an observation recorded by the Goncourt brothers to illustrate that 'a childhood impression is often responsible for the bent or the character of a whole life':

> I have been told Merimée was a man created uniquely by the fear of appearing ridiculous, and that the origin of that fear was this: when he was a child he was scolded; and on leaving the room he heard his parents laugh at the blubbering face he made during the reprimand. He swore then that no-one would ever laugh at him again, and he kept his word, maintaining a harsh, curt exterior which has now become part of his profoundest nature.[137]

What kind of evidence is it appropriate to demand for the existence of a causal relation between Merimée's childhood humiliation and his adult demeanour? Could not he himself supply it?

Matthew Erdelyi, a psychoanalytic researcher, reports that amnesia for some events can be overcome by the simple expedient of 'refocussing thought upon the forgotten material.'[138] Can such 'refocussing' be assimilated to the psychoanalytic procedure which purports to reconstruct the hidden process by which the inability of a paranoiac to acknowledge a homosexual passion becomes the conviction that he is being persecuted by those he unconsciously desires? Or by which a fetishistic requirement emerges out of the devastating infantile revelation that there are creatures without penises? No.

How does the subject's epistemic relation to the psychoanalytic etiology differ from his relation to the humanistic one? Consider the case of a man presented with the suggestion that he had lived his life like an unprepared schoolboy praying that the class period would end before he was called upon, and finding this felicitous and illuminating. Now suppose that there was just such a traumatic episode in his school life; the status of this episode as more than just an apt elucidation of his habitual self-feeling but as a causal explanation of it is not settled by the discovery of its historicity. That there

---

137. Lewis Galantiere, *The Goncourt Journals 1851–1870* (Doubleday, 1958), p. 174.
138. 'Repression, Reconstruction, and Defense' in Jerome Singer, ed., *Repression and Dissociation* (University of Chicago Press, 1990).

was an episode in the life of the subject when he had been called upon and humiliated does not establish its causal/etiological pretensions; its success, as what John Wisdom called 'a psychological fixed star,' cannot establish its etiological role. On the other hand the idea that yet to be undertaken epidemiological enquires can resolve questions such as these is ludicrous. What would strengthen our confidence that the invocation of the putatively originary traumatic episode was more than a device for clarifying, rather than explaining, current and recurrent self-feelings, would be evidence of its continuous coming to mind, with the appropriate apprehensions and humiliation-avoiding efforts. In the case of a psychoanalytic etiology there are no long-buried ruminations and resolutions to be recovered and, if a case can be made for a causal connection, this can only be through a circumstantially dense narrative.

There are two alternative epistemic constructions to be placed on the class of remarks of which this, from a biography of Percy Grainger, is a specimen: 'The flagellation which was an essential part of his sexuality was rooted in childhood experiences associated with his mother.' According to one, the truth of this claim depends on the role played by memories of maternal beatings in Grainger's recurrent lifelong erotic reveries; according to the psychoanalytic account, only a reconstruction of the unconscious mediating processes between his infantile sexual fantasies and his adult ones could explain them. We can give no general rule for determining when anamnesis confers epistemic authority with respect to such etiological claims.

The father of the novelist Walker Percy committed suicide when he was thirteen. A biography calls it the most formative influence of Walker Percy's life. Percy himself said, in his seventies, 'I was determined not only to find out why he did it but also to make damn sure it didn't happen to me.' This attests to a causal role for his father's suicide in forming his own attitude towards the act. Hemingway also had a father who committed suicide and whose example he was determined to avoid. But whether his father's example really did act as a disincentive to Hemingway's own inclination to suicide, whether he might not have committed suicide sooner if not for his determination to avoid his father's example, might seem to be out of reach of what anamnesis can tell us. This is not enough, however, to give what anamnesis can tell us any weaker epistemic claim on us than anything else we can bring to bear on the question. If the answer is not to be found in the subject's habitual, but insufficiently thematised, and only retrospectively, clearly discerned self-communings, where is it to be found?

The champions of controlled enquiry do not address the ostensible counter-instances from folk psychology adequately, if at all. The analysts do not show how the psychoanalytic examples, in which there is nothing to be remembered which could mediate the influence of the earlier events on the later, can be assimilated to the non-analytic ones. The Wolf Man does not stand to his witnessing the intercourse of his parents at 18 months as Miss Havisham stands to her jilting, or the Count of Monte Cristo to his enemies' persecution of him, or Shylock to Antonio's insults. On the other hand the troubling doubts raised by the Wolf Man as to the influence on him of his sister's seduction—'She played with my penis. But must that necessarily have such consequences or is it already a sign of sickness that something like that has consequences? I don't know . . .'[139]—arise in part because he has no mediating reminiscential ruminations which would show his sister's overtures at work on his sexual and affiliative proclivities.

One source of the mistaken assimilation of the rumination-mediated influence of the past to a psychoanalytic reconstruction, like that which Freud interpolates between the Wolf Man's primal scene and his adult character structure, may be that Freud sometimes produces accounts which are epistemically ambiguous with respect to these alternatives. Freud once imputed the adult's 'lasting impairment of self-esteem' to 'loss of love' in infancy. And in this kind of case all that prevents the infant's 'loss of love' from being just an elucidation of the adult's feelings ('Sometimes I feel like a motherless child'), is the imputed causal connection between them, which, unlike a 'further description'—a thematisation—the adult cannot confirm until he has overcome his amnesia, not merely for the traumatising events themselves, but for their role in his ruminative life. In Fitzgerald's *The Last Tycoon,* when someone wonders how the charismatic hero, Monroe Stahr, 'ever got to be Mr Stahr,' the narrator comments, 'I am afraid that Stahr could never have answered that one; for the embryo is not equipped with memory.' Suppose the embryo were equipped with memory; how much better placed would Stahr have been to say how he had become what he was? What foetal episodes could articulate intelligibly with the later character structure which made so profound an impression on those who encountered him? The narrator's response to the question how Stahr became Stahr illustrates the predominance of the early development paradigm at the same time that it illustrates how insusceptible the psychoanalytic version of this is to validation by the subject. But Freud does sometimes supply the kind of explanation to which memory is adequate—when off-duty, as it were—in his explanation of character structures akin to Monroe Stahr's. Freud once wrote '. . . he who has been the undisputed darling of his mother retains throughout his life that victorious feeling, that confidence in ultimate success, which not seldom brings actual success with it.' Though the *aperçu* is Freud's it is, nevertheless, not Freudian, for the mother's indulgence acts

---

139. Karin Obholzer, *The Wolf-Man, Sixty Years Later: Conversations with Freud's Patient* (Routledge, 1982), p. 37.

undistortedly without the mediation of symbolism or the primary process and is eligible for anamnestic retrieval in a way in which the shaping infantile episodes of Freudian theory are not.

It is difficult to produce arguments in favour of the comprehension-conferring powers of anamnesis which would be found persuasive by those who have not themselves made resolute attempts at anamnestic solutions to the conundrums they present themselves, and are convinced they have sometimes succeeded. Among the grounds for the conviction that the motivating rationales for certain behaviours were continuously present, but merely unobtrusive or warded off, is that it sometimes happens, when people arrive at a clearer picture of their natures, that they are struck in the light of it by how sensibly, yet without elaborate excogitation, they have managed their lives. For example, how right they were to marry or not to marry; to have no children or to have many; to eschew conventional ambitions or to seek their main satisfactions in public rather than private life. But, whether or not this mode of anamnesis can be counted as genuine self-knowledge, it is remote from anything we could call psychoanalytic.

The Past as Influence and as Metaphor

There is another function reference to the past may perform which may mislead us into thinking it has provided causal explanation when it has not. It may serve to clarify our feelings rather than explain them.[140] The use of past episodes as 'psychological fixed stars' reference to which may evince or evoke feelings as to current states is not uncommon. Proust's Marcel says of his lover's goodnight kiss 'what I at once call to mind in comparison is . . . the night on which my father sent Mama to sleep in the little bed by the side of my own.' In *The Magic Mountain* Hans Castorp reminisces about the likeness between a woman with whom he is infatuated and a schoolboy chum: 'As always whenever he set eyes on Clavdia the likeness reasserted itself which had puzzled him . . . Priboslav held his head like that.' It is clear that these are illuminations which can dispense with empirical corroboration. Even those who will allow Castorp no decisive say in the question as to the causal influence of his schoolboy infatuation on his adult one must concede that questions such as whether the one reminded him of the other, whether he could only, or best, convey the quality of one by reference to the other, were not matters to be arrived at by some objective empirical method but are issues as to which he is authoritative.

Episodes from our past may, thus, set us other than causal problems. We can do more than just imagine them to have been otherwise and speculate as to the difference it would have made to our lives. Memories may incite us

---

140. 'Explanation and Self-Clarification in Freud' in Cioffi, *Wittgenstein on Freud and Frazer* (Cambridge University Press, 1998).

to fathom their expressiveness as well as to assess the causal repercussions of the episodes of which they are memories. But though this kind of exploration, of my unhappiness, say, may leave me clearer as to who or what I blame it may yet leave me no wiser as as to who or what is really to blame.

A remark of the psychoanalyst Roy Schafer illustrates, though perhaps inadvertently, the difference between a past episode as a putatively pathogenic trauma with repercussions to be assessed, and a past episode as a topic of recurrent reminiscence with an implicit meaning to be elucidated: 'Trauma is given meaning by its victim: analysts promote insight into the profoundly disturbing sense that the analysand has given to the traumatic event.'[141] It is the epistemic ambiguity of the 'insight' which analysts are said to promote that provoked Wittgenstein's accusation of their having created an 'abominable mess.' Does Schafer mean that analysts have withdrawn from the task of determining what, in the remote infantile past of their patients, produced or contributed to the anomalous character structure with which they have to cope? This would evade the strictures of those who insist on how poor psychoanalytic infantile etiological explanations in general are and would be commendable, if it were more candid. But the question remains what is the character of this insight if it is not into the causal influence of the past?

In a penetrating commentary on the psychoanalytic enterprise John Wisdom drew a contrast between two kinds of matters on which an analysand might hope to be enlightened. Wisdom sees the psychoanalyst as someone who tries to uncover 'those models from the past which . . . powerfully influence our lives in the present, which dominate our thought, our talk, our feelings, our actions, in short, our lives.' Wisdom then contrasts two ways of uncovering these 'dominating models.' One is by the 'recalling and connecting things familiar but unrecognized'; the other by 'discovering new material.'[142] He sums up the contrast with a simile. One is like seeing clearly what has been creeping in the shadows and the other like applying a chemical to a surface on which something has been written in invisible ink. The trouble with this antithesis is that the non-empirical half of the enterprise—that with respect to whose success the subject is epistemically privileged—is not properly psychoanalytic. It is the general failure of analysts to recognize this which created what Wittgenstein called 'the abominable mess'.[143] The making out more clearly that which has been creeping in the shadows does not require an outsider's expertise at decipherment.

---

141. Roy Schafer, *Language and Insight* (New Haven and London: Yale University Press, 1978), p. 195.

142. 'Philosophy and Psychoanalysis' (abridged) in F. Cioffi, ed., *Freud* (Macmillan, 1970), p. 96.

143. See 'Wittgenstein on Freud's Abominable Mess' in Cioffi, *Wittgenstein on Freud and Frazer* (Cambridge University Press, 1998).

A picture puzzle in which we are to find a face is not like a code which must be broken. Wisdom seems unaware of how revisionist his conception of psychoanalytical self-revelation is.

The difference between illuminating juxtapositions like Marcel's of Albertine's kiss and his mother's, or Castorp's of Clavdia's manner of holding her head and his school chum's, and the interpretations Freud proffers is that Freud denies that what he is really doing is just putting things side by side in order to facilitate self-validating illumination. He insists he is providing an etiological explanation whose truth is independent of its acceptance by the subject. When one of his training analysands (Joseph Wortis) objected to the lack of a recognizable resonance in one of Freud's dream interpretations by complaining that it wasn't what he felt, he was rebuked that this showed that Wortis still hadn't learned the meaning of the term 'unconscious.'[144] So, though Grünbaum is correct to insist on the revisionism entailed by the hermeneutic abandonment of Freud's causal claims, he is obtuse to the presence of these revisionist germs in Freud himself. Even if Marcel's relation to Albertine would have been what it was without the causal influence exerted by his mother's good-night kiss it might still be his best means of elucidating the nature of his dependence on Albertine and the significance to him of her bedtime kisses.

Freud's successes at clarification mislead us into crediting him with explanatory achievements. One test of whether, when two states are said to be causally related, the claim is really just 'a good simile', a putting of two things side by side in the hope of thus bringing an experience to further articulation, is that when we discover the non-historicity of the ostensibly explanatory but surreptitiously clarificatory episode we are indifferent. Here is an example of clarification disguised as explanation. Desmond Morris sees as manifestations of the same underlying instinct, the act of 'watching television from the soft comfort of an easy chair' and the infantile experience of looking out of a window while safely cradled in mother's lap: 'cuddled snugly on the symbolic laps of our chair mothers we settle down with childlike security to view at a safe distance the chaos of the harsh adult world outside as portrayed on TV.'[145] This may succeed as simile while failing miserably as genetic hypothesis although we may not notice this and believe ourselves in possession of another triumph for the Freudian paradigm of infantile determination.

---

144. Joseph Wortis, *Fragments of an Analysis with Freud* (New York: Charter Books, 1963), p. 102
145. Desmond Morris, *Intimate Behaviour* (London: Jonathan Cape, 1971), p. 202.

Maternal Nipples as Causes of Metaphors

Here is an example of the confusion with which Wittgenstein taxes Freudians of treating a metaphor as an influence. In *NIL* Freud writes that interest in the penis has 'a powerful root in oral erotism; for, after weaning, the penis inherits something from the nipple of the mother's breast.'[146] Isn't this just a metaphor disguised as an influence?

Here are some possible scenarios of validation: While engaged in the anamnestic task of reconstructing their childhoods, patients recall that one day they became aware that for some time past the place of nipples in their oral erotic fantasies had been taken by penises (or perhaps by a particular penis). But this account is precluded from illustrating Freud's thesis by the unconscious nature of the developmental processes he is committed to. On the other hand, the scenario may be in the strictly psychoanalytical reconstructive mode: at a certain point in the analysis the retrospective narrative deployment of explanatory fantasies concerning nipples fails in perspicuity-conferring power and a switch to penises makes 'the order of the day as laid down by the unconscious' comprehensible once more. In the light of Wittgenstein's distinction between hypotheses and 'further descriptions' we can better appreciate the epistemic ambiguity of Freud's remark that in the case of Dora 'the udder of a cow has aptly played the role of an image intermediate between a nipple and a penis.' Dora need never have seen a cow's udder for the comparison, nevertheless, to perform a clarificatory function. The real as opposed to the ostensible role of hypotheses as to infantile transactions with nipples may be to clarify adult oral transactions with penises rather than explain them. To whom would such analogies be of no value? To those who find fellatio transparently delightful or irredeemably opaque; who find the nipple analogy too remote or too applicable.

The feebleness of Freud's etiological suggestions taken literally often invites us to take them figuratively instead. Sometimes Freud himself is happy to leave it an open question whether the adult practice of fellatio 'points to' an attempt to replace the infant's loss of the mother's nipple.[147] Why should an adult invert's practice of sucking penises 'point to' an attempt to replace 'the lost satisfaction in sucking the maternal nipple'? Would not sucking of another woman's nipple be a more convenient expedient? Isn't one woman's nipple more like another woman's nipple than a penis is like either?

For a better grasp of the two possible relations—causal, as contrasted with evocative/elucidatory—into which an allusion to an infantile past may

---

146. *NIL* (Hogarth, 1933), p. 131. See also Roy Schafer on the 'Phallus-breast equation' in *Language and Insight* (New Haven: Yale University Press, 1978), pp. 154–55.
147. 'Anatomical Distinction between the Sexes' in *On Sexuality* (Penguin, 1977), p. 335.

enter consider this apparently genetic account of the impression made on us by Florentine architecture in terms of the infant's experience of its mother's body. 'No-one will deny that the basis for this art was a thorough advertence to the human frame . . . which unconsciously endowed (their buildings) with the ambivalent infantine experiences of orifice, crevice, enfolding embrace; of members that project tautness and rotundity, of the hunger-filled and the contented mouth; in short, whatever sensuous experiences were primarily associated with the hard nipple, and the soft continuous breast . . .'[148] This parallel may work for some of us, and though it may even be causally true, and may even work *because* it is causally true, nevertheless, its working is distinct from either of these. It works because we say so but it isn't true just because we say so. What fails as explanation can succeed as metaphor.

Freud's Confusion of Causes and Reasons

There are two common exegetical errors in construing Freud's invocation of unconscious processes. One is to give them a character which permits patients a privileged relation with respect to them; the other is to deny them this privileged status. Since Freud confers both properties on his interpretations at different times, any monolithic characterisation of his view of interpretation is bound to be wrong. The problem is this. We want to understand the force of the frequently used expression 'analysis revealed' as it occurs in statements like, '. . . a woman may repress a sexual impulse only to find herself plagued by a disturbance of swallowing; analysis reveals that unconsciously a vaginal sensation has been displaced on to the mouth and pharynx.'

The expression 'analysis reveals' may mean that material was uncovered which made, not just the unconscious vaginal sensation, but the inference from it to the disturbances of swallowing, persuasive. But there is an alternative construal on what 'analysis reveals'—that when the repression is lifted the patient experiences the causal nexus between the vaginal sensation and the pharyngeal one. But can we make sense of this? And if we cannot, then an entire class of psychoanalytic interpretations is put beyond the range of the rationale of validation offered by Waelder and confusedly adopted by many analysts; a class so large as to almost sever the connection between psychoanalysis so construed and psychopathology.

The transformation of Freud into a high-powered agony aunt, though well-intentioned, deprives him of his distinctiveness. Freud did not just listen to his patients in the spirit of a confidante or confessor. He listened to to them as a physician listens to the sounds made by a patient's heart for evi-

---

148. Adrian Stokes, *Michaelangelo: A Study in the Nature of Art* (Tavistock Publications, 1955), p. 74.

dence as to what occasions his attacks of cardiac pain and breathlessness. Though it is normally assumed that the true grounds of our thoughts and feelings are outside the range of our own epistemic reach, and that we owe Freud a debt in compelling us to acknowledge the fact, we ought to be troubled by how often, when such claims are advanced, no efforts have been made to determine how the subject stands to the supposedly inaccessible psychoanalytically uncovered revelations, or even to clarify the distinction between conscious, but evaded, and unconscious in the sense which is distinctive of Freud—Freudianly unconscious.

Freud is sometimes a superb clarifier of thoughts, and it is this which is often behind our admiration for his penetration rather than the reason convention constrains us to give, that he discovered how to decode the manifestation of the unconscious. Freud's widely admired joke-reductions are not hypotheses about the causes of our laughter. They are commentaries on the point of the joke and are even assessable by people who did not find the joke funny and have never laughed at it.[149] Similarly with many of Freud's metapsychological energic hypotheses as to the difference between wit and humour, say.[150] We can make considerable headway with their appreciation while having no idea what it would be to do so if they were what they purport to be—accounts of subterranean transactions between energy systems—and treat them instead as schematic phenomenological analyses. Consider Freud's statement that the pleasure taken in comic movement is due to 'an innervatory expenditure which has become an unusable surplus when a comparison is made with a movement of one's own.' This can be read as a restatement in Freud's scientistic, energic jargon of what he had previously said without it; that in laughing at a comical movement we compare our movements with those of the clown, and the discrepancy between the effort it would take us and the effort it took him amuses us. What does Freud's alternative formulation in terms of economies in energic expenditure add but the illusion that he is a scientist penetrating beyond appearance to reality? Can we imagine bringing about the same energic state of affairs as that underlying our laughter at the clown while bypassing our observation of his antics and manipulating the energy levels directly? Could we, even in principle, directly observe the subject's psychic apparatus and infer from this whether his laughter belonged to wit, humour or the comic, as Freud has distinguished these? When, in the course of explaining humorous effects, the same state of affairs is described at one point as 'the superego speaking words of comfort to the ego' and at another as 'the displacement

149. 'The Technique of Jokes,' Chapter 2 of *Jokes and their Relation to the Unconscious* (London: Routledge, 1966).

150. *ibid.*, Chapter 7, 'Jokes and the Species of the Comic,' pp. 228–233; 'Humour,' *CP2*, p. 215.

of quantities of cathexis to the superego,' we have an example of the kind of thing which moved Wittgenstein to say that Freud's explanation 'sounded like science' but only did what aesthetics does—provided similes, put things side by side.

Misguided Objections to Introspective Access

There is a wrong way of dealing with the appeal to introspective access as a mode of validation of psychoanalytic interpretation. It is illustrated by Adolf Grünbaum and Edward Irwin. In *Foundations of Psychoanalysis* (p. 30) Grünbaum writes: 'Though the subject often does have direct and generally reliable access to the individual content of his mental states he/she has only inferential access—just like outside observers—to such causal linkages as actually connect some of his own mental states.' He repeats this in his reply to peer group criticisms in the July 1986 issue of *Behavioural and Brain Sciences* (p. 279). It is remarks like this which lead one to suspect that Grünbaum has not got the balance between self-promotion and intellectual effort quite right. Isn't the conception of mental life Grünbaum advances here a travesty? How would it apply to as familiar a phenomenon as seasickness, where the mental states connected are nausea and the perceived pitching of the deck?.

Grünbaum gives a mistaken objection to a putative example of the legitimacy of the patient's ultimate authority which invoked the case of Fräulein Elisabeth from Freud's *Studies on Hysteria*.[151] She was in love with her brother-in-law and while at her sister's deathbed had the unsisterly thought that he was now free to marry her. Grünbaum thinks that, though she can vouch for her having had the thought, and vouch for being later amnesic for it, she cannot vouch for the role of its shameful content in its banishment. On Grünbaum's view, when Wordsworth wrote, 'To me alone there came a thought of grief/a timely utterance gave that thought relief', he was only *inferring*—'like any outside observer'—that his relief was due to the same content that made the utterance timely. Grünbaum is able to remain oblivious of the doubtfulness of his thesis only by formulating it at an inappropriate level of abstraction—'mental states', 'mental content', 'causal linkage', as if each of these categories were conceptually homogeneous. Let us consider a perceptual 'mental state' like that of scrutinising the more delectable representations of feminine pulchritude in a *Playboy* centrefold and the affective 'mental state' of sexual arousal that may follow. It is not obvious, and not even plausible, that the subject in such a case has only 'inferential access' to the causal linkage between what he is looking at and his sexual excitement. Does a considerate lover who is extracting square

---

151. Howard Shevrin, *Behavioural and Brain Sciences* (1986), 9:2, p. 258.

roots in order to delay ejaculation merely *infer* the success of this enterprise, and would he have put it down to coincidence until controlled enquiry had persuaded him otherwise, if he were as scrupulous as Grünbaum? Grünbaum's mistake is due to an inadequate philosophic method, that of appealing to a general rule rather than directing attention to the phenomena themselves.

The right way to deal with the Freudian's invocation of 'psychoanalytically informed introspection' as a method of validation is to call attention to the particular phenomena they have committed themselves to explaining and assessing the confirmational adequacy of the subject's say-so in the light of the specific character of these phenomena. Can we make sense of the girl with the migraine headache, due to repressed defloration fantasies, coming to stand to the relation between her headaches and her defloration fantasies as the perusor of the *Playboy* centrefold, in my example, does to that between his erotic fantasising and his erection?

An analyst, Robert Langs, speaks of the 'cognitive mastery verbalised insight affords.' But psychoanalysis transcends, even if it encompasses, the provision of such 'verbalised insight.' The aim of accounting for a wide range of phenomena for which people seek relief, is not a matter of the provision of 'verbalised insights.' but of uncovering the unconscious ideation generating them. Consider vaginismus. Is what is called for by a patient's inability to tolerate penile intromission necessarily a 'verbalised insight' into this inability? In so far as this involves bringing to focus a subliminal or previously unacknowledged aversion to penetration or impregnation it may be welcomed by the patient as a recognizable illumination of her conscious state but this could not attest to its causal status or preclude the real cause having the kind of unconsciousness on which Freud normally insists, and which give his putative skills at translation their prestige.

In a sophistical defense of Freudian pretensions the philosopher Jonathan Lear writes, 'The central issue is, does the human soul have depth? Does it generate meanings that are not immediately available to consciousness.'[152] Lear's assumption that what is 'not immediately available to consciousness' is unconscious in Freud's sense—Freudianly unconscious—is philosophically primitive and is precisely the confusion with which Wittgenstein and others have taxed Freudians. This confusion may be a general feature of our culture and not confined to disingenuous apologists. In his review of *The Uses of Enchantment,* Bruno Bettelheim's book on fairy tales, John Updike illustrates the way in which psychoanalytic hypotheses are spontaneously and obliviously translated into a phenomenological mode.[153]

---

152. *Journal of the American Psychoanalytic Association,* Vol. 44, No. 2 (1996), p. 586.
153. John Updike, *Hugging the Shore* (London: Penguin, 1985), p. 653.

Updike says of Bettelheim's thesis that the frog prince is really an unconscious symbol of the penis: 'The resemblance between frogs or toads and male genitals need only be pointed out to be assented to.' (Poor Updike.) But in any case, Bettelheim's thesis concerns subterranean unconscious relations between networks of ideas such as require an expert analyst's 'laborious' efforts at decoding. If the phallic character of frogs is that readily recognisable it is not unconscious in Freud's sense.

Here are some instances of accesses of self-knowledge consequent on reflection which neither the Grünbaumian nor the psychoanalytic account does justice to. An analysand who had been blind from the age of three replied to the question what revelations she owed to her analysis, that it was the extent of her resentment over her affliction. It is difficult to see how to bring epidemiological considerations to bear on a case like this, or on what grounds we might challenge her account other than her own further reflections upon it. But neither is it dependent on any distinctive expertise such as Freud's apparatus of mechanisms, like condensation, displacement, and so forth, is meant to afford. Here is an example of an epistemic revelation which occurred outside analysis. A morbidly bereaved man realised one day that his reluctance to be comforted and his incessant recurrence to his bereavement had an ulterior motive—an attempt to detach himself from his own worldly failure. Is this not an advance in self-understanding? How is controlled enquiry meant to bear on it? It is our occasional success at resolving our own perplexities at this or that aspect of our lives or natures which provides our standard of epistemic achievement in this area. This success does not come via evidence of the kind we have in the case of the relation between smoking and lung cancer, rather in the form of uncovering Something which stood to us as Merimée's austere demeanour to his persistent memory of mockery at his childhood display of affect, and his resolve that it should not recur. But there is a tendency to confuse the rumination-mediated influence of the past with the unconscious causal repercussions to which psychoanalysis is committed, that is, to assimilate episodes like Merimée's humiliation to the Wolf Man's primal scene. And this is one of the major sources of the mistaken defense of psychoanalytic pretensions. A patient may be authoritative as to to the felicity of a mnemonic formulation of his feelings (Franz Alexander once gave one of the tasks of analysis that of helping the patient to put his feelings into words); and as to the veridicality of a narrative reconstruction of the themes on which his mind played its variations, but not with respect to the repercussions of infantile episodes which did not enter into the considerations which rationalised his subsequent actions and reactions. Although a circumstantially dense narrative, such as Freud attempts with respect to the Wolf Man's primal scene, may carry conviction, even without the patient's endorsement, if the narrative fails in persuasiveness, the patient's endorsement could not redeem it.

When Is a Patient's Say-so not an Eligible Mode of Validation?

Freud can neither dispense with avowal nor can he avail himself of it. He can't dispense with it because his pathogenic factors, his explanans, figure neither in well-attested laws nor, generally, in differentiatingly dense, tight-fitting narratives. He can't avail himself of it because his explanatory unconscious processes are, typically, not such as to be validated, or even just probatively enhanced, by the subject's endorsement. The *coitus a tergo* held to be the paramount influence in the formation of the Wolf Man's character is not as densely embedded in its aftermath as Miss Havisham's jilting, or Edmond Dantes's persecution. Yet neither is it a subject's own retrievable ground for later actions and reactions, as was the mockery to which Merimée was subjected.

That a migraine headache was the displacement upwards of a desire for defloration is typical of the interpretations Freud produces when confronted by the symptoms of hysteria, and yet it is too remote from Wisdom's perceptual example—the identity of a tantalisingly familiar but not immediately identifiable face—to allow of its being settled by the patient's belated acknowledgement. They are not the kind which we can coherently 'hope to be confirmed by the person's own self-understanding,' as Thomas Nagel thoughtlessly puts it.[154] James says of someone who feels that he knows but is momentarily unable to produce what he knows that his mind 'strains and presses in a direction which it feels to be right . . . the gap becomes no mere void but . . . an aching void . . . his mind quivers on the verge of its recovery.' This is not the way it is with the repressed ideation to which hysterical symptoms are imputed, which even if they are not themselves completely 'alien', nevertheless, produce effects which are only to be explained via causal inquiry. Elsewhere James suggests an alternative mode of validation. He speaks of 'Transitions, which at first sight startle us by their abruptness, but which, when scrutinised closely, often reveal intermediating links of perfect naturalness and propriety.'[155] An example of the kind of thing James has in mind is provided by an association experiment conducted, circa 1910, in which the unexpected response word 'Niagara' was produced to the stimulus word 'Pride'. The experimenter tells us he was finally able to fathom what mediated it when the subject produced the association 'Pride goeth before a fall.'[156] If we are to credit the role of unconscious fellatio fantasies in the production of Dora's cough this can only by done by considerations similar to those which persuade us that the proverb intervened between the

154. Thomas Nagel, 'Freud's Permanent Revolution.' *New York Review of Books* (May 12 1994).

155. William James, *Principles of Psychology*, Vol. I, p. 550.

156. E.W. Scripture in Carl Murchison, *Psychologies of 1930* (Oxford University Press, 1930).

stimulus word 'Pride' and the response word 'Niagara', and not by any variety of 'expanded awareness.' On the other hand, when a case is as circumstantially convincing as the link between the response word 'Niagara' and the proverb, it is a mistake to mechanically invoke the possibility which troubles Irwin and Grünbaum, that the proverb was produced by the association rather than producing it. The objection to be made to those who think Freud has produced good reasons for connecting the Wolf Man's sight of his parents copulating with his later difficulties is not that we have as yet no epidemiological grounds for linking the two, but rather the kind of doubts raised by Esterson and by Macmillan as to the authenticity of the items linking them, or, if this authenticity is conceded, of their constituting a sufficiently tight fitting narrative.[157]

It has been held significant that Freud's book is called 'The Interpretation of Dreams' rather than 'The Causes of Dreams', since the activity of interpretation is thought to preclude the appositeness of causal inquiry. But a causal inquiry need not be one which is confined to physical conditions or lawful connections but just one which may, though it need not, transcend the epistemic resources of the subject. Two considerations preclude the appropriateness of belated avowal as a criterion of the correctness of a psychoanalytic interpretation: the complexity of the mental content and its role in the production of the phenomena interpreted. The evidential implausibility of many explanations could be redeemed by the subject's corroboration were he epistemically authorised to give it. The fact that John is so common a name makes the hypothesis that someone so called was named after Pope John XXIII implausible, but his parent's statement that he was indeed named after John XXIII shows the implausible conjecture to be, nevertheless, true. But is this mode of confirmation available for typically psychoanalytic explanations? The problem which confronts us when we strive to retrieve something articulatable from an ineffable hinterland is not that which Freud was addressing in his interpretation of hysterical symptoms, where the unconscious mental contents imputed must be determinate and not amorphous if they are to produce the pathological effects assigned them. However difficult it may have been for Dora to put into words her feelings for Herr K they nevertheless had to be such as would account for her symbolic pregnancy and her consequent limp via the unconscious verbalisations Freud imputes to her. It is a mistake to assimilate the problem of determining whether Dora really had homo-erotic feelings for Frau K with that of determining whether the tickle in her throat really was produced by her unconscious fellatio fan-

---

157. Macmillan, *Freud Evaluated,* pp. 472–73; Allen Esterson, *Seductive Mirage* (Open Court, 1993), passim.

tasies. These problems are distinct. The doubt one gives rise to is method-ological—the possibility that the verbal formulation she comes to accept as apposite may not be authentic. The other doubt is conceptual. The patient's assent is not an appropriate means of determining whether unconscious ideation played a role in the production of the hysterical man-ifestations complained of. Dora's erotic feelings for Frau K stood to her allusion to Frau K's 'beautiful white body' not as a cause to its effect but as a thought at the back of her mind to its more explicit articulation, whereas Dora's fellatio fantasies had to pre-exist, in all their detail, the coughing they were invoked to explain. The appropriate objection to a large class of Freudian explanations is not, as is often argued, that the patient's endorsement may be the result of his suggestibility since, even if we assume that the patient's endorsement is completely uninfluenced by his analyst, it is often still without evidential value. When a piercing pain in a patient's forehead is said to have been caused by her conviction that she was the object of a piercing look there is no other construction to place on the remark than that it refers to an occurrence antecedent to the pain in her forehead. Similarly, if Schreber's nocturnal emissions were due to his homo-erotic fantasising, as Freud assures us, these fantasies must have been active *before* it was articulated during the analysis

What Makes Psychoanalytic Explanations Spurious Is not that They Lack the Support of Controlled Enquiry

Lines 37–41 of Coleridge's poem 'Kubla Khan' run:

> A damsel with a dulcimer
> In a vision once I saw.
> It was an Abyssinian maid,
> And on her dulcimer she played,
> Singing of Mount Abora.'

It has been conjectured that the phrase 'Mount Abora', which is not to be found in any atlas, is multiply allusive, and one of the allusions is to Book IV of *Paradise Lost* in which Milton speaks of 'Mt. Amara'. What kind of claim is this and how does one go about deciding on its credibility? The strongest interpretation it can bear is this: that Coleridge, with an explicit awareness of the sources of the allusions he wished to evoke, set about con-structing a proper name which would exploit the associations of Milton's lines on Mt. Amara. On this interpretation all the evidence which we might adduce as to Coleridge's reading is merely circumstantial and symptomatic, and what it is symptomatic of, what it is an inference to, is the deliberations in which Coleridge is presumed to have engaged. But an alternative account is open to us: Coleridge himself need not have been aware of the sources of the proper name, Mount Abora, or of the likely effects it would have on his readers, and yet the choice of this name be determined by his familiarity with the source to which the interpretation traces it. This kind of claim obviously cannot be settled by appealing to Coleridge who, at most, could confess his familiarity with the source. How then can it be settled? The similarity in the names of the two mountains together, with the fact that Coleridge had read Milton would not be sufficient to allay our suspicion that we might be confronted with a mere coincidence. But for most of us this question would be settled in favour of the causal interpretation ('No "Amara" in Milton, no "Abora" in Kublah Khan') by a reminder of the Miltonic context of the expression 'Mount Amara.' The line immediately preceding 'Mount Amara' runs: 'Nor where Abyssin kings their issue guard' thus linking up with Coleridge's 'Abyssinian maid'. And there is a thematic congruence as well.

Some critics have thought they detected an anagram of the name of Charles Dickens's lover, Ellen Lawless Ternan, in the names of several of the heroines of his novels subsequent to his meeting with her—Bella, in *Our Mutual Friend,* Estella, in *Great Expectations* and Helena Landless, in *The Mystery of Edwin Drood.* Now, is it reasonable to demand that someone privy to Dickens's relation with Ellen Ternan should have been able to predict that her name would turn up in the names of the heroines of his novels? If it is absurd to demand epidemiological or experimental evidence in support of these interpretations why isn't a similar exemption to be permitted psychoanalytic interpretations? It is this for which Freud was arguing in his 1920 essay on the homosexual girl. Our doubts as to the acceptability of Freud's etiological claims should not rest on their *post hoc* character but on other features which we feel distinguish them from warranted *post hoc* explanations such as those I have given. It is the most serious flaw in the rejection of clinical support for Freud's claims by Grünbaum, Erwin, and like-minded critics that they fail to do this. Just as it the most serious flaw in psychoanalytic apologetic that, though it contains a plausible defense of the potential probative value of clinical data, it fails to show that the most widely accepted and distinctive of Freud's diagnostic and developmental theses are supported by such data. In a justification of the Freudian rationale for clinical interpretation—of what he calls 'the fitting together of two gestalts'— Fritz Schmidl gave as an example the famous case of the disappointed bride in *Introductory Lecture* 17. Freud explained her puzzling compulsion to go several times a day to a room with a stained table cloth and gratuitously ring for the housemaid by tracing it to her husband's failure to consummate on their wedding night. This is how Schmidl justifies Freud's claim that she was re-enacting the traumatic events of that night:

The symptom can be broken down into the following elements:

(a) Patient runs from one room into the other.

(b) She rings for her maid.

(c) She takes up a certain position in order to enable the maid to see a certain spot.

(d) This spot is a mark on a tablecloth.

(e) The process is repeated several times within a day.

(f) The elements (a) to (e) form part of one symptom.

The 'gestalt' of the allegedly traumatic wedding night is broken down by Schmidl into a similar pattern.

(a) During the wedding night the husband ran from his bedroom into that of the patient.

(b) He expressed his anxiety about the maid missing the blood spot on the bed linen by saying, "It is enough to disgrace one in the eyes of the maid who does the bed."

(c) He made a mark with red ink on

(d) the bed linen.

(e) He repeated his going from his to the patient's bedroom several times.

(f) The fact that all this happened during one night, the wedding night, combines the elements (a) to (e) into a unit.[158]

Pace Erwin there is nothing wrong with Schmidl's argument (though doubts may be raised as to the authenticity of the data constituting the gestalt fit and as to whether, in any case, it reaches the Amara/Abora or Ellen Lawless/Estella, Bella, Helena Landless level).

How are disputes as to whether an acceptable level of articulation between the symptom and its interpretation has been reached to be settled? A very natural way of attacking arguments of this kind is the production of reductios; that is, the production of admittedly fanciful or tendentious specimens with the same degree of circumstantiality as the disputed one. It is not reasonable to demand evidence of a regularity of which the imputed connection is an instance. The objection to the claim advanced by Thomas Nagel and others that Freud provided good grounds for his infantile etiologies would then be, not the un-Nicomachean argument that they lack epidemiological support, but that they are not supported by sufficient circumstantial detail to make the connection credible.

---

158. Fritz Schmidl, 'The Problem of Scientific Validation in Psycho-analytic Interpretation', *International Journal of Psychoanalysis* (March–April 1955), p. 110.

Has an Oedipal etiology ever been laid out, as Schmidl lays out the case of the table cloth compulsion, and retained its credibility? Has such a laying out, in the forty years since Schmidl produced his argument, even been attempted? If it is attempted with any of Freud's case histories, and the connections are freed of the rhetoric which surrounds them there, it will be apparent how feeble they then show themselves to be. One manageable example is that of the Rat Man's 'great obsessive fear.' The juxtaposition of his fear that his father will be subjected to a torture in which ravenous rats are introduced into his rectum with the Rat Man's infantile belief that birth is *per anum,* and his equation of rats with babies, and the use of the mechanism of reversal to get from babies emerging from the anus to rats entering it, loses all credibility when once it is realised that 'the great obsessive fear' was a literal reproduction of the torture that had been described to him the day before the symptom made its first appearance, thus rendering any alternative explanation of its content gratuitous. These undermining considerations are remote from those invoked by those who are determined not to admit the probative value of any clinical data.

The Production of Reductios in the Assessment of Psychoanalytic Interpretations

Where the preferred interpretation does apparently manifest a dense circumstantial fit close examination of how this appearance of fit was achieved may bring it into question. Reductios are a way of accomplishing this.

The following example may illustrate how, by exploiting the ubiquity of expressions capable of *double entendre,* a spurious air of demonstration and consecutiveness can be lent to an interpretation which is, nevertheless, untenable and tendentious. When Freud was expecting his fifth child he wrote to his friend Wilhelm Fliess that he intended to name it Wilhelm in his honour. He made the same offer before the birth of his next child, but they were both girls. Suppose now that someone, recollecting that Freud spoke of 'some unruly homosexual component' in his feelings for Fliess, saw in this offer of Freud's, not just the traditional gesture of affection and esteem it normally is taken for, but the disguised expression of Freud's unconscious wish to bear Fliess a child. It is not difficult to weave this initially outrageous suggestion into a coherent story. It has been pointed out that in his letters to Fliess, Freud, when referring to their projected meetings, repeatedly used a term which is capable of a sexual construction—the term 'congress'. For example, 'Where shall we have our next congress' and 'Our congress will be a great refreshment and relief.' Another illustration of the homosexual suggestions of Freud's images occurs in the sentence, 'I am busy rethinking out something which will cement our work together and put my column on your base.' In another letter, in anticipating his next meeting with Fliess, Freud speaks of himself as 'lubricated for reception'.[159] If we also recall Freud's assertion that the idea of fire is 'permeated with sexual symbolism, the flame always standing for the male organ . . .'[160] we will see still more repressed manifestations of sexual feeling in an already lover-like letter which begins, 'I live gloomily and in darkness until you come and then I . . . kindle my flickering light at your steady flame and feel well again.' Though this account of Freud's promise to name a child after Fliess in terms of a sublimated wish to have intercourse with him is as cogent as any of Freud's own, for many of us it would, nevertheless, constitute a reductio of Freud's hermeneutic procedure rather than a demonstration of his desire to be impregnated by Fliess. Of course in this kind of case the reductio may fail because the Freudian has the option of welcoming it as a further illustration of the illuminating power of what Thomas Nagel calls 'rudimentary Freudianism.' But the cost of this tactic would be to admit all hermeneutic effort to the same status as the Freudian since the level of cogency in my Freud-Fliess example is often met. It is obvious therefore why an alternative response is normally preferred.

On the Licit Role of Imponderable Data

This alternative way of dealing with the problem of reductios is by adducing the evidential weight of publicly untransmissible data which, when taken into account, destroys the analogy to the reductio and thus restores the credibility of the psychoanalytic interpretation. The argument is that the convincingness of Freudian interpretations does not rest on their manifest cogency alone but on additional data which the analyst who puts them forward cannot (or did not) state explicitly. Evidentially unconvincing interpretations are like certain hilarious incidents which fall flat in the telling. You have to have been there. The argument we must assess is thus: There are areas of discourse in which judgements are made and deferred to in spite of the fact that the publicly available grounds for them are acknowledged to be inadequate, for instance: clinical medicine and connoisseurship. What gives these judgments their authority is not their grounds but their source. 'Berenson says it is not a Raphael'; the great diagnostician says that the record of a high blood-urea is a laboratory mistake or the result of collecting the blood into a contaminated tube. In these cases we trust the judge because his judgement has so often been vindicated by ponderable evidence. (In fact insight has been defined as 'successful invalid inference'.)

---

159. *The Complete Letters of Sigmund Freud to Wilhelm Fliess* (Belknap Press, 1985), p. 193.
160. *IL* (Penguin, 1991), p. 196.

We trust Skoda (the pioneer of auscultation) because Rokitanski (the great nineteenth-century pathologist at Vienna General) so often tells us that the post mortem shows that Skoda was right as to the condition of the patient's organs. Chemical analysis tells us that the art critic who was suspicious of certain Caravaggios was right as to their being forgeries. An analogous claim is made on behalf of particular psychoanalytic reconstructions and for Freud's general view of infantile sexuality. His record of intuitively inferred but later objectively validated claims entitles him to credence even where the evidence he is able to present is inadequate. Claims such as these can't be impugned except by impugning the astuteness or trustworthiness of those who make them. And this is what condemns our reductios to inconclusiveness. In order to cast doubt on Freud's claims it is not sufficient to lay out Freud's jigsaw and demonstrate how ill-fitting the pieces are. Freud concedes this and falls back on grounds which he has but can't transmit just as Berenson could not transmit the impression that produced the judgement that a painting was not a Raphael. Ernest Jones also appealed to imponderable data to account for the unpersuasiveness of many published cases: 'a given interpretation, which can be put in a sentence, may be based on several hours of detailed observation, most of which, the individual utterances of the patient, the tone, the emotional gestures, etc., are impossible to reproduce, although it is just those that inevitably convince one of the validity of the inference drawn.'[161] Robert Waelder supplements his case for penis envy in a three-year-old with an appeal to 'her mother's intimate knowledge of the details of her everyday life,' and by the child's 'happy smile of relief' when offered the penis envy interpretation. 'It would have been possible to convince others of what was conveyed by this smile if it had been present on film.' Since it was not filmed the reader has to take Waelder's word for the child's 'happy smile of relief' as well as for what it 'conveyed'[162] This is why psychoanalysis has been dubbed a 'testimonial' science. How can psychoanalytic claims based on data such as this be assessed independently of judgments as to the astuteness and disinterestedness of the analyst—and pre-eminently of Freud?

Asessing Trade-off Arguments: Freud's Legacy

A trawl through psychoanalytic apologetic yields a diversity of rationales for clinging to the conventional view of Freud's greatness, from those in the spirit of Auden's lines on Paul Claudel—'for writing well'—to the discovery

---

161. Ernest Jones, *Papers on Psychoanalysis* (Baillière, Tyndall and Cox, 1923) p. 414; See also Oberndorf, *A History of Psychoanalysis in America* (Harper Torchbooks, 1964), p. 123.

162. Robert Waelder, 'The Problem of the Genesis of Psychical Conflict in Infancy.' *International Journal of Psychoanalysis* (1936), p. 458.

of a subtext whose sublimity more than compensates for the falsity or inanity of the text. The most common and the most suspect of responses to the case against Freud takes the form of some indeterminate concession as to its justice coupled with the defence that these are more than compensated for by his merits—often also indeterminate. The archetypal trade-off fable is one of Freud's own jokes. When the disciples of the Great Rabbi at Cracow learn that the rabbi of Lemberg, whom he had seen die in a clairvoyant vision, was hale and hearty they, nevertheless, refused to be shaken in their admiration. 'That makes no difference. The "Kuck" (look) from Cracow to Lemberg was a magnificent one, whatever you may say.' It was in this spirit that Havelock Ellis wrote: 'Despite the validity of radical criticisms of most of his results Freud is to be recognised as one of the greatest masters in thought.'[163]

Some trade-offs ask us to do more than merely overlook Freud's evidential deficiencies because of the poetic power of his vision. They insist on his compensatory epistemic achievements. The psychiatrist Anthony Storr, while acknowledging that Freud 'became a guru', objects to Frederick Crews' lack of appreciation of the positive aspects of Freud's legacy. But Storr's concessions leave us puzzled as to what these positive aspects could be since he argues that though 'Freud was a great clinical observer . . . well aware of the requirements of scientific truth', he unfortunately 'abandoned them and became a guru interpreting psychological data in terms of his own theoretical preconceptions.' Storr is unforthcoming as to when the guru took over from 'the great clinical observer.'[164] Just when did this 'abandonment of the requirements of scientific truth' in the interest of his own prepossessions occur? Was Freud 'a great clinical observer' when he decided Dora's cough was due to her repressed wish to suck her father's penis (as early as 1900), and did he begin interpreting psychological data in terms of his own theoretical preconceptions at a later stage? And was this before or after he explained the Wolf Man's constipation as due to a repressed desire to be buggered by his father while himself having intercourse with his mother and being reborn through his own rectum?

Freud's Legacy and the Undervaluation of Folk Psychology

It is arguable that what we indubitably owe to Freud—the genitalisation of psychopathology—is of questionable value, whereas what is said to be the legacy he bequeathed bears a striking resemblance to the legacy he inherited. If we wish to assess our indebtedness to Freudian explanatory

---

163. Havelock Ellis, 'Freud's Influence on the Changed Attitude towards Sex'. *American Journal of Sociology* (November 1939), pp. 309–317.

164. Anthony Storr, *The Times* (London, 12 June 1997).

modes we need some idea of the pre-Freudian use that was made of the unconscious and cognate explanatory notions in vernacular discourse, and in literature, rather than in abstract speculations as to the nature of the mind. For this purpose a novel or a memoir is more likely to be instructive than more academic productions. Though it is not without interest that the phrase 'unconscious cerebration' should have provoked 'a regrettable contention for priority' between two medical psychologists in the 1850s it is much more pertinent that in *Anna Karenina* Tolstoi speaks of one of his characters as concealing his feelings 'from others and even from himself, ' and that the central figure of *The Kreuzer Sonata* (1889) says: 'Finally I attain what I had unconsciously sought: the inability to see the cowardice, the stupidity of my position.' It is the currency of such modes of expression rather than the echo of abstruse controversy which accounts for the common reader's feeling of 'obscure relevance to common knowledge'[165] when first encountering Freudian theory.

Henri Ellenberger argued that 'Much of what was credited to Freud was diffuse current lore.'[166] Evidence that this still needs saying is provided by a distinguished analyst, Kurt Eissler, who is so struck by the way in which an observation made by Galton, in a paper published in 1879, anticipates Freud that he refers to it as 'astounding'. The statement which Eissler finds astounding runs, 'The more I have examined the working of my own mind . . . the less respect I feel for the part played by consciousness. I begin, with others, to doubt its use altogether as supervisor, and I think that my best brain work is wholly independent of it.'[167] It is very doubtful that contemporary readers of Galton's paper were at all astonished by this remark. Several years earlier Eduard Hanslick, the music critic, complained of Wagner's *Die Meistersinger* that its composition was too much the 'product of cerebration' and insufficiently under the dominance of 'the magic power of the "unconscious" which should play the first role in the conception of every work of art.'[168] I suspect that what we have in both Galton's remark and Hanslick's is a Romantic commonplace.[169]

Both the ubiquity and the paradoxical character of self-deception seem to be part of the vernacular inheritance on which Freud both drew and impinged. Pip, in *Great Expectations,* reflects on the puzzle posed by what

---

165. Edna Heidbreder, 'Freud and Psychology, *The Psychological Review* (May 1940), p. 192.

166. Henri Ellenberger, *The Discovery of the Unconscious* (London: Allen Lane, 1970), p. 548.

167. Kurt Eissler, *Medical Orthodoxy and The Future of Psychoanalysis* (International Universities Press, 1965), p. 79.

168. Eduard Hanslick, *Music Criticisms, 1846–99* (Penguin, 1963), pp. 121–22.

169. See M.H. Abrams, *The Mirror and the Lamp* (Oxford University Press, 1958), Chapter Eight, 'The Psychology of Literary Invention'.

he calls 'self-swindling': 'An obliging stranger, under pretence of compactly folding up my banknote for security's sake, abstracts the notes and gives me nutshells, but what is his sleight of hand to mine, when I fold up my own nutshells and pass them on myself as notes!' The paradoxical character of self-deception has rarely been so graphically put and yet this is unlikely to have struck many of his nineteenth century readers as a revelation. And aren't the errors which Freud's theory purports to account for continuous with the 'indirect misdeeds' of George Eliot's Bulstrode in *Middlemarch* who, though 'he shrank from a direct lie', engages in those 'acts which are not taken account of in the consciousness, though they bring about the end we fix our mind on and desire?'

There is thus evidence to suggest that the invocation of unconscious self-serving or self-protective devices before Freud was not a profound insight to which certain gifted spirits were able to break through, though only in an impressionistic, unscientific fashion, but a commonplace explanatory mode which was employed from time to time when the occasion seemed to call for it. The Freudian notion of displacement finds its analogue in Sainte-Beuve's confession that in his head he kept, 'a drawer, a pigeonhole, that I have always been afraid to look squarely into. All my work, all that I do, the spate of articles I send forth—all that—is explained by my desire not to know what is in that pigeon hole. I have stopped it up, plugged it with books, so as not to have the leisure to think about it . . .'[170] We can be fairly sure that the interest of this communication was purely personal and that none of Sainte-Beuve's listeners was staggered by the notion of someone behaving as he described for the reasons he gave. Any one who reflects on his naive, psychoanalytically uninformed speculations of what motivates him and his fellows will be surprised at how little that is not doubtful has been added to them by empirical investigation or systematic reflection, by Freud or anyone else.

Freud's Legacy: The Genitalisation of the Cultural Landscape

Let us consider what is an indisputable Freudian legacy—the widespread diffusion of the unconscious sexual symbolism which Freud, in the first of his introductory lectures, listed as one of the major sources of the opposition to psychoanalysis

The conferring of unconscious sexual significance on phenomena is the most ubiquitous feature of Freud's influence on discursive life and amounts to what might be called a genitalisation of our hermeneutic propensities.

---

170. Lewis Galantiere, ed., *The Goncourt Journals 1851–1870* (Doubleday Anchor Books, 1958), p. 193.

Here is a sampler: We are told that when Aladdin rubbed his lamp he was unconsciously masturbating, as was Jack when climbing the bean stalk; that when the ghost of Hamlet's father says 'Remember me!' he is expressing a wish to be restored to his pre-castratory state ('Re-member me!'); that the appeal of the story of the little mermaid who gave up her tail to become human and suffered intensely as a result is due to the universality of castration fear; that both Santa Claus's prominent belly and his obsession with climbing down chimneys are sexual symbols; that the Mickey Mouse of the cartoons as well as being phallic in shape 'actually moves, what's more, in urgent spasm and jerks . . .' just like an ejaculating penis; that the cataclysmic fissure in Poe's *The Fall of the House of Usher* represents the female genitalia; that the 'cavity of importance' which Jane Austen's Catherine Morland (in *Northanger Abbey*) suspects lies concealed behind a small locked door is her own genital organ; that the asparagus stalks painted by Proust's Elstir are phallic and that the madeleine-impregnated tea is a drop of semen; that one of the perks of being a member of parliament is the symbolic significance of the fact that they take their seats in a chamber in which they are continually passing motions; that the practice of lighting one cigar from another probably has a homosexual significance; that the reason the minor key is sad and the major not, is that the minor is evocative of limpness and thus castration and the major of virility as evidenced in the German terms for these *Moll* (soft) and *Dur* (hard); that playing cricket involves the repeated endurance of symbolic castration as when bowled or caught out (I suppose something similar could be said of baseball). And so on and so on. We can say with certainty of these *aperçus* that they would have been impossible without Freud—that it is Freud's distinctive legacy with which we are confronted. The only question is whether they represent genuine advances in understanding.

Our minds having been naturalised in polymorphous perversity many interpretations which strike us as cogent may only reflect our own education, reading, and prepossessions. It is an awareness of this that distinguishes a candidly speculative from a dogmatic outlook; and it is the difficulty of distinguishing these that explains the prolongation of the controversy as to Freud's epistemic status. When Bruno Bettelheim writes that that Little Red Ridinghood's grandmother is a mother surrogate whom Red Ridinghood wants out of the way so that she can pursue her incestuous passion for her father (the huntsman), or indulge her id pleasures with the wolf unhindered, he is, for some, making an illuminating application of what Thomas Nagel calls the 'the reality and pervasive influence of the unconscious, and of the impact of infantile sexuality on the rest of mental life.' But to disparagers of this outlook Freudian hermeneuts, like Bettelheim, seem more assimilable to those animals which go about spraying their distinctive scent throughout an area so as to lay claim to it.

Consider, for example, the rival Adlerian and Freudian explanations as to why sufferers from travel phobia find it easier to use private than public transport. This is how it looks to an orthodox Freudian like Fenichel: the greater fear of public transport is a manifestation of the patient's 'unconscious fear of loss of control over his bodily processes, e.g., urination, defecation, ejaculation.' Adler's account, on the other hand, sees in the same symptom the manifestation of the patient's will to dominate. The patient will not travel in a tram because he must always feel himself in 'the driver's seat.' Is the question raised by these rival interpretations 'Who is right?' or is it rather 'Who can spray higher?' It is obvious that for most of this century Freudians could. Can they still?

When the heroes in a Jack Le May Western make a fire to send out meaningless smoke signals in order to scare off some Comanches who they hope will misinterpret them as signs of their numerousness a recent critic sees this—in accordance with contemporary neo-Sausserean preoccupations—as illustrating 'the detachment of the signifier from its signification.'[171] A few decades ago someone bent on hermeneuticising such a text would more likely have seen the smoke signals as apotropaic phallic symbols evocative of ejaculatory power. In both the Saussurean and the Freudian case a flag is being hoisted over a familiar terrain, and it is being claimed for the intellectual fatherland. If we were to say that a leg was being cocked, and a spray emitted, to stake out a territorial claim we might be suspected of cocking our own leg in the service of a rival sociobiological dispensation. However, there are grounds for thinking that as cogent an account of Freudian hermeneutics is being given by the sociobiological analogy as Freudian hermeneutics gives of its subjects. The least that can be said against many psychoanalytic interpretations is that they can be denied with the same impunity as they are asserted, and are themselves subject to the same hermeneutic reduction as they dispense. The only question is whether there are many of which this could not be said.

Trade-off: 'Now, Any Ass . . .' The Asininity/Insight Ratio

Freud's fanciful pseudo-explanations, precisely because they are so brilliant, perform a disservice. Now any ass has these pictures available for use in "explaining" symptoms of illness.[172]

---

171. Christine Bold, *Selling the Wild West* (Bloomington: Indiana University Press, 1987), p. 132.

172. Wittgenstein, *Culture and Value* (Blackwell, 1980), p. 55.

In order to persuade us of the value of a 'rudimentary Freudianism' Thomas Nagel gives examples in which what would have been otherwise unexplained is rendered intelligible by the application of one of Freud's 'pictures'. But, even if we concede the veridicality of the instances Nagel gives, the overall assessment of his argument would require us to make some rough estimate of the occasions on which we would have been better off without a patrimony of 'rudimentary Freudianism.' It is this problem which is raised by Wittgenstein's remark, 'Now any ass has these pictures available for "explaining" symptoms . . .' This suggests that in order to assess the epistemic value of Freud's influence we would have to arrive at some intuitive asininity/insight ratio.

Nagel's example is of a banker's son who abjured the family business against his father's wishes. His tendency to mysteriously fall asleep whenever he listened to the stock market report made 'expressive sense' when he recalled some repressed episode involving a promise to his father to listen to the stock market reports. This example is meant to stand in for 'countless others', but unless these 'countless others' involve infancy and sexuality, both of which Nagel makes claims for, they would fall short of what an apologist needs.

This is Freud providing the template for the plethora of interpretations invoking genital ideation to explain neurotic symptoms. He is explaining why certain organs though healthy fail to function normally. 'Analysis shows that where activities like playing the piano, writing or even walking are subjected to neurotic inhibitions it is because the physical organs brought into play—the fingers or the legs—have become too strongly eroticized. As soon as writing, which entails making a liquid flow out of a tube on to a piece of white paper, assumes the significance of copulation, or as soon as walking becomes a symbolic substitute for treading upon the body of mother earth, both writing and walking are stopped because they represent the performance of a forbidden sexual act.'[173] And this is a psychiatrist applying Freud's picture of 'symbolic substitution' to conscript soldiers with back problems:

> To understand the significance of 'bent back' as an expression of distaste for army service it is necessary to consider the indirect means of representation (symbolization) which the patient unconsciously uses . . . The spine is a favourite phallic symbol, as closer psychiatric examination of patients with 'bent back' shortly convinces us . . . they feel themselves to be psychologically castrated, to lack all the qualities of the combative and active males of the species that they see all around them. In these patients, unconsciously the spine is a phallic symbol.'[174]

---

173. Freud, *Inhibitions, Symptoms and Anxiety* (London: Hogarth, 1961), pp. 3–4.
174. D.W. Abse, *The Diagnosis of Hysteria* (Bristol: John Wright and Sons, 1950), p. 16.

And this is the analyst Otto Fenichel using the notion of hysterical 'genitalisation' to explain a monosymptomatic hysteria:

> This 'genitalization' may consist of objective changes within the tissues, for example, hyperemia and swelling, representing erection; or it may be limited to abnormal sensations imitating genital sensations. A patient suffering from cardiac neurosis related that the continual palpitation of his heart was accompanied by the feeling that his heart was getting larger and larger, that his whole chest was becoming more and more tense, up to a certain, almost unbearable, point, and that then the whole process would stop, the palpitation would cease and his heart would 'shrink' again. These sensations represented an increasing erection, finally ending with orgasm.'[175]

Nagel's argument is as good as specimens like these are convincing.

Freud's Legacy: 'Darkness Is not News'

> Very few can boast of hearts which they dare lay open to themselves, and of which, by whatever accident exposed they do not shun a distinct and continued view. (Samuel Johnson, *Life of Pope*)

There are few defences of Freud which do not invoke some variant of the argument from resistance. This is how it was put in Seaborn Jones's book, *Treatment or Torture*:[176] 'The insights of . . . Freud have been absorbed so slowly and incompletely not because of their intrinsic difficulty but because of their affective unacceptability;' which is to say, not because they are hard to take in but because they are hard to take. This is often accompanied, as with Jones, by a confession of an original antipathy to Freudian ideas. 'I have now recovered from the intense distress I suffered when Father Christmas faded into a myth. I am beginning to accept—and this is a much more difficult adjustment—the survival within myself and within my friends. of a savage, ruthless, fearful infant.'[177] There are good reasons for thinking that many Freudians are as attached to the idea of themselves as 'savage, ruthless, fearful infants' as Jones once was to his belief in Father Christmas. In any case, the degree of pre-Freudian obliviousness to the extent of our depravity is grossly overestimated, and Freud can be suspected of exploiting the vanity of his readers—'Most people aren't tough enough to take this'.

When Thomas Nagel writes that 'Freud is a natural target for the enemies of self-knowledge,'[178] he prompts speculation as to whether his pre-Freudian life was spent in a locked room with nothing to read but back

---

175. Otto Fenichel, *The Psychoanalytic Theory of Neurosis* (London: Routledge, 1946), Chapter XII, 'Conversion', p. 232.

176. Seaborn Jones, *Treatment or Torture* (Tavistock, 1968), p. 224.

177. *ibid.*

178. 'Freud's Permanent Revolution', *The New York Review of Books* (12 May 1994).

numbers of *St. Nicholas,* and the exploits of Frank Merriwell or the Bobbsey
Twins. Nagel's argument was spelled out by a London psychoanalyst who
speculated that Freud is attacked because 'He said that civilisation was a
veneer over polymorphous perversity, incest, rapaciousness, man as a wolf to
other men . . . all these things, that I cannot bear to know about my friends
and myself.'[179] Apologists like Nagel overestimate our resistance to revelations of our depravity: viciousness loves company. But not only is darkness
'not news' (as the sociologist Erving Goffman put it) but there are those
who find the concept of a reprobate unconscious itself appealing. Someone
once accounted for the early hostility to psychoanalytic explanations by saying that patients preferred, for the sake of their peace of mind, to call their
problems 'medical' rather than psychological, but it is no extravagant conjecture that many achieved a similar tranquillity by calling their problems
'unconscious.' If so, to the other attractions of the unconscious must be
added the attraction of the idea that we are innocently oblivious of our perverse whimsies, our scatological reveries, our murderous, familial resent-
ments and our persecutory feelings and violent retaliatory fantasies in
general. Just as someone may be HIV positive and not know it, so, it is
soothingly suggested, someone may nurture perverse, criminal, and degrad-
ing desires yet not know it. Though it is true that Freud may have persuaded
people to indict themselves of shameful thoughts and fantasies, of which
they sincerely thought themselves innocent, it is as likely that he permitted
them to acquit themselves of their intermittent indulgence in fantasies which
were no less shameful and not only conscious but familiar.

Candour as to this was sometimes an embarrassment to Freud—a distinguished friend whose dreams Freud was regularly interpreting later
reported, 'All the dreadful things which Freud had suggested I might have
concealed from myself and suppressed I could honestly assure him had
always been clearly and consciously present in my mind.'[180] I think that a lot
of people are uncomfortably aware of having engaged in erotic reveries concerning inappropriate others and this is mistakenly counted in Freud's
favour. Studs Lonigan, the eponymous hero of James T. Farrell's novel, even
gets to the point of masturbating because he is excited by a glimpse of his
sister's nudity. To think in Freudian rather than Catholic, self-inquisitorial
terms may have advantages—as hypocrisy often does. It may permit someone to think in cool rather than hot terms, such as could disrupt ratioci-

---

179. Paul Williams, *Sunday Times* (26 June 1994).
180. The classical scholar Heinrich Gomperz relates this in his autobiography. It is quoted
in Macmillan, *Freud Evaluated,* p. 277. Freud himself tells of a celebrated poet who abandoned
his objection to the idea that he had sexual feelings for his mother as soon as Freud explained
that they need not have been conscious.

nation and resolve. A man who is able to persuade himself that his incestuous feelings for a pubescent daughter or step-daughter are unconscious can think of appropriate ways of distancing himself without dwelling too disturbingly on his intermittent awareness of her loveliness and desirability.[181]

This counter-charge that it is the Freudians who are guilty of bad faith and self-deception in denying or ignoring the appeal of their ideas was not just a mechanical *tu quoque*. The analyst in Mann's *Magic Mountain,* who reminded his listeners 'of secret suffering, of shame and sorrow, of the redeeming power of the analytic,' has an obvious affinity to Freud. ('"Come unto me" he was saying, though not in those words, "Come unto me all you who are weary and heavy laden." And he left no doubt of his conviction that all those present were weary and heavy-laden.') In the course of remarks on the general question as to the influence of affective and/or ideological forces in the acceptance and propagation of ill-founded views Simon and Gagnon shrewdly compare the popularity of Freudian revelations with those of Kinsey. 'When the Kinsey studies reported that very large numbers of men had masturbated, other men who had done so felt better.' Isn't it natural to suspect that the enthusiasm that greeted Freud's dubious thesis of universal bisexuality was, for many, just their way of sticking one toe out of the closet? But this of course is nowhere general enough to account for the massive endorsement Freud's ideas received. This was due, I think, to the paradoxical fact that it was the sexual impulse as it is directly, if intermittently, known in all its importunacy and lawlessness, rather than laboriously inferred via Freud's 'method' that made its pre-eminence so plausible.

I suspect that what many are indebted to Freud for is not self-knowledge but absolution. It may be that what enables some of Freud's critics to be less inhibited in their rejection of him is that they are comparatively at ease with their more risible sexual quirks and don't feel so strong a need for some intellectual justification ('polymorphous perversity, don't you know'). John Hospers, who raised this issue, resolved it the opposite direction, '. . . we all have secret wishes and defenses . . . but the people who are most nearly free from this (are) the psychoanalysts . . . viewing with a certain detached and half-humorous unconcern the feelings and foibles which it would make most philosophers squirm to have mentioned.'[182] Hospers's boast seems to be that, though we are all miserable wankers, psychoanalysts don't worry about it. That habitual trafficking with the notion of the unconscious tends to promote a greater degree of obtuseness to the quotidian world than is

---

181. The terms 'hot' and 'cool' derive from Walter Mischel's work on self-regulation in children.

182. John Hospers, *Psychoanalysis, Scientific Method, and Philosophy,* ed., Sidney Hook (New York: Grove Press, 1959), p. 344.

possible to the rest of us is suggested by what an analyst said of a patient's 'unformulated ideology about sex'—'He felt that women should not hesitate about sexual relations with him. They should do so without demanding love and attachment. He should be free to leave them at any time he felt like it. However, they should give him deep love and should admire him. They should not be too much hurt when he leaves them.'[183] What I find incongruous in this is, that even if it does not indicate a profound self-ignorance in the analyst himself, it certainly shows him obtuse to the wishful fantasies of the generality of the men of his culture since the 'sexual ideology' he describes is held by too many of them to be treated as pathognomic of neurosis.

It would have been better if Nagel had concentrated on the issues and postponed his judgement that Freud's critics were 'enemies of self-knowledge' until it had been established that their rational grounds for questioning Freud's epistemic pretensions were so inadequate as to warrant speculation of this kind.

The Idea of a Pathos

> If there existed in science and medicine an analogue of literary criticism, we should investigate not only what people have reason to believe in, but the kind of thing they want to believe . . .[184]

Any satisfactory account of the infatuation with Freud would have to address the 'pathos' of psychoanalytic ideas, in the sense of 'pathos' employed by Arthur Lovejoy when, in the introduction to *The Great Chain of Being*, he speaks of 'the susceptibility to diverse kinds of metaphysical pathos as an influential cause in the determination of speculative tendencies.' He defines 'metaphysical pathos' as 'any description of the nature of things, any characterisation of the world to which one belongs, in terms which, like the words of a poem, awaken through their associations and through a sort of empathy they engender, a congenial mood or tone of feeling'.[185] One kind of metaphysical pathos to which psychoanalysis has some affinity, and to which its appeal has been imputed, is the animistic pathos, of which an apt account is given by Gilbert Murray. In his *Five Stages of Greek Religion*, Murray speaks of the innate tendency of men everywhere to imagine a personal cause for every striking phenomenon: 'If the wind blows it is because some being is blowing with his cheeks; if a tree is struck by lightning it is

---

183. Paul Schilder, 'The Social Neurosis'. *The Psychoanalytic Review* (1938), p. 5
184. Peter Medawar, 'Science and Literature' in *The Hope of Progress* (Wildwood House, 1974), p. 36.
185. Arthur Lovejoy, *The Great Chain of Being* (New York: Harper and Row, 1960 [1936]), p. 11.

because someone has thrown his battle axe at it. In some Australian tribes there is no belief in natural death. If a man dies it is because "bad man killed that fellow.[186] Freud himself acknowledged this affinity: 'The psychoanalytic assumption of unconscious mental activities appears to us . . . a further development of that primitive animism which caused our own consciousness to be reflected in all around us.'[187]

However, a difficulty in accounting for the response to Freud in terms of susceptibility to an animistic pathos is that whereas to some of his contemporaries Freud signified the supercession of a medical/materialist view of mental illness by a voluntaristic/hermeneutic one, to others he represented a daring extension of nineteenth-century medical materialism. For example, whereas Thomas Mann sees in Freud's 'unmasking of happening as really doing . . . the innermost core of psychoanalytic theory', one of Freud's earliest British supporters saw him as 'dominated by the the the prevailing urge to find mechanistic explanations for everything in the cosmos.'[188]

The following quotations illustrate the varied and incompatible impressions that Freud provoked: '. . . in his eager search for causes, he took as his standard the rigid kinds of causation studied by the physicist, and so became committed to a mode of conceiving the manifestation of human effort which does not do them justice.'[189] On the other hand the Marxist theorist Christopher Caudwell complained that 'the psychology of Freud and his followers . . . instead of being causal and materialistic . . . is religious and idealistic.'[190] Egon Friedell, an Austrian cultural historian, also took Caudwell's view: 'the decisive importance that he attaches to the power of the word—the creative Logos—is an unequivocal admission of the supremacy of the spiritual over the physical.'[191] The literary critic Alfred Kazin stood this account on its head: 'Freud always emphasised the organic and the physical, rather than the social and the cultural . . . it is precisely Freud's old-fashioned, scientific rationalism, his need to think of a man as a physical being, rather than a 'psychological one', that explains the primacy of Freud's discoveries.'[192] E.E.G. Boring attempted to capture this incoherence by speaking of 'psychoanalytic philosophy's loose and indeterminate mixture of

---

186. Gilbert Murray, *Five Stages of Greek Religion* (London: Watts and Co., 1935), p. 23.

187. 'The Unconscious', *CP IV* (Hogarth, 1925), p. 104.

188. T.N. Mitchell, 'Critical Notice of *Beyond the Pleasure Principle.*' *British Journal of Medical Psychology* (1922), pp. 232–243.

189. J.J. Putnam 'The Work of Sigmund Freud.' *Journal of Abnormal Psychology* Vol. XII, No. 3, (August 1917), p. 151.

190. Christopher Caudwell, *Studies in a Dying Culture* (London: John Lane, 1938), p. 160.

191. Egon Friedell, *Cultural History of the Modern Age* (1932), Vol. III, pp. 480–81.

192. Alfred Kazin, 'The Freudian Revolution Analysed.' in Benjamin Nelson, ed., *Freud and the Twentieth Century,* (London, 1958), p. 15.

voluntarism and determinism.'[193] A similar observation was made several
decades earlier by a German psychiatrist, Oswald Bumke: '. . . though some
have thought psychoanalysis is materialist in its views of the psyche and have
opposed it for that reason, others like Thomas Mann felt that Freud's doctrine of the libido was a reaction against the mechanistic tendencies of the
last century'[194] In Bumke's view these contradictory impressions were due
to an ambivalence in Freud himself. Sandor Rado attempted to resolve these
contradictions by dividing Freud's development into an early, though never
completely superseded, fruitful mechanistic phase, up to about 1905 or so,
and a barren animistic phase thereafter.[195] This doesn't work. What Rado
calls Freud's animism is just as pronounced in the works of his early phase
such as *Studies on Hysteria* and *The Interpretation of Dreams* as in any of his
later works. A particularly striking example of the contradiction is that provided by the contrast between the view of a prominent analyst and Freud
scholar and founder of the Freud Archives, Kurt Eissler, and an Irish
Freudian. Kurt Eissler sees a source of resistance to Freud's conception of
the neurosis in the fact 'that a pathophysiological theory of neurosis would
meet the requirements of Christian metaphysics better than would a psychogenic theory. The idea of a physical poison penetrating into the brain
and affecting the mind seems less offensive to Catholic religionists than the
idea of a mind that falls sick in itself and by itself . . . an evil effect of the
body upon the mind is not, in this framework of belief, inherently offensive,
since nothing good is to be expected, after all, from corrupted flesh; but a
disease of the mind whose source lay in the mind would imply—even
though remotely—a dysfunction of the soul.'[196] Eissler seems to live in
some alternative universe in which the Manicheans prevailed. In any case, at
least one Catholic religionist, Jonathan Hanaghan of Dublin, saw Freud
quite differently: 'the fundamental value of Freud is that . . . for the first time
since the days of the miracles of Jesus he gave form and substance to unextended mind and spirit . . . he showed purpose at work in the form of wish
fulfillment . . .'[197]

The ancient rhetorician Quintilian drew a distinction between metaphors
which animate the inanimate and those which inanimate the animate. Freud
proffers us both. Though at certain times we are encouraged to see human
undertakings as just movements of energy from one locale to another, at

---

193. E.B.G. Boring, 'Was This Analysis a Success?' *Journal of Abnormal Psychology* (1940),
p. 7.

194. Bernard Sachs, 'Bumke's Critique of Psychoanalysis.' *Mental Hygiene* (July 1932), p.
409.195. Sandor Rado, 'On the Retransformation of Psychoanalysis into a Medical Science.'
Comprehensive Psychiatry, Vol. 3, No. 6 (December, 1962).

196. Kurt Eissler, *Medical Orthodoxy and the Future of Psychoanalysis* (International
Universities Press, 1965), p. 255.

197. Jonathan Hanaghan, *Freud and Jesus* (Dublin: The Runa Press, 1966), p. 136.

others we are persuaded to see even natural death, 'that which no man chooses,' the paradigm of an ostensibly passive undergoing, as in reality the successful consummation of the subject's secret strategy for escape from 'the clamour of life.' Freud's theory simultaneously elevates and degrades. On the one hand, it encourages us to see our most considered choices as, ultimately, discharges through their continuity with their blatantly discharge-like infantile prototypes. On the other hand, not just neuroses, but afflictions as varied as infertility, spontaneous abortions, appendicitis and death itself, are given a noumenal character which belies their passive surface appearance in that they are really the upshot of 'intentions and motives such as operate in everyday life.' Two antagonistic demands threaten a true perception of our common world: one is the compulsion to see in nature the operation of motives and intentions similar to those which animate us and beings like us, the other to see ourselves as ultimately passive as a river flowing towards the sea. Perhaps it uniquely characterises Freud's psychoanalysis that it gratifies both.

Why Are They Picking on Freud?

'Why pick on Freud?' asked Frank Sulloway.[198] The fact that someone of Sulloway's scholarly standing could ask so plaintively provides the best of reasons. How did Freud become the Dulcinea del Toboso of so large a segment of the intelligentsia? Sulloway protested that other psychological theories were as bereft of empirical support as Freud's without being so vehemently denounced for it. Perhaps so. But were these other theories accompanied by the claim that they had been validated by all competent and disinterested investigators? And more to the point, were these claims, like the Freudian ones, accepted? No other theory attained the institutional and cultural status of Freud's. What other theory has had a critic of Freud scolded editorially by institutions as established as the *New York Times*?[199] In *Pears Cyclopedia*, a one-volume compendium of human knowledge, we are informed of the influence of bowel training in the production of adult character traits such as 'fussiness, punctuality, belief in discipline, and extreme but repressed aggressiveness', and of the child's Oedipus complex on 'its attitude towards the opposite sex throughout life.'[200] If it be objected that the reference work in question is largely addressed to quiz

198. Frank Sulloway, 'Grünbaum on Freud.' *Free Inquiry* (Fall 1985), p. 25. It took five more years for Sulloway to work out an answer to his question and when he did (preface to the 1992 edition of *Freud: Biologist of the Mind*) it was one that had been around for over half a century and which he could have worked out for himself had there been the will.

199. 29 March 1921: 'He Needs to get the Facts.' 'He' was G.K Chesterton who had shown himself insufficiently appreciative, and failed to realise that psychoanalysis champions sexual rectitude.

200. 'The Self.' *Pears Cyclopedia*, 1966–67 (Pelham Books).

game addicts, the same cannot be said of academic monuments such as the *International Encyclopedia of the Social Sciences,* where the fact that Freud's theory of infantile sexuality has not attained universal acceptance is traced to unanalysed infantile complexes in the dissidents. In another contribution in the same work—the entry on phobias—we are told authoritatively that fear of going insane is really a displacement upwards of the fear of castration— the head standing in for the penis. And has it been said of any but Freudian theory that '. . . on the basis of your past history and general laws, the psychoanalyst can not only explain why you have the dreams that you do, why you feel aggression toward this person and affection toward the other, and why you feel guilty in the situation you do, but also predict what conflicts will arise, what course therapy will take, and whether it will achieve certain desired results'? And we are informed of this mythical achievement, not by an analyst, but by an analytic philosopher in a tradition of epistemic rigour so scrupulous that it questioned our entitlement to anticipate tomorrow's dawn.[201]

To deal with criticism of the psychoanalytic movement without taking account of the representativeness of these endorsements is like telling the story of the Cold War without mentioning the activities of the Soviet Army. And yet these citations fall short of what the critic wishes to convey as to the traditional 'taken for granted' status of Freudian theory. Imagine that someone who had witnessed at first hand the operation of the *de facto* Jim Crow of the 1940s was trying to describe what it was like. How could something as pervasive as the force of gravity be conveyed by documentation as to this or that particular discriminatory employment practice, or restricted covenant, or patronising remark? So it was with the psychoanalytic culture in which we were immersed. Whatever we can document falls short of the intimidatory ambience that constrained judgement on Freud and psychoanalysis over so prolonged a period.

Revisionism Without Anachronsim

Can't we imagine a more candid epistemic revisionism—one which concedes both that indefensibly inflated claims were traditionally made and accepted and the extent to which they still are? Critics would then be confronted with the argument that nothing they have said has succeeded in showing that Freud did not discover novel and momentous phenomena. It is one thing to show that Freudian confirmation claims were spurious and

---

201. John Hospers, *An Introduction to Philosophical Analysis* (London: Routledge, 1963), pp. 181–82.

quite another to show that Freudian instantiation claims were. Revisionist apologists fall into two main classes, substantive and epistemic. Substantive revisionists may be divided between those who, while retaining an indeterminate number of Freudian theses, abandon those that large and influential groups have objected to, and those who reject most of them but wish to continue to make use of some general assumption which was, nevertheless, distinctively Freudian, for example, that the formative events of childhood can be reconstructed from the material produced during the analytic hour.

I have argued that Freud's substantive theses, though instantiatable, are not falsifiable, and thus pose the problem of how they could be abandoned on ostensibly empirical grounds. Epistemic revisionists, are not open to this objection since, while making some indeterminate concessions to critics, they nevertheless retain the bulk of Freud's major claims while modifying their form, for example, from 'all' to 'many' or 'some'. They may further wish to qualify their retreat from universality by withdrawing any implication that particular instances are *known* to occur, in favour of some reduced claim that there is some degree of support for their occurrence.

The Incoherence of Substantive Revisionism

Whichever thesis the substantive revisionist has decided to abandon he will be confronted with an embarrassment. Suppose he denies that there is any such phenomenon as penis envy. How can he show previous instantiation reports not to have been veridical? Suppose he meets this objection by confining his revisionism to the generalising component of the traditional theory and merely maintains that not *all* women who choose to find fulfillment in activities other than motherhood and marriage are displacing their penis envy. How can he show that the failure of revisionists to detect this mechanism is not, nevertheless, compatible with its presence? What can be said against penis envy clinically has always been said against it. Why have arguments that have been rejected for half a century suddenly become cogent? And the same embarrassment will arise whichever thesis he wishes to jettison. Without a clear account of the empirical grounds on which a thesis has been rejected the charge of opportunism becomes the most plausible explanation of theory change.

Non-substantive, epistemic revisionism is spared this embarrassment because it does not claim to have discovered classical psychoanalysis to be false; it merely concedes that it is as yet unproven. Many epistemic revisionists seem to await validation of Freudian theory as pious Jews do the Messiah, which is odd since until very recently these revisionists were insisting that he had already arrived and died for our sins. Why have they placed their confidence in an investigatory method which after almost a century has generated no results as to which there is consensus among fellow practitioners?[202]

Epistemic Revisionism: The Retreat from Laws to Instances

Those who relinquish the more readily assessable general claims of Freudian theory have certainly retreated to a less vulnerable position. But it is one which they can no longer distinguish from that of a systematic communal delusion. Might they not be mistaking their familiarity with a vocabulary and an architectonic and a sense of solidarity with their fellow Freud-speakers, for genuine knowledge? The least such apologists can be charged with is a failure of reflexivity. The critics of psychoanalysis may concede that conversancy with Nagel's 'rudimentary Freudianism' is a *sine qua non* of a complete education while, nevertheless, deeming it akin to a social accomplishment, like speaking French, rather than an epistemic achievement, like mastering the principles of nutrition or antisepsis. Amnesia for the germ theory of disease and thus of the practices based on it would exact a higher price than just social isolation. It is denied that amnesia for what we owe to Freud would entail analogous losses. I do not say that this is so but that discriminating its being so from its not being so is a more arduous enterprise than the class of revisionists to which Thomas Nagel belongs show themselves aware.

In 1480 Marsilio Ficino complained to his friend Giovanni Cavalcanti: 'The safety ensured you by the benevolence of your Jupiter standing in the sign of the Fish is denied me by the malevolence of my Saturn retrogressing in the sign of the Lion.' Are present-day apologists capable of even formulating the possibility that their vaunted Freud-indebted understanding of human nature may bear no more relation to reality than Ficino's? But though there is a strong possibility that a day may come when the analytically indoctrinated, swapping insights about 'massive amounts of anal material' and 'good breasts' and 'bad breasts', will be perceived as we now perceive the exchange between Ficino and Cavalcanti, the nature of the revisionist case (unassessable instantiation claims rather then demonstrably spurious confirmation, test survival claims) precludes my being sure of this.

No such doubts assail me as to the epistemic pretensions of classical psychoanalysis, though even my own formula—the issuing of spurious reports

---

202. Frederick Crews was able to point out in his comment on Thomas Nagel's *New York Review of Books* piece that though both Nagel and Wollheim exalt psychoanalytic method they cannot agree as to what it authorises them to assert (*The Memory Wars*, pp. 282–84).

that the theory has been confirmed—does not capture the feature of the situation which I am most concerned to convey—the gratuitous social standing of the theory in the light of its manifest deficiencies; a social standing which caused normal intellectual processes to be suspended in its favour to the point where expositors became unaware of their own tendentiousness. Though classical psychoanalysis is a pseudoscience rather than just an erroneous one, because it comprises blatantly untenable claims that the theory advanced had survived prolonged investigation, its interest transcends that of other pseudosciences because of the extent to which these claims were accepted and assimilated into the culture.

For well over half a century an enormous number of intelligent, highly educated, even intellectually distinguished, people thought themselves to have good reasons for crediting claims on grounds which even apologists now concede were manifestly inadequate. Why then were they credited? I have suggested one reason in my remarks on the influence of Lovejoy's 'metaphysical pathos'. But there is a more obvious source which has often been noted. It is what one writer called 'the cause of unashamedness.' Society now feels less in need of a medical rationale for exercising restraint in interfering with sexual life. The fact that many people, homosexuals pre-eminently, were either intimidated from expressing their sexuality in the only way natural to them, or punished for doing so and even rendered odious in their own eyes, was once felt insufficient grounds for protest without the invocation of a hygienic, psychodynamic rationale for tolerance. That this is much less so today may provide one reason for the enhanced willingness to abandon Freud's emphasis on the pathogenic potency of sexual repression. I do not think it plausible to maintain that this came about because, in the fullness of time, facts came to light of which previous generations of Freudians were ignorant. Rather the situation is that described by George Bernard Shaw:

> The moment we want to believe something, we suddenly see all the arguments for it, and become blind to the arguments against it. The moment we want to disbelieve anything we have previously believed we suddenly discover not only that there is a mass of evidence against it but that this evidence was staring us in the face all the time . . .[203]

This is a more recognisable account of the transition from classical psychoanalysis to whatever it is that is replacing it than revisionist apologists themselves have been able to give. The final irony is that recognition of the

---

203. George Bernard Shaw, *The Intelligent Woman's Guide to Socialism and Capitalism* (London: Constable, 1929), p. 460.

accuracy of a Shavian account of the changing content of psychoanalytic theory teaches as chastening a lesson as to the helplessness of our intellect in its struggle with our interests and our affects as any taught by psychoanalysis itself; and more convincingly.

2

Wittgenstein's Freud

Introduction

Wittengstein's remarks on Freud do not form part of one continuous exposition. Most of them were not intended for publication. Some are sketchy to the point of incomprehensibility. Others are apparently, and perhaps even ultimately, inconsistent. Nevertheless, they seem to me to offer a more illuminating characterization of Freud than any other and one of the few which can be confronted with its subject without producing acute feelings of incongruity.

There are three habits of mind which it is natural to refer to Freud. One is the tendency to see a large segment of human life as comprising the pursuit of ends of which the agent has no cognizance, even to the point of seeing as instances of purposive activity what would have formerly been considered happenings and of redrawing the customary boundary between what we undertake and what we undergo. Another, the pursuit of hidden meanings, the readiness to see a wide range of phenomena, from dreams, errors and the symptoms of neurotics to works of art and the anonymous productions of culture—like legend and myth—as the distorted manifestation or symbolic gratification of unconscious impulses. (Everything is what it is *and* another thing.) Third, the tendency to trace the personalities of adults, their interests, attitudes, sexual proclivities and susceptibility to neurotic illness, to the influence of infantile sexual vicissitudes.

In what follows I try to elicit and assess Wittgenstein's answer to the question of how the currency of these habits is to he accounted for, by examining two more determinate questions: What is Freud really up to when he proffers interpretations of symptoms, errors, dreams, and so forth? What is the character of the claim that these phenomena are 'mental acts', are motivated, are wish-fulfilments? Freud himself has more answers to these

This essay first appeared in Peter Winch, ed., *Studies in the Philosophy of Wittgenstein* (Routledge, 1969), and is reprinted by permission.

questions than he chooses to be aware of. However, all of them involve him in the claim that he is in some sort explaining these phenomena, that he is accounting for their occurrence. A proto-typical Freudian utterance would have the following features: It would assert of some phenomenon like a slip of the tongue, a lapse of memory, a reminiscence, a dream, a phobia, an hysterical symptom, or an obsessive thought, that though it might appear to be something which the patient had passively suffered, it was, nevertheless, motivated, purposive, and that by submitting the item to free association and/or translating it according to certain rules, a wish would be arrived at, often of an infantile sexual character, of which the patient may have been unaware but which had been secretly at work, waiting for an opportune moment to contrive its gratification. About such remarks Wittgenstein holds the following views: They are not hypotheses; their production is more a consummatory than an instrumental activity. Neither the wish-fulfilling and symbolic character of the events they purport to explain nor their connexion with sexuality are matters of evidence. If such remarks have come widely to be accepted and made models for still other remarks, this is not to be attributed to any explanatory use to which they can be put but to the appeal they exert, an appeal partly to be explained in terms of their invocation of the notion of hidden meaning and of sexuality.

In the *Introductory Lectures,* Freud refers to 'the displeasing proposition that mental processes are essentially unconscious' and says, 'By thus emphasizing the unconscious in mental life, we have called forth all the malevolence of humanity.' In the *New Introductory Lectures,* he speaks of 'the burdens under which we groan—the odium of infantile sexuality, the ludicrousness of symbolism'. In his 1925 paper on 'The Resistances to Psychoanalysis', he attributes this odium 'above all to the very important place in the mental life of human beings which psychoanalysis assigns to what are known as the sexual instincts'. And in accounting for the popularity of Adler he said: 'Humanity is ready to accept anything when tempted with ascendancy over sexuality as the bait.'

A succinct way of giving Wittgenstein's view of Freud is simply to state that he stands these propositions on their heads. In a letter to Norman Malcolm, he said of Freud: 'He always stresses what great forces in the mind, what strong prejudices work against the idea of psychoanalysis but he never says what an enormous charm this idea has for people just as it has for Freud himself.'[1] In the first of the conversations with Rush Rhees on Freud, he says of the notion of the unconscious: 'It is an idea which has a marked

---

1. Norman Malcolm, *Ludwig Wittgenstein: A Memoir* (London, 1958), p. 44. Freud was not always so disingenuous about this. In 1893 he wrote to his friend Fliess: 'The sexual business attracts people; they all go away impressed and convinced, after exclaiming: No one has ever asked me that before.' Freud, *Origins of Psychoanalysis* (New York, 1954), Letter 14.

attraction.'[2] In the third of the lectures on Aesthetics, he says about Freud's sexual interpretation of a dream: 'The connexions he makes interest people immensely. They have a charm. It is charming to destroy prejudice. . . . It may be the fact that the explanation is extremely repellent that drives you to adopt it'; and of psychoanalytic explanations in general that many 'are adopted because they have a peculiar charm. The picture of people having unconscious thoughts has a charm. The idea of an underworld, a secret cellar. Something hidden, uncanny . . . A lot of things one is ready to believe because they are uncanny.'[3]

I

In what way are psychoanalytic explanations uncanny? Consider the protective, interest-serving relationship in which the unconscious so often stands to its possessor: Ferenczi's unconscious makes him forget a witticism which might have caused offence and embroiled him in controversy; Jones's causes him to mislay his pipe when he is suffering from the effects of over-smoking and to find it again when he has recovered; an engineer's (who has reluctantly agreed to work one evening) to put out of commission the equipment necessary for the task; a house physician's to absent himself during duty hours without detection; a keen classicist's to present herself with a coveted antique Roman medallion which she finds she has unwittingly packed among her belongings; that of girls with beautiful hair to 'manage their combs and hairpins in such a way that their hair comes down in the middle of a conversation'. Freud's unconscious permits him to forget to keep professional engagements which are not lucrative and to miss a train connection while travelling to Manchester via Holland and thus fulfil a long-cherished with to see Rembrandt's paintings without defying his elder brother's request not to break his journey. On one occasion it admonished him before visiting a patient to take particular care not to repeat a diagnostic error.

It also assuages the sense of guilt by punishing moral breaches. In support of this view Freud cites a correspondent who informs him that he has observed how often men who turn round to look back at passing women in the street meet with minor accidents such as colliding with lamp-posts.

Along with this benevolence you must also consider the unconscious's superiority in performance as compared with that of the person whose unconscious it is. Freud freely acknowledged his inferiority to his unconscious in performing arithmetical calculations or aiming accurately. He relates that on one occasion when he received news that a seriously ill

2. Cyril Barrett, ed., *Ludwig Wittgenstein: Lectures and Conversations* (Oxford, 1966), p. 43.

3. *Lectures and Conversations*, pp. 24–25.

daughter had taken a turn for the better and his unconscious had decided
that a sacrificial act of thanksgiving to fate was in order, he impulsively
kicked a slipper at a little marble statue of Venus, knocking it to the ground,
where it broke. The fact that he did not hit any of the objects which were
closely grouped around it, he attributes to the superior aim of the unconscious mind. Freud gives another example of the superior dexterity of the
unconscious: the manner in which he broke the marble cover of his inkpot.
'My sweeping movement was only apparently clumsy; in reality it was
exceedingly adroit and well directed, and understood how to avoid damaging any of the more precious objects that stood around. It is my belief that
we must accept this judgement for a whole series of seemingly accidental,
clumsy movements . . . they prove to be governed by an intention and
achieve their aim with a certainty which cannot in general be credited to our
conscious voluntary movements.' (Elsewhere Freud speaks of the 'unconscious dexterity' with which objects are mislaid 'if the unconscious has a
motive in doing so'.) Freud also informs us that apparently clumsy movements can be most cunningly used for sexual purposes'. One such which he
relates 'was accomplished with the dexterity of a conjurer'. This was when
Stekel, in extending his hand to greet his hostess, undid the bow of her
gown without being aware of any dishonourable intention.

Rank, Freud reports, has provided evidence of the superior ability of the
unconscious to see under unfavourable conditions: it enabled a girl, who
coveted a cheap piece of jewellery, to find on the pavement, a note for
exactly the amount required. 'Otherwise it would be impossible to explain
how it was, that precisely this one person, out of many hundreds of passers-
by—and with all the difficulties caused by poor street lighting and the dense
crowds—was able to make the find.'

Don't these stories remind you of something? Don't they illustrate the
degree to which the notion of the unconscious meets the same demands as
those which produce the invisible companion phantasies of our childhood?
Though we know what Freud would have said to this suggestion: that invisible companion phantasies are endopsychic perceptions of the operation of
unconscious agencies.[4]

It may seem strange but it is undeniable that accounts in which the rôle
assigned to the unconscious is a punishing rather than a benevolent one are
found equally gratifying. In this connexion Freud writes of a class of patients

---

4. In *The Red and the Black* Stendhal attributes this same relish in the masterfulness of the
unconscious to his Mathilde de la Mole:

'As she made these reflections, Mathilde's pencil was tracing lines at random on a page
of her album. One of the profiles she had just completed amazed and delighted her; it was
strinkingly like Julien. "It's the voice of Heaven! Here's one of the miracles of Love"! she cried
in rapture. "Quite unconsciously I've drawn his portrait."

'She rushed off to her room, locked herself in, applied herself to her task, and tried hard whom he describes as 'those wrecked by success', people who fall mentally ill 'precisely because a deeply rooted and long-cherished wish has come to fulfilment'. He cites the case of a teacher who developed melancholia when offered promotion and of a woman who broke down when the obstacles to her marriage to the man she loved were removed.[5] The 'peculiar attraction' of such explanations can be illustrated by contrasting them with the case of the cricketer who was perfectly happy as long as he scored no runs, but broke into tears if he scored more than fifty. If this were all, one could have added him to Freud's list as a particularly striking case of self-punishment consequent on success, and predicted a great bibliographical future for him in the literature of psychoanalysis. But he was diagnosed as a diabetic whose distress was induced by the effect on his blood sugar level of the exertion of running between the wickets. When he was given glucose sweets to suck he was able to score a century without too much anguish. Don't we feel that by unimaginatively responding to so banal a form of treatment be forfeited his claim to our interest?—though we could restore this interest if we could be persuaded that, as Freud once remarked when he came upon an organic determinant of an illness, 'the neurosis had seized upon this chance event and made use of it for an utterance of its own'.[6]

This remark brings us to another characteristic of the unconscious; one which reinforces Wittgenstein's suggestion as to its affinities and the source of its appeal. It is alluded to rather cryptically in the *Introductory Lectures* in the remark that 'the neurosis of hysteria can create its symptoms in all systems of the body (circulatory, respiratory, etc.)'.[7] Though this could be construed as simply an allusion to the phenomenon of hypochondriacal conviction which does not involve any assumption of mental control over physical processes, there is reason to believe that Freud means more than this. In the case history of Dora, Freud explains how Dora was able to make use of an organically based disorder of the throat, which induced coughing and aphonia, to express symbolically her unconscious love for a man by falling ill when he was away and recovering when he returned. That the periods did not invariably coincide is attributed by Freud to the fact that 'it became necessary to obscure the coincidence between her attacks of illness

to draw a portrait of Julien. But she could not do it; the profile sketched by accident still remained the best likeness. Mathilde was enchanted by this; she saw in it a clear proof of a grand passion.'

All the examples referred to on pages 95 to 96 are from *The Psychopathology of Everyday Life*. James Strachey's translation has an index of all the examples Freud uses.

5. Sigmund Freud, 'Some Character Types met with in Psychoanalytic Work (1915), *Collected Papers,* Vol. IV (London, 1956), pp. 324–25.

6. Sigmund Freud, 'Fragments of an Analysis of a Case of Hysteria' (1905), *Collected Papers,* Vol. III (London, 1925), p. 123.

7. Sigmund Freud, *Introductory Lectures on Psychoanalysis* (1915–17), (London, 1922), p. 259.

and the absence of the man she secretly loved, lest its regularity should betray her secret'.[8] Unlike Jane Austen's Kitty Bennett, Dora had complete discretion in her coughs and timed them beautifully.

Since Freud isn't clear as to whether the wish produces, or merely exploits the catarrh, this example might seem open to an alternative construction. More conclusive evidence of his proclivity for this mode of thought, along with a suggestion that he was nervous about making it too explicit, is contained in a letter to Groddeck: '. . . it is not necessary to extend the concept of the unconscious in order to include your experience with organic disorders. In my article about the unconscious which you mention, you will find a small footnote: "We shall save for mention in another connexion a further important prerogative of the unconscious." I shall tell you what I kept back there, namely the assertion that acts of the unconscious have intense plastic effects on somatic processes in a manner impossible to achieve by conscious acts.'[9] Further evidence on this point is to be found in Ernest Jones's biography, where we arc told that at the end of 1916 Freud was considering writing a book, the essential content of which was 'that the omnipotence of thoughts was once a reality. Our intention is to show that Lamarck's conception of need which creates and modifies organs is nothing else than the power unconscious ideas have over the body, of which we see the remains in hysteria—in short, "the omnipotence of thoughts".'[10]

We can account both for this conviction of Freud's and for our readiness to be convinced by varying slightly his judgement on Adler: 'There is nothing humanity won't accept with ascendancy over matter as the bait.'

II

But what is noteworthy in Freud is not just the credulity he evinces, and evokes, towards the outlandish but the tendentious way in which be describes the commonplace. This brings us to another of Wittgenstein's theses: that in Freud's hands the notions of unconscious mental acts and of wish-fulfilment are notations.

Among the most reliable indicies of a notation is the advancing of a thesis in the company of its own counter-examples. The principle at work is

---

8. Freud, *Collected Papers,* III, p. 49.
9. Ernst Freud, ed., *Letters of Sigmund Freud* (London, 1961), Letter 176.
10. Ernest Jones, *Sigmund Freud: Life and Work* (London, 1957), Vol. III, p. 335. Freud explicitly endorses the felicity of Wittgenstein's term 'uncanny'. In his account of 'the peculiar quality . . . which arouses in us the feeling of uncanniness' (*Collected Papers,* IV, pp. 368–69), Freud invokes just those features which we have seen to characterize his notion of the unconscious. See also the essay 'Animism, Magic and the Omnipotence of Thought' in *Totem and Taboo,* Footnote 25, Strachey Translation: '. . . we invest with a feeling of uncanniness those impressions which lend support to a belief in the omnipotence of thoughts'. It is as if he were constructing his explanations to a formula.

that all putative counter-instances are to be considered clandestine specimens of confirmatory instances. If we examine Freud's investigation of
errors, of which he said that it was 'the prototype of every psychoanalytic
investigation' and that it was 'better calculated than any other to stimulate
a belief in the existence of unconscious mental acts', we see how great is
the notational component in the claim that 'acts of a mental nature, and
often very complicated ones, can take place in you . . . of which you know
nothing'. Less than a quarter of the 250 or so examples which *The
Psycholpathology of Everyday Life* came to contain are even apparently illustrations of the phenomena they are said to exemplify, 'of a will striving for
a definite aim'.

Consider those cases of forgetting which Freud describes as 'forgetting
from a motive of avoiding unpleasure'. Let us suppose that the empirical
facts are not in question, i.c. that there is a tendency for names or words or
intentions with unpleasant associations to be forgotten. Is there anything in
this fact which demands description in terms of the behaviour of an unconscious agency which censors the thoughts of the subject in the interests of
his peace of mind? Freud says of these cases 'the motive of forgetting actu-
ates a counter-will'. But he also compares them with the flight reflex in the
presence of painful stimuli. Why then do they demand description in terms
of an unconscious agency any more than this does? Is my inability to hold
my hands above my head for an indefinite period to be ascribed to the vic-
tory of a counter-will to lower them? 'Couldn't the whole thing have been
differently treated?'[11] Considerations like these suggest that what Freud
often sees as instances of the operation of unconscious agencies really regis-
ter his determination to describe familiar facts in a novel and congenial
idiom.

In *Zettel*, § 444, Wittgenstein compares Freud's theory that all dreams
are wish-fulfilments with the thesis that every proposition is a picture. '. . .
it is the characteristic thing about such a theory that it looks at a special,
clearly intuitive case and says: that shows how things are in every case. This
case is the exemplar of all cases.'[12] And in the 'Conversations on Freud', he
says of this theory of Freud's, 'it is not a matter of evidence' but 'is the sort
of explanation we are inclined to accept. . .[13] Some dreams obviously are
wish fulfilments: such as the sexual dreams of adults for instance. But it
seems muddled to say that all dreams are hallucinated wish-fulfilments.'[14]

---

11. *Lectures and Conversations*, p. 45.
12. In his autobiography Freud neatly exemplifies this habit of mind. 'The state of things
which he (Breuer) had discovered, seemed to me, to be of so fundamental a nature, that I could
not believe it could fail to be present in any case of hysteria if it had proved to occur in a single one,' *An Autobiographical Study* (Hogarth Press, 1950), p. 36.
13. *Lectures and Conversations*, p. 42.
14. *ibid.*, p. 47.

Even those dreams which are incontestably wish-fulfilments don't justify the inferences which Freud draws from them. Consider Freud's anchovy dream. On nights on which he has eaten anchovies he wakes thirsty, but not before he has dreamt of gulping down draughts of cold water, This is certainly an instance of wish-fulfilment. As is the case of the hungry dreamer who dreams of a delicious meal. But Freud goes on to say of this last example: 'The choice was up to him of either waking up and eating something or of continuing sleep. He decided in favour of the latter.'[15] What is there in these examples to justify the assumption of a supervisory agency accompanying the phenomena and regulating their manifestations? If I succeed in waking at a predetermined hour, must I assume that some delegate of myself has kept vigil through the night? 'Unconscious mental acts', 'choice', 'decision': If it were a matter of Penelope unravelling her web in a nocturnal trance, or Lady Dedlock sleep-walking her way to Captain Hawdon's grave, there might then be some justification for the voluntaristic connotations of these idioms.

Freud has various devices for dealing with counter-examples. The most notorious occurs in Chapter 4 of *The Interpretation of Dreams*. A patient recounted a dream in which something she wished to avoid was represented as fulfilled. Freud comments: 'Was not this in sharpest opposition to my theory that in dreams wishes are fulfilled? No doubt . . . the dream showed that I was wrong. *Thus it was her wish that I might be wrong, and her dream showed that wish fulfilled.*'[16] (Freud's italics.) Nor is he timid about generalizing this solution. 'Indeed it is to be expected that the same thing will happen to some of the readers of the present book: they will be quite ready to have one of their wishes frustrated in a dream if only their wish that I may be wrong can be fulfilled.'[17] Anxiety dreams are dealt with either by invoking the masochistic wish for pain or the super-ego's satisfaction in inflicting punishment on the ego.

The problem that most dreams have a neutral or indifferent content is dealt with by means of the distinction between the latent and the manifest content of the dream, It is the latent content which constitutes the fulfilment of the wish, the manifest content being a consequence of distortion.

Wittgenstein comments on this in the second conversation: 'The majority of dreams Freud considers have to be regarded as camouflaged wish-fulfilments and in that case they simply don't fulfil the wish. *Ex hypothesi*, the wish is not allowed to be fulfilled and something else is hallucinated instead. If the wish is cheated in this way, then the dream can hardly be called a fulfilment of it. Also it becomes impossible to say whether it is the wish or the

---

15. Sigmund Freud, *An Outline of Psychoanalysis* (London, 1949), p. 36.
16. Sigmund Freud, *The Interpretation of Dreams* (London, 1954), p. 151.
17. Freud, *The Interpretation of Dreams*, p. 158

censor that is cheated. Apparently both are, and the result is that neither is satisfied. So that the dream is not an hallucinated satisfaction of anything.'[18]

The applicability of these remarks is not confined to the dream theory but extends to Freud's account of the neuroses, where one is often equally at a loss to see the grounds for Freud's insistence that the symptoms of the disorder represent the fulfilment of a wish, or of the wish to frustrate the wish, or both.

Consider his explanation of epileptoid attacks like those from which Dostoevsky suffered in his youth. Deathlike seizures of this kind 'signify an identification with a dead person, either with someone who was really dead or with someone who was still alive and whom the subject wished dead', in which case the attack has the significance of a punishment. 'One has wished another person dead and now one is this other person and is dead oneself . . .' Thus Dostoevsky's 'early symptoms of deathlike seizures can be understood as a father-identification on the part of his ego, permitted by his superego as a punishment. "You wanted to kill your father in order to be your father yourself. Now you *are* your father, but a dead father . . . now your father is killing you."'[19] And this is how Freud derives a wish-fulfilment from a young girl's attempt at suicide: She was simultaneously punishing herself for a death-wish against her mother and gratifying it since 'the girl's identification of herself with her mother makes this "punishment-fulfilment" again into a wish-fulfilment'. i.e. if I *am* my mother and I kill *myself*, I kill my mother and my mother's murderer.[20]

Interpretations like these are the conceptual equivalents of impossible objects. But to speak of Freud's conceptual confusion in this context is to slight his grammatical genius, his ingenuity in devising unconstruable idioms. It is as if one were to attribute the self-contradictory structures in M.C. Escher's prints to his inability to draw.

(We tend to be diffident about characterizing explanations like these because it is so difficult to be sure one has got hold of them. But why shouldn't this resistance to paraphrase be the most important thing about them? Why shouldn't it be the essence of the matter? What a psychoanalytic explanation tells us is itself.)

Though 'the peculiar attraction' of the uncanny goes far towards explaining the appeal of the idioms in which psychoanalytic explanations are couched it is inadequate as an account of why Freud employs them. In the *Blue Book* Wittgenstein says of the thesis that there exist unconscious

---

18. *Lectures and Conversations*, p. 47.
19. Sigmund Freud, 'Dostoevsky and Parricide' (1928), *Collected Papers*, Vol. V (London, 1957), pp. 229 and 232.
20. Sigmund Freud, 'The Psychogenesis of a Case of Homosexuality in a Woman' (1920), *Collected Papers*, Vol. II (London, 1948), p. 220.

thoughts: '. . . it is just a new terminology and can at any time be translated into ordinary language'.[21] Later, after remarking on how we may be 'irresistibly attracted or repelled by a notation', he says: 'The idea of there being unconscious thoughts has revolted many people. . . . The objectors to unconscious thoughts did not see that they were not objecting to the newly discovered psychological reactions, but to the way in which they were described. The psychoanalysts, on the other hand, were misled by their own way of expression into thinking that they had done more than discover new psychological reactions: that they had in a sense discovered conscious thoughts which were unconscious.'[22] These remarks seem to me mistaken in seeing in the notion of unconscious thoughts a disinterested notational compulsion and in thinking that they merely record 'newly discovered psychological reactions' which 'can at any time be translated into ordinary language'. The notion of unconscious thoughts is not a detachable excrescence which can be removed leaving a neutral core of 'phenomena and connexions not previously known'.[23] Its function is to give a self-authenticating character to psychoanalytic method.

When Freud says 'we call a process unconscious when . . . it was active at a certain time although at that time we knew nothing about it'[24] he is not merely succumbing to the appeal of a notation, not just adopting a form of description which 'adds nothing to what we know but only suggests a different form of words to describe it'.[25] For what other manner of speaking would enable him to insist on the irrelevance of any doubts as to the existence of such connexions not based on the use of a specialized method of introspection? What has been taken for conceptual audacity was really prudence.

Making the reference of his claims an imperceptible process, contemporary with the 'act' it is supposed to explain, enables Freud to combine the compatibility with an agent's candid disavowal of a hypothesis about the causes of his behaviour, with the invulnerability to counter-example of Collingwood-type reconstructions of an historical agent's grounds for his action. The objection to. speaking in this connexion of the 'abominable mess' made by Freud's disciples in confusing cause and reason,[26] is that it represents the state of affairs too much as one of helpless confusion and overlooks the way in which the confusion is ingeniously exploited in the interests of the theory. In the notion of reasons which are ultimately self-intimating causes there is more grammatical flair than grammatical muddle.

21. Ludwig Wittgenstein, *The Blue and The Brown Books* (Oxford, 1958), p. 23.
22. Wittgenstein, *The Blue and The Brown Books*, p. 51.
23. G.E. Moore, 'Wittgenstein Lectures in 1930–1933', *Mind*, Vol. 64. (1955), p. 15.
24. Sigmund Freud, *New Introductory Lectures* (London, 1949), p. 95.
25. Wittgenstein, *The Blue and The Brown Books*, p. 136.
26. Moore, *Mind*, Vol. 64. (1955), p. 20.

By encapsulating the thought inside the agent's head, Freud is enabled to dispense with the surroundings and by making it unconscious to dispense with the agent's assent as well. Once we grasp that it is not the hypothesis of the existence of unconscious wishes which gives Freud's theory its distinctive character but the assumption that psychoanalytic method affords a unique access to them, many puzzles surrounding psychoanalytic claims are dissipated.

III

Wittgenstein thinks psychoanalytic explanations are like aesthetic explanations; but it doesn't help us to know this unless we know what he thinks aesthetic explanations are like. All that is certain is that he thinks they are unlike explanations in terms of brain mechanisms. But though, when he says that the giving of a cause cannot resolve our puzzlement over an aesthetic impression, he sometimes means that the giving of the physical substrate of the impression cannot answer our question (e.g. an account of the state of the olfactory nerve while we are smelling a rose doesn't shed light on the aesthetic question why it smells pleasant),[27] he doesn't always mean only this.

In his remarks on Frazer in the same series of lectures something else is in view. According to Moore, 'He said that it was a mistake to suppose that why, e.g., the account of the Beltane festival "impresses us so much" is because it has "developed from a festival in which a real man was burnt" . . . Our puzzlement as to why it impresses us' (which Wittgenstein said was an aesthetic question), 'is not diminished by giving the causes from which the festival arose, but is diminished by finding other similar festivals: to find these may make it seem "natural", whereas to give the 'causes from which it arose cannot do this.'

Darwin is taxed with a similar mistake in supposing that 'because our ancestors when angry wanted to bite' is a sufficient explanation of why 'we show our teeth when angry'. I am not sure of the force of 'sufficient' here and not sure how the question of why we show our teeth when angry is like the question why the account of the Beltane festival impresses us. And there are other puzzles connected with these remarks. The question to which Fraser is supposed to have given a mistaken reply is never raised by Frazer, whose main interest (in *Balder the Beautiful*) seems to be whether the point of Fire festivals is to reinforce the sun's heat by sympathetic magic or to destroy evil and threatening things. Also, the method recommended by Wittgenstein to relieve us of our puzzlement as to why we are impressed— '. . . finding other similar festivals'—sounds like a description of what Frazer

---

27. Moore, *Mind*, Vol. 64 (1955), p. 18.

is doing a good deal of the time: 'Bonfires at the Ponggol festival in Southern India . . . bonfires at the Holi festival in Northern India . . . the fire walk in China . . . the fire walk at the Hindu festival . . . the fire walk among the Badagas . . . the fire walk in Japan etc., etc.' I have said enough to show why it is difficult to have much confidence in the construction one puts on these remarks. Nevertheless, it is hard not to feel, at some points, an almost Spenglerian disdain for causal inquiry at work; that, for example, Wittgenstein hasn't misremembered the question that Frazer set himself but just feels that his own is more interesting and Frazer's an error of sensibility. But there is an alternative and plausible construction that might be put on these remarks which falls short of attributing to Wittgenstein an antipathy to causal questions. Wittgenstein may just be calling attention to an error which there is a natural tendency to make. The error in question might be described as looking for consummation in the wrong place; an instance of which is asking for the etiology of a phenomenon where what we really want is an analysis of the impression produced on us by the phenomenon. For example, we often think we are interested in the past when it is really the experience of pastness which absorbs us. We forget that the peculiar impression ruins make on us is not accounted for by discovering how they came to be in that condition. Someone who embarked on a course of astronomical study in the vague hope of shedding light on the nature of the impression made on him by the night sky when the stars are out is also making this kind of mistake. Again, the peculiar impression made on us by the distinctive movements of achondroplastics ('a friendliness was in the air as of dwarfs shaking hands') is not elucidated by an account of the endocrinology of the condition. And yet when Wittgenstein speaks of 'the sort of explanation one longs for when one talks of an aesthetic impression' one doesn't feel that it is just the analysis of an impression that he wants: even that is still too much like a hypothesis.

A clue to what he does have in mind is provided by a comparison he makes in the second lecture on Aesthetics between aesthetic remarks and expressions like 'What is it I wanted to say?' and 'What people really want to say is so and so'.[28] In *Philosophical Investigations*, § 334, of the expression 'So you really wanted to say . . .', Wittgenstein says 'We use this phrase in order to lead someone from one form of expression to another'. This suggests to me that the kind of remark which Wittgenstein thinks aesthetic puzzlement calls for is one which, though it may seem to be describing or explaining a certain past state of mind, is really prolonging an experience in a particular direction; like the angle-trisector who, when shown the proof that what he was attempting to do was impossible, says 'That this was the

---

28. *Lectures and Conversations*, p. 37.

very thing he was trying to do, though what he had been trying to do was really different', or the regular pentagon-constructor who, in similar circumstances, says '"That's what I was really trying to do" because his idea had shifted on a rail on which lie was ready to shift it'.[29] The Egyptian intellectuals of the twenties, who declared that their countrymen were Arabs, exemplify a related phenomenon, as do the estranged couple who say they never loved one another: these are statements which, though apparently descriptive of the past, really serve to orient their utterers to a projected future; and like some interpretations of the analyst 'make it easier for them to go certain ways . . . make certain ways of behaving and thinking natural for them'.[30]

Often these remarks take the form of an analogy; the finding of something to which we feel we stand in a similar relation as to that which puzzles or impresses us.

In Moore's notes Wittgenstein speaks of Aesthetics as a matter of 'giving a good simile' and of 'putting things side by side'. And in the third lecture on Aesthetics he speaks of 'the explanation we should like to have when we are puzzled about aesthetic impressions. . . . the puzzlement I am talking about can only be cured by peculiar kinds of comparison . . .'[31] In the second conversation he says: 'When a dream is interpreted it is fitted into a context in which it ceases to be puzzling. In a sense, the dreamer re-dreams his dream in surroundings such that its aspect changes.'[32] In the *Brown Book,* in discussing what an explanation in Aesthetics is like, he says: '. . . it may consist in finding a form of verbal expression which I conceive as the verbal counterpart of the theme . . . the word which seemed to sum it up'. There is some inadvertent testimony from the analyst Wittels that psychoanalytic explanation may also be a matter of 'the word which seemed to sum it up'.[33] He speaks of '. . . neurotic patients who were peculiarly ready to adopt the use of the word "castration" as soon as they heard me employ it. Their reminiscences then tended to assume some such form as the following: "My mother castrated me when I was a little boy. But the one who especially castrated me was my paternal grandfather. Yesterday my mistress castrated me."'[34] Freud gives a sexual explanation of obsessive thinking. He speaks of the tendency to 'sexualize thinking and to colour intellectual operations with the pleasure and anxiety which belong to sexual processes proper . . . investigations become a sexual activity . . . the thought process itself

29. Moore, *Mind,* Vol 64, (1955), pp. 9–10.
30. *Lectures and Conversations,* p. 44–45.
31. *ibid.,* p. 20.
32. *Lectures and Conversations,* p. 45.
33. Wittgenstein, *The Blue and The Brown Books,* pp. 166–67.
34. Fritz Wittels, *Sigmund Freud* (London, 1924), pp. 160–61.

becomes sexualized . . . the gratification derived from reaching the conclusion of a line of thought is experienced as sexual gratification . . . (the feeling that comes from settling things in one's mind and explaining them replaces sexual satisfaction)'.[35] We can easily imagine that someone on reading these words might have a delighted feeling of recognition and be moved to assent. But would it follow that they constitute a hypothesis? When in this connexion Karl Abraham points out that 'In Biblical Hebrew the word to "know" is used for the sexual act. A man is said to know his wife', and that 'the comparison of mental and sexual acts is not uncommon. We speak for instance of the conception of a poetical work'; or when Freud says of Leonardo 'He had merely converted his passion into a thirst for knowledge . . . at the climax of intellectual labour, when knowledge had been won, he allowed the long restrained affect to break loose and flow away freely . . .', aren't these once again simply a matter of 'giving a good simile', of 'placing things side by side'?

Consider Baudelaire's comparison of the act of love to an application of torture—'. . . these sighs, these groans, these screams, these rattling gasps. . . . What worse sights can you see at any inquisition? These eyes rolled back like sleepwalkers, these limbs whose muscles burst and stiffen as though subject to the action of a galvanic battery, etc., etc.' Contrast our state of mind as we read these words with that in which we take in Freud's observations on the sadistic nature of coitus, or his characterization of sexual consummation as a minor form of epilepsy ('a mitigation and adaptation of the epileptic method of discharging stimuli').[36] No one would confuse his gratitude to Baudelaire for momentary relief from the burden of being high-spirited about his sexuality with the appreciation of a discovery or the consideration of a hypothesis, but with Freud this is happening all the time.

'The attraction of certain kinds of explanation is overwhelming. At a given time the attraction of a certain kind of explanation is greater than you can conceive. In particular, explanations of the kind "this is really only this".' This remark of Wittgenstein's brings out what most discussions of Freud, even when they are critical, miss—the compulsive quality of Freud's interpretations. 'There is a strong tendency to say: "We can't get round the fact that this dream is really such and such" . . . If someone says "Why do you say it is really this? Obviously it is not this at all", it is in fact even difficult to see it as something else.'[37] Try telling someone who is psychoanalytically oriented that Van Gogh's mutilation of his ear may have had no connexion with castration, or that Oedipus's blinding of himself was not a castration-

---

35. This passage is an amalgam of remarks in Freud's *Leonard da Vinci* (London, 1963), p. 114 and in his 'Notes upon a Case of Obsessional Neurosis' (1909), *Collected Papers*, III, p. 380.

36. Freud, 'Dostoevsky and Patricide', *Collected Papers*, V, p. 226.

37. *Lectures and Conversations*, p. 46.

substitute and you meet not so much with incredulity as bewilderment. He will have difficulty in giving your statement sense. He behaves as if he had learned the expression 'castration-symbol' ostensively. This is simply what castration-substitute *means*. 'The correct analogy is the accepted one.'

IV

In Moore's account of the 1933 lectures Wittgenstein is reported as saying 'that Freud did not in fact find any method of analysing dreams which is analogous to the rules which will tell you what are the causes of stomach ache'.[38] But aren't repressed thoughts the green apples of Freudian psychopathology? We might ask how Freud manages to detect allusions to castration, defloration, birth, intercourse, menstruation, masturbation, etc., etc., on so many occasions if he has not discovered rules analogous to those 'which will tell you what are the causes of stomach ache'. And in the second conversation, in contrasting the real character of psychoanalytic interpretations with their apparent character, Wittgenstein describes what 'might be called a scientific treatment of the dream . . . one might form a hypothesis. On reading the report of the dream, one might predict that the dreamer can be brought to recall such and such memories. And this hypothesis might or might not be verified.'[39] But isn't this what Freud does? Doesn't Freud produce instances where the interpretation is tied to some independently authenticatable event? But before we accept this argument we must look more closely at Freud's reconstructive achievements. When we do, we find that they are almost invariably inconclusive in one of the following ways: either the inferred event is ubiquitous, or it was known independently of the procedure which ostensibly inferred it. In either ease the reality of the inferred event wouldn't, in itself, show the validity of the means by which it was arrived at.

If we doubt this and consult the case histories to reassure ourselves on the point, we find that either the events or scenes reconstructed have too great an independent probability to support the validity of the interpretative technique (as with Dora's urinary incontinence), or they were known independently of the analysis (as with the severe beating Paul had from his father and the castration threats to which Little Hans was exposed). The apparent exception to this is, what is often regarded as Freud's greatest reconstructive achievement, the discovery that a patient, at the age of 18 months, saw his parents engage in 'a coitus a tergo, thrice repeated',[40] at five in the afternoon. This certainly doesn't lack circumstantiality. What it lacks is corroboration. Freud is aware of this and falls back on a coherence argument.

---

38. Moore, *Mind*, Vol. 64, p. 20.
39. *Lectures and Conversations*, p. 46.

It might be felt that even if these objections hold of the cases Freud reported at length, he does assure us that he has produced reconstructions to which these objections do not apply; where the reconstructed events were not known in advance and were independently authenticated through 'lucky accidents'. For example, Marie Bonaparte's servants confirming Freud's suspicion that she had witnessed intercourse before the age of one.[41] But for this to count in favour of the claim that Freud discovered the laws according to which repressed memories are distorted, we should have to know how often Freud gave reconstructions which contained primal scenes; and we have reason to believe that it was very often. That he should have failed to report those which were not corroborated doesn't involve attributing to him any improbable degree of disingenuousness, since he himself tells us that he attached no importance to this kind of authentication, convinced as he was that his reconstructions must have been essentially true in any case:

> I should myself be glad to know whether the primal scene in my present patient's case was a phantasy or a real experience; but taking other similar cases into account I must admit that the answer to this question is not in reality a matter of very great importance. These scenes of observing parental intercourse, of being seduced in childhood, and of being threatened with castration are unquestionably an inherited endowment, a phylogenetic inheritance. . . .[42]
>
> If they can be found in real events, well and good; but if reality has not supplied them, they will be evolved out of hints and elaborated by phantasy. The effect is the same, and even today we have not succeeded in tracing any variation in the results according as phantasy, or reality, plays the greater part in these experiences.[43]

With phylogenetic inheritance to fall back on Freud deprives himself of any way of discovering that his reconstructions are mistaken and his principles of interpretation invalid. He fails to see this because he exploits an unconscious presumption that the complexity of an interpretation, the number of cross-references it contains to incidents in the life of the patient, '. . . the long thread of connexions that spun itself out between a symptom of the disease and a pathogenic idea', is an index of its truth. We underestimate enormously the possibility of producing such an appearance of intricate coherence where the items are not genuinely related.

In justifying his conviction as to the reality of a primal scene Freud said: 'Everything seemed to converge upon it . . . the most various and remark-

---

40. Freud, 'From the History of an Infantile Neurosis' (1918), *Collected Papers*, III, p. 508.

41. Jones, *Freud—Life and Work*, Vol. III, p. 129.

42. Freud, 'History of an Infantile Neurosis', *Collected Papers*, III, p. 576.

43. Freud, *Introductory Lectures*, p. 310.

able results radiated out from it [and] not only the large problems but the smallest peculiarities in the history of the case were cleared up by this single assumption . . . [the analyst] will disclaim the possession of the amount of ingenuity necessary for the concoction of an occurrence which can fulfil these demands.'[44]

Wittgenstein doubts this: 'Freud remarks on how after the analysis of it, the dream appears so very logical. And of course it does. You could start with any of the objects on this table—which certainly were not put there by your dream activity—and you could find that they all could be connected in a pattern like that, and the pattern would be logical in the same way.'[45]

Either Wittgenstein's table was more cluttered than mine or he shared Freud's genius for constructing associative links between any two points, for I have not been able to produce patterns anywhere near as convincing as Freud's. But the force of this consideration is weakened if we remember that Freud lays his own table: 'The material belonging to a single subject can only be collected piece by piece at various times and in various connexions.'

But it is the elasticity and multiplicity of the rules which do most to reduce the *a priori* improbability of producing associative links to and between his patients' dreams, symptoms, reminiscences, etc., and sexual themes though there are really none. The link between the unconscious thought and its manifestation is often simply that in both something is inside something, or something is going into something, or something is coming our of something, or something is being detached from something, etc., etc.

It is this which enables Freud to see an allusion to castration anxiety in a symptom of obsessional neurotics 'by means of which they manage to ensure themselves continual torment. When they are in the street they are constantly watching to see whether some acquaintance will salute them first, by taking off his hat, or whether he seems to wait for their salute; and they give up a number of their acquaintances who they imagine no longer salute them or do not return their salute properly . . . the source of this excess of feeling can easily be found in relation to the castration complex.'[46] (Something is being detached from something.)

And to see an incestuous desire for his mother in 'Little Hans's' inability to venture out of doors. This phobia involves a 'restriction on his freedom of movement. . . . It was, therefore, a powerful reaction against the

---

44. Freud, 'History of an Infantile Neurosis', *Collected Papers*, III, p. 256.

45. *Letters and Conversations*, p. 51.

46. Freud, 'Connection between a Symbol and a Symptom' (1909), *Collected Papers*, II, p. 163.

obscure impulses to movement which were especially directed against his mother.' That a horse should have been the object of his phobia lends itself to the same construction. 'For Hans, horses had always typified pleasure in movement. . . but since this pleasure in movement included the impulse to copulate, the neurosis imposed a restriction on it and exalted the horse into an emblem of terror.'[47] (Something is moving.)

And to see defloration in the following example: 'Do you know why our old friend E. turns red and sweats whenever he sees a certain class of acquaintance. . . . He is ashamed, no doubt; but of what? Of a phantasy in which he figures as the deflowerer of every person he comes across. He sweats as he deflowers because it is hard work. . . . Moreover, he can never get over the fact that at the university he failed to get through in Botany so he carries on with it now as a "deflowerer".'[48]

'It is all excellent similes.' Freud turns his patient into a walking rebus.

Though the interpretations tell their own story there is some interesting testimony on this point from an American psychiatrist who underwent a training analysis with Freud: 'I would often give a whole series of associations to a dream symbol and he would wait until be found an association which would fit into his scheme of interpretation and pick it up like a detective at a lineup who waits until he sees his man.'[49]

It seems that Freud stood to his patients' associations, dreams, symptoms, reminiscences and errors more as the painter to his pigments than as the sleuth to his traces of mud and cigar ash.

The implications of this are that instead of seeing in 'condensation', 'displacement', 'representation by the opposite', etc., etc., laws governing unconscious processes, we recognize them as recipes for the construction of associative chains to preselected termini; not mechanisms by whose operation the symptom, dream, etc, was constructed, but devices for 'working a piece of fancy into it'.

V

As to the thesis that infantile experience determines adult character, e.g. the rôle of primal scenes, Wittgenstein once again locates its persuasive power in its attractiveness, 'the attractiveness of a mythology', of 'explanations which say this is all a repetition of something which has happened before', thus 'giving a sort of tragic pattern to one's life. . . . Like a tragic figure carrying out the decrees under which the Fates had placed him at birth.'[50]

---

47. Freud, 'Analysis of a Phobia in a Five Year Old Boy' (1909), *Collected Papers,* III, p. 280.
48. Sigmund Freud, *Origins of Psychoanalysis* (New York, 1954), Letter 105.
49. J. Worth, *American Journal of Orthopsychiatry,* Vol. X (1940), pp. 844–45.
50. *Lectures and Conversations,* p. 51.

An objection which might be brought against Wittgenstein here is that he comes to this conclusion while discussing no topic other than clinical interpretation. What of the objective evidence for the pathogenic power of infantile sexual occurrences and the developmental claims about infantile sexuality? Surely these provide a sufficient explanation of how the themes of infancy and sexuality came to figure so prominently in psychoanalysis, without the necessity of invoking 'charm' or the appeal of the repellent?

Wittgenstein's failure to mention these topics might lend some credence to Professor Wollheim's suggestion that his view of Freud is to be put down to a combination of ignorance and envy. On the other hand, perhaps Wittgenstein noticed something which Professor Wollheim missed. If, undisheartened by the extravagance of this supposition, we re-examine Freud to see what basis there might be for it, we find that far from constituting an objection to Wittgenstein, his implicit dismissal of Freud's etiological and developmental claims alerts us to a certain peculiarity of psychoanalytic discourse which has gone largely unnoticed: the extent to which Freud dehistoricized his theory so that the etiological and developmental claims, which ostensibly underpinned his interpretations, were actually derived from them.

When we reread Freud in the light of Wittgenstein's remarks the conviction forces itself on us that the end of analysis, to serve which the rest of the theory exists, is the construction and emission of interpretations; that it is this activity which must at all costs be sustained; that if Freud had come to the conclusion that his views as to infantile sexual life were mistaken the stream of interpretations would not on that account have been halted.

This might seem an idle speculation which there is no way of checking and which is in any case extremely implausible. It is therefore worth mentioning that Freud himself once discussed the possibility that 'what analysts put forward as being forgotten experiences of childhood . . . may on the contrary be based on phantasies brought about on occasions occurring in later life'. This is his comment: 'And if this interpretation of the scenes from infancy were the right one . . . The analysis would have to run precisely the same course as one which had a naïve faith in the truth of the phantasies . . . A correct procedure, therefore, would make no alterations in the technique of analysis, whatever estimate might be formed of these scenes from infancy.'[51]

---

51. Freud, 'History of an Infantile Neurosis', *Collected Papers*, III, p. 522. In these remarks Freud is anticipating a contingency very like that which overtook him in 1897 when he concluded that in many cases the sexual interference which he had stated was the specific cause of hysteria had not taken place and which he met by assigning to infantile sexual phantasies the pathogenic role vacated by infantile seductions. And he is meeting it with the same tenacity.

But, if interpretations containing allusions to infantile sexuality are to be advanced in spite of a disbelief in the occurrence of infantile sexual phantasies, Freud's convictions as to the rôle of infantile sexuality in the etiology of the neuroses cannot be his ground, but only his pretext, for interpreting symptoms in infantile sexual terms.

Just as often as Freud tells us that the psychoanalytic theory of infantile sexual development has been or could be confirmed by the direct observation of children, just so often does he imply that we are to expect nothing of the kind. '. . . Direct observation has fully confirmed the conclusions drawn from psychoanalytic investigation and thus furnished good evidence for the reliability of the latter method of investigation.'[52] But elsewhere it is psychoanalytic investigation which confirms the reliability of our observation of infantile sexual life: '. . . we call the doubtful and indefinable activities of earliest infancy' towards pleasure sexual because, in the course of analysing symptoms, we reach them by way of material which is undeniably sexual'.[53] 'But those phases of the sexual development . . . which are of the greatest interest theoretically (are) gone through so rapidly that direct observation alone would perhaps never have succeeded in determining (their) fleeting forms. Only by the help of psychoanalytic investigation of the neuroses has it become possible to penetrate so far back . . .'[54] And of observations on small children: 'They do not carry such complete conviction as is forced upon the physician by psychoanalyses of adult neurotics.'[55] His account of his grounds for the conviction that the key to the neuroses is to be found in infantile sexual life is infected with the same ambivalence. 'If anyone should enquire where he is to look for an incontestable proof of the etiological importance of sexual factors in psychoneuroses—since . . . a specific etiology in the form of particular infantile experiences is not forthcoming—then I would indicate psychoanalytic investigation of neurotics as the source from whence the disputed conviction springs.'[56] It has not generally been realized how often Freud implies (what his practice confirms) that the character of a child's infantile sexual life is to be determined by waiting until he is an adult and then psychoanalysing him.[57]

---

52. Sigmund Freud, 'Three Contributions to the Theory of Sex', *The Basic Writings of Sigmund Freud* (New York, 1938), p. 594.
53. Freud, *Introductory Lectures,* p. 273.
54. Freud, *Introductory Lectures,* p. 274–75.
55. Freud, *The Interpretation of Dreams,* p. 258.
56. Sigmund Freud, 'My Views on the Part Played by Sexuality in the Etiology of the Neuroses' (1905), *Collected Papers,* Vol. I (London, 1948), p. 281.
57. 'An analysis which is conducted on a neurotic child . . . cannot be very rich in material; too many words and thoughts have to be lent to the child and even so the deepest strata may turn out to be impenetrable to consciousness. An analysis of childhood disorder through the medium of recollection in an intellectually mature adult is free from these limitations.' (From the 'History of Infantile Neurosis', *Collected Papers,* III, p. 475.)

But the character of Freud's claims concerning infantile life is often such that even the patient's acquiescence cannot assuage our doubts; it merely raises the Ballard problem of *Philosophical Investigations*, § 342, and *Zettel*, § 109, in a more acute form. If it is a matter of 'dim impulses which it is impossible for the child to grasp psychically at the time',[58] if we are to 'consider how little the child is able to give expression to its sexual wishes and how little it can communicate them',[59] aren't we justified in treating the patient's assent as Wittgenstein treats Ballard's reminiscence of the period before he knew language? 'Are you sure—one would like to ask that this is the correct translation of your wordless thoughts into words? . . . These recollections are a queer memory phenomenon, and I do not know what conclusions one can draw from them about the past of the man who recounts them.'[60]

When Freud says of the influence of infantile castration fears that 'psychoanalytic experience' has put it 'beyond the reach of doubt',[61] this is not hyperbole. He means it. What allows him to mean it is his intermittent conviction that his achievement consists in having defeated the malice of nature in compelling men to observe each other's minds through so opaque a medium as a human skull by providing access to the thing itself.[62] Wittgenstein has brought us to feel that this is an ambition which not even God could reasonably entertain.

The behaviour of patients under analysis, which began as evidence of the vicissitudes through which they had passed, gradually became criteria for the ascription of these vicissitudes. To say of a patient that he had entertained such and such wishes, or had repressed such and such phantasies, is to say that he now behaves towards the analyst in such and such a way, responds to the proffered interpretations in such and such a manner. Interpretation has been dehistoricized. The notion of truthfulness has replaced that of truth. The narration of infantile reminiscences has been assimilated (incoherently) to the narration of dreams.

Conclusion

When, in Moore's notes, Wittgenstein speaks of Freud as giving accounts which sound like science when, in fact, they are only 'a wonderful representation',[63] he may be referring to the extent to which the world,

58. Freud, 'Female Sexuality' (1931), *Collected Papers*, V, p. 265.
59. Freud, *New Introductory Lectures*, p. 155.
60. Ludwig Wittgenstein, *Philosophical Investigations* (Oxford, 1953), Section 342.
61. Freud, 'Dostoevsky and Patricide', *Collected Papers*, V, p. 231.
62. 'The unconscious is the true psychical reality.' (Freud, *The Interpretation of Dreams*, p. 613.)
63. Moore, *Mind*, Vol. 64, p. 20.

conceived of psychoanalytically, is just the everyday world taken over again with an altered expression. An illustration: in the grammatical phantasies which constitute the libido theory we can see the operation of a typically metaphysical motive in the way in which the quotidian world disappears from view behind the permutations of the libido, e.g. the metapsychological account of why we mourn our dead; of why, as Freud puts it, 'the ego never abandons a libido-position willingly'. If the fact that we grieve for our dead is perplexing, by reference to what is it to be rendered intelligible? 'The adhesiveness of the libido'? It seems that a Freud-person would have no difficulty in feeling grief—'that pattern in the weave of our lives'—for a second, or, if he did, it would be from the same causes which make it difficult to empty a bath tub or a bottle of glue in a second. Nevertheless Freud is sometimes in the position of the impressionistic painter of *Philosophical Investigations*, § 368: 'I describe a room to someone, and then get him to paint an impressionistic picture from this description, to show that he has understood it. Now he paints the chairs which I described as green, dark red; where I said yellow he paints blue—that is the impression which he got of that room. And now I say: "Quite right! That's what it's like."'

I think it is this sort of thing which Wittgenstein was referring to when he said that Freud had genius and therefore might 'find out the reason of a dream',[64] even though 'if you are led by psychoanalysis to say that really you thought so and so, or that really your motive was so and so, this is not a matter of discovery but of persuasion',[65] and that 'there is no way of showing that the whole result of analysis may not be "delusion".'[66]

Freud certainly produced statements to which an enormous number of people have said 'yes', but there are good grounds for assimilating his achievement to that of the anonymous geniuses to whom it first occurred that Tuesday is lean and Wednesday fat, the low notes on the piano dark and the high notes light. Except that instead of sensory impressions we have scenes from human life.

In this paper I have tried to demonstrate the impossibility of accounting for Freud's preoccupations, or our preoccupation with Freud, without invoking what Wittgenstein called 'charm'. We were caused to re-dream our life in surroundings such that its aspect changed—and it was the charm that made us do it.

---

64. *ibid.*
65. *Lectures and Conversations*, p. 27.
66. *ibid.*, p. 24.

3

Freud and the Idea of a Pseudoscience

I

A successful pseudoscience is a great intellectual achievement. Its study is as instructive and worth undertaking as that of a genuine one. In this chapter I shall maintain that psychoanalysis is such a pseudoscience; that the character of this claim has often been misunderstood; and that when it is understood its intractability is less surprising. Psychoanalysis may be described as an attempt to determine the historicity and/or pathogenicity of episodes in a person's infantile past and the character of his unconscious affective life and its influence over his behaviour, by the manner in which he responds to assertions or speculations concerning these—not however, just *any* attempt, but a particular, historically identifiable one which issued in a body of aetiological and dynamic theses, the abiding core of which is the claim that 'only sexual wishful impulses from infancy are able to furnish the motive force for the formation of psychoneurotic symptoms' (Freud, 1949*b*, pp. 605–6).

In attempting to assess the genuinely empirical character of such an enterprise the statements which we must subject to scrutiny are not merely those in which the claims that are the ostensible object of investigation are advanced, but also those which describe, or enable us to infer, what the procedures of investigation are. A pseudoscience is not constituted merely by formally defective theses but by methodologically defective procedures. We could express this mnemonically by saying: the notion of a pseudoscience is a pragmatic and not a syntactic one.

The contrary view is partly the result of preoccupation with a narrow and untypical range of examples (e.g., the dormitive powers of opium) and

This essay first appeared in Robert Borger and Frank Cioffi, eds., *Explanation in the Behavioral Sciences* (Cambridge University Press, 1970), and is reprinted with the permission of the Syndics of the Cambridge University Press.

partly a function of the calculus-dominated assumption that the logical character of a thesis can always be determined by inspection.

In his paper 'Can psychoanalysis be refuted?' (Farrell, 1961) B.A. Farrell argues that when we ask 'whether a generalization about some *specific* unconscious process or state is true or not—for example, the generalization about unconscious Oedipal wishes . . . we presuppose that these generalizations about specific unconscious process can be refuted in principle. We have discovered no reason so far for saying that this presupposition is false in any way that matters.'

But the real difficulty is that it can't be *true* in any way that matters. Refutability in principle is not an adequate criterion of the genuinely empirical character of an enterprise. (Not is it the criterion advanced by Popper in the paper which Farrell alludes to—Popper, 1957.) If it were, none of the specimens we would naturally proffer as examples of pseudo-diagnostic, pseudo-therapeutic or pseudo-explanatory claims would qualify. The efficacy of the high-potency micro-dose, the propensity to melancholy of those born under Saturn, the immunity to appendicitis of people ignorant of the existence of the vermiform appendix; these claims are eminently refutable and, as far as most of us are concerned, have been refuted. But they are nonetheless pseudoscience. For an activity to be scientific it is not enough that there should be states of affairs which would constitute disconfirmation of the theses it purports to investigate; it must also be the case that its procedure should be such that it is calculated to discover whether such states of affairs exist. I use the word 'calculated' advisedly. For to establish that an enterprise is pseudoscientific it is not sufficient to show that the procedures it employs would *in fact* prevent or obstruct the discovery of disconfirmatory states of affairs but that it is their function to obstruct such discovery. To claim that an enterprise is pseudoscientific is to claim that it involves the habitual and wilful employment of methodologically defective procedures (in a sense of wilful which encompasses refined self-deception). The necessity for this provision becomes clear if we consider cases like the following.

Lind's failure to employ a placebo control group when he tested the efficacy of lemons in the prevention of scurvy would, had a placebo effect been operative and the lemons prophylatically or therapeutically inert, have prevented him from discovering this. But this would not justify our characterizing his procedure as pseudoscientific, since he was not aware of the placebo effect and therefore could not be said to have been attempting to avoid the discovery that his theory was mistaken. If today, however, someone failed to employ placebo control groups in making therapeutic tests this might well justify the characterization 'pseudoscience'. Our hesitation in so characterizing it would be due to doubts as to whether there might not be moral or practical reasons for failure to undertake the necessary tests.

Consider, as an illustration, the following piece of apologetic offered by Brian Inglis on behalf of homeopathic medicine:

> The difficulty has been to *prove* that the homeopathic micro-dose works . . . It is no use the homeopaths replying that the proof lies in the results they have achieved; these are dismissed by the profession as self-deception or, at best, as placebo-effect. Why not—doctors ask—allow the homeopathic contention to be proved or disproved by experiments, double blind, with controls? This is a challenge the homeopaths have been unwilling to take up, and they would have been foolish if they had, for it would have been a negation of their founder's third principle: that no two patients are alike for purposes of treatment . . . Two patients with the same symptoms, or the same patient with the same symptoms but in a different mood—may require very different prescriptions. Homeopathic treatment cannot be given 'blind'. (Inglis, 1964, pp. 83–84)

If we find this an unconvincing defence against the charge of 'pseudoscience' this is not because of any formal deficiencies in the assertion that the homeopathic micro-dose works, but because of non-syntactic considerations like the failure (which Inglis's excuses, even if valid, don't explain) to rule out the effect of suggestibility by seeing whether the micro-dose is effective even when administered surreptitiously; to say nothing of the non-existence of homeopathic veterinarians.

Though Inglis argues that 'homeopathic treatment cannot be given blind' it is piquant to note that it is over a century since the most eventful occasion on which it was. In *Science and Health* Mary Baker Eddy relates the following incident:

> A case of dropsy, given up by the faculty, fell into my hands . . . as she lay in her bed, the patient looked like a barrel. I prescribed the fourth attenuation of Argentum nitratum with occasional doses of high attenuation of Sulphuris. She improved perceptibly . . . learning that her former physician had prescribed these remedies, I began to fear an aggravation of symptoms from their prolonged use, and told the patient so; but she was unwilling to give up the medicine while she was recovering. It then occurred to me to give her unmedicated pellets and watch the result. I did so, and she continued to gain. Finally she said that she would give up her medicine for one day, and risk the effects. After trying this, she informed me that she could get along two days without globules; but on the third day she again suffered, and was relieved by taking them. She went on in this way, taking the unmedicated pellets—and receiving occasional visits from me—but employing no other means, and she was cured. (Eddy, 1875, p. 156)

If Mrs Eddy had always reasoned this well we should never have heard of her.

In what follows I shall attempt to show that there are a host of peculiarities of psychoanalytic theory and practice which are apparently gratuitous and unrelated, but which can be understood when once they are seen as manifestations of the same impulse: the need to avoid refutation. I shall proceed by arguing that the apparent diversity of the ways in which the correctness of psychoanalytic claims may be assessed—observation of the behaviour of children, enquiry into the distinctive features of the current sexual lives or infantile sexual history of neurotics, awaiting the outcome of prophylactic measures based on Freud's aetiological claims—all resolve themselves into one which itself ultimately proves illusory: direct appreciation or, as Freud variously formulates it, 'Translating unconscious processes into conscious ones' (Freud, 1950, p. 382); 'Filling in gaps in conscious perception' (Freud, 1950, p. 382); '. . . constructing a series of conscious events complementary to the unconscious mental ones' (Freud, 1949*b*, p. 24); '. . . [inferring] the unconscious phantasies from the symptoms and then [enabling] the patient to become conscious of them' (Freud, 1924*b*, p. 54).

II

It is characteristic of a pseudoscience that the hypotheses which comprise it stand in an asymmetrical relation to the expectations they generate, being permitted to guide them and be vindicated by their fulfilment but not to be discredited by their disappointment. One way in which it achieves this is by contriving to have these hypotheses understood in a narrow and determinate sense before the event but a broader and hazier one after it on those occasions on which they are not borne out. Such hypotheses thus lead a double life—a subdued and restrained one in the vicinity of counter-observations and another less inhibited and more exuberant one when remote from them. This feature won't reveal itself to simple inspection. If we want to determine whether the role played by these assertions is a genuinely empirical one it is necessary to discover what their proponents are prepared to call disconfirmatory evidence, not what *we* do.

An example of this is provided by what Freud calls his 'Libido Theory' of the neuroses. Freud makes many remarks whose bearing seems to be that the sexual nature of the neuroses is an inference from the character of the states which predispose towards them, or of the vicissitudes which induce them, for instance, that their causes are to be found 'in the intimacies of the patient's psycho-sexual life'. The importance of this claim for our present purpose is that it would relieve our doubts about the validity of the psychoanalytic method if the inferences to which it leads as to 'which the repressed impulse is, what substitutive symptoms it has found and where the motive for repression lies' were corroborated by independent investigation of the patient's sexual life, as, for example, Freud's aetiology of the actual neuroses was (presumably) corroborated. But the claims which constitute Freud's libido theory are only apparently assessable by an investigation of the relation between the patient's sexual life and his accesses of illness.

Here are some assertions by means of which the impression that they are so assessable is produced.

Whenever a commonplace emotion must be included among the causative factors of the illness, analysis will regularly show that the pathogenic effect has been exercised by the ever present sexual element in the traumatic occurrence (Freud, 1924*a*, p. 281) . . . human beings fall ill when . . . the satisfaction of their erotic needs in reality is frustrated (Freud, 1962, p. 80). . . . patients fall ill owing to frustration in love—(owing to the claims of the libido being unsatisfied . . .) (Freud, 1950, p. 87). People fall ill of a neurosis when the possibility of satisfaction through the libido is removed from them—they fall ill in consequence of 'frustration' . . . in all cases of neurosis investigated the factor of frustration was demonstrable. (Freud, 1956, pp. 310, 353)

These statements certainly look like hypotheses. But our hopes that Freud might be placing a limit on the kinds of events or states which are conducive to the onset of neurosis and might then go on to tell us what these are, are dashed when we read: 'We see people fall ill who have hitherto been healthy, to whom no new experience has presented itself, whose relation to the outer world has presented no change . . .' Though they rise again when Freud goes on to say: 'Closer scrutiny of such cases shows us nevertheless that a change has taken place . . . the quantity of libido in their mental economy has increased to an extent which by itself sufficed to upset the balance of health and establish the conditions for a neurosis . . . this warns us never to leave the quantitative factor out of consideration when we are dealing with the outbreak of the illness.' But what are these changes in the mental economy which 'closer scrutiny' reveals? Once again Freud keeps the word of promise to our ears and breaks it to our hopes: 'We cannot measure the amount of libido essential to produce pathological effects. We can only postulate it after the effects of the illness have manifested themselves' (Freud, 1924*b*, p. 119).

For instance, this is how the apparent counter-examples constituted by the war neuroses are assimilated to the libido theory. Freud says that those who had observed 'traumatic neuroses, which so often follow upon a narrow escape from death, triumphantly announced that proof was now forthcoming that a threat to the instinct of self-preservation could by itself produce a neurosis without any admixture of sexual factors' but that 'any such contradiction has long since been disposed of by the introduction of the concept of narcissism, which brings the libidinal cathexis of the ego into line with the cathexis of objects and emphasises the libidinal character of the instinct of self-preservation . . .' (Freud, 1961, p. 43). In any case 'Mechanical concussions must be recognised as one of the sources of sexual excitation' (Freud, 1922, p. 39).

Consider in this connection Freud's account of the relation of neurosis to the perversions: 'Neuroses are related to perversions as negative to positive. The same instinctual components as in the perversions can be observed in the neuroses as vehicles of complexes and constructors of symptoms' (Freud, 1962, p. 76). And elsewhere: 'The path of perversion branches off sharply from that of neuroses. If these regressions do not call forth a prohibition on the part of the ego no neurosis results; the libido succeeds in obtaining a real though not a normal satisfaction' (Freud, 1956, p. 368).

We might take this to imply that Freud is ruling out the occurrence of a condition in which perverted sexual impulses are being gratified and the pervert is nevertheless suffering from neurotic symptoms. But no. Freud tells us that we are not to be surprised at the existence of such states of affairs: 'Psycho-neuroses are also very often associated with manifest inversion' (Freud, 1938, p. 575). The symptoms may then express the patient's repressed conviction of the unacceptability of his perverted practices (Freud, 1925a, p. 335).

And this is how Freud reconciles his view that delusional attacks of jealousy are due to surplus libido with the fact that he came across a case in which the attacks 'curiously enough appeared on the day following an act of intercourse'—: '. . . after every satiation of the heterosexual libido the homosexual component likewise stimulated by the act forced for itself an outlet in the attack of jealousy' (Freud, 1924b, 235).

Freud also maintains that 'homosexual tendencies . . . help to constitute the social instincts': 'It is precisely manifest homosexuals and among them again precisely those that struggle against an indulgence in sensual acts who distinguish themselves by taking a particularly active share in the general interests of humanity—' (Freud, 1925a, p. 447).

Does it follow that homosexuals indulge their tastes at the expense of their philanthropic impulses? That Casement would have been more solicitous on behalf of the exploited natives of Putomayo and the Congo had he been more chaste? Or does it not follow? The following formula could cope with either contingency: 'In the light of psychoanalysis we are accustomed to regard social feeling as a sublimation of homosexual attitudes towards objects. In the homosexual person with marked social interests, the detachment of social feeling from object choice has not been fully carried out' (Freud, 1924b, p. 243).

But on occasions on which counter-observations are too vividly present to him, Freud's claim that the neuroses have sexual causes takes this form:

> It did not escape me . . . that sexuality was not always indicated as the cause of neurosis; one person would certainly fall ill because of some injurious sexual condition, but another because he had lost his fortune or recently sustained a severe organic illness . . . every weakening of the ego from whatever cause must have the same effect as an increase in the demands of the libido; viz., making neurosis possible . . . the fund of energy supporting the symptoms of a neurosis, in every case and regardless of the circumstances inducing their outbreak is provided by the libido which is thus put to an abnormal use. (Freud, 1956, p. 394)

And on a later occasion, in connection with the case of a businessman in whom 'The catastrophe which he knows to be threatening his business induces the neurosis as a by-product', Freud says that nevertheless 'the dynamics of the neurosis are identical' with those in which 'the interests at stake in the conflict giving rise to neurosis are . . . purely libidinal . . Libido, dammed up and unable to secure real gratification, finds discharge through the repressed unconscious by the help of regression to old fixations' (Freud, 1950, p. 471).

It is fair to conclude that though the introduction of the term 'libido' permits Freud to give the impression that claims are being advanced as to the nature of the vicissitudes which precipitate, or the states which predispose to, the development of neurotic disorders, in fact a convention has been adopted as to how these vicissitudes and states are to be described. 'Sexual trauma' has been extended in the direction of pleonasm; 'non-sexual conflict' no longer has a use. Whenever necessary these terms are employed in a 'typically metaphysical way, without an antithesis' (Wittgenstein).

III

Consider some typical psychoanalytic scenery as it occurs in Freud's reconstructions of infantile sexual life. One sequence shows the child complacently fondling his penis while entertaining obscure projects of doing something in relation to his mother with it, subsequently discovering that this activity is frowned upon, but meeting with incredulity the threat that persistence in it will result in his sexual organ being taken from him until, on observing with horror the wound where his sister's penis should be, he abandons his defensive scepticism and initiates a struggle against his masturbatory impulses and the incestuous phantasies which accompany them. In another sequence the child is speculating as to the nature of the sexual transactions between his parents and on its relation to the puzzle of birth, deciding that the orifice of parturition and intercourse is the anus, yearning to usurp his mother's sexual place with his father and to bear him a child, but once again rejecting these wishes when the facts of female anatomy convince him that a precondition of their fulfilment would be his own submission to castration.

These accounts of infantile sexual life are startling, but, once we have got over being thrilled by them, ultimately trivial contributions to natural history, with as much human relevance as the fact that we once had gills. Their claim to our attention rests on two things: their explanatory value and the evidence they afford of the validity of psychoanalytic method.

Our confidence in Freud's reconstructions of his neurotic patient's infantile sexual life, and therefore in his claim that adult neuroses are continuations or recrudescences of infantile ones, might be justified by the endorsement of the validity of psychoanalytic method afforded by the accuracy of those portions of the reconstructions which are held to characterize childhood in general and can thus be confirmed by the contemporary observation of children. That Freud recognizes that at least some of their significance resides in this latter fact is indicated by this remark in the *Three Essays on Sexuality:* 'I can point with satisfaction to the fact that direct observation has fully confirmed the conclusions drawn from psychoanalysis and thus furnished good evidence for the reliability of the latter method of investigation' (Freud, 1938, p. 594). And on many occasions Freud does say that his clinically derived theses regarding the infant's sexual life could be tested by systematically observing the behaviour of children. In the case history of Hans he refers to the observation of children as a 'more direct and less roundabout proof of these fundamental theories' and speaks of 'observing upon the child at first hand, in all the freshness of life, the sexual impulses and conative tendencies which we dig out so laboriously in the adult from among their own debris'. He even implies that the facts to which he has called attention are so blatant that one must take pains to avoid noticing them. For example in his paper 'The sexual theories of children' he says 'one can easily observe' that little girls regard their clitoris as an inferior penis. In his paper 'The resistances to psychoanalysis' he writes of the Oedipal phase: 'At that period of life these impulses still continue uninhibited as straightforward sexual desires. This can be confirmed so easily that only the greatest efforts could make it possible to overlook it' (Freud, 1925*b*, p. 172). And again:

> In the beginning my formulations regarding infantile sexuality were founded almost exclusively upon the results of analysis in adults . . . It was, therefore, a very great triumph, when it became possible years later to confirm almost all my inferences by direct observation and analysis of children, a triumph that lost some of its magnitude as one gradually realised that the nature of the discovery was such that one should really be ashamed of having to make it. The further one carried these observations on children, the more self-evident the facts became and the more astonishing was it too that so much trouble was taken to overlook them.

But on occasions when Freud is under the necessity of forestalling disconfirmatory reports he forgets the so-easily-confirmable character of his reconstructions of infantile life and insists on their esoteric only-observable-by-initiates status. In the preface to the fourth edition of *Three Essays on Sexuality* we are told that 'none, however, but physicians who practise psychoanalysis can have any access whatever to this sphere of knowledge or any possibility of forming a judgment that is uninfluenced by their own dislikes and prejudices. If mankind had been able to learn from direct observations of children these three essays could have remained unwritten' (Freud, 1953,

p. 133). This retreat to the esoterically observable in the face of disconfir-matory evidence is a general feature of psychoanalytic apologetic. A reviewer of the NYU symposium on psychoanalysis and scientific method meets the challenge to demonstrate the empirical status of these claims by offering to provide a list of child-analysts who will vouch for them (Waelder, 1962).

B.A. Farrell has made the following defence of this mode of dealing with disconfirmatory reports: 'We have to remember that almost any negative finding—such as that over female penis envy—can be countered by analysts claiming that it is necessary to postulate such girlish envy in order to account for the material thrown up in analysis. The strength of this reply can only be resolved, presumably, by settling the validity of psychoanalytic method' (Farrell, 1961). Something seems to have gone wrong with this argument. The question of the bearing of empirical observation of children on reconstructions based on the use of psychoanalytic method cannot be post-poned until the validity of that method is resolved, since the only way of resolving the validity of that method is by determining whether, and to what extent, it accords with empirical observation of children. Farrell's argument illustrates a tendency to implicitly dehistoricize psychoanalytic reconstruc-tions, since it is obvious on reflection that what women felt or underwent as infants cannot depend upon what 'it is necessary to postulate in order to account for the material thrown up in analysis'. But aside from the intrinsic objectionableness of such a procedure for determining the character of infantile mental life, it renders the observation of children futile for the pur-pose of validating psychoanalytic method. Freud's peripheral awareness of this would account for a lack of candour in his expositions. The expression 'direct observation' alternates with 'direct analytic observation' as if they were synonymous, so that it only becomes clear after several rereadings that when Freud speaks of 'the direct observation of children' he is referring to the psychoanalytic interpretation of infantile behaviour. That is, Freud in attempting to dispel our doubts as to the validity of psychoanalytic method by appeals to 'direct observation', proffers us a copy of the same newspaper, this time with his thumb over the banner.

But there is apparently another way of testing the validity of psychoana-lytic method. It might seem that there can be no question of the genuinely empirical–historical character of those clinical reconstructions which incor-porate references to the external circumstances of the patient's infantile life, such as that he had been threatened with castration or been seduced, or seen his parents engaged in intercourse. These at least are straightforwardly testable and their accuracy would therefore afford evidence of the validity of psychoanalytic method; for if the investigation into the infantile history of the patient revealed that he had had no opportunity of witnessing intercourse between his parents (the primal scene), or that he not been sexually abused, or not threatened with castration, this would cast doubt on the validity of the interpretative principles employed and on the dependability of the anamnesis which endorsed them.

But Freud occasionally manifests a peculiar attitude towards independent investigation of his reconstructions of the patient's infantile years. In 'From the history of an infantile neurosis' he writes: 'It may be tempting to take the easy course of filling up the gaps in a patient's memory by making enquiries from the older members of the family: but I cannot advise too strongly against such a technique . . . One invariably regrets having made oneself dependent on such information. At the same time confidence in the analysis is shaken and a court of appeal is set up over it. Whatever can be remembered at all will anyhow come to light in the course of further analysis' (Freud, 1925*a*, footnote on p. 481). In the same paper he even expresses misgivings about the value of child analysis: '. . . the deepest strata may turn out to be inaccessible to consciousness. An analysis of childhood disorder through the medium of recollection in an intellectually mature adult is free from these limitation' (Freud, 1925*a*, p. 475).

This preference is expressed as early a *The Interpretation of Dreams* (Freud, 1949b, p. 258), where Freud remarks of the death wish of children against the same-sexed parent: 'though observations of this kind on small children fit in perfectly with the interpretation I have proposed, they do not carry such complete conviction as is forced upon the physician by the psychoanalysis of adult neurotics.' (This is as if Holmes, having concluded from the indentation marks on his visitor's walking stick that he was the owner of a dog smaller than a mastiff and larger than a terrier, instead of glancing with interest in the direction from which the animal was approaching were to turn once again to a more minute inspection of the stick.)

Finally Freud makes assurance double sure by dispensing with the patient's anamnesis altogether. In the case history of the Wolf Man he says: '. . . it seems to me absolutely equivalent to a recollection if the memories are replaced . . . by dreams, the analysis of which invariably leads back to the same scene, which reproduce every portion of its content in an indefatigable variety of new shapes . . . dreaming is another kind of remembering . . .' (Freud, 1925*a*, p. 524).

These remarks suggest that the foundering of the seduction theory on the failure of independent investigation of the alleged seductions to authenticate their occurrence had an influence on the development of psychoanalytic practice similar to that exerted on Percival Lowell, the astronomer of Martian Canals fame, by his failure to detect the canals under especially favourable conditions with a more powerful telescope than he customarily used.

> Finding out that the seeing of canals occurred oftener and less ambiguously when the smaller telescopes were used, Lowell used these instruments far oftener

in his work than the more powerful ones, claiming that magnification of atmospheric perturbation with the larger telescopes vitiated their use for the observation of the canals . . . Lowell never used Mexico as an observation post again and he never again relied upon the splendid 24-inch telescope for observation of Mars . . . (Hoffing, 1964, p. 33)

Freud's reliance on dream interpretation to determine the historicity or pathogenicity of an individual's infantile sexual past ('dreaming is another kind of remembering') plays a role in his practice similar to that of the small telescope in Lowell's.

However if, by some chance, circumstances from the patient's infantile past which were at variance with Freud's reconstructions did come to light, the validity of his interpretative principles would not thereby be imperilled. This is how Freud deals with the fact that according to his clinical experience 'it is regularly the father from whom castration is dreaded, although it is mostly the mother who utters the threat': 'We find that a child, where his own experience fails him, fills in the gap in individual truth with prehistoric truth; he replaces occurrences in his own life with occurrences in the life of his ancestors. Wherever experiences fail to fit in with the hereditary schema they become remodelled in the imagination. We are often able to see the schema triumphing over the experience of the individual . . .' (Freud, 1925a, pp. 557 and 603).

Nor does Freud restrict this device to paternal castration threats. He extends it to 'memories' of seduction and of the primal scene as well. 'These primal phantasies of seduction, castration and witnessing parental intercourse) are a phylogenetic possession . . . If they can be found in real events, well and good; but if reality has not supplied them they will be evolved out of hints and elaborated by phantasy . . . the individual, where his own experience has become insufficient, stretches out beyond it to the experience of past ages' (Freud, 1956, p. 379).

If 'memories' of infantile events which prove never to have occurred are to be taken as due to an 'analogy with the far-reaching instinctive knowledge of animals', how could Freud ever discover that the discrepancy between his reconstruction of the patient's infantile life and the independently ascertained facts of his infantile history was not an instance of 'the phylogenetically inherited schema triumphing over experience' but was due to the invalidity of his reconstructive procedures?

Freud sometimes offers a therapeutic rationale for his conviction as to the authenticity of his reconstructions, asserting that it rests on the fact that anamnesis of the reconstructed scenes, fantasies, impulses or what not, dissipates the symptoms which are held to be the distorted manifestations of their repression. In 1909 he wrote: 'Starting out from the mechanism of cure, it now became possible to construct quite definite ideas of the origin

of the illness.' And 'it is only experiences in childhood that explain susceptibility to later traumas' since '. . . it is only by uncovering these almost
invariably forgotten memory traces and making them conscious that we
acquire the power to get rid of the symptoms' (Freud, 1962, pp. 48 and 71).

But we are also told that 'marked progress in analytic understanding can
be unaccompanied by even the slightest change in the patient's compulsions
and inhibitions' (Freud, 1924*b*, pp. 221–22). And that he often 'succeeded
in . . . establishing a complete intellectual acceptance of what is repressed—
but the repression itself is still unremoved' (Freud, 1950, p. 182), and that
'Quite often we do not succeed in bringing the patient to recollect what has
been repressed. Instead . . . we produce in him an assured conviction of the
truth of the construction, which achieves the same therapeutic result as a
recaptured memory' (Freud, 1950, p. 368).

So that as well as patients who do not recall their infantile sexual
impulses and retain their symptoms and patients who do recall their infantile sexual impulses and relinquish their symptoms, we have patients who do
not recall their infantile sexual impulses but nevertheless relinquish their
symptoms, and patients who do recall their infantile sexual impulses and
nevertheless retain them. And since this is just what we might expect to find
if there were no relation between the anamnesis of infantile sexuality and the
remission of the neurotic symptoms, it is fair to conclude that there is no
support from this source for the authenticity of Freud's reconstructions.

I conclude that the reconstructions of infantile sexual history which
Freud proffers are pseudo-narratives: the space in which he locates the incidents which comprise them is *a priori* unoccupied.

IV

In his stimulating introduction to the Pelican edition of Freud's *Leonardo*,
B.A. Farrell writes: 'What distinguishes Freud's essay about Leonardo from
the usual run of narratives is that it uses the technical generalisations of psychoanalytic theory' (Farrell, 1963, p. 13). I shall argue that what distinguishes Freud's narrative, as it distinguishes many of his narratives, is its
abstention from determinate inference. For Freud does not use his 'technical generalisations' to infer the character of Leonard's adult sexual life from
his knowledge of Leonardo's infantile sexual history, nor does he use them
to infer Leonardo's infantile sexual history from his knowledge of
Leonardo's adult sexual life. What he does is to link, through the use of a
variety of idioms and a plethora of mechanisms and interpretative principles,
what is already 'known' of Leonardo's childhood with what is already
'known' of his adult character, selecting from the conflicting traditions
about Leonardo what best serves this purpose.

Consider how Freud proceeds to demonstrate 'the existence of a causal
connection between Leonardo's relation with his mother in childhood and

his later manifest, if ideal (sublimated), homosexuality'. He works backwards from Leonardo's adult attitude towards sex to see what in his infantile years might hold a determinant consonant with the psychoanalytic thesis of the overwhelming predominance of infancy and settles on Leonardo's early years of uninterrupted possession of his mother as a determinant of his homosexuality. Because, Freud says, 'we . . . know from the psychoanalytic study of homosexual patients that such a connection does exist and is in fact an intimate and necessary one' (Freud, 1963, pp. 137–38).

But in the first two edition of *Three Essays on Sexuality* (1905 and 1910) Freud had this to say of the infantile determinants of male inversion:

> in the case of men a childhood recollection of the affection shown them by their mother and others of the female sex who looked after them when they were children contributes powerfully to directing their choice towards women . . . The frequency of inversion among present-day aristocracy is made somewhat more intelligible by . . . the fact that their mothers give less personal care to their children. (Freud, 1957, p. 229)

The Leonardo essay was published in 1910. In the next edition of *Three Essays on Sexuality,* published in 1915, this passage was supplemented as follows: '. . . on the other hand, their early experience of being deterred by their father from sexual activity and their competitive relation with him deflect them from their own sex . . .' (Freud, 1957, p. 229). So it would seem that it was only after Freud had enrolled the (supposed) absence of Leonardo's father among the determinants of his homosexuality that this became a homosexuality-inducing mechanism. And a counter-intuitive one at that. For our natural expectation on being told that a child has escaped the castration-anxiety inspiring presence of a father during his crucial years is that this would minimize the possibility of his erotic feelings towards his mother undergoing a pathogenically intense repression. That this is an expectation which Freud intermittently encourages, and further evidence of the *ad hoc* character of his post-Leonardo emendation of the circumstances favouring the development of homosexuality, is indicated by his remarks on 'retiring in favour of the father': '. . . another powerful motive urging towards the homosexual object-choice [is] regard for the father or fear of him; for the renunciation of women means that all rivalry with him (or with all men who may take his place) is avoided' (Freud, 1924*b*, p. 241).

What then is there which, had he found or failed to find it in the accounts of Leonardo's infancy, would have shaken Freud's view that the 'accidental conditions of his childhood had a profound and disturbing effect on him'? Whenever advances in Leonardo studies deprive some environmental circumstances to which Freud had assigned an explanatory role of its historicity, we are told that this does not necessarily impugn Freud's account of Leonardo's infantile reveries and preoccupations. This is true, but it then becomes difficult to see what revelation short of his having died at birth could do so.

As another instance of the ease with which the variety of mechanisms at Freud's disposal enables him to press into the service of the thesis of infantile pathogenicity, whatever parental circumstances the childhood history of his subject happens to provide, consider his account of how inevitable it was, given the character of Dostoevsky's father, that he should have come to possess an over-strict super-ego:

> If the father was hard, violent and cruel, the super-ego takes over these attributes from him, and in the relations between the ego and it, the passivity which was supposed to have been repressed is re-established. The super-ego has become sadistic, and the ego becomes masochistic, that is to say, at bottom passive in a feminine way. A great need for punishment develops in the ego, which in part offers itself as a victim to fate, and in part finds satisfaction in ill-treatment by the super-ego (that is, the sense of guilt). (Freud, 1950, p. 231)

This is not at all implausible. But neither is this:

> The unduly lenient and indulgent father fosters the development of an over-strict super-ego because, in the face of the love which is showered on it, the child has no other way of disposing of its aggressiveness than to turn it inward. In neglected children who grow up without any love the tension between ego and super-ego is lacking, their aggressions can be directed externally . . . a strict conscience arises from the co-operation of two factors in the environment: the deprivation of instinctual gratification which evokes the child's aggressiveness, and the love it receives which turns this aggressiveness inward, where it is taken over by the super-ego. (Freud, 1930, footnote on p. 117)

That is, if a child develops a sadistic super-ego, either he had a harsh and punitive father or he had not. But this is just what we might expect to find if there were no relation between his father's character and the harshness of his super-ego.

As a final illustration of the use which Freud makes of the indefiniteness and multiplicity of his pathogenic influences and of the manner in which they enable him to render any outcome whatever an intelligible and apparently natural result of whatever circumstances preceded it, consider the contrast between his accounts of two children—Hans, who was almost five and Herbert, who was four. Herbert figures as a specimen of enlightened child-rearing in a a paper of 1907, 'The Sexual Enlightenment of Children', where he is described as 'a splendid boy . . . whose intelligent parents abstain from forcibly suppressing one side of the child's development'.

Although Herbert is not a sensual child he shows 'the liveliest interest in that part of his body which he calls his weewee-maker' because 'since he has never been frightened or oppressed with a sense of guilt he gives expression quite ingenuously to what he thinks'. On the other hand the unfortunate

Hans was a 'paragon of all the vices'—his mother had threatened him with castration before he was yet four, the birth of a younger sister had confronted him 'with the great riddle of where babies come from' and 'his father had told him the lie about the stork which made it impossible for him to ask for enlightenment upon such things'. Thus, due in part to 'the perplexity in which his infantile sexual theories left him' he succumbed to an animal phobia shortly before his fifth year.

We learned from Jones's biography that Hans and Herbert are the same child, the account of Hans written *after* and that of Herbert *before* he had succumbed to his animal phobia (but not before the events to which Freud later assigned pathogenic status). Freud even decides as an afterthought that Hans's/Herbert's 'enlightened' upbringing would naturally have contributed to the development of his phobia: 'Since he was brought up without being intimidated and with as much consideration and as little coercion as possible his anxiety dared to show itself more boldly. With him there was no place for such motives as a bad conscience or fear of punishment which with other children must no doubt contribute to making the anxiety less' (Freud, 1925a, p. 284). This belongs with Falstaff's account of why he ran away at Gadshill.

Freud's general accounts of his infantile theory show the same elusiveness and adjustability in relation to counter-example. He makes claims which appear to commit him to a distinctive infantile sexual history for neurotics, and thus seem vulnerable to refutation, while at the same time insisting on the universality, or at least, the undetectability of the pathogenic features invoked.

'At the root of the formation of every symptom are to be found traumatic experiences from early sexual life' (Freud, 1950, p. 117). But since 'Investigation into the mental life of normal persons then yielded the unexpected discovery that their infantile history in regard to sexual matters was not necessarily different in essentials from that of the neurotic' (Freud, 1924a, p. 279), the occurrence of 'traumas' in the childhoods of neurotics can hardly afford us grounds for belief in their causal relevance. This must lie in some pathological repercussion of the 'traumas' which distinguishes neurotic childhoods from normal. What are those repercussions? 'The important thing . . . was how he had reacted to these experiences, whether he had responded to them with repression or not' (Freud, 1924a, p. 279). Then is it in repression that the differentia between neurotic and non-neurotic childhoods lies? It seems not. For not only is 'no human being spared such traumatic experiences' but 'none escapes the repression to which they give rise' (Freud, 1949a, p. 52). 'Every individual has gone through this phase but has energetically repressed it and succeeded in forgetting it' (Freud, 1950, p. 172). So once again the differentia must lie elsewhere.

Let us suppose it to have been the case of those early patients of Freud's whose illness he mistakenly attributed to their having been seduced in infancy, that their illness was not a function of their infantile sexual history at all, and not merely not a function of their having been seduced. How could he have discovered the one as he discovered the other? What would have stood to his view concerning the infantile fantasy theory of the neuroses as the discovery that not all his patients had had 'a passive sexual experience before puberty' (Freud, 1924*a*, p. 142) stood to the seduction theory of the neuroses? But it must be conceded that this consideration is insufficient to establish that Freud's infantile sexual aetiology is without content. For the universality of a putative causal factor does not necessarily impugn its status as a pathogenic agency.

If Freud had discovered features of infantile life whose pathogenic power depended on the presence of an inherited predisposition to respond pathologically to normal contingencies this would have been an important discovery even though those features were not abnormal interventions. Though it would not be a theoretically satisfying answer to the question why certain individuals are neurotic it would be of great practical and humanitarian interest. For we might, by adopting extraordinary measures, prevent the predisposition from having pathological outcomes, as we do, for example, in the case of phenyl-pyruvic oligophrenia, where infants with a metabolic disposition to make poisons of ordinarily innocuous nutrients are provided with a special diet which enables them to escape the usual pathological outcome of such a predisposition; or as we do in the case of children with a tendency to protruding teeth, where braces are fixed to the teeth to ensure normal development. But with Freud's post-seduction theory of the neuroses it is impossible to say what he believes stands to the neuroses as the failure to put braces on the teeth of a child with a tendency to protrusion stands to his adult mouth deformation.

At first it looks as if precautions against castration fears might. But because of the ubiquity of castration surrogates, because, that is, any attempt to control the child's sexuality (of which infantile incontinence is, according to Freud, a manifestation) can induce castration anxiety and thus initiate pathological developments and because the failure to intervene in the child's sexual life is in itself a pathogenic agency—('Complete freedom . . . would do serious damage to the children themselves' [Freud, 1933, p. 191]) and because furthermore, 'the power of refractory instinctual constitutions can never be got rid of by education' (Freud, 1933, p. 1920)—there is no ostensibly psychoanalytic child-rearing regimen whose failure to protect against neuroses could be said to have disconfirmed Freud's claim of infantile pathogenesis.

Freud is well aware that when a putatively pathogenic factor is discovered to be widely distributed this casts doubt on the genuiness of its relation to the illness. Before his abandonment of the seduction theory he said: 'Of course if infantile sexual activity were an almost universal occurrence it would prove nothing to find it in every case' (Freud, 1924*a*, p. 205). His awareness of this may account for his increased tendency to treat the patient's infantile sexual vicissitudes as *grounds for* rather than *causes of* his neurotic illness; since the explanatory status of a motive is not called into doubt because of the absence of a general connection between it and the behaviour it is invoked to explain.

It finally becomes clear that Freud's assertion that 'the factors which go to form neuroses are to be found in the patient's infantile sexual life' (Freud, 1925*a*, p. 303) is not an epidemiological claim in the sense in which the seduction theory of the neuroses was, since the contingencies about which Freud is explicit are neither manipulable nor differentiating. We would convey more of its real character if we characterized it as cryptoverstehen (although, as I hope to show, it is really pseudo-verstehen).

The explanation of these equivocations, evasions and inconsistencies is that Freud is simultaneously under the sway of two necessities: to seem to say and yet to refrain from saying which infantile events occasion the predisposition to neuroses. To seem to say, because his discovery of the pathogenic role of sexuality in the infantile life of neurotics is the ostensible ground for his conviction that the neuroses are manifestations of the revival of infantile sexual struggles and thus for the validity of the method by which this aetiology was inferred: to refrain from saying, because if his aetiological claims were made too explicit and therefore ran the risk of refutation this might discredit not only his explanations of the neuroses but, more disastrously, the method by which they were arrived at. Only by making these prophylactic and pathogenic claims can his preoccupations and procedures by justified, but only by withdrawing them can they be safeguarded. So the 'quantitative factor' to which Freud invariably alludes in his exposition of the aetiology of the neuroses, and his insistence on the importance of the inherited constitution, are not examples of scientific scrupulousness. They are devices for retaining a preoccupation long after any reasonable hope of enhancing one's powers of prediction and control by means of it have been exhausted.

It could be argued that the counterfeit character of Freud's infantile aetiology could be conceded without substantially reducing our estimate of his contribution to the understanding of neuroses. For there is an alternative construction to be put on Freud's claim that the neuroses are sexual disorders: that it be understood as a claim not about the causes but about the character of neurotic disorders. In other words, that Freud's theory of the neuroses be treated as an answer not to a 'what happened to him?' question but to a 'what's wrong with him?' question. On this view, infantile sexuality stands to the neuroses somewhat as the upright posture of the human species does to the fallen arches of some of its members, and neurotics are persons who are so constituted that for unknown reasons, out of memories of their infantile sexual life, they make illnesses. And that this is so would be demonstrated by the fact that the neurotic symptomatology serves, expresses, or alludes to sexual interests, interests which ultimately date from infancy. Or to use Freud's own formulations: 'The aetiological importance of sexual factors' would rest on 'the delicate but firm inter-relationship of the structural elements of the neurosis' (Freud, 1924a, p. 150); 'the logical structure of the neurotic manifestations' (p. 150); 'the inevitable completion of the associative and logical structure' (p. 201); 'the structural connections between symptoms, memories and associations (p.179); 'the copious and intertwined associative links' (Freud, 1949b, p. 191).

V

Let us see how these rather figuratively expressed criteria work in practice. Freud says of Dora's attack of acute abdominal pain accompanied by a high fever and succeeded by a dragging right foot that it is 'a typical example of the way in which symptoms arise from exciting causes which seem to be entirely unconnected with sexuality'. This is how the appearance of uncon-nectedness is dissipated: 'What then was the meaning of this condition, of this attempted simulation of perityphlitis? . . . I asked Dora whether this attack had been before or after the scene by the lake. Every difficulty was resolved at a single blow by her prompt reply: "Nine months later . . ." Her supposed attack had thus enabled the patient with the modest means at her disposal (the pains and the menstrual flow) to realise the phantasy of child-birth.' But 'What was all this about her dragging her leg . . . ? That is how people walk when they have a twisted foot. So she had made a "false step": which was true indeed if she could give birth to a child nine months after the scene by the lake.' If this is what Freud considers 'a typical example of the way in which symptoms arise from exciting causes 'which seem to be entirely unconnected with sexuality', we must ask how he could ever dis-cover that the symptoms had arisen from causes which were in fact, and not just apparently, unconnected with sexuality.

Since in this instance Dora did not confirm Freud's account of the nature of her limp (assuming for the moment that it was the kind of thing which she could confirm) and since the symptoms were no longer there to confirm it by 'entering into the discussion', on what does Freud rest his conviction that in Dora's 'simulated attack of perityphlitis' and its sequelae there was an allu-sion to her feelings of regret at the outcome of the scene by the lake? On the fact that both menstrual discharges and babies come out of the vagina, on the coincidence between the period required for gestation and that which elapsed between Herr K's overtures and her abdominal attack and on the possibility of placing a sexual construction on an idiom ('false step') which might be used in connection with her limp. How is the probative, evidential value of such considerations to be assessed? How do we assess them elsewhere?

What we do in assessing such claims is to make intuitive judgements of the likelihood of the events, between which the relation of allusion is said to hold, occurring independently of each other. Let us examine some examples of blatantly spurious allusiveness and see on what our conviction that they are spurious rests.

In *La Vita Nuova,* Dante argues that the date of Beatrice's death, 9 June 1290, was determined by her relation to the Trinity and other significant numerical values:

> according to the computation used in Italy, her most noble spirit departed hence in the first hour of the ninth day of the month; and, according to the computation used in Syria, she died in the ninth month of the year . . . in which the perfect number was nine times completed, within that century wherein she was born into the world . . . Why this number was so propitious to her may be possibly explained thus. According to Ptolemy, and according to Christian truth, the heavens that move are nine . . . so this number was propitious to her, indicating, as it did, that at her birth all the nine moving heavens were in the most perfect conjunction. This is one reason; but when the matter is scanned more closely, and in conformity with infallible truth, this number was her very self. I speak by way of similitude meaning thus:—The number three is root of nine, because without any other number, multiplied by itself, it makes nine, it being obvious that three times three makes nine. If, then, three is by itself the author of nine, and the author of miracles is in Himself three, Father, Son and Holy Ghost, which are Three and One, this lady was accompanied by the number nine, in order to show that she was a Nine, in other words a miracle, whose only root is the adorable trinity. (Dante, 1871, pp. 59–60)

In the sixth chapter of Newton's *Observations on the Prophecies of Daniel,* Newton argues that the identity of the fourth of the beasts mentioned by Daniel with the Roman Empire and therefore his miraculous anticipation of its downfall is attested by the coincidence between the number of horns of the fourth beast and the number of kingdoms into which the Empire was fragmented, since if to the seven kingdoms listed by Sigonious you '. . . add the Franks, Britons and Lombards . . . you have the ten; for these arose about the same time with the seven' (Newton, 1841, p. 48).

As a last illustration of spurious allusiveness consider the proof produced by a cleric encountered in India by Thomas Babington Macaulay that Napoleon was the Beast mentioned in the thirteenth chapter of 'Revelations': if 'Bonaparte' is written in Arabic omitting only two letters it yields the number 666.

A felicitous characterization of what is going on in these specimens and of the manner in which they differ from bona fide enquiries is provided by Pareto. I have adapted it slightly to give it greater generality.

Case 1. We have a (datum D) which is assumed to (allude to) certain facts
A . . . Our purpose is to determine A. If our effort is successful, we shall be following the line *DA* . . . But, if our venture . . . chances to fail, we get not to *A*,
but to *B*, and imagine, though mistakenly, that *B* is the source of *D*.

Case 2. From a (datum D), the idea is to draw certain conclusions, *C*, which
are generally known in advance . . . the quest is not for *C* (*C* being already
known), but for a way of getting to *C*. Sometimes that is done deliberately. A
person knows perfectly well that *C* does not follow from *D*, but he thinks it desirable to make it seem to . . . But more often, the search for a road that will
lead from *D* to *C* is not consciously premeditated . . . Quite without conscious
design he brings the two sentiments together over the path of *DC* . . . The person who is trying to persuade others has first of all persuaded himself. There is
no trickery.

In the first case . . . the search is for *A*. In the second case . . . the search,
deliberately or unconsciously, is for the route *DC* . . . the search for the path *DC*
is represented in all sincerity as a quest strictly for *A* . . . the person . . . is using
an *interpretation DC* suitable for getting him to the desired goal . . . Those two
termini are fixed. The problem is simply to find a way to bring them together.
(Pareto, 1963, pp. 385–87)

This gives us an account of the motivation for spurious allusions. But
how is it done? How is the impression of allusiveness created? Martin
Gardner has some enlightening remarks on this problem in his examination
of the claims of Pyramidologists to have found allusions to scientific truths,
such as the axis of the earth, its polar radius, its mean density, the mean tem-
perature of its surface and the period of precession of its axis, and so forth,
in the dimensions of the Great Pyramid.

It is not difficult to understand how (Pyramidologists) achieved these astonishing scientific correspondences. If you set about measuring a complicated structure like the Pyramid, you will quickly have on hand a great abundance of lengths
to play with. If you have sufficient patience to juggle them about in various ways,
you are certain to come out with many figures which coincide with important
figures in the sciences. Since you are bound by no rules, it would be odd indeed
if this search for Pyramid 'truths' failed to meet with considerable success.

Take the Pyramid's height, for example. Smyth multiples it by ten to the
ninth power to obtain the distance to the sun. The nine here is purely arbitrary.
And if no simple multiple had yielded the distance to the sun, he could try other
multiples to see if it gave the distance to the Moon, or the nearest star, or any
other scientific figure. (Gardner, 1957, pp. 176–77)

How do these specimens differ from the genuine allusiveness which psychoanalytic apologetic is compelled to maintain is exemplified by Freud's
accounts of symptom-formation, dreams, errors, etc.? 'How would it be
possible', asks Merleau-Ponty, 'to credit chance with the complex correspondences which the psychoanalyst discovers? How can we deny that the
psychoanalyst has taught us to notice echoes, allusions, repetitions from one

moment of life to another?' These remarks express a typical reaction to Freud's interpretations and it must be conceded that on a great number of occasions Freud does produce an overwhelming impression of cogency in his demonstrations that some contemporary item of behaviour contains an allusion, to a remote event of infancy, say. But could it be that this cogency is illusory and that it arises, as for the credulous in the cases cited, because we overlook the enormous discretion he enjoys in the selection and characterization of the data he explains and because of our assumption that he undoes the work of distortion and arrives at his interpretation by the application of antecedently formulated rules?

Consider, in the light of these suspicions, one of the devices which Freud employs to get an allusion to fellatio into Leonardo's vulture reminiscence: 'Its most striking feature was after all that it changed sucking at the mother's breast into being suckled, that is into passivity and thus into a situation whose nature is undoubtedly homosexual.' Thus Leonardo's account of the bird inserting its tail between his lips and beating about with it could not be merely a distorted reminiscence of nursing at his mother's breast but must be a fantasy of sucking at a penis, since sucking a nipple is active but sucking a penis passive. I will forbear asking where Freud derives his assurance that sucking a penis is passive rather than active since it might be felt that I was polemically exploiting the fact that it is not a question on which anyone is likely to pronounce authoritatively. But I will point out that it doesn't sort well with the view, also expressed by Freud, that fellatio is a revival of the infantile demand for the breast. And this suggests that the decision as to the passivity of the breast in relation to the nursing child's mouth is due to Freud's prior knowledge of the tradition according to which Leonardo was homosexual. For example he writes: 'The mother is in every sense active in her relations to her child; it is just as true to say that it is she who gives suck to the child as that she lets it suck her breast' (Freud, 1933, p. 148). And 'The first sexual or sexually tinged experiences of a child in its relation to the mother are naturally passive in character. It is she who suckles, feeds . . .' (Freud, 1950, pp. 264–65).

Consider, too, one of the mechanisms which Freud employs to derive Leonardo's homosexuality from his infantile relation to his mother. 'By repressing his love for his mother he preserves it in his unconscious and from now on remains faithful to her. While he seems to pursue boys and to be their lover he is in reality running away from the other women who might cause him to be unfaithful'. So the unconscious which is driven by incestuous urges is nevertheless, like a good bourgeois, respectably monogamous. But does not this sexual attachment of the homosexual to his mother contradict the revulsion which Freud says her penisless state inspires in him? And if the reply to this is that it is the phallic mother to whom his unconscious is attached and to whom he is under the compulsion of remaining faithful, how is this end served by 'seeking his sexual object in men who through other physical and mental qualities remind him of women's (Freud, 1924*b*, p. 66)?

But Freud has an answer to these philistine objections which brings us to another feature of psychoanalytic theory which has been found puzzling but is easily accounted for on the assumption that its function is to avoid refutation: Freud's insistence that the unconscious contains no contradictions. Its effect is to allow Freud to reserve the right to determine *a posteriori* what the logical implications of any interpretative claims advanced are. An extended exposition of this property of the unconscious occurs on the following occasion: Freud is anticipating an objection that his account of a patient's symptoms as due to an unconscious wish to be penetrated by his father's penis and bear him a child plus an unconscious conviction that castration was a precondition of this wish being fulfilled conflicted with another interpretation which presupposed that the patient was unconsciously convinced that the anus was the orifice of intercourse and birth; 'That it should have been possible . . . for a fear of castration to exist side by side with an identification with women by means of the bowel admittedly involved a contradiction. But it was only a logical contradiction—which is not saying much. On the contrary, the whole process is characteristic of the way in which the unconscious works' (Freud, 1925*a*, p. 557). But the first of the two accounts which Freud attempts to reconcile by this device itself presupposes that the unconscious is aware of contradiction, for it is this which brings the desire to play a passive sexual roles *vis-à-vis* the father in conflict with the desire to retain the penis. And one cannot help noticing that the unconscious, which 'has no logic' and knows nothing of contradictions, is nevertheless constantly involved in the drawing of inferences. For example, in the case history of Hans, Freud describes the following as a 'typical unconscious train of thought.': 'Could it be that living beings really did exist which did not possess widdlers? If so, it would not longer be so incredible that they could take his own widdler away and, as it were, make him into a woman' (Freud, 1925*a*, p. 179). But if there is no 'No' in the unconscious ('In the unconscious No does not exist and there is no distinction between contraries' [Freud, 1925 a, footnote on p. 559]), then there can be no 'If', "So', or 'Thus' either.

VI

With the principle that 'it is not necessary that the various meanings of a symptom be compatible with one another' (Freud, 1925*a*, p. 65) ready to be invoked in case of need the risk involved in the proffering of an interpretation would seem to be minimal.

But all these arguments may be beside the point, for Freud's interpretations may belong to a class of claims for which arguments from independent probability and related considerations have no relevance; and which are only confirmed or otherwise by the event. On this view the interpretative principles are rules of thumb whose justification is that in conjunction with imponderables, which can only be discriminated through talent and experience, they lead to correct inferences about unconscious processes. The congruity of the patient's behavior and associations with the proffered interpretation would then be symptoms and not criteria of its correctness, so that production of spurious allusions, which show just as intricate an interrelatedness as Freud's putatively genuine ones, would have no weight.

When Alastair Fowler, a literary critic, investigating numerological allusions in Renaissance poetry, is considering the claim that 'The Amorous Zodiac' embodies an allusion to the lunar month, he concedes that 'the probability against its having the same number of stanzas as there are days in the lunar month . . . is not very great', but goes on to argue:

> while a routine caution about probabilities should certainly be observed, we should also remember that, unless it is observed in moderation, many intentional patterns will be neglected. For a Renaissance poet was not in any way obliged to construct statistically improbable configurations. The pattern he intended might well be one that had a good chance of occurring at random . . . imponderables ought to influence our statement about numerological patterns . . .

It is on this model that we are sometimes invited to construe Freud's interpretations. The associative patterns produced or elicited by the analyst would then not themselves constitute the content of his interpretative inferences but would merely be symptomatic of their correctness. But their correctness as to what? As to—'something that was then going on in him'. And this construal of Freud's interpretations has, for him, an additional advantage, in that many of them not only fail to stand up to tests of independent probability but are difficult to unpack in dispositional terms at all.

Dora, Paul, etc., could no more *act* as if they had entertained the unconscious thoughts which figure in Freud's reconstructions and to which he attributes their symptoms, then Freud could have *acted* as if he had dreamt the dream of the Botanical Monograph. Such phenomena are intrinsically linguistic. Having is here tied to telling. But aren't the surroundings which would allow Freud's reconstructions to bear this sense missing too?

John Wisdom has remarked that the insistence on a behavioural elucidation of Freud's claims concerning a patient's unconscious is mistaken and has made the following suggestion as to how they might be construed: 'If someone modifies the use of "there is in X's mind hatred of Y" so that X's introspection at the time is not given its normal weight we may still give it a sense in which X's subsequent introspection, what appears later in X's mind, is still what finally settles the truth of the statement. A statement about a hidden hatred is still a statement such that (the patient) has a way of verifying it which no other could have' (Wisdom, 1961). We might well allow a belated avowal or even a belated disavowal-repudiating avowal to confirm an imputation of the kind Wisdom mentions. But the bulk of Freud's interpretations is not susceptible of this sort of elucidation. Wisdom's are conceptually bowdlerized examples of the sort of questions which confront us in attempting to understand them; questions such as whether a belated avowal could transform a happening, like falling, say, into an action. Or a physiological event like menstruation into a performance. Or confirm that a pain or a fear or a delusion was effected and not suffered. Could Paul (the man with the rats) belatedly confirm that, when in a mood of mingled resentment and longing, due to his lady's being away looking after her sick grandmother, he was overcome by a compulsion to cut his throat succeeded by the thought 'No, you must go and kill the old woman', the underlying *unconscious* train of thought was really 'I should like to kill that old woman for robbing me of my love. Kill yourself, as a punishment for these savage and murderous passions', only in reverse order, à la White Queen, the punitive command coming first and the outburst which pro-voked it afterwards (Freud, 1925*a*, p. 326)?

The impression that Freud's assertions concerning a patient's uncon-scious mental processes are such that the patient's 'subsequent introspec-tion' might confirm them is an impression which Freud needs to create. For if we can be persuaded to locate the differentia between phenomena which are mental and those which are not inside the agent we won't be troubled by our inability to give an account of just what it is that is implied by the ascription to someone of an unconscious mental state—the picture of inaudible, internal deliberations, non-introspectable but retrospectable, will distract us and keep us happy.

When Freud writes '. . . of many of these latent states we have to assert that the only point in which they differ from states which are conscious is just in the lack of consciousness of them' (Freud, 1925*b*, p. 101). 'We call a process unconscious when . . . it was active at a certain time, although at that time we knew nothing about it' (Freud, 1933, p. 95), he is, in these for-mulations, indulging in something less innocuous than a mere ontological bent and it is only by considering their relation to testability that we can understand Freud's insistence that in these occult transactions is to be found 'the true essence of what is mental'.

Consider the idioms in which Freud's interpretations are typically phrased. Symptoms, errors, etc., are not simply *caused by* but they 'announce', 'proclaim', 'express', 'realize', 'fulfil', 'gratify', 'represent', 'imi-tate', or 'allude to' this or that repressed impulse, thought, memory, etc. Consider the term 'allusion'. It is typically used short of its full force, in a strained sense, like that in which one might say that a hangover is an allu-sion to alcoholic over-indulgence or a winter sun-tan to a Mediterranean holiday. In one of his dream interpretations Freud advances the claim that the red, camellia-shaped blossoms which his patient reported carrying were 'an unmistakable allusion to menstruation' and supports this by a reference to La Dame aux Camélias who signalled the onset of her menstrual periods by replacing her usual white camellia with a red one (Freud, 1949*b*, p. 319). Though we can give a sense to the statement that the dream blossoms owed their shape and colour to the dreamer's familiarity with 'La Dame aux Camélias', and that if menstrual blood were green, they too would have been green, it is not the sense which Freud requires, for it is not the kind of thing to which the dreamer could attest. She might agree but she could not corroborate. But Freud contrives by the use of such idioms as 'allusion' to get us to assimilate his explananda to a class of actions and reactions, enquiry into which naturally terminates in our receipt of the agent-subject's account of the matter, such as the course taken by his thoughts during a brown study. The cumulative effect of this is that in contexts where it would otherwise be natural to demand behavioural elucidation or inductive evidence, this demand is suspended due to our conviction that it is intentional or expressive activity which is being explained; while in contexts where we normally expect an agent's candid and considered rejection sufficient to falsify or disconfirm the attribution of expressiveness or intention, this expectation is dissipated by Freud's talk of 'processes', 'mechanism', and 'laws of the unconscious'.

Suppose we take as a paradigm of disguised expressiveness the case of the minister in *La Symphonie Pastorale,* who keeps a record of his struggle to desist from masturbating, but in order to ensure his privacy takes the precaution of writing 'smoking' for 'masturbating'. We have no difficulty in understanding this. But if we now replace this secret meaning by an unconscious reference to masturbation, isn't any residual feeling of understanding we may have just a shadow cast by our paradigm?

But our descent into unintelligibility is, on most occasions, concealed from us by the gentleness of the declivity, the succession of subtle dislocations of sense to which the idioms in which the interpretations have been couched were subjected. To free ourselves we have to make explicit the tacitly performed assimilations which produce the illusion of intelligibility and hide from us the extent to which the absence of the normal surroundings deprives Freud's interpretations of sense. When we do so we see these reconstructions of Freud's to be pseudo-soliloquies.

Conclusion

Examination of Freud's interpretations will show that he typically proceeds by beginning with whatever content his theoretical preconceptions compel him to maintain underlies the symptoms, and then, by working back and forth between it and the explanandum, constructing persuasive but spurious links between them. It is this which enables him to find allusions to the father's coital breathing in attacks of dyspnoea, fellatio in a *tussis nervosa*, defloration in migraine, orgasm in an hysterical loss of consciousness, birth pangs in appendicitis, pregnancy wishes in hysterical vomiting, pregnancy fears in anorexia, an accouchement in a suicidal leap, castration fears in an obsessive preoccupation with hat tipping, masturbation in the practice of squeezing blackheads, the anal theory of birth in an hysterical constipation, parturition in a falling cart-horse, nocturnal emissions in bedwetting, unwed motherhood in a limp, guilt over the practice of seducing pubescent girls in the compulsion to sterilize banknotes before passing them on, and so forth.

It might be felt that these criticisms are biographical in character and of only limited relevance to the question of the pseudoscientific status of psychoanalysis. This objection overlooks the fact that they do not deal with private episodes in Freud's history but with matters of public record, which we have expounded and discussed on innumerable occasions without their having aroused in us any but the most easily placated misgivings. The questions and objections which force themselves upon us when we *do* make a resolute attempt to understand Freud's claims as we would others encountered in the course of an explanatory enquiry have a blatancy which must cause us to suspect the spirit in which we originally received them. They set us problems in the phenomenology of psychoanalytic conviction.[1]

If psychoanalytic claims are not genuine hypotheses this is not because of any inspectable formal deficiencies they display but because this is not the role which they played in the lives of those who originated and transmitted them, nor of those who have since repeated, adapted or merely silently rehearsed them. We did not interpret dreams, symptoms, errors, etc., because it was discovered that they were meaningful, but we insisted that they were meaningful in order that we might interpret them. And if we reflect on the kind of thesis this is and the kind of evidence it involves, we will not find it surprising that it should prove incapable of demonstration and give rise to intractable disagreement, for it is not a question of proving of some isolated thesis of psychoanalysis that it fails to meet a particular criterion but of discerning a pattern in the total ensemble.

But if Freud's transactions with his patients' symptoms, dreams, associations, reminiscences, and so forth, are not explanatory, what are they? To what genre do they belong? One of our difficulties is that we have no commonly accepted label for them. 'Pseudoscience', though a correct characterization, is a merely negative one which performs too general an assimilation. We can only illuminate their character by comparisons.

In this paper I have assembled reasons for concluding that whatever Dante was doing when he found a trinitarian allusion in the date of

---

1. Problems towards whose solution Wittgenstein has made some fruitful suggestions—see Chapter 2 above.

Beatrice's death; whatever the cleric encountered by Macaulay was doing when he demonstrated Bonaparte's identity with the Beast mentioned by St John; whatever Pyramidologists are doing when they discover allusions to mathematical and scientific truths in the dimensions of the Great Pyramid; whatever St Augustine was doing when he expounded the significance of St Peter's catch of 153 fish; whatever Newton was doing when he identified the subdivisions of the Western Roman Empire with the ten horns of the fourth Beast mentioned in the Book of Daniel—it is this which Freud is doing when he 'lays bare' the secret significance of his patients' dreams, symptoms, errors, memories and associations, and explains 'what the symptoms signify, what instinctual impulses lurk behind them and are satisfied by them and by what transitions the mysterious path has led from those impulses to these symptoms'.

REFERENCES

Dante. 1871. *La Vita Nuova*. Trans. Theodore Martin. Edinburgh.

Eddy, Mary Baker. 1875. *Science and Health with Key to the Scriptures*. Published in Boston by the Trustees under the Mary Baker Eddy will.

Farrell, B.A. 1961. Can Psychoanalysis be Refuted? *Inquiry*.

Freud, S. 1922. *Beyond the Pleasure Principle*. London.

———. 1924*a*. *Collected Papers*. Vol. 1. London.

———. 1924*b*. *Collected Papers*. Vol. 2. London.

———. 1925*a*. *Collected Papers*. Vol. 3. London.

———. 1925*b*. *Collected Papers*. Vol. 4. London.

———. 1930. *Civilization and its Discontents*. London

———. 1933. *New Introductory Lectures on Psychoanalysis*. London.

———. 1938. *The Basic Writings of Sigmund Freud*. Trans. A.A. Brill. New York.

———. 1949*a*. *An Outline of Psychoanalysis*. London.

———. 1949*b*. *The Interpretation of Dreams*. London.

———. 1950. *Collected Papers*, Vol. 5. London.

———. 1953. *The Standard Edition of the Complete Works*, Vol. 7. London.

———. 1956. *General Introduction to Psychoanalysis*. London.

———. 1953. *The Standard Edition of the Complete Works*, Vol. 11. London.

———. 1961. *Inhibitions, Symptoms, and Anxiety*. London.

———. 1962. *Two Short Accounts of Psychoanalysis*. London.

———. 1963. *Leonardo da Vinci*. London.

Gardner, Martin. 1957. *Fads and Fallacies*. New York.

Hofling, Charles K. 1964. Percival Lowell and the canals of Mars. *Br J. med. Pscyhol.* 37.

Inglis, Brian. 1964. *Fringe Medicine*. London.

Marmor, Judd, 1962. Psychoanalytic therapy as an educational process. *Psychoanalytic Education*, vol 5. New York. In the series *Science and Psychoanalysis*. (Ed. Jules H. Masserman.)

Newton, Isaac. 1841. *Observations on the Prophecies of Daniel*. London.

Pareto, V. 1963. *The Mind and Society: A Treatise on General Sociology*, vol. 1. New York.

Popper, K. 1957. Philosophy of science: a personal report. *British Philosophy in Mid-Century*. Ed. C.A. Mace. London.

Waelder, R. 1962. Psychoanalysis, scientific method and philosophy. *F. Am. psychoanal. Ass.* 10, No. 3.

Wisdom, John. 1961. Review of *Psychoanalysis, Scientific Method and Philosophy*. Ed. Sidney Hook. *Q. Jl. exp. Psychology* 13, No. 1.

4

Wollheim on Freud

I

What is it that we want to know about Freud? These are, I think, most of the major questions, some of which survive prolonged frequentation: How did the theme of sexuality, and particularly infantile sexuality, get into the theory of the neuroses; and how was it kept there? Just how does Freud's conception of sexuality differ from the common view with which he contrasts it? What are we to make of Freud's claim that symptoms, errors, etc., are really actions and how are we to bring it into relation with the other idioms in which Freud characterized these phenomena and with the explanation of them which he actually proffers? What is the force of Freud's claim that these phenomena have meaning and that we know their meaning but do not know that we know it? And how are we to assure ourselves that the meanings which Freud arrives at by employing his interpretative technique and/or principles are the correct ones? What is the status of the death instinct and why was it introduced?

Before I go on to assess Wollheim's answers to these questions, I had better say that the value of his book may not depend on their adequacy for he devotes considerable attention to topics I have not mentioned, such as the posthumously published *Project for a Scientific Psychology* of 1895 and the over-all coherence of Freud's later metapsychological speculations. If you find nothing problematic about the character of statements such as that 'at the very beginning, all the libido is accumulated in the id' and 'at first the whole available quantity of libido is stored up in the ego' but would like to see how they can be reconciled with one another, or if you wonder what, since the energy of the id is libido, the energy of the superego can be, and are happy to be told that the answer is aggression, then Wollheim's book can

This review of Richard Wollheim, *Freud* (London: Fontana Modern Masters, 1971) first appeared in *Inquiry*, Vol. 15, 1–2 (Summer 1972) and is reprinted by permission.

be of considerable use to you. He has some elegant and concise exposition in places and sometimes makes the involved relations of Freud's later thought surveyable.

II

How did the theme of sexuality get into the theory of the neuroses? As to this question, there are two views; though one would not gather this from Wollheim's account. This would matter less if the one he gives were not almost certainly the wrong one. According to Wollheim, Freud's 'new estimate of the importance of sexuality' was due to the fact that 'the trail of free associations in which he now put his trust ended in sexual ideas'. According to the view I should like to recommend, the theme of sexuality was not put into the theory of the neuroses by the associations of Freud's patients. It was always there. However, the view which Wollheim does not explicitly mention nevertheless makes its presence felt by goading him into absurd reconstructions in an attempt to undercut it.

Wollheim presents us with the standard picture of Freud's being dragged kicking and screaming toward a sexual etiology of the neuroses. On page 11 he refers to the theme of sexuality as 'a disturbing note' which Freud 'only reluctantly' took account of. On page 33 he writes that 'Freud's views [as to the importance of sexuality] changed slowly, very much against the grain'. To support this view Wollheim quotes from Freud's 1888 essay in Villaret's *Medical Dictionary*. But Freud's retrospective denial that he had entertained a sexual etiology for hysteria before he began the practice of psychoanalysis is sufficient to induce an acute scotoma in Wollheim and he completely misreads (I can't even say misinterprets) the passage he quotes from. 'As regards what is often asserted to be the preponderant influence of abnormalities in the sexual sphere upon the development of hysteria, it must be said that its importance is as a rule over-estimated' (p. 33). These words don't mean what Wollheim takes them to mean. They allude not to psychosexuality but to diseases of the internal genitalia like the ovaries.

In the next sentence, Freud makes this clear by citing as reasons for his judgement that 'the influence of abnormalities in the sexual sphere has been overestimated' the fact that 'hysteria has been observed in women with a complete lack of genitalia', and that 'the majority of women with diseases of the sexual organs do not suffer from hysteria'.

And in the following sentence, the last in the paragraph, he states unequivocally the view which Wollheim (and not only Wollheim) is at such pains to deny he held before he began the practice of psychoanalysis, even in its crudest form. 'Conditions related functionally to sexual life play a great part in the etiology of hysteria (as of all neuroses), and they do so on account of the high psychical significance of this function, especially in the female sex' (Standard Edition, Vol. 1, p. 50).

After this illustration of Wollheim's propensity to scotomization, it is not surprising that he fails to notice the incoherences in Freud's account of *how* rather than when he came upon the influence of sexual factors in the neuroses. Wollheim gives as one of the influences which led Freud to an appreciation of the importance of sexuality the discovery of the pathogenic character of masturbation and *coitus interruptus* in neurasthenia (in the inclusive sense). Though Freud did say this, he also, when apprehensive about the admission that he was convinced of the relevance of sexuality before undertaking his investigation of the psychoneuroses, said the opposite. In his *Autobiographical Study,* he wrote, 'Under the influence of my surprising discovery [of the role of sexuality in the psychoneuroses] I now took a momentous step. I went beyond the domain of hysteria and began to investigate the sexual life of so-called neurasthenics'.

So much for sexuality. What of infantile sexuality? How did it come to be the specific factor in the production of neurotic illness? Wollheim's answer is once again that the free associations of Freud's patients invariably led to it.

The 'traumatic event' . . . from which the ideas ['which made themselves felt in the symptoms'] derive, was eventually located right back in infancy, and—a more disturbing note—if the patient's associations were to be trusted, it was found invariably to have a sexual character. (p. 11)

But at this stage (1895–6) the 'sexual character' in question was confined to responses to sexual interference passively endured by the child, rather than its own sexuality. Wollheim thinks this 'implausible' view a tribute to the strength of Freud's reluctance to 'credit the infant with wishes and impulses from which tradition and orthodoxy had tried so hard to protect it'.

. . . one way in which Freud tried to block the road to infantile sexuality was— though he tried hard not to think of it in this light—by invoking a quite scandalous hypothesis about the family life of the Viennese *bourgeoise*. (p. 39)

(The scandal wasn't confined to the *bourgeoise*. Freud thought infantile seduction much more common in working class families but believed that their 'inferior intellectual and moral development' had a prophylactic effect.) 'In the so-called "seduction theory", we can see the lengths to which Freud was prepared to go in accounting for the facts of mental disorder as he saw them without compromising the innocence of childhood' (p. 11). So that according to Wollheim, far from the seduction theory's suggesting that Freud nurtured an overreadiness to discover pathogenic factors from sexual life in his patient's history, it is evidence of the lengths to which his puritan aversion to ascribing sexual impulses to children could take him.

Is it really plausible to suggest that Freud, who implicated his father in sexual assaults on his brothers and sisters and had persuaded himself that he harbored an unconscious craving for sexual connection with his nine-year-old daughter, would have been subject to inhibitions about attributing infantile sexual feelings to his patients? This is a step that had been taken long since by other psychopathologists; in 1886 Krafft-Ebing observed, 'Every physician conversant with nervous affections and diseases incident to childhood is aware of the fact that manifestation of sexual instinct may occur in very young children'. In any case, Freud was already committed to the capacity of infants to experience sexual pleasure in his etiology of the obsessional neuroses, which were due to their having first undergone the seductions with pleasure and then repeated the experience with younger children.

There are other reasons why Freud's belated recognition of infantile sexuality is not open to the construction Wollheim puts upon it. The realization that his patients were recollecting fantasies and not events would have given him no warrant for universalizing their infantile experience. And if we modify Wollheim's question for him so that it becomes, 'Why did Freud not attribute infantile incestuous fantasies to *his patients* if not because of an aversion to sexuality?', the answer is because the transition from seductions to fantasies of seduction is a transition from an intervening to a non-intervening factor. And Freud would have been left not with an infantile sexual etiology of the neuroses, but a mere precursor abnormality. He would have found his way back to a specialized version of the theories of inherited neuropathic temperament which it was his boast to have superseded.

Another consideration is that universalizing infantile sexuality would have been of no use to him in resolving his etiological problem. We must remember that the reasoning that took him into the patient's infancy was that the etiological agent must have both determining and traumatic power. If he were to settle for a universal contingency like infantile sexuality he would have lost this justification for his emphasis on infancy. And Freud was perfectly aware of this point. In 1896 he wrote, 'Of course if infantile sexuality were an almost universal occurrence it would prove nothing to find it in every case'. Far from coming to his rescue, the recognition of infantile sexuality would have called the etiological status of the infantile fantasies into doubt, as indeed, it eventually did. Perhaps the most frequently expressed criticism of Freud's post-seduction theory was why a factor that was universal ('a typical fantasy of the oedipal period') should be credited with the production of neurotic illness.

Wollheim seems to feel that Freud has met this objection by his invocation of the constitutional factor.

> Freud never ceased to respect the constitutional factor, which carried the implication that one individual might fail to tolerate, or to find compatible, what another could readily accommodate. (p. 146)

What Freud thought of the constitutional factor when invoked to safe-guard the etiological pretensions of theories other than his own can be inferred from his comments on Rank's birth trauma. 'No body of evidence has been collected to show that difficult and protracted birth does in fact coincide with the development of a neurosis.'

> If however we try to find a place for the constitutional factor by qualifying his statement with the proviso, let us say, that what is really important is the extent to which the individual reacts to the variable intensity of the trauma of birth, we should be depriving his theory of its significance and should be relegating the new factor introduced by him to a position of minor importance: the factor which decided whether a neurosis should supervene or not would lie in a differ-ent, and once more an unknown field. (*The Problem of Anxiety*, revised edition, [London 1961], pp. 65–66)

It seems that only Freud's deuces are wild.

But Wollheim is quite right to attempt to explain how it is that Freud came to maintain the seduction theory, for it certainly requires explaining. Maybe it happened like this: beginning with hysterical symptoms which per-tained to what we would now call erotogenic zones, anal pains, say, and going, in accordance with his requirement that the explanatory episode must have determining as well as traumatic power, in search of one which involved the anus he fetched up against a (quite authentic) experience in which the child was sodomized. This placed the symptoms less obviously connected with sexuality, like nausea, in a new light, and he repeated the procedure with respect to them and with similarly successful outcomes. Freud's willingness to credit the authenticity of the seductions may have also received some reinforcement from his discovery of his own incestuous incli-nations towards his nine year-old daughter.

So much for the seduction theory itself. Our question now is how did the mistaken reconstructions come about? Freud gradually allowed himself to be guided by more and more tenuous links between the symptoms and the putatively pathogenic episodes to which he attributed them, with fewer inhibitions about telling the patient what it was he was expected to remem-ber, until at some point he committed himself to a reconstruction which 'met with contradiction in definitely ascertainable circumstances' and he found himself at a loss. But why, if this is the way things went, did not Freud himself tell us so?

In later years, Freud recurred on several occasions to the seduction episode, and his accounts are significantly inconsistent both with each other and with what he said at the time. On one occasion, he explained the seduc-tion error in the following terms:

> one was readily inclined to accept as true and etiologically significant the state-ments made by patients in which they ascribed their symptoms to passive sexual experiences in early childhood. (*Collected Papers*, Vol. 1, [London 1924])

I won't say that this statement is a lie, since as we all know, a lie is an interested falsehood propagated by someone not Freud. But it is blatantly untrue. And in two respects. First, in that Freud went out of his way at the time to assure his readers that his conviction as to the veridicality of the seduction episodes was not based on the patients' statements. Second, in that though the patients may have made misleading statements as to the *occurrence* of the seduction episodes (though even this is doubtful), they did not make statements in which they ascribed their condition to the seduction episodes. Freud said at the time,

> [patients] are generally indignant if we tell them that something of the sort is coming to light; they can be induced only under the strongest compulsion of the treatment to engage in reproducing the scenes . . . they still try, even after going through them again in the most convincing fashion, to withhold belief by emphasizing the fact that they have no feeling of recollecting these scenes as they had in the case of other forgotten material.

and 'patients assure me emphatically of their unbelief'. How are these remarks to be reconciled with Freud's later accounts that his patients related 'stories' of infantile seduction to him or 'told me they had been seduced by their fathers'?

Perhaps some of his patients did come to believe that they remembered these seduction episodes, but I suspect that they did so only after having been assured by Freud of their veridicality. In a letter to Fliess (28 April 1897), he reports responding to a new patient's confession of having suffered advances from her father at the age of eight by assuring her 'that similar and worse things must have happened to her in infancy'. And that the sexual etiology of neuroses is something in which Freud already had a special investment is suggested by the following remark in a letter to Fliess (letter 21) of August, 1894, apropos of some reflections by Möbius on neuroses: 'fortunately he is not on the track of sexuality.'

Why does it matter? It matters because it gives us good reason for believing that what Freud really discovered in 1897, but could not bring himself to acknowledge, was that the infantile incestuous material produced by his patients was a function of his own interest in the subject. The discovery of the falsity of some of his infantile reconstructions placed Freud in the following dilemma: if the incestuous material produced with such uniformity by his patients had no historical warrant, how was it to be accounted for? Either it was an artifact of Freud's method, due partly to the effect of his preconceptions on his patients' thoughts, dreams, reminiscences, etc., and partly to the enormous discretion he permitted himself in interpreting these; or his reconstructions were correct except in one point: they were reconstructions of fantasies and not of events. And we are expected to be overwhelmed at Freud's 'moral courage' in opting for the latter alternative!

Why is Wollheim so anxious to assure himself that Freud had a decided aversion to the theme of infantile sexuality at the time that he arrived at the seduction hypothesis? Isn't it just a tribute to the worrying power of the contamination thesis—the view that the incestuous material produced by Freud's patients was a function of his own expectations and, occasionally, explicit suggestions? That this is the natural construction to put on the seduction theory episode is suggested by the fact that Freud himself felt so; for why else was the admission that he had abandoned the seduction theory delayed for over eight years (or as Wollheim prefers to put it, 'only slowly assimilated into the published work')? So much for how the theme of infantile sexuality got into the theory of the neuroses. Now as to how it was kept there.

III

On page 108 we are told that one of the sources of

> [the] privileges or liberties in which Freud confirmed sexuality, and which have so often been contested by his more pious or respectable critics . . . is an extended inquiry into the history of sexuality, which traces it to a time before that at which it is ordinarily found.

Among the evidences for the validity of this inquiry, Wollheim cites 'that provided, profusely, by the psycho-neuroses [for] . . . the neuroses reveal, or make reference to, infantile impulses . . .' (p. 111). This is too reminiscent of Dewey's Vermont farmer who weighs his pigs by placing them on one end of a plank, piling rocks on the other end until the plank balances, and then guessing the weight of the rocks. What authorizes us to make inferences concerning infancy from the behavior of neurotics undergoing analysis?

Wollheim has one more try at answering this question on a later page (154) which deals with transference. The transference 'provided evidence for infantile sexuality, since, in repeating infantile attitudes, it invariably exhibits them permeated with sexuality'. But how does one exhibit infantile attitudes permeated with sexuality? Or better, to descend to the details of Freud's infantile reconstructions, how does a woman exhibit the fact that she experienced intense disappointment at her lack of a penis and blamed her mother for this? How does a male patient exhibit the fact that he had entertained passive sexual wishes toward his father but was intimidated from indulging them by the prospect of castration? What we need in the way of elucidation is a circumstantial first-hand account of how this works. Wollheim intimates in his Preface that he is just the man to give it us. But for some reason he won't. In any case, he doesn't.

If we turn to Freud's own account in his paper, 'Repetition, Recollection, and Working Through', our suspicions as to the dubiousness of the whole procedure are not allayed. Freud is explaining how one gains a knowledge of the fantasies of early childhood through transference behavior.

> The patient . . . does not remember how he came to a helpless and hopeless deadlock in his infantile searchings after the truth of sexual matters hut he produces a mass of confused dreams and associations, complains that he never succeeds at anything, and describes it as his fate never to be able to carry anything through. He does not remember that he was intensely ashamed of certain sexual activities but he makes it clear that he is ashamed of the treatment to which he has submitted himself, and does his utmost to keep it a secret. (*Collected Papers,* Vol. 2, [London, 1924], p. 369)

Doesn't the connection between the infantile fantasies and the behavior said to exhibit them seem rather tenuous? Why then does Freud think them proof of the correctness of his speculations as to the fantasies of early childhood? 'One is compelled to believe in them by irresistible evidence in the structure of the neuroses.' But haven't we heard something like this before? In presenting his reasons for crediting the occurrence of infantile seductions, he adduced, in the first of the seduction trilogy, 'the delicate but firm interrelationship of the structural elements of the neuroses'; in the second, 'the logical structure of the neurotic manifestations', and in the third, 'the inevitable completion of the associative and logical structure'.

The point to bear in mind is this. The method, technique, mode of procedure, call it what you will, through which Freud came to grief in the mid-nineties, the method which led him to the construction of nonveridical seduction episodes, is the same method on which he based his reconstruction of infantile fantasy life. With this difference: that his post-seduction infantile reconstructions are so tenuously linked to the workaday world that never again could the fate of the seduction theory overtake them—'contradiction in definitely ascertainable circumstances'.

Wollheim's account of Freud's extension of the notion of sexuality sees it as a protest against 'the absurd narrowness of the conventional definition'.

> To bring out the inadequacy of the conventional definition, Freud . . . went on to point out that there are many forms of behaviour deviating from the norm in object, or in aim, or both, and yet which we could not but think of as sexual. (pp. 109–10)

This makes it sound as if it were Freud's merit to have insisted boldly, in the teeth of prim denials, that fellatio was a sexual activity. Wollheim rescues his account from this absurdity at the cost of rendering it pointless. It was not, he argues, the popular *use* of the term which Freud corrected but only the popular *definition*. In this connection Wollheim refers mysteriously to the 'discrepancy between the way in which the notion of sexuality was ordinarily defined and the way in which it was in fact employed' (p. 110). I would have supposed that you learn what the popular definition of sexual is by seeing what it is that people call sexual. For what occasion would popular opinion have for proffering explicit definitions of sexuality?

The reason why Wollheim's account is beside the point is that the objections to Freud's extended use of the term sexual most often came up in explanatory contexts, and it was its concertina-like character, not its mere breadth, that was viewed with suspicion. Whenever the question of the sexuality of his infantile pathogenic factors comes up, Freud acts as if the only possible objection to his use of the term 'sexual' must be due to insistence on restricting it to genital activity, and proceeds to treat his audience to an account of adult perversions to justify his extension of the term to oral and anal interests. But this is not at all the source of our perplexity as to why Freud insists on characterizing his pathogenic factors as sexual. That perplexity has its origin in the fact that though Freud speaks as if he were denying something, excluding the possibility that some nonsexual interpersonal vicissitude might be pathogenic for the neuroses, it becomes increasingly difficult to say what infantile transaction Freud would concede to be nonsexual. Under these circumstances his denial that 'other mental excitations' could lead to repression becomes comparatively empty of content. Consider the occasion on which he vindicates his infantile sexual etiology against an apparent counter-example—the effect on the Kaiser's character of the natal injury which crippled his arm—by pointing out that the real determinant was his mother's attitude toward this, 'She withdrew her love' (*New Introductory Lectures* [London, 1933], p. 87). We have come a long way from nongenital sexuality.

IV

What is it that Freud is saying about the nature of symptoms? Wollheim goes about answering this question in a strange way for a philosopher of his time and place. He tells us that symptoms are the expression of thoughts, that they are actions, that they are substitute gratifications, that they are compromises, thus reperpetrating the very idioms which have stupefied us. What we need to be given are the examples and analogies on the basis of which these idioms were introduced and which presumably suggested them, so that we can form some idea of what residual force an expression like 'action' or 'gratification' has when applied to a symptom.

The first thing to be clear about is something which talk of Freud's conceptual innovation with respect to the notion of action obscures. It leads Wollheim to take the mistaken view that 'the desires expressed in symptoms . . . are of a form to which [the distinction 'between the expression of a certain desire and its satisfaction'] does not apply' (p. 91). But there are symptoms which stand in a quite straightforward instrumental relation to the desires they attempt to satisfy. Consider the case of Dora's cousin who produced gastric pains in order to avoid having to attend her sister's wedding.

It was not the pains themselves that constituted the gratification, but the conventional exemption from social obligations that suffering them involved. They were a stratagem for realizing a wish, not its consummation. The requirement of the bedtime ritual girl that the door between her bedroom and her parents' be kept open was intended to ensure that since they could be overheard they did not have intercourse. And even the inefficacious rituals with the eiderdown and the bolster and bedstead are described by Freud in instrumental idioms as attempts at magical intervention. And there are many other similar examples.

On page 91, Wollheim writes, 'it might be objected that Freud's view of the symptom requires us to believe that many involuntary acts are really actions that we undertake. This is an objection that has already arisen over the parapraxis, but it might seem that the implausibility is much greater here, in the case, say, of tics or attacks of vomiting than it was with forgetting names or bungling actions.'

Wollheim's list of phenomena which Freud requires us to think of as actions is heavily bowdlerized, and the examples he gives are not the most troubling ones. Among the phenomena which Freud requires us to think of as actions are delusions, phobias, and the hallucinations of *delirium tremens*. That developing a phobia is for Freud just as much an intelligent performance as deciding what suit to make trumps is implied by some remarks in the *New Introductory Lectures*.

> In the case of phobias one can see clearly how [an] internal danger is transformed into an external one . . . in his phobia he makes a displacement and is now afraid of an external situation. What he gains thereby is obvious; it is that he feels he can protect himself better in this way.

In *The Problem of Anxiety,* this point was elaborated on in the following terms:

> The anxiety belonging to a phobia is conditional: it only emerges when the object of it is perceived—and rightly so, since it is only then that the danger situation is present. There is no need to be afraid of being castrated by a father who is not there. On the other hand, one cannot get rid of a father: he can appear whenever he chooses. But if he is replaced by an animal, all one has to do is avoid the sight of it—that is its presence—in order to be free from anxiety and danger. 'Little Hans', therefore, imposed a restriction on his ego. The young Russian had an even easier time of it, for it was hardly a deprivation for him not to look at a particular picture book any more. If his naughty sister had not kept showing him the book with a picture of the wolf standing upright in it, he would have been able to feel safe from his fear.

But Wollheim keeps all this to himself.

What of those symptoms which do not lend themselves to a full-fledged instrumental account? Has Wollheim's characterization of them as satisfactions or gratifications any more warrant here? Consider the story of Alnaschar, the barber's fifth brother. One day when he was squatting in his accustomed place in the bazaar with his entire capital of glassware at his feet, he fell into a brown study in which he imagined a succession of entrepreneurial coups that enabled him to marry a highborn lady who, when she displeased him, he would spurn with his foot. At this point out goes Alnaschar's foot and down comes his display of glassware to lie in shards at his feet.

Though Freud invites us to assimilate symptoms to Alnaschar's fantasy, often the most natural way to construe them, and all that Freud himself has any warrant for, is as like his outflung foot; their relation to the thoughts seems to be that of expressive concomitants and not gratifications. The fellatio component in Dora's cough represented the very affair we are told she became ill in order to disrupt. 'Gratification', as Wollheim, following Freud, employs it, is pseudo-functional, phantom-homeostatic.

In his account of how symptoms may be said to gratify the wishes they express, Wollheim attempts to repair a deficiency in Freud's view by introducing the notion of a presuppositional relation between desires and beliefs. 'If a desire presupposes a belief, then that belief receives support from the desire.' E.g., '. . . the point of Dora's desires is to reinforce the beliefs that would have to be true if the desires were to be . . . satisfied' (p. 135). How does one decide which of the innumerable beliefs to which the desire expressed in a symptom might be said to stand in a presuppositional relation is that which it is designed to reinforce?

The bedtime ritual girl's dealings with the eiderdown presupposed that her mother was capable of conceiving, but was it an attempt to reinforce that belief? Dora's aphonia presupposed Herr K's absence, but can't be construed as desiring it. The tablecloth ritual presupposed the disappointing wedding night which it was, we are told, an attempt to correct, but it did not reinforce that belief, and even less was it the function or the point of the ritual to reinforce it. So Wollheim's analysis would seem to have no generality: but neither does it illuminate the cases to which Wollheim applies it.

Consider Wollheim's account of Dora's pseudo-appendicitis. It represented a pregnancy, and therefore argues Wollheim, that which is the normal prelude to pregnancy, intercourse. So the unconscious, whose exemption from logic permits it to equate an attack of abdominal pain accompanied by a menstrual discharge with an accouchement, is nevertheless incapable of forgoing the requirement that intercourse must have preceded conception (and by nine months too, so that though intermittently lacking logic it nevertheless possesses arithmetic). The arbitrariness of the whole proceeding becomes apparent when we consider that we could just as easily argue that since Dora did not have sexual relations with Herr K, her (symbolic) pregnancy presupposes the belief that she conceived virginally, and therefore reinforces it. In fact, this is just what Freud does argue. Dora who had realized a phantasy of childbirth through her abdominal pain was now able to identify herself unconsciously with the Madonna, because, Freud tells us, like the Madonna she had given birth while yet a virgin.

Whether we are attempting to follow Freud's explanation of dreams, errors, or symptoms, the same question obtrudes itself. What is the relation of the agent-subject to the unconscious processes which eventuated in the phenomena?

The question that Freud addresses to Dora with respect to her gastric pains, 'Who are you copying?' employs the language of intentionality and assimilates her case to that of Marx's beard which he is said to have modeled on that of a bust of Zeus. Is Dora's cousin's stomach-ache the occulted or latent intentional object of her mimicry as Zeus's beard was the manifest intentional object of Marx's, or its cause in a nonintentionalistic sense?

All Wollheim gives us in this connection are a few opaque phrases and an allusion to Freud's argument from post-hypnotic compliance.

> . . . a man may know something, or something about himself, without knowing that he knows it: a point which Freud thought was proved beyond doubt by hypnosis and hypnotic suggestion (p. 75).

Just what was it that Freud thought was proved beyond all doubt? As often as Freud recurred to the evidence of post-hypnotic compliance he never made it clear just what it was that he believed the subject of the experiment at first professed himself ignorant of, and later remembered. Is it merely the activities of the hypnotist during the subject's trance? But why invoke the specialized phenomenon of post-hypnotic compliance for such a banal phenomenon as recall? The subject would on this construction not *remember* having acted in compliance with an order of which he was unaware, he would merely *infer* that he had done so from his memory of the order and his knowledge of hypnotic phenomena. But this would assimilate the unconscious to the merely forgotten, beyond which Freud was insistent on extending it. This suggests that Freud really thinks of the experiment as showing that what is recalled is the act of compliance itself; just as, in the case of the missed train connection, Freud later remembered seeing the sign reading 'Hook of Holland' of which he was oblivious at the time. But how much sense can we make of the notion of the belated recognition of noumenal agency detected not inductively but by a subsequent act of introspection? In this instance, as too often, when Wollheim completes his elucidations we are left to do the real work for ourselves.

V

How are we to assure ourselves that the meaning Freud proffers as the source of the symptoms is the correct one? As always when Wollheim broaches the issue of evidence there is something forced and unnatural in the way that the discussion develops. On page 91 we are told that 'once the sense is realized or the wish becomes conscious, the symptom vanishes'. Only Wollheim doesn't say at this point, what emerges much later, that there are special criteria for the sense's being realized and the wish's being made conscious; criteria so special that the sense's being realized and the wish's being made conscious are compatible with their nonfulfilment.

On a later page (151), Wollheim writes, 'But the phrase' "making what is unconscious conscious" is deceptive. Merely to tell a man of his unconscious wishes is not necessarily to make those wishes conscious'. This is badly put. Freud's point (and Wollheim's) is not that merely telling a man of his unconscious wishes is not necessarily to make those wishes conscious, but that his merely accepting that they are his unconscious wishes is not sufficient to do so: that is, we are no longer to take a patient's awareness that he harbors certain wishes as evidence that they have been made conscious. ('We succeed in . . . establishing a complete intellectual acceptance of what is repressed—but the repression itself is still unremoved' [*Collected Papers*, Vol. 5, p. 82].) Wollheim continues: 'The original wishes might remain unconscious; if, that is, repression persisted, now manifesting itself in the form of resistance.' One suspects a certain disingenuousness in retaining the word 'resistance' to designate the non-occurrence of the 'inner change in the patient' which must accompany mere recognition of the unconscious impulse if it is to have been made conscious, when it has hitherto been used to refer to the reluctance of the patient to accept interpretations or his failure to produce material confirmatory of them. The effect of its retention is to blind us to the fact that no criterion but therapeutic inefficacy is provided for determining when this kind of resistance has been encountered.

Wollheim concludes with a scathing quotation from a paper of 1910 about those inexperienced in psychoanalysis who imagine that knowledge of the unconscious is in itself important. But the fault of those who arrived at this conclusion was in simplemindedly believing that Freud means what he says, and therefore concluding that to enlighten a patient as to the significance of his symptoms is to deprive them of that insulation from uptake on which their ability to constitute gratifications depends. And this was not a matter of the popular conception of psychoanalysis lagging behind the development of Freud's thought. For in the same year in which they were chided for their *naïveté* Freud made his most extravagant claims as to the therapeutic value of uptake. In his address to the second international psychoanalytic congress, Freud told his colleagues:

> You know that the psychoneuroses are substitutive gratifications of instincts the existence of which one is forced to deny to oneself and to others. Their capacity to exist depends on this distortion and disguise. When the riddle they hold is

solved and the solution accepted by the sufferers these diseases will no longer be able to exist. There is hardly anything like it in medicine: in fairy tales you hear of evil spirits whose power is broken when you can tell them their name which they have kept secret. . . . Diseased people cannot let their various neuroses become known—their apprehensive overanxiousness which is to conceal their hatred, their agoraphobia which conceals disappointed ambition, their obsessive action which represents self-reproaches for evil intentions . . . Disclosure of the secret will attack at its most sensitive point 'the etiological equation' from which the neuroses descend. . . . (*Collected Papers*, Vol. 2, [London, 1924], p. 292)

With the discovery that 'the wish' can be 'simultaneously conscious and unconscious' (p. 151), the symptom-remission rationale for the correctness of an interpretation, on which Freud once leaned so heavily, is no longer really available. If we can invoke so many explanations of why the persistence of the symptoms is compatible with the correctness of the interpretation (that recognition of the wish is unaccompanied by an inner change; that the symptom is overdetermined ['One need not be surprised or misled if a symptom seems to persist with undiminished force though one of its sexual meanings has already been resolved' (1908).]; that the patient is self-punitively determined to cling to his illness) we will have made it almost impossible to discover that an interpretation, in terms of repressed sexuality, say, has failed in therapeutic efficacy simply because it is wrong and the theory from which it derives false.

Isn't there a rather obtrusive asymmetry between the old advantage from illness which depended on certain contingent features of the patient's situation which could he altered and the new (dis)advantage from illness which depends on its punishing character and is therefore not a contingent feature of the situation since illnesses are necessarily incapacitating? We might discover empirically that the advantage from illness played only a negligible role or none at all if the illness persisted when the patient was deprived of advantage or granted it unconditionally. But how would we discover that the illness was not self-punishing? The only suggestion Freud offers is that it sometimes happens that the patient contracts an organic illness or has a serious misfortune and the superego, satisfied that an adequate level of suffering is being maintained, relents and the neurosis disappears. (Not such a bad chap after all.)

We are told that the ego courts suffering in order to atone to the omniscient superego for its unlawful wishes and also from masochistic motives of enjoyment. But why should the superego be placated by the ego's indulgence in masochistic pleasure? Does its omniscience fail it at this point? I don't believe Wollheim understands these sentences. I don't believe they are understandable. The surroundings are missing. But I don't know how this point is to be enforced.

An expression which Wollheim repeatedly employs in connection with the issue of validation, whose familiarity he mistakes for intelligibility, and thus leaves completely unelucidated, is 'the associations showed'. (He twice invokes it when there is no warrant for it in the cases he supposes himself to be paraphrasing; on page 90 he speaks of 'the Rat Man's association from "getting rid of his *dick*" to "getting rid of Dick"'. There was no such association. In the original record of the case Freud says of the Dick-dick pun, 'This came from me and he did not accept it'. And on page 92, of Dora's pseudo-appendicitis, 'through her associations Freud equated this with a hysterical pregnancy'. Not true. Freud put the verbals on her.)

On page 90 we are told of '[a] woman patient . . . given to hysterical vomiting' that '[her] associations showed that this represented . . . [a] wish that she might be continuously pregnant . . . by as many men as possible', and are assured that '[in] the symptom both these wishes are represented . . . as fulfilled'. I understand how the association might show that she had these wishes but how could they show that 'in the symptom they are represented as fulfilled'?

The inordinately discretionary character of Wollheim's conception of what associations can show inadvertently comes to light in his account of why Paul (the man with the rats) suddenly decided on a drastic slimming regimen. He was in a murderous rage with a rival called Dick which in German means 'fat' ('dick'). This acted as a switch word causing his repressed rage to manifest itself as a determination to lose weight (infelicitously referred to by Wollheim as 'getting rid of his "dick"' which, given the context, has distracting connotations). The arbitrariness of this proceeding is brought out by the fact that Freud used the connection between 'Dick' and 'dick' to support the thesis that Paul was expressing a suicidal attack on *himself* as expiation for the violence of his feelings toward Dick; not, as Wollheim has it, expressing a murderous attack on Dick.

As an illustration of the way in which Wollheim allows himself to get out of touch with the concrete practice of explanation from which Freud's formulations draw whatever interest they have, preferring rather to ensconce himself in flattering delusions of synoptic grasp, consider his account of how the mechanisms of symptom formation in phobias, compulsions, and paranoia differ from that in hysteria.

Whereas

[in] hysteria there is an associative chain running from the repressed idea and terminating in a bodily conversion, which is the symptom. [In the other neuroses there is] an intermediary stage . . . 'substitutive formation', in which a conscious or preconscious idea is substituted for the repressed idea, and it is this idea that is expressed in the symptoms and that forms the core of the neurosis. In obsessional neurosis, the substitution takes the form of reaction-formation, in which an idea opposed to the original idea is intensified: in paranoia, it takes the

form of projection, in which the original idea is referred away and treated as a perception of the external world: in anxiety-hysteria, it takes the form of displacement, from which the phobias derive . . . (p. 149)

Has Wollheim forgotten that, though no paranoid, Dora *projected* her own self-reproaches onto her father; that her disgust at Herr K's kiss was a *projection* of her revulsion for her own leucorrhoea; that the same disgust was a *displacement* upward of her genital excitation which she then *reversed* into an experience of nausea, thus combining mechanisms Wollheim thinks distinctive of phobias and obsessions respectively; that the patient who Freud said gave him his first insight into the nature of obsessional disorder *displaced* his self-reproaches from his perverse and exploitatory sexual practices onto scruples about the circulation of unsterilized bank notes; that the account of hysterical loss of vision which he himself recounts on page 125 invokes the mechanism of *reaction formation*; that the sensation of Herr K's penis pressing against Dora's waist was *displaced* upward into a sensation of pressure against her thorax: that the girl with the bedtime ritual expressed *directly*, i.e. in a manner which Wollheim thinks distinctive of hysteria, her fear of the prospect of her mother's pregnancy by her dealings with the eiderdown and of her parents' having sexual relations by her manipulation of the bolster and bedstead: that the tablecloth lady similarly expressed *directly* her wish that her husband had been potent on his wedding night through her compulsive ritual (and along an *associative* route [bed and board] indistinguishable from that which occurs in the construction of hysterical symptoms); that similarly, the Wolf Man's fear of swallowtail butterflies was formed in accordance with an *associative mechanism* and not displacement; that Paul's slimming compulsion, of which Wollheim himself gave an account, proceeded along the associative route Dick-dick and *directly* expressed his murderous (or self-murderous) impulse. Perhaps Wollheim would say that none of these pertain to the 'core of the neurosis' to which he was referring.

VI

Wollheim devotes several pages (179–86) to expounding the significance of the death instinct, the great theoretical innovation which transformed self-destructiveness from an aberration due to the deflection of aggressiveness inward into a primal force alongside that of self-preservation, so that, to vary Ernest Jones's joke, charity and murder both begin at home. But in his account of Freud's theory of the death instinct, Wollheim seems to be incapacitated by a tin ear. Confronted with a speculation that 'the most universal endeavour of all living substance is to return to the quiescence of the inorganic world', that 'the mute but powerful death instincts desire to be at peace', that 'the goal of life is death', Wollheim finds it appropriate to remark that 'Freud required of even the most abstract or speculative of his hypotheses that it should not be assessed otherwise than as part of a theory that is, in its overall intentions, empirical' (p. 181), and: 'From a certain way in which the mind functions, Freud inferred the death instinct' (p. 184). Someone once remarked that a man was nothing but a bundle of protoplasm on his way to becoming manure. Is it plausible to suggest that he was calling attention to the nitrogen cycle?

Wollheim tells us that Freud 'rested his case partly on the facts of sadism and masochism' (p. 181). Consider sadism: how are we to get from 'sexual satisfaction linked to the condition of the sexual object's suffering pain, ill treatment and humiliation' to 'the universal endeavour of all living substance to return to the quiescence of the inorganic world'? The latter is more reminiscent of the maiden aunts in *Arsenic and Old Lace* than the Marquis de Sade.

As for sexual masochism, it was plausibly explained in the narcissism essay of 1914 as a desire, not for pain, but for the sexual excitation it stimulates. In the later metapsychological works it becomes a 'mysterious' phenomenon which is only explicable when seen as a manifestation of the fusion of Eros with the death instinct. But again, what has the 'drive to re-establish an original inorganic state' to do with Mlle. Lambercier-Wanda-Ayesha-Dragon Lady fantasies or the desire to have prostitutes address one as 'tu'? Ernest Jones himself maintained that there was so little objective support to be found for Freud's theory of the death instinct that one had to consider 'subjective contributions to its inception' and found these in the narcissistic satisfaction it affords.

That there is nothing tendentious in the view that Freud's conception of 'death as a point towards which the life of the individual moves' gives to death a congenial aspect it had hitherto lacked can be supported by considering some remarks made by Simmel, in his essay on ruins, written several years before *Beyond the Pleasure Principle*. The sight of ruins is tragic rather than sad, argued Simmel, because destruction 'is not something coming senselessly from the outside but rather the realisation of a tendency inherent in the deepest layer of the existence of the destroyed', an impression lacking, Simmel continued, 'when we describe a person as a ruin'. Freud's theory obliterated this difference and gave to human extinction 'that metaphysical calm which attaches to the decay of a material work as by virtue of a profound a priori' which Simmel found in ruins.

It is difficult to bring the theory of the death instinct as presented by Wollheim into relation with the concept which consoled Karen Horney for the premature death of her brother, at first felt as 'totally senseless', by persuading her 'that something in him had wanted to die', but later prompted the misgiving 'that it is too much of what we want to believe', since it 'smuggles omnipotence back into the *Es*'; or with that which prompted Freud himself to remark that if his essay had been produced by another man who had recently lost a beloved daughter, he would have presumed a connection between the two. One would be hard put to divine from Wollheim's account what the connection could possibly be.

In his Preface, Wollheim reminds us that on several occasions Freud referred to the majority of human beings as worthless. Instead of recognizing this corrupt and self-indulgent sentiment for an aberration quite at variance with the quality of moral greatness in Freud to which we respond (and which by a kind of halo effect reduces many of us to the level of credulity manifested by Wollheim in this book), Wollheim reports it with an air of sharing Freud's fastidiousness. The quality I mean is the freedom from censoriousness which makes us feel that if anyone must know and relate our shameful secrets we should prefer it to be Freud.

But Wollheim locates Freud's greatness elsewhere. To illustrate Freud's remoteness from 'the kind of bland and mindless optimism that he so utterly and heroically despised', Wollheim chooses to end his book with the following quotation from *Civilisation and its Discontents* to serve as his 'envoi'.

> I have not the courage to rise up before my fellow-men as a prophet, and I bow to the reproach that I can offer them no consolation; for at bottom that is what they are all demanding—the wildest revolutionaries no less passionately than the most virtuous believers.

Nietzsche was more discerning:

> Of all the means of consolation there is none so efficacious as the declaration that no consolation can be given. This implies such a distinction that the afflicted person will raise his head again.

The troubles of our proud and angry dust are from eternity and had better not fail.

5

The Myth of Freud's
Hostile Reception

When did Freud arrive? What was the situation on which he impinged? What sort of reception did he receive and how it is to be accounted for? There is a received answer to these questions: that due to their painful truth Freud's views only slowly became known and then only to be reviled in a manner almost unprecedented.

In his life of Freud, Ernest Jones tells us that 'in the first years of the century Freud and his writings were either quietly ignored or else they would be mentioned with a sentence or two of disdain as if not deserving any serious attention.'[1] Abraham Brill also paints a picture of Freud 'surrounded by a sceptical and hostile world . . . his theories of the neuroses . . . rejected and derided by the neurologists and psychiatrists of his time'.[2]

These remarks are more misleading than the necessity of representing a complex situation in a mnemonic formula can justify. Not only because of the fact, documented by Bry and Rifkin and endorsed by Henri Ellenberger in his monumental *Discovery of the Unconscious,* that 'for the time during which Freud was supposed to have been ignored' he received 'a great many signs of recognition and extraordinary respect', but for another reason.[3] In the passages I quoted, Jones speaks broadly of 'Freud and his writings', and Brill refers quite as broadly to 'the theories of the neuroses which (Freud) formulated during this period'. We all think we know to which writings and

This first appeared as the introduction to Frank Cioffi, ed., *Modern Judgements: Freud* (Macmillan, 1973), and is reprinted by permission.

1. Ernest Jones, *Sigmund Freud: Life and Work,* vol. 2 (London, 1958), p. 123.
2. A. Brill, *Lectures on Psychoanalytic Psychiatry* (London, 1948), p. 7.
3. Ilse Bry and Alfred H. Rifkin, 'Freud and the History of Ideas: Primary Sources, 1886–1900', in *Science and Psychoanalysis,* vol. 5 (New York, 1962), p. 28; Henri Ellenberger, *The Discovery of the Unconscious* (New York, 1970) particularly pp. 450, 454–55.

to which theories these remarks refer but like most accounts of Freud's reception during the decade or so after *Studies on Hysteria,* they mislead by their failure to take note of a rather surprising fact, to appreciate the significance of which a certain amount of background is needed. Sometime between 1893 and 1895 Freud came to believe that a sexual seduction in early childhood was an indispensable precondition for the development of psycho-neurotic illness. He proclaimed this conclusion in three papers published in 1896, one of which was also delivered as a lecture to his Vienna colleagues.

Freud was confirmed in this conviction by one of his own dreams, which he interpreted as evidence of an unconscious wish to have sexual relations with his nine-year-old daughter. But some time later an infantile reminiscence of having been excited by the sight of his mother naked suggested an alternative explanation of the appearance of seduction material in his patients' productions: that they were distorted reminiscences of the children's erotic impulses towards the cross-sex parent. In any case, for whatever reason, by September 1897 Freud had changed his mind and decided that the seduction theory was mistaken.

The startling fact referred to above is that Freud did not *publicly* repudiate the infantile seduction theory of hysteria until eight years later. Its bearing on the question of Freud's reception is that it is difficult to say at this date how much of the incredulity and derision Freud encountered in those years was provoked by claims which he himself had already privately rejected and which form no part of what came to be known as psychoanalysis. As late as 1909, Emile Kraeplin, in the eighth edition of his textbook, was still under the impression that Freud adhered to the seduction theory.[4]

We have seen how misleading is the contention that the usual response to the views that we today associate with Freud was silence or derision. It is more difficult to decide whether his celebrity was so long delayed that an explanation is called for. Our problem is threefold. When do we start counting? When do we stop? And how long is long?

Writing in 1932, Frank Alexander said of Freud's theories: 'All these concepts are today not only generally accepted, but they have already become emotionally assimilated, and like the theory of evolution or the cos-

---

4. This fact doesn't seem to have been taken in properly by students of the psychoanalytic movement. Marjorie Brierly, Marthe Robert, Erik Erikson, J.A.C. Brown, and J.C. Burnham all appear to confound, at least intermittently, the date at which Freud publicly renounced the seduction theory with the date at which he privately abandoned it. Other writers seem to forget that he ever held it. For example, David Stafford-Clark, in his book *What Freud Really Said* (London, 1967), cites as evidence of the unreasoning incredulity and hostility with which Freud's views were met, the criticism he received on the occasion on which he addressed the Society of Neurologists and Psychiatrists in 1896 with Krafft-Ebing in the chair. This was the meeting at which Freud expounded the infantile seduction theory, which he himself later described as having collapsed 'under the weight of its own improbability'.

mological doctrine of the planetary systems are now an integral part of modem thinking . . . .'[5] When did this state of affairs come about?

In his useful book on Freud's precursors, Lancelot Law Whyte refers to 'the years after the First World War when psychoanalysis was a novelty', thus evincing a common misconception. It is true that the character in Scott Fitzgerald's *This Side of Paradise* (1920), who describes herself as 'hipped on Freud and all that' is an advanced female, and that as late as 1918 H.L. Mencken could write: 'hard upon the heels of . . . the Montessori method, vers libre and the music of Stravinsky, psychoanalysis now comes to intrigue and harass the sedentary multipara who seek refuge in the women's clubs from the horrible joys of home life.'[6]

But Alfred Kuttner, who helped Brill with his translation of *The Interpretation of Dreams* and did much to publicise psychoanalysis among American intellectuals, remarked in 1922 in his contribution to the book *Civilization in the United States* that 'Freud after an initial resistance rapidly became epidemic in America'. In her contribution to the same volume the sexual reformer, Elsie Clews Parsons refers to the age as 'this post-Freudian day'.[7] A year later D.H. lawrence referred to the Oedipus complex as 'a household word . . . a commonplace of tea table chat'.

An allusion in Clifford Allen's *Modern Discoveries in Medical Psychology* (London, 1937) to a period around 1914 when 'society ladies became interested in psychoanalysis and went about talking of their complexes', provoked Ernest Jones to object that

> we have several times come across vague allusions to this supposed craze of society women for psychoanalysis, but we have never seen it placed in time so precisely. Unfortunately the author does not locate it in space so definitely as in time. Viennese society had certainly other things with which to occupy itself in 1914, at the beginning of the war, and London had hardly heard of the subject at that time.[8]

But it is to New York that Dr Allen's remark, though no doubt hyperbolic, has some application. By 1916 there were some five hundred self-styled psychoanalysts practising there. And it was there that Mabel Dodge Luhan conducted a salon at which psychoanalysis was a favourite topic of discussion and which Freud's American translator, the analyst Abraham Brill, was invited to address.

Mrs Luhan, who was analysed by both Brill and Smith Ely Jelliffe, though no mere society lady, did go about talking of her complexes:

---

5. F. Alexander, 'Psychoanalysis and Medicine'. *Mental Hygiene,* XVI (January 1932), pp. 63–84.

6. H.L. Mencken, 'Rattling the Subconscious'. *The Smart Set* (September 1918), p. 138.

7. Harold E. Sterns ed., *Civilization in the United States* (New York, 1922), p. 311.

8. *International Journal of Psychoanalysis,* XVIII (1937), pp. 483–84.

I enjoyed my visits . . . it became an absorbing game to play with oneself, reading one's motives, and trying to understand the symbols by which the soul expressed itself . . . I longed to draw others into the new world where I found myself: a world where things fitted into a set of definitions and terms that had never even been dreamt of. It simplified all problems to name them. There was the Electra complex, and the Oedipus complex and there was the libido with its manifold activities . . .[9]

Among those who argue that Freud's celebrity was unduly belated are Shakow and Rapaport, but they overlook the fact that Freud's works were written in a foreign language which, though it may have been known to a number of doctors and psychologists, had to be translated before they were accessible to the educated public.[10] The *Three Essays on Sexuality* was translated in 1910 as were the lectures which Freud delivered at Clark University. What is generally considered his greatest work, *The Interpretation of Dreams*, was not translated into English until 1913, and he was completely untranslated until Brill produced a selection of his papers on the psychoneuroses in 1909.

Though in the absence of agreed criteria the reader must decide for himself just how long long is, these facts do much to mitigate the impression of belated celebrity that may be produced by thinking of Freud's claims on the attention of the English-speaking world as dating from the turn of the century.

Perhaps the most useful observation to make with respect to the cultural climate in which Freud's early works appeared is the felt continuity of his explanatory modes and intuitions with literary culture and folk wisdom, with what Dr Johnson referred to 'as remarks on life, or axioms of morality as float in conversation and are transmitted to the world in proverbial sentences', rather than with esoteric scientific or philosophical speculation.

The reviewer of *Studies on Hysteria* for the *Neue Freie Presse* observed of the Breuer-Freud theory of hysteria that it was 'nothing but the kind of psychology used by poets'—and by the rest of us, he might have added. The following stanza from one of the songs in Tennyson's *The Princess* was often cited, both before and after Freud, as illustrating what the *Studies on Hysteria* (1895) referred to as 'strangulated affect':

Home they brought her warrior dead
She nor swooned nor uttered cry;
All her maidens, watching, said,
She must weep or she will die.[11]

---

9. Mabel Dodge Luhan, *Makes and Shakers* (New York, 1936), pp. 439–40.

10. D. Shakow and D. Rapaport, *The Influence of Freud on American Psychology* (Cleveland, Ohio, 1964).

11. This poem was sufficiently familiar that another of its lines, the one recording the abreaction, 'Like summer tempests came her tears', could, with a change of gender, be used as the title of the penultimate chapter of *The Wind in the Willows*.

Malcolm's injunction to Macduff ('Give sorrow words; the grief that does not speak/Whispers the o'er-fraught heart and bids it break'), or the incident in *Persuasion* when Captain Wentworth, encountering Anne Elliot after Louisa Musgrove's accident at Lyme Regis, comments, 'I am afraid you must have suffered from the shock, and the more from its not over-powering you at the time', might just as appositely have been invoked.

What also tends to be insufficiently stressed in the standard accounts of the intellectual climate in which Freud's work appeared is the currency of his sexual themes, particularly with reference to the neuroses, but even in their more general bearings.

The reviewer of *The Studies on Hysteria* for *Brain* remarked, on its pub-lication in 1895: 'It is interesting to note a return, in part at least, to the old theory of the origin of hysteria in sexual disorders.' However, the implica-tion that Freud was reviving a view which was moribund would seem to be unwarranted. If we consult the entry on hysteria in Hack Tuke's dictionary of medical psychology, published in 1892, we find it stated that:

> Among the activities artificially repressed in girls, it must be recognized that the sexual play an important part and, indeed, the frequent evidence given of dammed up sexual emotions . . . have led many to regard unsatisfied sexual desire as one of the leading causes of hysteria . . . forced abstinence from the gratification of any of the inherent and primitive desires must have untoward results.[12]

The view that it was the function of hysterical attacks to provoke rape was advanced in 1890 by an American physician, A.F.A. King:

> . . . In prudish women of strong moral principle whose volition has disposed them to resist every sort of liberty or approach from the other sex [there occurs] a transient abdication of the general, volitional, and self-preservational ego, while the reins of government are temporarily assigned to the usurping power of the reproductive ego, so that the reproductive government overrules the govern-ment by volition and thus forcibly compels the woman's organism . . . to allow, invite, and secure the approach of the other sex, whether she will or not, to the end that nature's imperious demands for reproduction shall be obeyed.

Dr King then proceeds to the following idyllic account of the likely sequence of events in a community uncorrupted by civilization:

> Let us picture ourselves a young aboriginal Venus in one of her earliest hysteri-cal paroxysms. . . . Let this Venus now be discovered by a youthful Apollo of the woods, a man with fully developed animal instincts but without moral, legal or religious restraint . . . He cannot but observe to himself: this woman is not dead; she does not look ill; she is well-nourished, plump and rosy. He speaks to her;

---

12. H.B. Donkin, 'Hysteria'. *A Dictionary of Psychological Medicine*, vol. 1 (London, 1892), p. 620.

she neither hears, apparently, nor responds. Her eyes are closed. He touches, moves and handles her at his pleasure; she makes no resistance. What will this primitive Apollo do next? . . . The course of nature having been followed, the natural purpose of the hysteric paroxysm being accomplished, there would remain as a result of the treatment—instead of one pining, discontented woman —two happy people and the probable beginning of a third.[13]

But this alertness to the less blatant manifestations of sexuality in human life was not confined to medical contexts.

At the beginning of the Victorian era, a diarist recorded his conviction that a young woman's dismay at the prospect of ending her platonic association with an older man 'was sexual though she did not know it'. (It enhances the piquancy of this observation that the young woman concerned was Queen Victoria; the man was Lord Melbourne and the diarist Greville.) And consider the following reflections on the relations between sexuality and the appreciation of beauty:

> . . . Some of the most conspicuous elements of beauty ought to be called sexual . . . because they owe their fascination in a great measure to the participation of our sexual life in the reactions which they cause. Sex is not the only object of sexual passion. When love lacks its specific object, when it does not yet understand itself, or has been sacrificed to some other interest, we see the stifled fire bursting out in various directions. One is religious devotion, another is zealous philanthropy, a third is the fondling of pet animals, but not the least fortunate is the love of nature, and of art . . .[14]

We would confidently have cited these remarks as a striking example of Freud's influence in facilitating the tendency to see the operation of sexuality in areas previously considered remote from it if we did not know that it is what Santayana was telling his classes at Harvard in the early nineties.

I shall follow Shakow and Rapaport in dividing the factors which influenced responses to Freud into intrinsic and extrinsic.[15] Among the extrinsic sources two major ones are those relating to Freud's national and ethnic affiliations and to the peculiar solidarity of the psychoanalytic groups.

Several authors (and Freud himself) suggest that anti-semitic feeling played a role in the hostility incurred by psychoanalysis. This may have been true of central Europe, but there is little sign of it in the English literature. The only examples I have noted are two pointed allusions to Freud as an 'oriental' in American reviews of *The Interpretation of Dreams,* and a bit of high-spirited nonsense on the subject of circumcision from Roy Campbell twenty years later.

---

13. A.F.A. King, 'Hysteria'. *American Journal of Obstetrics,* XXIV (1891), pp. 513–32. If *Ueber Hysterie* (Berlin, 1892) by 'King' is a translation of this, then it was in Freud's library.
14. George Santayana, *The Sense of Beauty* (New York, 1961), p. 53.
15. Shakow and Rapaport, *op. cit.*

On the other hand, Freud did come in for a share of the general opprobrium of things German which characterised the years during and immediately after the First World War. Charles Mercier saw Freud as just a new and more unsavoury addition to the 'monstrous regiment of German professors that has so long afflicted us'. W.H.B. Stoddart, one of Freud's earliest British champions, apprehessive in 1915 about 'asking readers to accept as a scientific truth, doctrines which have had their birth in Austria and Germany . . .', disarmed them with the assurance that 'as a matter of fact, Freud himself has no German blood in him' but is a pure Jew'.[16] Christine Ladd-Franklin attributed the more objectionable aspects of psychoanalysis to the fact that 'the German mind is to a certain extent undeveloped when contrasted with the logical and moral sanity of the non-German civilized nations . . . psychoanalysis is most intimately bound up with German kultur.'[17]

An article in the New York Times contrasted Freud's attitude towards the war unfavourably with that of Karl Kraus. Freud was described as having 'taken up the cudgels for Germany', and exception was taken to his having expressed the hope that 'impartial history will furnish the proof that this very nation in whose language I am writing . . . has sinned least against the laws of human civilisation'. In the immediate post-war atmosphere these unexceptionable sentiments passed for xenophobic ravings and Freud's great essay, 'War and Death' with its moving evocation of 'fellowship in civilisation' was described as 'a little less than a justification of the Prussian theory of the supremacy of the state over morals and ethics'.[18] On the occasion of its translation into English in 1916 the psychiatrist E.E. Southard characterised it as 'a subtle apology for the central powers', and 'an admirable essay in propaganda Teutonica.'

That these remarks were not simply rationalisations of an antecedent antipathy to psychoanalysis is suggested by the fact that at about the same time William Alanson White, whom C.P. Oberndorf describes as one of the 'most effective American propagandists for psychoanalysis',[19] was moved by anti-German feeling to propose that 'the time has come to free American psychiatry from the domination of the Pope at Vienna', and that the American Psychoanalytical Association ought therefore to be dissolved.

Franz Alexander and Sheldon Selesnick have tried to clarify the nature of the opposition Freud provoked by distinguishing between 'psychoanalytic thought' and 'the psychoanalytic movement', their point being that some of

---

16. W.H.B. Stoddart, *The New Psychiatry* (London, 1915), p. iv.
17. Christine Ladd-Franklin, 'Freudian Doctrines'. *The Nation* CIII (19 October 1916), p. 373.
18. 'More German than Germans'. *New York Times Magazine* (24 August 1919), p. 11.
19. C.P. Oberndorf, *A History of Psychoanalysis in America* (New York, 1964), pp. 135–36.

the early opposition to psychoanalysis was due to dubious organisational features of the psychoanalytic associations rather than any wholesale hostility to
psychoanalysis itself.[20] They based this view on an exchange of letters
between Freud and the distinguished Swiss psychiatrist Eugen Bleuler, one
of Freud's earliest non-Viennese adherents, concerning Bleuler's refusal to
join the newly constituted International Psychoanalytic Association. Their
quotations show that this was due to Bleuler's suspicion that the aims of the
new association were medico-political rather than scientific (and not, as
Ernest Jones maintained, to Bleuler's sharing his countrymen's proclivity for
isolation as evidenced by the Swiss attitude towards international organisa-
tions like the United Nations and the League).

One of the episodes which troubled Bleuler was the exclusion of a psychiatrist called Isserlin from attendance at a psychoanalytic meeting because
of his persistent criticism. At first Freud dismissed the matter as trifling and
countered with the demand that Bleuler should sever his relations with those
German psychiatrists who were hostile and derisory. But in a later letter
Freud advanced as proof of his open-mindedness his toleration of Adler,
who 'is so against my inner convictions that he makes me angry every week.
Yet I did not demand his exclusion, his boycott, nor even his decapitation'.
(The delightfully Red Queen flavour of this last remark is due to the trans-
lators' English rendering; it is safe to assume that Freud was referring to the
restraint he had shown in not removing Adler as head of the Vienna Society
rather than on not removing Adler's head.)

Bleuler was unpersuaded and persisted in his conviction that 'the introduction of the closed door policy scared away a great many friends and made
some of them emotional opponents'. Alexander and Selesnick comment that
the Isserlin affair became a kind of test case for the sectarianism of the analytic societies and conclude that 'because of the soundness of its basic concepts and investigative methods, psychoanalysis did not need the dubious
help of rigid organisational measures.[21] The latter gave at least a nucleus of
validity to some of the criticisms levelled against psychoanalysis.'

According to the received view the answer to the question why Freud's
'doctrines and methods were found so despicable' lay 'in Freud's explicit
and narrow emphasis on sexuality. . . . To be told that sexual conflict was the

---

20. F. Alexander and S. Selesnick, *Archives of General Psychiatry*, vol. XII (January 1965),
pp. 1–9.

21. There is corroboration as to these 'rigid organisational measures' from another source.
Max Graf, an early member of Freud's Wednesday circle (and the father of Little Hans) writes:
'Freud . . . insisted that . . . if one followed Adler and dropped the sexual basis of psychic life,
one was no more a Freudian. In short, Freud as the head of the church banished Adler; he
ejected him from the official church. Within the space of a few years, I lived through the whole
development of church history: from the first sermons to a small group of apostles, to the strife
between Arius and Athanasius.' 'Reminiscences of Professor Sigmund Freud'. *Psychoanalytic
Quarterly*, XI (1940), p. 473.

cause of all neurosis and a fear of incest lay at the bottom of everything was hateful and Freud was duly hated. . . .'[22]

Ernest Jones spoke in this connection of an 'odium sexicum'. And there are quite a few recorded responses to Freud which render this characterisation an apt one. In 1915 Charles Mercier, writing in the *British Medical Journal*, characterised psychoanalysis as 'the sedulous inculcation of obscenity'. The reviewer of Freud's *Three Essays on the Theory of Sexuality* for the *New York Medical Journal* described it as 'pornography gone to seed'. S. Weir Mitchell, the inventor of the famous 'rest cure', (not to be confused with S.W. Mitchell, an editor of the *British Journal of Medical Psychology* and one of Freud's supporters) threw a book of Freud's into the fire (we are not told which) because it was 'filthy'.

Boris Sidis, a famous New England psychopathologist, made a violent attack on Freud on this score:

> Psychoanalysis is a conscious and more often a subconscious or unconscious debauching of the patient. Nothing is so diabolically calculated to suggest sexual perversion as psychoanalysis. Psychoanalysis . . . is a menace to the community . . . Better Christian Science than psychoanalysis![23]

There is no doubt that methodological objections to Freud's claims were occasionally no more than rationalisations of the shock and revulsion they induced. An illustration is provided by Adolf Wohlgemuth's account of how he went about testing on himself Freud's assertion of universal bisexuality in men.

> I looked out for and seized opportunities to contemplate at ease and unobtrusively . . . men of all sorts and conditions . . . the martial figure of the dashing soldier or the brainy and intellectual countenance of the thinker, the athlete, or the delicate and dreamy artist—all men who would probably please and whose exterior decidedly attracted me. I contemplated them and dwelt upon their personal advantages, having constantly in mind the purpose of the experiment. I imagined the preliminary period of a sexual approach; but I think it unnecessary to enter here into further details of this process, and will state at once the result of these experiments. I have been unable to come across the least trace of any homosexual propensity in my experiences.[24]

The reasoning on the basis of which Wohlgemuth was persuaded to submit himself to this ordeal is worth retrieving, if only to illustrate that the production of arguments which defy parody was not a monopoly of the Freudians.

---

22. Lancelot Law Whyte, *The Unconscious Before Freud* (New York, 1960), pp. 167–68.
23. Boris Sidis, *Symptomatology, Psychognosis, and Diagnosis of Psychopathic Disease* (Boston, 1914), p. vii.
24. A. Wohlgemuth, *A Critical Examination of Psychoanalysis* (London, 1923), pp. 57–59.

. . . When looking at a woman and indulging in sexual phantasies it is a well-known fact that, with the normal man, the impulse of contrection (i.e. touching), to use Moll's term, occurs. From this I reasoned that a similar experience must occur in the homosexually disposed individual with regard to another male. If therefore, I were to indulge in such phantasies, whilst contemplating a man, as would cause an impulse to contrection when practised with respect to a woman, I, as a trained observer, should certainly be able to detect any incipient conative tendencies and affective experiences, if they be present.

Nor did so rigorous an experimentalist as Wohlgemuth neglect to control for the possibility that his failure 'to detect any incipient conative tendencies and affective experiences' might evidence a general enfeeblement rather than the absence of specifically homosexual inclinations. Recalling ungallantly that 'a great number of women exert . . . a repulsive affect . . . ' he reasoned that

if such women are made the object of similar experiments as those described above with men, and if in spite of the primary repulsion, sexual conative tendencies, an incipient libido, be detected to be present, such a fact would certainly tend to prove my introspection reliable . . . I chose then as suitable subjects for these experiments . . . old and decrepit women, and such as were afflicted with some nauseating complaint, women of varying degrees of cleanliness, or rather uncleanliness. in all these cased I have invariably been able to discover decidedly sexual conative tendencies and unmistakable libido . . . I have, therefore no hesitation whatever in affirming that Freud's statement, that there are homosexual tendencies in every man at some time or another, to be a groundless assertion.

Though Wolgemuth's self-experiment constitutes one of the most engaging episodes in the martyrology of science, it is otherwise worthless. As Wohlgemuth himself conceded in his reply to J.C. Flugel's criticism, 'My argument does not touch the real point at issue'.

The bad arguments which Freud occasionally provoked tempted Freudians to the convenient inference that all the methodological objections by which they were plagued sprang from a reluctance to acknowledge the truth of their claims and could be ignored. But at the same time that Freud and his advocates were invoking the revulsion produced by his emphasis on sexuality to account for the opposition which he met, critics of psychoanalysis were plaintively demanding how mere rational argument could be expected to make headway against doctrines so alluring.

Bernard Sachs, for example, wrote: 'It is the sex appeal of Freudian doctrines that has given psychoanalytic writing their great vogue among literary and professional people.'[25]

---

25. Bernard Sachs, 'Bumke's Critique of Psychoanalysis'. *Mental Hygiene* (July 1932), p. 409.

At about the same time Robert Woodworth attributed 'the popular interest in psychoanalysis . . . largely to the freedom with which Freud and his disciples have handled the problem of sex.'[26]

Italo Svevo, who combines mockery of the pretensions of psychoanalysis with mockery of its disparagers in proportions which it is difficult to assess, has the hero of *The Confessions of Zeno* (1922) reflect:

> . . . They have found out what was the matter with me. The diagnosis is exactly the same as the one that Sophocles drew up long ago for poor Oedipus: I was in love with my mother and wanted to murder my father . . . I listened enraptured. It was a disease that exalted me to a place among the great ones of the earth; a disease so dignified that it could trace back its pedigree even to the mythological age.

But there were more creditable reasons for being favourably impressed by Freud's emphasis on man's instinctual nature. William Morton Wheeler, a distinguished zoologist, in a paper read at Harvard in 1917, scornfully contrasted academic psychologists who 'merely hint at the existence of such stupendous and fundamental biological phenomena as those of hunger, sex, and fear . . . and whose works . . . read as if they had been composed by beings that had been born and bred in a belfry, castrated in early infancy, and fed continually for fifty years through a tube with a stream of liquid nutriment of constant chemical composition' with the psychoanalysts who 'have had the courage to dig up the subconscious, that hotbed of all the egotism, greed, lust, pugnacity, cowardice, sloth, hate and envy which every single one of us carries about as his inheritance from the animal world.'[27]

This indictment was endorsed, though less colourfully, by at least one academic psychologist. L.L. Thurstone, in a symposium on the contribution of 'Freudism' to psychology, conceded the 'gross deficiencies in the subject matter of psychology' to which psychoanalysts had called attention.

> They are constantly searching for the relation between the fundamental cravings and wants of people and the ways in which these wants are expressed and satisfied . . . and that relation is more important as a determinant of personality and conduct, than the stimulus-response relation to which we scientific psychologists have given most of our effort.[28]

Another set of objections centred about the supposed immoral therapeutic and prophylactic implications of Freud's theory of the neuroses. It was asserted that analysts prescribed intercourse as a therapeutic measure;

---

26. Robert Woodworth, *A Quarter Century of Learning* (New York, 1931), p. 140.

27. W.M. Wheeler, 'On Instincts'. *Journal of Abnormal Psychology*, XV, nos 5-6 (December 1920–March 1921), p. 316.

28. L.L. Thurstone, 'Influence of Freudism on Theoretical Psychology'. *The Psychological Review*, XXI, no. 3 (May 1924), p. 180.

that, in any case, the effect of the treatment was to alienate the patient from the prevailing sexual code, and that analysts had sexual relations with their patients.

A reviewer in the *British Medical Journal* warned that psychoanalytic therapy 'contains an element of danger for the patient who . . . may receive advice from her psychoanalytic physician repugnant to the ordinary code of morality.'[29]

Bernard Sachs claimed that 'the good affects of psychoanalytic therapy have been heralded by patients because they have been encouraged, if not ordered, to violate the prevailing code of morality.' This sounds like an agreeable fantasy but, in fact, it was more than that. Whatever the practice of analysts may have been, it is certain that there were physicians who did recommend intercourse to their patients and that some of these did so on what they took to be Freud's authority.

Freud's apprehensiveness about this trend caused him to denounce it as 'wild psychoanalysis' in a paper of 1910, which, however, leaves an exaggerated impression as to the extent to which the prophylactic and therapeutic value of intercourse was an unwarranted inference from Freud's writings. A careful reading of Freud's paper, which was often cited to refute those who understood Freud to hold that sexual abstinence was in itself pathogenic, and which Brill was careful to include in the second edition of *Selected Papers in Hysteria,* shows that the mistake made by the physician, who was the subject of Freud's remonstrance, was not that he had misunderstood Freud, but that he had misdiagnosed his patient, confounding an anxiety-hysteria with an anxiety-neurosis; the right treatment but the wrong illness, as it were.

Pierre Janet in an address to the International Congress of Psychiatry in 1913 drew the implication that Freud's explanation of the neuroses committed him to holding that a visit to a brothel would have as much therapeutic effect as psychoanalytic sessions. This provoked Ernest Jones to accuse him of deliberate, malicious prevarication. But it is more likely that Janet was merely guilty of carelessly confounding Freud's aetiology of the 'actual' neuroses with that of the psychoneuroses, thus erroneously extending to the latter the pathogenic role Freud had assigned to sexual abstinence in the former.

But the accusation that Freud and his followers 'corrupted' their patients had a source more difficult to allay than simple misunderstanding of the distinction between the actual and the psychoneuroses in doubts as to the correctness, and sometimes even as to the candour, of Freud's theory of sublimation.

---

29. *British Medical Journal* (5 July 1913), p. 24.

Paul Bjerre, a Swedish analyst, raised this issue in his book *The History and Practice of Psychoanalysis.* If, he asked, a sexual desire always lies at the base of a neurosis how can merely psychic treatment work? 'It is very easy to suspect that analysts might . . . advise sexual congress as a cure for neuroses.' Bjerre went on to say that some analysts, in fact, did so but that 'Freud holds aloof from them' in consequence.[30]

It is thus understandable that a common inference from Freud's writing should have been, as one indignant critic put it, that 'absolute continence is unnatural and incompatible with mental health'.[31]

A character in an Aldous Huxley short story of the same period remarks to another that it is better that she should have sexual thrills than repressions: 'Read Freud. Repressions are the devil.'

The New York Times found it necessary to contradict this misconception editorially:

> . . . While it is true that the Freudians teach that many mental, and some physical, ills are the result of 'repressions', they seek the cure for these ills not in 'Do as you please', but in turning the repressed energies to high and proper uses— 'sublimation', they call it. Whoever does anything else—who finds in psychoanalysis license instead of liberty—is not a follower of Freud . . . but a charlatan, certainly ignorant and probably vicious.[32]

Whereas *The New York Times* accepted Freud's doctrine of sublimation at its face value, some shared Jung's view that the notion of sublimation was 'a pious wish structure invented for the quieting of inopportune questioners'. Jung's suspicion with regard to sublimation is dramatised in Thomas Mann's *The Magic Mountain,* in the comments of Hofrat Behrens, the director of the sanitarium:

> This cursed libido! . . . We have psychoanalysis, we give the noodles every chance to talk themselves out—much good it does them! The more they talk the more lecherous they get. I preach mathematics . . . I tell them that if they will occupy themselves with the study of mathematics they will find in it the best remedy against the lusts of the flesh. Lawyer Paravant was a bad case; he took my advice, he is now busy squaring the circle, and gets great relief. But most of them are too witless and lazy, God help them.[33]

---

30. P. Bjerre, *The History and Practice of Psychoanalysis* (Boston, 1916), p. 138.

31. G.M. Cullen, 'Psychoanalysis Attacked'. *The Living Age* (1921).

32. *New York Times* (29 March 1921), p. 14, col. 5.

33. With characteristic perspicacity Mann has discerned Freud's own, at least intermittent, view of the matter. Sentiments similar to those of Hofrat Behrens are expressed by Freud's in a letter to Pfister of January 1909, in which he states that since sublimation is 'too difficult for most patients our cure generally issues in the search for gratification'. Ernest Jones, *Sigmund Freud: Life and Work,* Vol. 2 (London, 1958), p. 489.

No account of the sources of the hostility towards psychoanalysis would be complete which failed to mention the trepidation aroused by the psychoanalytic notion of the 'transference'. It was the transference, the aim, as Freud put it, 'of attaching the patient to the person of the physician', which provoked one critic to ask rhetorically, 'Who after learning of this would submit his young daughter to psychoanalysis?' A reviewer in the *British Medical Journal* was content to issue a friendly warning:

> . . . The situation contains elements of danger for the professional reputation of the psychoanalyst, and it would not be prudent for him to neglect any of those precautions usually observed by members of the profession in the clinical examination of hysterical women.[34]

Much of the anti-psychoanalytic literature of the time is prone to somewhat coy innuendoes as to the kind of relationship between the patient and his physician which the practice of transference encouraged. For example, Bernard Sachs remarked: 'We all know the mischief that has been wrought by this whole transference business. And as far as the patient's emotional reactions to the psychoanalyst are concerned, the less said the better.[35] (In his *A History of Psychoanalysis in America*, C.P. Oberndorf records that this was a common accusation and tells of a quick-witted woman he was analysing who, when warned that analysts have sexual relations with their patients, replied, 'Poor Dr Oberndorf, he sees six patients a day.')
Joseph Jastrow wrote:

> I cannot close my eyes nor those of the reader to the disquieting tales of the abuse of the relation of analyst-patient . . . in which the transference eased the way of abuse . . . remember that not all analysts are saints and the rest can be left to the reader's imagination.[36]

What Jastrow was content to leave to his readers' imagination was made explicit by Gilbert Seldes in his book *Can Such Things Be?* (New York, 1931), to which Jastrow referred them. Seldes relates stories of 'the translation of the verbal intimacy which the method involved into physical intimacy between practitioners and patients'. One concerns 'a handsome American matron' who left her husband to have an affair with her Viennese analyst. 'The husband bought a hussar's whip and matched a duelling scar on the psychoanalyst's cheek with half a dozen welts, until the whip broke. He returned to America and got a divorce and the custody of his three children.' As for the woman, Seldes relates that the member of the American Medical Association of Vienna who told him the story 'saw her himself not so long

34. *British Medical Journal, op. cit.*
35. Sachs, *Mental Hygiene.*
36. Joseph Jastrow, *The House That Freud Built* (New York, 1959), p. 238.

ago at the races in Baden-Baden—a heavily rouged and powdered travesty of her formerly wholesomely alluring self in company with a notorious South American profligate.' Though some today might regard this story as inadvertent testimony to the regenerative powers of psychoanalytic treatment, we can be sure Seldes's American readers, for whom consorting with a South American was half way towards miscegenation, would not have seen it in this light.

But what is significant about Seldes's remarks in their bearing on Freud's standing at the time is the pains which he takes to contrast the 'irresponsible practitioners' of his anecdotes with the 'leaders of the science themselves' who 'were the simplest and most honest of men.' One of the subtitles of the chapter on psychoanalysis runs 'While real scientists perfect theories to benefit mankind, quacks practise on Americans!'—the 'real scientists' being Freud and those for whom he vouched.

There were three major methodological criticisms of Freud. These were that Freud took no precautions against suggesting aetiologies to his patients, that his methods of interpretation were arbitrary, and that he abused the term sexual and its cognates. Of those. the most frequently iterated was the charge of suggestion. This may have been felt to have particular weight since Freud's seduction error was sometimes attributed to it.

A neurologist writing in *Brain* in 1911 objected to 'the so-called facts of psychoanalysis' that

> we may put into (the patient's) mind just what we want to find there. We know that Freud gave up that portion of his theory which relates to sexual assaults, because he found that his patients had misled him. And if the master of this method may be deceived, how much more his disciples?[37]

That Freud's replies to these misgivings (for example in the twenty-eighth of the *Introductory Lectures*) were not found convincing is indicated by the fact that almost two decades later Bernard Hart, one of Freud's earliest sympathisers, repeated the objection in his *Psychopathology: Its Development and Its Place in Medicine* (London, 1928):

> The preconceptions of the analyst, the particular moments at which he sees fit to intervene in the patient's narrative, the emphasis which he directs to certain features of the narrative, the point at which he deems the flow of associations to have reached the significant element, all these are abundantly able to produce decided alterations in the subsequent functioning of the patient's mind.

In one of the earliest assessments of Freud to be published in the United States, J.J. Putnam, later to be one of Freud's staunchest American advocates, objected that

---

37. J.A. Ormerod, 'Two Theories of Hysteria'. *Brain*, XXXIII (January 1911), p. 287.

. . . When the physician is fully imbued with the belief in the sexual origin of the patient's illness, he must, by virtue of the closeness of this relationship, be in a position to impress his view, unconsciously, upon his patients, and might easily draw from them an acquiescence and an endorsement which would not in reality be as spontaneous as it seemed.[38]

But Putnam came to feel, after further experience with Freud's method, that his original objections and apprehensions were unfounded. Others retained their misgivings. And still others came to feel the force of these objections after having initially discounted them (for example, Frederick Peterson, Boris Sidis, Samuel Tannenbaum and, most notoriously, Jung).

Another frequent source of misgiving was the impression of arbitrariness produced by Freud's interpretative procedures and by his employment of symbolism in particular. In 1912 an American psychologist, Frederick Lyman Wells, referred to symbolism as 'the phase of psychoanalysis to which the most legitimate objections are raised'.[39]

'There is absolutely nothing in the universe which may not readily be made into a sexual symbol,' objected Knight Dunlap, a professor of psychology and author of the first book explicitly devoted to the refutation of psychoanalytic claims.

. . . All natural and artificial objects can be turned into Freudian symbols. We may explain, by Freudian principles, why trees have their roots in the ground; why we write with pens; why we put a quart of wine into a bottle instead of hanging it on hooks like a ham; and so on.[40]

The psychiatrist Pearce Bailey was less witty but blunter: 'Freud and his industrious followers . . . make symbols mean what they like.'[41]

In 1925 Aldous Huxley, writing in an American journal, confided that

it was the machinery of symbolism, by which the analyst transforms the manifest into the latent dream content, that shook any faith I might possibly have had in the system. It seemed to me, as I read those lists of symbols and those obscene allegorical interpretations of simple dreams, that I had seen this sort of thing before. I remembered, for example, that old-fashioned interpretation of the Song of Solomon . . . I had never, even in infancy, whole-heartedly believed that the amorous damsel in the Song of Songs was, prophetically, the Church and her

---

38. J.J. Putnam, 'Recent Experiences as the Study and Treatment of Hysteria at the Massachusetts General Hospital; with Remarks on Freud's method of Treatment by "Psychoanalysis"'. *Journal of Abnormal Psychology*, vol. 1 (April 1906), pp. 40–41.

39. F.L. Wells, 'Review of *Psychoanalysis: Its Themes and Applications* by A.A. Brill'. Journal of Abnormal Psychology, vol. 7 (1912–13), p. 447.

40. Knight Dunlap, 'The Pragmatic Advantage of Freudo-analysis'. *Psychoanalytic Review*, 1 (1913), p. 151.

41. P. Bailey, 'Hero Myths According to Freud'. *New Republic* (13 march 1915), p. 161.

lover the Saviour. Why should I then accept as valid the symbolism invented by Dr. Freud? There are no better reasons for believing that walking upstairs or flying are dream equivalents of fornication than for believing that the girl in the Song of Solomon is the Church of Christ.[42]

Many comments on Freud's deployment of his sexual terminology manifest the irritated bewilderment Hans Castorp felt towards Dr Krokowski's lectures on psychoanalysis.

> . . . The speaker employed the word 'love' in a somewhat ambiguous sense so that you were never quite sure where you were with it, or whether he had reference to its sacred, or its passionate and fleshly aspect—and this doubt gave one a slightly seasick feeling.[43]

But often it was neither the mere breadth of Freud's notion of sexuality nor its concertina-like character which was found troubling, but the suspicion, as Freud himself put it, that his 'unwarrantable expansion' of the term sexual 'was in order that (my) assertion regarding the sexual origin of the neuroses and the sexual significance of symptoms might be maintained' (last paragraph of the twentieth of the *Introductory Lectures*). For example, the psychotherapist, Dr T.A. Ross spoke of a 'certain equivocation' on the part of Freudians:

> The statement is made by them that sex is at the bottom of every neurosis, and when people hold up their hands at this statement, the further statement is made that by sex they mean all sorts of manifestations of love . . . that, in short, the term sex for the Freudian is a much wider one than for other people. And yet when one comes to the case material which has been given frequently in great detail in the Freudian literature, one finds that the sex manifestations there described are just what anyone else would call sex manifestations.[44]

The same complaint was made by a member off influential group of Philadelphia neurologists:

> When anyone now accuses the disciples of the newer psychology of laying greater stress on sexual matters as a cause of mental trouble than they deserve, the work 'libido' is claimed to be used symbolically . . . I refuse to make charges of bad faith, but I do not think the disciples of Freudism are altogether frank in their statements as to their use of the word. I think their enthusiasm has made them a little disingenuous. The present explanation was not given till adverse criticism had been made.[45]

---

42. Aldous Huxley, 'Is Psychoanalysis a Science?' *The Forum*, LXXII (1925), pp. 316–17.
43. Thomas Mann, *The Magic Mountain* (London, 1960), p. 130.
44. T.A. Ross, *An Introduction to Analytical Psychotherapy* (New York, 1932), p. 82.
45. Charles W. Burr, 'A Criticism of Psychoanalysis'. *American Journal of Insanity*, XXXI, no. 2 (October 1914), p. 244.

That there was some warrant for this suspicion may be inferred from a sample of the elucidations of the sexual theory proffered by Freud's expositors. One of them observed:

> Many have strongly objected to Freud's theory principally on account of the term 'sexual', translating it for themselves to mean sexual in the narrowest sense . . . Rather does it embrace life and love and creation, indeed, the whole diffused tendency to seek expression, starting with mother-love and graduating to the power to not only create life but to be capable of any creative work.[46]

Another argued that:

> The meaning of sexual manifestations in the Freudian sense . . . covers a broad and comprehensive field of activity, whether bodily desires or mental longings. It embraces all desires, instincts, wishes, ambitions—like hunger, sex, acquisition, aspiration, the social sense, love of art, etc. This is a far cry from the narrow vulgar conception of the term which seems to be understood by the men opposing the Freudian psychology.[47]

Nor can it be said that these equivocations were restricted to ill-informed or faint-hearted apologists. It was a founder-member of the New York Psychoanalytic Society who explained that psychoanalysis used the word sex 'in so broad a sense that even the most puritan minded need not be startled . . . without any implication necessarily of any moral unfitness or physical grossness'. And Ernest Jones himself, in the original preface of his book *Papers on Psychoanalysis*, elucidated Freud's conception of sexual instinct in terms of its affinity to 'Schopenhauer's and Nietzsche's "Wille Zur Machte", Bergson's "Élan Vital", Shaw's "Life Force", and the "vital impulse" of so many writers all of which,' Jones concluded, 'are equivalent to what Freud termed "Libido"'[48] And yet, a few years later, Jones was authoritatively defining libido as 'nothing less than sexual hunger'. No wonder Hans Castorp felt sea-sick!

Another feature of Freud's work often selected for comment was what may loosely be termed his explanatory style. However, there were radical divergences as to what this explanatory style amounted to, what its affinities were. Some found these in mechanistic physics or biology, others in teleology and animism. There was ample warrant in Freud's writings themselves for either assimilation.

The philosopher Paul Carus, contrasting Schopenhauer's animistic account of gravitation in terms of the stone's will to fall with Freud's explanations, observed that whereas

---

46. *The Medical Record*, LXXXIV (9 August 1913), p. 258.
47. *Journal of American Medical Association* (28 March 1914), p. 1036.
48. Ernest Jones, *Papers on Psychoanalysis* (London, 1913), p. xi. This account of libido was deleted from subsequent editions.

some philosophers take features typical of the highest and most complicated forms of existence and generalise them to explain the nature of lower forms. Others do the reverse, they generalise the lowest forms and explain all higher features as mere repetition of simpler modes of activity . . . Freud generalises the lower . . . so as to cover the higher.[49]

On the other hand, *Harper's Weekly* found in Freud's views 'a great advance on the hopeless materialistic stand-point of the doctors of a quarter of a century ago . . . Freud lays great stress on the purpose underlying neu-rotic reactions.'[50] Neither view can be written off as just a popular misun-derstanding. A New York analyst writing in a medical journal in 1915 contrasted the contemporary medical mind 'brought up in the school of the natural sciences, saturated with mechanistic explanations' and predisposed to 'what metaphysicians designate as materialism' with 'the practice of psy-choanalysis (which) demands the idealistic view'.[51]

To an extent the contradiction is only apparent. Someone who was struck by the contrast between Freud's emphasis on the influence of mental conflict on the disposition to neurotic illness with the theories of hereditary degeneracy held by some of Freud's contemporaries might mark this aware-ness by characterising Freud's views as 'idealistic'; while those who were struck rather by the biological or carnal nature of the impulses in question might use the same term to characterise the mental-moralistic views which Freud also supplanted.[52]

This, however, did not exhaust the sources of ambiguity. There remained the question of how Freud conceived these pathogenic wishes to exert their influence. Though the explanatory factors which Freud invoked might be in some sense 'materialistic', their mode of operation was often characterised in animistic idioms: it is as if an itch were to be credited with both the incli-nation and the ability to scratch itself.

Among those who were struck rather by this aspect of Freud's explana-tions was Sidney Hook who felt that since 'the unconscious works more intelligently to attain its ends than does ever active intelligence . . . Freud's unconscious is in line with the élan vital of Bergson, the super-empirical ent-elechies of Driesch and the "soul spook" of McDougall. . . .'[53]

---

49. Paul Carus, 'Wrong Generalisations in Philosophy: Schopenhauer and Freud'. *The Monist*, XXIII (1913), p. 150.

50. *Harper's Weekly* (24 June 1911), p. 6.

51. Mary Isham, 'Some Implications of Psychoanalysis'. *New York Medical Journal* (21 August 1915), p. 390.

52. The psychiatric schools of thought that predominated between the period of the decline of the Nancy school of suggestion (c. 1890) and the rise of the psychoanalytical school (1910) were chiefly rationalistic, moral, exhortative, and re-educational. They appealed to the reason of the patient, to his conscious thinking and feeling.' Iago Galdston, *Progress in Medicine* (New York, 1940), pp. 260–61.

53. S. Hook, 'Marxism, Metaphysics and modern Science'. *The Modern Quarterly*, IV (1927), p. 389.

The authors of a history of science, summing up the controversy over the theory of evolution, write:

> Those who had external reasons for wishing to rebut the new doctrine tended to exaggerate the technical objections, flogging the genuine difficulties still facing the theory of evolution for more than they were worth: meanwhile, Darwin's henchmen were tempted in return to play down these difficulties in public, for fear of giving prejudiced objectors too much of a foothold.[54]

With the qualification that it is still an open question just how much the technical objections to Freud were worth and that Freud's advocates have not been dead long enough to be designated 'henchmen', this account fits equally well the controversy over the empirical warrantability of Freud's theories.

But there is a striking feature of Freud's role in our lives to which the controversial literature over his contribution to psychopathology does not do justice—the feature which provoked Alfred Kazin to remark that

> psychoanalytical literature has replaced the Bible as the place to which people turn for an explanation of their suffering, and a source of consolation.[55]

The same feature is ironically noted in Thomas Mann's account of Dr Krokowski's lectures:

> . . . With open arms he summoned all and sundry to come unto him. 'Come unto me,' he was saying, though not in those words, 'come unto me, all ye who are weary and heavy laden.' And he left no doubt of his conviction that all those present *were* weary and heavy laden. He spoke of secret suffering, of shame and sorrow, of the redeeming power of the analytic.

We find it in Hans Sachs's remark that reading *The Interpretation of Dreams* was 'the moment of destiny' for him: . . . 'when I had finished the book I had found the one thing worthwhile for me to live for; many years later I discovered that it was the only thing I could live by.'[56] The same note of exaltation sounds in a remark Jung addressed to Freud in the early years of their association—'to know your science means to have eaten from the Tree of Paradise'. And also in Theodore Dreiser's comparison of Freud to 'a conqueror who has taken a city, entered its age-old hoary prisons, there generously proceeding to release from their gloomy and rusted cells the prisoners of formulae, faith and illusions which have wracked and worn man for hundreds and thousands of years.'[57]

---

54. Stephen Toulmin and June Goodfield, *The Discovery of Time* (London, 1967), p. 259.
55. Alfred Kazin, 'The Freudian Revolution Analysed', Benjamin Nelson, ed., *Freud and the Twentieth Century* (London, 1958), p. 15.
56. Hans Sachs, *Freud: Master and Friend* (Cambridge, Mass., 1944), p. 1.
57. Theodore Dreiser, 'Remarks', *Psychoanalytic Review* (July 1931), p. 250.

In a paragraph in which he discusses his relation to Nietzscbe, Dostoievsky and Freud, André Gide speaks of having found in Freud '*rather an authorisation than an awakening.* Above all (he) taught me to cease doubting myself, to cease fearing my thoughts, and to let those thoughts lead me to those lands that were not after all uninhabitable since I found (him) already there.'[58]

These remarks suggest that a potent source of Freud's 'redeeming power' is his skill in easing what G.K. Chesterton, in an essay on Freud, called 'our monstrous burden of secrecy'.[59]

George Orwell has left a vivid record of the liberating effect this sort of realisation can have:

> . . . Now and again there appears a writer who opens up a new world not by revealing what is strange but by revealing what is familiar. . . . Here is a world of stuff which you supposed to be of its nature incommunicable, and somebody has managed to communicate it. The effect is to break down, at any rate momentarily, the solitude in which the human being lives.[60]

Though Orwell was referring to James Joyce's *Ulysses* his words are strikingly evocative of what many have felt towards Freud. And they suggest an answer to D.H. Lawrence's dismissive view that once we have gotten over the excitement of realising 'how thrillingly immoral things really are', we will forget the concepts of psychoanalysis 'as we have forgotten so many other catch words' and will once again be just where we were'.[61]

There is good reason to think that we shall never again be where we were; that though the extent, and even the precise character, of Freud's 'scientific' achievement will remain a matter of dispute for some time to come, what is not disputable is that Freud broke down, and not just momentarily, one of the solitudes in which we lived.

---

58. André Gide, *Pretexts* (London, 1959), p. 306.
59. G.K. Chesterton, 'The Game of Psychoanalysis'. *Century*, CVI (1923), p. 38.
60. George Orwell, 'Inside the Whale'. *Selected Essays* (London, 1957), pp. 11–12.
61. D.H. Lawrence, *Fantasia of the Unconscious* (London, 1961), p. 126.

6

Symptoms, Wishes, and Actions

We want to understand those sentences in which Freud invokes unconscious wishes, thoughts, motives, processes to explain why a patient dreamt a certain dream, forgot a certain name, made a certain slip, is afflicted with certain symptoms, acted or reacted in a certain manner. Particularly we want to understand in what sense symptoms express, fulfil, or gratify unconscious wishes: that is, how Freud believes himself to have explained Miss Lucy's olfactory hallucinations, Fraülein Elisabeth's leg pains, Dora's throat disorders, Hans's fear of horses, the Rat Man's obsessive thoughts and practices, the Wolf Man's constipation, the homosexual girl's choice of jumping from a height as a means of suicide, the matron's delusions of jealousy, the father-infatuated girl's bedtime rituals, the separated wife's transactions with the tablecloth, and generically: hysterical convulsions. hysterical paralyses, hysterical blindness, phobias, obsessions, compulsions and delusions.

This enterprise would involve attempting to elucidate and bring into some intelligible relation with one another the following diverse if not contradictory accounts by Freud and his expositors of just what his theory of the influence of unconscious wishes comes to: 'highly complicated mental acts . . . can be performed unconsciously . . .' (Freud, *Introductory Lectures*); 'There reigns in the unconscious a quite uninhibited flow towards the imaginary fulfilment of the wish that stirs it . . .' (Ernest Jones); 'Freud's view of the symptom requires us to believe that many involuntary acts are really actions which we undertake, (Wollheim). 'In the symptoms the wish is represented as fulfilled' (Wollheim); 'Freud's theory was one of unconscious wishes not unconscious reasons, (Peters); 'The concepts which psychoanalytic theory seeks to extend are precisely those in terms of which rational agents give accounts of their own conduct and that of other rational agents' (Flew); 'hysteria or neurotic obsessions are attempts to seek grat-

---

This essay first appeared in *Proceedings of the Aristotelian Society,* Vol. XLVIII (1974), and is reprinted by courtesy of the Editor.

ification or to avoid pain which go unrecognised both by the agent and by others' (MacIntyre); '(the patient) really does know the meaning of his (dreams. symptoms. errors), only he does not know that he knows, and therefore thinks that he does not.' (*Introductory Lectures*).

How are the 'highly complicated mental acts' related to the 'uninhibited flow towards imaginary fulfilment?' Which of them produces the symptom? Why are the characterisations of Peters and Flew so strikingly at variance? How can the pains and parenthesis which hysterics complain of be 'actions which they undertake'? How does a phobia 'represent a wish as fulfilled'? In what sense can an object of complaint be a gratification'? What is the force of 'knows but does not know that he knows'?

It is this last question, which I shall refer to as the self-intimation issue, that I believe to be both the most important and the most in need of elucidation and I should like to put it more elaborately than the others. In what epistemic relation does the patient stand to the explanation of the symptoms, dreams, errors, and so forth, which Freud proffers him? For example, Freud believed that the red camellias which one of his patients was carrying in her dream signified menstruation. Could the dreamer come to know what the cammellia signified in the way in which 'la dame aux camélias', on whose practice of signalling the onset of her menstrual periods by changing from her usual white camellia to a red one, knew what her camellia signified?

I

On one occasion (in *The Interpretation of Dreams*) Freud meant to refer to Hannibal's father, Hamilcar Barca, but wrote the name of Hannibal's brother, Hasdrubal, instead. We know that Freud meant to refer to Hamilcar Barca and not to Hasdrubal because he tells us so. Freud also maintained that the occurrence of the name of Hannibal's brother instead of that of his father was the fulfilment of an unconscious intention. Do we know this, too, because he tells us so? It has been argued that Freud was mistaken as to his unconscious intention and that the occurrence of the name Hasdrubal was the consummation of an unconscious intention to refer, not to Hannibal's brother, as Freud maintained, but to his brother-in-law and predecessor in-command, also called Hasdrubal. How is this issue to be decided? By self-surveillance? Or introspection?

Our inability to say on the basis of Freud's own words what his answers to these questions are is the most crucial ambiguity in psychoanalytic theory. In his accounts of dream interpretation, for example. Freud leaves us in doubt as to whether he is in search of something to which the dream stands as his own water-quaffing dreams, which he was able to produce experimentally, stood to the anchovy-induced thirst by means of which he instigated them, or to the transparent thirst assuaging point which the dreamer would himself give them irrespective of whether he recalled eating anchovies or not. (It is this ambiguity which Wittgenstein may be referring to when he speaks of 'the abominable mess' created by Freudians in confounding the proffering of reasons with the advancing of hypotheses.)

To anticipate my main conclusions: Freud so characterises the relation between wishes and the phenomena they are invoked to explain that it is often impossible to say whether the wish is conceived to act causally or to act by providing an agent with reasons. My second conclusion is that Freud characterises the relation between the subject and the explanations of his symptoms, dreams, errors, and so forth, incoherently, in some places conferring a self-intimating character on them, and at others withholding it, and that either construction renders his more characteristic claims unassessable if not unintelligible.

I want first to show the inadequacy of two closely related views of Freud's conception of the relation of wishes to symptoms—that of Richard Peters that they are discharge-like phenomena to be accounted for in terms of wishes construed as operating causally rather than as providing reasons and that of Richard Wollheim's that rather than intelligently pursuing the wishes that account for them, they represent them 'as fulfilled'. Though these views are different they concur in slighting a pervasive and essential feature of Freud's notion of the unconscious—its ratiocinative character. When Freud says 'tendencies exist in human beings which can effect results without their knowing of them' he does not mean merely that, as Wollheim puts it, 'in the symptom the wish is represented as fulfilled.' He is referring to the intelligent, even cunning, pursuit of ulterior ends.

Even by Peters's own criterion Freud does not conceive of his explicanda as happenings, for Peters says of happenings that they cannot be characterised as 'intelligent or unintelligent, correct or incorrect, efficient or inefficient.' But Freud speaks of the 'skilfulness with which hysterical attacks are carried out.' Hysterical conversions are said to be sometimes expedient but more often morally craven. Freud speaks of the symbols in a dream as being 'used by' the dreamer, and of the dream picture as 'chosen' by him, and of the dreamer as 'drawing a parallel.' Part of one dream is described as 'extremely subtly designed' to mislead, and Freud refers to one of his patients 'as the cleverest of all my dreamers'. The motives for forgetting resolutions are described as 'achieving their ends by craft.' One of his own errors is described by Freud as 'a trick' which he 'brought off.' In another example cited by Freud the 'unfulfilled wish . . . neatly hatched the plot.' All these idioms sort ill with the passivity implied by the discharge view.

We might put Freud's persistent use of deliberative, voluntaristic idioms down to a poetic bent extraneous to his real thesis and detachable from it. But this won't do. It is not just Freud's exposition but his examples themselves which compel us to interpret the Freudian wish as not just a 'directive tendency,' as Peters calls it, but a full-fledged motive such as we invoke in explaining consciously-pursued aims. The Rat Man's illness, which made it impossible for him to take the examinations which would qualify him to practise law is explained in terms of his unconscious desire to delay a marital decision which might bring him into conflict with his father's wishes. The bedtime ritual girl of *Introductory Lecture* 17 is said to have become ill in order to avoid marriage and remain with her father. The tablecloth lady in the same lecture became ill so that she might be separated from her husband without scandal. Frau K in the Dora case history fell ill when this would discourage her husband's insistence on his conjugal rights. We are even told that 'Tongue biting in hysterical attacks occurs more readily when the physician's questions have drawn the patient's attention to the difficulties of a differential diagnosis.' But it isn't only the generalised advantage from illness that Freud invokes as a motive but more specific objectives as well.

The Wolf Man's constipation is explained in terms of his desire to be administered an enema. Hysterical vomiting is explained as an attempt to punish by disfiguring through emaciation. The bedtime ritual girl's insistence on the door between her parent's bedroom and her own being left open is explained as a way of preventing their having sexual relations. A girl with a counting compulsion is said by Freud to be unwillingly trying to keep her mind off troubling thoughts. Phobias in general are explained as chosen in order to reduce the number of occasions of fear by transferring the fear from a less, to a more, readily avoidable object.

Then there are those occasions on which Freud invokes the goal of amnesia (or agnosia) and speaks as if the creation of the symptom was a stratagem unconsciously employed by the patient to prevent the recall of certain memories or the recognition of certain impulses. For example, we are told of Miss Lucy, the English governess of *Studies on Hysteria*. 'The gain consists in the crowding out of the unbearable idea.' He says of Fräulein Elisabeth, 'She succeeded in sparing herself the painful consciousness that she was in love with her sister's husband by creating for herself bodily pains instead.' On another occasion he says that 'she . . . created for herself the hysterical pain . . . she repressed the erotic idea . . . and changed the sum of affect into somatic sensations of pain.' This account is generalised in the eighth *Introductory Lecture* where he calls the tendency to disguise or avoid painful thoughts the 'most prodigious motive for symptoms and errors'.

Let us turn to errors. In his exposition of Freud's theory Wollheim speaks of the wish which was operative in Freud's forgetting the name Signorelli as 'erupting'. If this is so, it makes the Signorelli case an unrepresentative one. To speak in general of Freud's error-explaining wishes as 'erupting' is as infelicitous as describing the wish to win at chess as erupting into checkmate.

Consider Freud's account, in the sixteenth of the *Introductory Lectures*, of those patients who fail to close the doors between his waiting room and his study, the prominence of which gives it some sort of paradigm status. He notes that it only happens when the waiting room is empty and their privacy is therefore not threatened. So the error can be characterised as prudent.

And there is a further point. Not only can a discharge phenomenon not be prudent but neither can it be rude. Yet this is just what Freud tells us of the failure to close the consulting room doors. '. . . anyone who behaves this way . . . belongs to the rabble and deserves to be received with coldness.' And there is something characteristically gratuitous about Freud's construction. Let us agree that, as Freud says. the patient's forgetfulness 'betrays his attitudes to the physician.' So far, mere nonratiocinated expressiveness. But Freud goes further in the direction of a rational or, as I prefer to say, instrumental, conception in his claim that the patient, having expected the notorious Dr. Freud's waiting room to be crowded with applicants and finding it deserted, 'must somehow make the physician atone for the superfluous respect he had been prepared to show him.' Thus the consulting room doors example is fully instrumental. It is uptake-seeking; the failure to close the doors between the waiting room and Freud's consulting room is meant to offend and Freud is duly offended.

The errors in the following cases are just as straightforwardly instrumental: The duty officer forgetting to put out the light during an unauthorised absence and thus concealing the fact that he was away; the engineer, who had reluctantly agreed to work overtime, turning a valve in the wrong direction thus putting the equipment out of commission and permitting him to go home; Stekel repeatedly interchanging the names of two foreign patients because 'he was able in this way to let each of his patients know that he was not the only (foreigner) who had come to Vienna in search of medical advice.' These acts necessitated just those calculations and deliberations that their perpetrators would have been involved in had they been unscrupulous enough to undertake them intentionally.

This can even be illustrated with respect to dreams. If we ask what did dreaming the dream accomplish, or what was the point of dreaming the dream, there is sometimes an answer other than that it provided a disguised gratification of an unconscious wish. For example, Freud's dream of sex play with his infant daughter was not just intrinsically but instrumentally gratifying. Freud explains it by invoking his desire to believe that even respectable fathers may entertain sexual inclinations towards their pre-pubescent daughters and thus relieve him of his doubts as to the authenticity of the paternal seductions in which at that point he wished to believe. The distressing dream of one patient. which she had put forward as a counter-example to Freud's wish fulfilment theory, is explained by Freud in terms of her desire to reject some interpretations which he had proposed and so to persuade herself of his fallibility. A homosexual girl patient of Freud's has a series of dreams which when interpreted reveal that contrary to her waking pronouncements she wishes to become heterosexual and start a family. But Freud eventually discovers that they are 'lying dreams' dreamt with the intention of misleading him as to the prospects for a cure and ensuring his disappointment.

These interpretations involved not just dream-work but a dream-worker who cunningly contrives that welcome inferences should naturally be drawn from the manifest content of the dream. The dream in these cases is designed to provoke a certain kind of uptake.

There is another distinct role which ratiocination play in Freud's explanations. In his pioneering study, Richard Peters compared symptoms and psychoanalytic explicanda in general to the leap of a motorist stung by a wasp, who reflexively lets go of the wheel. But even when Freud is purporting to account for non-instrumental, intrinsic gain, what an unconscious wish explains does not characteristically stand to it as being stung by a wasp stands to the subsequent agitation. Because of the role he gives to concealment Freud's patients are just as often, in terms of Peters's example, like a motorist who. having been stung, prudently waits to pull in at the first lay-by for a jump and a shout.

In his paper, 'Dream Interpretation in Psychoanalysis' (1912, *Collected Papers*, Vol. 2, p. 310) Freud is explicit as to this. 'The more the patient has learnt of the method of dream interpretation the more obscure do his later dreams become . . . All the acquired knowledge serves as a warning to the dream work.' We don't see how dreams or symptoms can be the discharge-like product of the primary process if disguise enters into their construction since this is not a discharge but a taking-account-of phenomenon. 'Indifference to the path along which discharge takes place' is not easily reconciled with the idea of acquiring knowledge and heeding warnings.

II

Let us turn to those cases in which Freud's explicanda are not implied to be instrumentally related to the achievement of an ulterior objective but which do answer to Wollheim's account of the wish being 'represented as fulfilled' (or are meant to) and which Freud describes as providing intrinsic or primary gain. Are they necessarily discharge-like? What analogies are we proffered in terms of which we are to understand Freud's account of the gain provided by symptoms, dreams, and so forth? They are said to be like someone hallucinating, or like someone manifesting rage or joy, or like someone confessing a shameful or burdensome secret, or like someone enacting a charade, or like someone withdrawing his hand from a flame. An analogy which we are only occasionally proffered but which on many explanatory occasions is the most plausible and appropriate, though it is inconsistent with Freud's gratification thesis, is that of someone moving his lips and gesticulating while thinking to himself

Freud maintains that the symptom is a 'compromise' between the satisfaction of an impulse and its repression. How are the gratificatory and repressive components in the compromise related? Is a symptom like the muffled sounds that escape a man who is gagged where it is the expressive component which is purposive and action-like? Or is it like a man trying to control a fit of coughing in church where the expressive component is discharge-like and it is the repressive component which is action-like? Or is it like the outcome of one man trying to shout for help while another has a hand clapped over his mouth where two conflicting purposes are operative? Or is it like a man belching through a gag where one mechanical process is impeded by another? And if symptoms are simultaneously like all of these which aspects of the symptom are correlated with which explanations'?

I shall argue that Freud so expresses himself that these possibilities are often not distinguishable from each other. It might seem a limitation on the rational/instrumental construal of Freud's explanations that many of them fail to render the symptoms intelligible as even a misguided action is rendered intelligible by finding its point. For example, Freud says of the bedtime ritual girl that '. . . fear of an erection of the clitoris expressed itself by the imposition of a rule to remove all going clocks and watches.' and of 'the most urgent bowel movement of the wolf man's life' that it was a manifestation of his magnanimity. These are difficult to fit into a rational means-end schema. And so is Dora's limp as an attempt to gratify her passion for Herr K, or the tablecloth lady's summoning her servant to see the stain and her desire to raise her husband in public esteem. The unconscious reason for the homosexual girl's attempt at suicide could intelligibly be 'to punish my father' but not 'to gratify my wish to have a child by my father.' But this apparent limitation on a means-end conception of what Freud thought was going on is lifted if the operative wish is held to be that of representing a state of affairs rather than that of bringing it about We could understand how the homosexual girl's desire to bear her father a child was instrumentally implicated in her act if what she wished was to represent or portray rather than gratify her desire by means of it.

At this point it is the very criterion for an action with which we have been working that breaks down. Imagine someone trying to represent the battle of Waterloo at the dinner table, 'Let the salt-cellar stand for Mont St. Jean, the sugar bowl for Waterloo, the mustard-pot for Napoleon' is neither intelligent nor unintelligent, but it is not a discharge or happening either. Why shouldn't Dora's limp similarly stand for the sexual consummation of her love for Herr K? (But this means that we are left with no way of telling whether an instance of intrinsic, primary gain has been brought about to enact a fantasy or was merely causally related to one as salivation is related to sumptuary fantasies and erection to erotic ones.)

It is doubtful whether our extension of Freud's voluntarism can even stop at the concession that though disguised gratifications are to that extent, actions, blatant gratifications, like erotic dreams are discharge phenomena since they ignore the necessity for seemliness. This is because Freud sometimes uses idioms which encourage us to assimilate the dreamer-patient to someone who doesn't just hallucinate an oasis when lost and thirsty but takes the trouble to draw one.

Freud's treatment of forgetting illustrates the same ambiguity and equivocation although here it is the ratiocinative deliberative account which often seems strained. On the one hand the tendency to forget what is disagreeable is compared with the 'flight reflex in the presence of painful stimuli.' On the other Freud speaks of the motives for forgetting as 'achieving their ends by craft.' Even if there are cases where forgetting is more like dropping a hot object or flinching at a blow than we had formerly suspected, this in itself doesn't make it like planning a campaign or threading a needle. We could understand the forgetting of things with painful associations on the everyday model of the avoidance of reminders, which we sometimes employ as a conscious tactic, for example, Leontes's injunction on mention of his dead son, Mamillius: 'Cease . . . he dies to me again when talked of.' But many examples put a strain on this construction. In the celebrated Aliquis example there is no suggestion that forgetting Dido's words permitted the subject obliviousness to his apprehensions of his girlfriend's unwelcome pregnancy. And in the case of forgetting the name of someone who is distasteful the transaction with the thought of that person is actually prolonged. When Freud forgot, while on vacation, the place name 'Nervi' because of its association with 'nerve doctor' he was, nonetheless, perfectly aware that he was a vacationing nerve doctor. The middle-aged divorcee who forgot the name Jung, because she did not wish to be reminded that she was no longer young, nevertheless herself mentioned the subject of youth in the course of the conversation. Are we to see such cases like these as nevertheless action-like, the result of stupid or pointless precautions, like the person so tactful that he won't speak of rope even to a man being hanged? Or as discharge phenomena?

We are at a loss, in such cases, whether to take the error as being a stupid action with respect to the aim of oblivion, or an intelligent one with respect to some other aim, or no action at all. The upshot is that when we turn to Freud's description of the dream-work, say, we don't know whether we are being asked to assimilate it to the familiar phenomenon of being reminded of something by something or the equally familiar phenomenon of making something stand for something, or using something to remind someone of something.

What kind of considerations would settle which Coleridge was doing when he called the mountain of which the Abyssinian maid sings in *Kubla*

Khan 'Mt. Abora', a name not to be found in any atlas? We understand this
question so long as it is conscious passivity or agency which is in question.
We stop understanding it when it becomes a matter of unconscious passivity or agency. The impression we are left with is that the background against
which we are accustomed to make the distinction between actions and happenings, passive and active, the deliberate and the accidental, is missing.

In the case of Mt. Abora we can imagine the following alternative
accounts: Coleridge considers and then rejects the expression 'Mt. Abora'
which 'just came to him', as we say, because its connection with two rivers
mentioned by Bruce and the general theme of rivers of paradise render it
insufficiently evocative. Though it sounds right to him he suspects this may
be for reasons of its idiosyncratic associations for him alone which would not
hold for his readers. It then occurs to Coleridge that his sense of 'Abora's'
appropriateness is due to its calling up Milton's 'Mt. Amara' which also figured in a false paradise and is thus due to its public and cultural and not
merely its personal reverberations. This settles him; to the words, 'It was an
Abyssinian maid/and on her dulcimer she played/singing,' he adds, 'of Mt.
Abora.' We can also spin a story which would cause us to say that the influence of Mt. Amara was causal; Coleridge is congratulated on its felicity in
reinforcing the false paradise theme with an echo of the lines on false par-
adises in Milton and confesses that this had never occurred to him. But
when the claim is that the occurrence of Mt. Amara in Milton was an unconscious determinant of Coleridge's choice then I don't see how we can decide
whether this determinant operated as a reason for Coleridge's choice or
merely exerted a causal influence on it. The surroundings are missing.

A familiar paradigm often tacitly appealed to in Freud's account of symptom formation is the story of the barber of King Midas. You may recall from
your schooldays that Apollo gave King Midas donkey's ears to show what he
thought of his musical taste, and that Midas kept them hidden under his hat
except when having his hair cut. His barber, who was threatened with a horrible death if he revealed the condition of the king's ears, found keeping the
secret to himself so burdensome that he was driven to seek relief by digging
a deep hole in a remote place and whispering into it, 'King Midas has donkey's ears.' Put King Midas and the barber in the same head, replace whispering by symbolising or disguisedly representing and we have Freud's
theory of dream and symptom formation in so far as he can be said to have
one theory.

On many occasions we are puzzled to know whether we are to understand the point of the symptom to be to secure uptake and thus alter states
of information, or merely to relieve feelings in the way the barber did.
Expositions tend to obscure this distinction. For example, when Wollheim
reports at one point that Frau K fell ill when her husband was at home, 'her
purpose being to avoid her conjugal duties with K,' and at another that her

illness was used 'to demonstrate her aversion for K' he takes himself to be merely repeating the same claim. But in fact there are three claims here. One is that the pathogenic wish is the wish to avoid sexual relations with her husband, another that it is the wish to convey her distaste for such relations and the third that it is the wish to disguisedly, self-referringly, express her distaste for them.

Freud does sometimes speak as if the wish which impelled the symptom, error, or what-not, was the wish to communicate: 'A communicating agency has been able to say what it wanted but not in the way that it wanted.' And this is the impression that several expositors have received and passed on: but as a general claim about the character which Freud assigns to symptoms, etc., it is quite unwarranted and is only countenanced because it is confused with the related but distinct thesis that the symptom gratifies the wish to mimic a communication.

Erik Erikson says of the cases in *Studies on Hysteria* 'the symptoms were delayed involuntary communications: using the whole body as spokesman, they were saying what common language permits common people to say directly: "He makes me sick," "She pierced me with her eyes," "I could not swallow that insult."' And Charles Rycroft thinks Freud's revolutionary discovery is that 'neurotic symptoms are meaningful disguised communications.' When Wollheim, following Freud, says that Dora used her throat disorders to demonstrate her love for Herr K. he too is invoking a communication rationale. What is it (among other things) that gets gratified here but a communicative itch? But since it is, like the barber's, an uptake-avoiding one (she obscured 'the coincidence between her attacks of illness and the absence of the man she loved lest its regularity should betray her'), what Dora's aphonia illustrates is not the wish to communicate but the wish to utter.

B.A. Farrell says that when Leonardo, recording his childhood reminiscence of being visited in his cradle by a 'vulture,' laid particular emphasis on the big tail of the bird, 'it was a way of telling us that there was a time when he was curious about his mother's body.' Farrell doesn't explain why Leonardo should want to tell us this. What we have in Freud's account of this incident is either the barber paradigm again, i.e. an uptake avoiding, mimic-communication, or no communication at all but inadvertent self-revelation.

In his explanatory practice Freud gives us plenty of warrant for asserting that if a symptom is indeed 'a substitute formation for an unperformed action' then the action in question is the making of a statement. Moreover, the statement in question need not be a wish—a desire expressed in words. It is not just the content of the representation that constitutes it a gratification but the very act of representation itself. Many of Freud's examples bear this out if a forced construction is not put upon them. Thus when it is an unconscious *wish* which is represented this is doubly wish-fulfilling, for in addition to the content which represents the desired state of affairs, there is the wishing itself which constitutes a gratification in that it too was under repression. Not only did we lack the desired state but we didn't own to wanting it. It follows that even when what is manifested is not a wish but a different thought content—a resolution, an apprehension, or a rebuke—it is still wish-fulfilling merely in virtue of its being a representation.

There is a persistent ambiguity in Freud as to whether the wish that was 'fulfilled', by his Hamilcar-Hasdrubal error, say, was Freud's wish that his half-brother Emmanuel should have been his father rather than Jacob, or Freud's wish to acknowledge, in some form, that Emmanuel rather than Jacob had been his father. (After all, it was not the wish that Emmanuel be his father that Freud had prevented from being realised by truncating his account of the associations to the Rome dreams, but his wish to say so.) 'I finally told him what I thought of him—that he was a rogue' gratifies the wish to have told him that he was a rogue, not the wish that he be a rogue. The barber's whispering, 'King Midas has donkey's ears' was not meant to satisfy the wish that King Midas have donkey's ears, but just the wish to reveal that he had.

In *The Psychopathology of Everyday Life* Freud says of a parapraxis in which the speaker dropped a piece of pie from a fork he was lifting to his mouth in the middle of an anecdote about a desirable post he had narrowly missed being appointed to, 'the obtrusive thought thereupon disguised itself as a symptomatic act which expressed symbolically what was meant to be hidden and in this way afforded the speaker relief which arose from unconscious sources.' This semantic, or utterance-surrogate, theory is also exemplified by the unlucky gambler whose failure to take his personal possessions with him when he leaves represents, according to Freud, the reproach, 'You have made me destitute.' And by the elderly honeymooner whose symptomatic act expresses, according to Freud, his apprehension that he would be unable to consummate. And by Dora's playing with her reticule; Freud could have said that she was gratifying symbolically her masturbatory urges but what he says is that she was attempting to say something with respect to them: that she wished to indulge them—a 'pantomimic *announcement.*' (My italics)

The woman whose practice of leaving the best of everything she is given to eat corresponds to cessation of sexual relations with her husband ('she had given up the best') can't be fulfilling a repressed wish since she is re-enacting symbolically what is already the case. So it was a surrogate expression of regret and not a wish-fulfilment. It would have illustrated Freud's explicit theory better if the woman who said of her husband's unrestricted diet, 'he can eat and drink whatever I want' did not 'wear the breeches in the family,' for then it could have been a wish-fulfilment and not just a gratuitous revelation of the actual state of affairs, i.e. a surrogate-boast. (A case cited by Rycroft of a patient whose right hand became paralysed because of the death of his mother 'who had been his right hand' shows that the tradition is being kept up.)

Why does Freud call symptoms gratifications? Does he notice a lessening of the intensity of the wish consequent on its symbolic manifestation? Do maidens seek defloration less intensively after their migraine attacks? Certain symptoms may illustrate what students of magic and ritual call 'mimetic intensification' so that though the overt manifestations of the unconscious fantasy don't themselves constitute the gratification they, nevertheless, enhance it. Mimetic intensification is exemplified by the faint, fleeting smile that played about Walter Mitty's lips as, proud and disdainful, he faced an imaginary firing squad. But when Walter Mitty, attempting to remember his shopping list, startled a passer-by by saying 'puppy biscuit' out loud he wasn't gratifying anything. Had he muttered 'pocketa-pocketa-pocketa' in the course of his great surgeon fantasy we might invoke mimetic intensification to bring it under the gratification thesis. What reason is there for thinking that phenomena like Dora's limp, or Freud's climbing one flight of stairs too many, are not like 'puppy biscuit' rather than like 'pocketa-pocketa-pocketa?' and thus not gratificatory. We understand how hysterical attacks accompanied by vigorous pelvic thrusts and clonic-tonic contractions might afford sexual relief, or suggest that they did, in a way in which we don't understand how a chronic symptom like a paralysis can; but we obligingly project behind the appearance of the unaccommodating cases a story which would make sense of them. If symptoms are to be rendered intelligible through assimilation to these standard cases of relief through expression, then this must be via the similarity in the surroundings, what goes on before and after, and not by reference to 'the yet uncomprehended process in the yet unexplained medium' (Wittgenstein). What we want is not what a libidometer or psychoanalytoscope will one day reveal but the lineaments of gratified desire or something like them.

III

In his remarks on psychoanalysis Wittgenstein suggests that the appropriate mode of assessment for psychoanalytic interpretations is the subject's endorsement, since they pertain to reasons and not causes. as with Freud's explanations of jokes, for example. But there is a profound disanalogy between the symptom-work and the joke-work. We can't lead the patient from one end of the symptom to the other as we can lead him from one end of the joke to the other. One is in the nature of a supplementation, what Wittgenstein calls 'a further description,' the other is not and must be supported as a hypothesis is supported.

We could say of the interpretations of symptoms what Wittgenstein said of the interpretation of dreams—that they are not all of one kind. Just as there are interpretations which 'still belong to the dream in a way.' so there are interpretations which still belong to the symptom 'in a way.' But I should maintain that those interpretations which still belong to the symptom—further detail concerning the content of obsessional thoughts, for example—are essentially pre-Freudian in their conceptual character.

In the case where a patient accepts as apposite or felicitous the analyst's characterization of a rebuke she had suffered as 'like a slap in the face' we may concede her special privileged relation to the suggestion and the inappropriateness of describing her as entertaining or accepting an hypothesis. But can we allow that she stands in a privileged relation to the claim that the attack of facial neuralgia she suffered on that occasion was a conversion of the thought-content 'like a slap in the face?'

Freud's account of Elisabeth von R's tender feelings for her brother-in-law 'which had been able to conceal themselves behind the mask of sisterly affection' is also typical of the pre-Freudian, humanistic unconscious. To sharpen your sense of the distinction contrast Freud's reconstruction of her thoughts at the deathbed of her dead sister, 'Now he is free and I can be his wife' with his interpretation of her hysterical pains, 'In place of mental pains which she avoided physical pains made their appearance.' She stands in no privileged relation to Freud's claim that it was because she avoided mental pain that physical pain made its appearance.

John Wisdom replies to the objection to Freud that 'one cannot, in the ordinary sense of the word, fail to be aware of one's hatred or of one's wish when one tries to detect it introspectively' by arguing that one can 'give a psychological word or phrase a more dispositional use' without giving it a more behaviouristic one. He then suggests that claims about hidden feelings might be construed as follows: 'There is in X's mind hatred (love, contempt) for Y . . . is less a matter of whether at the moment, upon reflection it appears (so) and more a matter of how it would feel if, for example, this or that were to happen.'

This is plausible but is it Freud? How much of the theory of the unconscious will this enable us to salvage? For one thing Wisdom speaks of 'hidden feelings,' but what of the hidden processes to which Freud is so often committed? Would we allow that a claim about what an hysteric was unconsciously doing or undergoing at a certain time, could be settled by what she 'would feel if this or that were to happen?' And what of the unconscious wishes manifesting themselves as symptoms in the following typical specimen: 'the paralysed leg of a hysterical girl expresses her unconscious wish for a penis in that the leg is stiff and at the same time it reveals her acceptance of her castration in that she is paralysed' (L. Eidelberg, ed., *Encyclopaedia of Psychoanalysis*). What would this girl have to 'feel if this or that were to happen' in order for us to find this claim worthy of credence?

A patient might ultimately come to realise that she harboured a particular unconscious impulse, for example, a defloration or pregnancy fantasy, in
the way Wisdom suggests, but what of the relation between the impulse and
its supposed manifestations. such as migraine or vomiting—its efficacy in
producing symptoms, dreams, errors? Could she 'realise' this, too, in the
same way? What we need in the case of claims that phenomena like these are
due to an unconscious wish or motive is not mere evidence of possession but
evidence of implementation. And this the patient's subsequent introspection
is in no position to give us. If the interpretation is to be supported it must
be as a hypothesis is supported. But this puts a greater burden on behavioural evidence than it can normally bear. We are aware of this in an obscure
way and so think in terms of the prospect of the patient's ultimate recognition without confronting this criterion with any interpretative specimens
concrete or typical enough to reveal its inappropriateness. Moreover the
absurdity of the criterion of retrospective self-intimation often extends
beyond the question of evidence to the question of intelligibility. Would we
even understand what Dora meant if she retrospectively assured us that on
the occasion of Herr K's sexual overtures she had displaced a sensation of
pressure from her thigh to her thorax, or that she had transformed the experience of excitation in the genitals into one of disgust at the glottis? Even if
we confine ourselves to claims respecting the mere possession of unconscious wishes, thoughts, or feelings rather than to their somatic expression,
there are striking differences between those examples which illustrate
Wisdom's account of their character and those which are distinctively characteristic of Freud. Freud illustrates Wisdom's view of how a later experience
might induce a recognition of what one had hitherto been unconsciously
feeling in his account of a patient's realisation that she had been hiding her
infatuation for her brother-in-law under a 'mask of sisterly affection' when,
at her sister's deathbed, the thought overwhelmed her, 'Now he is free and
can marry me.' But the use Freud makes of the notion of the unconscious
here is essentially pre-Freudian and could have been made at any time before
him. And it was. Wisdom's notion is just as clearly illustrated by the following episode in *Anna Karenina*.

> At first Anna sincerely believed that she was displeased with [Vronsky] for dar-
> ing to pursue her; but soon after her return from Moscow, having gone to a
> party where she expected to meet him but to which he did not come she dis-
> tinctly realised by the disappointment that overcame her, that she had been
> deceiving herself and that his pursuit was not only not distasteful to her, but was
> the whole interest of her life.

That the notion of self-discovery, and thus of the unconscious, employed
in these two examples is not centrally Freudian is indicated by the fact that
Anna did not have to wait for the ball at which Vronsky did not appear to
learn 'that his pursuit was not only not distasteful to her but was the whole

interest of her life.' Tolstoy himself implies this when he says she had been deceiving herself. We don't say of those whose ignorance pertains merely to what they would feel under unrealised circumstances that they are deceiving themselves. And this shows that we are still not dealing with the Freudian unconscious in such cases. Notice that in his account Wisdom says that what is hidden in one's mind 'is less a matter of whether at the moment, on reflection it appears so', but on a full-fledged Freudian view is not at all a matter of what at the moment, on reflection it might appear. This would still only be what Freud is careful to distinguish as 'preconscious'. Further information in cases like Anna's functions to bring into the focus of consciousness things of which we were 'aware in a nascent penumbral way' and 'relations which were felt though not implicitly recognised' rather than to provide the basis of fresh inferences. When Freud says that the patient knows the meaning of his symptoms. dreams, errors, and so forth, this is not the sort of thing he means, or needs to mean.

In the first chapter of *The Ego and the Id,* in his discussion of the distinction between conscious and unconscious, Freud says, 'The thought which was previously unnoticed is not recognised by consciousness but often seems entirely alien . . .' He alludes in the same paragraph to the anti-Freudian tactic of 'seeking refuge from the unconscious in what is unnoticed or scarcely noticed.' The subject who is presented with the thought which is unconscious is described by Freud as 'being quite unaware of the fact.' And there are many other occasions on which Freud employs idioms which indicate how different is his concept from the one defended by Wisdom. But this view is incoherently combined with one which conceives the patient, nevertheless, to stand in a privileged relation to explanations of his condition.

In the sixth of the *Introductory Lectures* Freud asks, 'Where and in what connection is it supposed to have been proved that a man can possess knowledge without knowing that he does so?' and offers a proof taken 'from the sphere of hypnotic phenomena'—the fact that the subject who had been placed in an hypnotic trance will, though initially oblivious, come to remember the activities in which he had then engaged. 'Since in the end he had knowledge without having learnt it from any other quarter in the meantime these recollections were in his mind from the outset. They were merely inaccessible to him. He did not know that he knew . . . his case was exactly similar to what we assume the dreamer's to be.' But what is the post-hypnotic subject, who denies that he knows what went on during the hypnotic interlude, wrong about? The sense in which he knows (he is capable of recollecting it) is not the sense in which he denied that he knew. The fact that Freud thinks that the phenomenon of post-hypnotic reminiscence supports his argument in favour of the existence of unconscious thoughts indicates that he thinks of the hypnotic subject not as finally remembering what occurred during the hypnotic trance or state but as 'remembering' what was 'going on in him' at the time he denied any knowledge of it. The recollections were unconsciously present and thus he 'knew' them but he did not know that he knew. But this misdescribes the situation. It was not 'mental processes going on in him' when he protested ignorance, that the hypnotic subject belatedly recalled, but his public activities during the hypnotic episode. Suppose that, as sometimes happens, there was no amnesia and he had answered that he did know, would it be mental processes 'going on within him' that he was confessing conversancy with? Wouldn't this just be a pretentious way of saying that he did recall what had happened and could tell us?

If we turn to another place where Freud invokes hypnotic phenomena, the 1912 'Note on the Unconscious', we find that there it is not mere recall of the hypnotic episode after protests of obliviousness which he invokes but the phenomena of posthypnotic compliance with an order, for example opening an umbrella at a particular cue. Freud's appeal to the post-hypnotic subject's realisation that a particular action was undertaken in compliance with an hypnotically implanted suggestion to show that a dreamer may similarly come to know the meaning of his dream also shows that he intermittently harbours a self-intimationist conception of the unconscious. If Freud is not under the dominance of some such presupposition why introduce the fact of the hypnotic subject's later recollection at all, and with such fanfare, 'Lo and behold . . . ?' The argument in favour of unconscious mentality, as a non-self-intimationist would construe it has just as much force without the emphasis on the fact that the subject could be brought to recollect the occasion of the instruction. And by choosing from among post-hypnotic phenomena an action like opening an umbrella Freud makes the claim that the subject later knew why he had done it easy to interpret in its strong, self-intimationist sense. Had he taken the case of someone being told he would hallucinate, or feel pain, or that his nose would bleed, it would have seemed less plausible to construe the subject's realisation that he had been complying with a post-hypnotic suggestion as a self-intimating one.

The subject in the post-hypnotic suggestion case arrives at a conviction that his apparently unmotivated act was the result of a suggestion made to him while he was in the hypnotic state. But why are we to say, as Freud insists, that he knows that it was? Isn't it because Freud so sets the example up that we are told what happened and so know that he is right? But this has no parallel when we turn to the dream. For if we knew of something which stood to the dream as the publicly pronounced post-hypnotic suggestion stood to the opening of the umbrella we would not require the dreamer's corroboration.

Some philosophers have tended to treat statements of the form 'X unconsciously wants P', 'X unconsciously feels P', 'X unconsciously thinks

P', as if it were a matter of indifference what replaces P. We want to know what it means to say that a girl's convulsively contracting arm represents the ejaculation of her fantasized penis though she doesn't know it, but we are only told what it means to say that someone hates his father though he doesn't know it. Attempted elucidation of interpretations tends to overlook the number of occasions on which the unconscious wish figures in occurrent rather than dispositional claims.

Since we are quite habituated to real-reason discourse, discourse in which, without doubting an agent's candour, motives are, nevertheless, imputed to him, because the manner in which his behaviour co-varies with the grounds-providing features of his circumstances is not otherwise, or not as simply, explicable, we fail to notice that many psychoanalytical explanations in terms of unconscious wishes are not assimilable to real-reason discourse because they are not capable of behavioural but only of introspective validation; which, if I may be permitted an Irishism, they are also incapable of. A typical class of psychoanalytic interpretations are pseudo-soliloquies and the idioms in which they are couched are due to the necessity of creating the impression that the harbourer of unconscious thoughts and wishes can come to stand to them in the same relation as he does to his conscious thoughts and wishes. The effect of conferring an ultimately self-intimating character on Freud's imputations of unconscious processes is that it protects Freud's more elaborate interpretations from the charge of unintelligibility.

In this paper I have recorded the comments, questions, distinctions which, it seems to me, force themselves on anyone who makes a determined attempt to understand Freud's claims as to the influence of unconscious wishes. Casting about for a phrase which would serve as a mnemonic summary of my general impression of the use Freud makes of this notion I found that William James had prophetically said it for me: 'The distinction between conscious and unconscious mental states is the sovereign means for believing what one likes.'

7

Was Freud a Liar?

The story of how Sigmund Freud discovered the Oedipus complex, and thus the main source of neurotic tribulation, is a celebrated one, which has fired imaginations and warmed hearts from the shores of Asia to the Edgware Road. Let me remind you of how it goes.

In the mid-nineties of the last century, Freud, a Viennese physician, who specialised in the treatment of nervous disorders, had a succession of patients who recalled an occasion in infancy in which they had been sexually molested, usually by one of their own parents. This came as a great shock to Freud, as he had no inkling of the pathogenic potency of sexual life and was, indeed, reluctant to credit it. Nevertheless, he believed his patients' stories, and, when he had heard about a dozen or so, duly reported that he had discovered the specific cause of psychoneurotic disorder: a passive sexual experience before puberty. In other words, a seduction. To continue the story in the words of Freud's biographer, Ernest Jones, 'Freud found that several of the seduction stories were simply untrue: there had been no seduction. But he held fast to the fact that the patient had told him these stories, with the result that he discovered the importance of infantile fantasy life in the genesis of the neuroses.' How did Freud do this? How did he turn the seduction mistake into a discovery about the role of parents in infantile fantasy? Well, the story continues, Freud brilliantly penetrated the patients' false memories of being seduced by a parent, and found, concealed behind them, their own infantile wishes for sexual relations with the parent.

In this article I want to persuade you that, with the exception of the claim that Freud was practising medicine in Vienna during the 1890s, this story has about as much historicity as that of George Washington and the cherry tree or King Alfred and the cakes. The truth of the matter can be briefly stated, though not briefly documented. Freud did not base his

This was a talk first broadcast on BBC Radio 3 in October 1973, and first printed in *The Listener* (7 February 1974). It is reprinted by permission.

seduction theory on stories of infantile seduction related by his patients. In any case, his patients did not tell him any fictitious seduction stories. And the seduction stories of whose truth they were eventually persuaded did not normally involve parents, and so are unlikely to have been transformations of fantasies concerning parents. Further, Freud could not, for a variety of reasons, have been surprised by the discovery that his patients' illnesses had sexual causes. Rather, it is likely that it was Freud's own preconceptions concerning the influence of sexual life that incited his patients to accept sexual cause for their difficulties.

I think what really happened was this: at first, Freud was exhilarated by the way in which his patients produced confirmation for his seduction theory. Then he discovered that some of the seductions had never happened. He had been warned by the reviewers of his first book on hysteria of the serious risk that his method produced false convictions in his patients as to the correctness of his explanations. And his critics, it seemed, were right. What a humiliation! Freud now put all his enormous resourcefulness into mitigating, if not entirely evading, this humiliation.

Freud had to account for the consistency with which he had arrived at the seduction scenes. Either the seductions were authentic, or Freud's method of reconstructing the infantile past of his patients was invalid. But many of the seductions had proved fictitious, so it must have been Freud's method that was invalid. Freud solved this dilemma by falsifying one of its horns. It then became: 'Either the seductions are authentic or my patients are self-deceived and their confessions false. But the seductions are fictitious, therefore my patients' confessions are false.' But there was still a difficulty. Might not the alleged confessions of his patients be attributed to their suggestibility? Might the confessions not be the result of his own preconceived views as to the role of sexuality in nervous disorders? Freud resolved this difficulty by obliterating from his consciousness the fact that he had any preconceived views as to the influence of sexuality.

It is an established part of psychoanalytic folklore that Freud came slowly and reluctantly to an acknowledgment of the role of sexuality in the production of neurotic illness. And, like most psychoanalytic folklore, it derives directly from Freud's repeated assertions of it. But it is completely untrue. Freud was searching for the sources of neurotic disorders in the sexual life of his patients before he began practicing psychoanalysis even in its most primitive and rudimentary forms. And by the mid-1890s, when he put forward the seduction theory, he was already subjecting his patients to an aggressive cross-examination as to their sexual habits.

We are all familiar with the way in which legends grow imperceptibly more and more remote from the historical facts. The striking thing about the legend of Freud's progression from real seduction to Oedipal fantasies is that it did not grow. It sprang fully armed from the brow of Freud. And so it confronts us with the embarrassing but unavoidable question—was Freud a liar? In attempting to account for the grossness of the discrepancy between Freud's accounts of the seduction episode and what really happened, I did not overlook the possibility that Freud simply lied. I finally rejected it because it is more plausible to assume that Freud suffered a massive amnesia than that he foolishly gave accounts which are so blatantly incompatible with the published evidence. What makes it even more likely that in Freud's case we have, not lies, but memory errors, is that we know Freud to have been particularly prone to such memory errors. There was, for example, the cocaine episode. Freud had been an uncritical advocate of the medical value of cocaine when it was first introduced in the early 1880s. He defended himself from the criticism which followed the discovery of its dangers by arguing that these dangers were conditional on its being administered by injection. When administered by mouth, as Freud himself had advocated, it was harmless. In fact, Freud had advocated the administration of cocaine by injection. Not only did Freud overlook this in his reply to criticism, but he seems to have become permanently amnesic with respect to it. The topic of cocaine comes up again in Freud's associations to the dream which inaugurated the psychoanalytic study of dreams—the dream of Irma's injection. One of the themes of this dream was the injurious effects of cocaine. In his associations Freud repeated that he had never advocated its use by injection. It seems that dream analysis, which is capable of plumbing the depths of the unconscious is, nevertheless, not able to uncover common or garden self-deception.

So far I have merely shown that there is nothing extravagant in putting down Freud's grossly distorted account of the seduction episode to a failure of memory: I have not yet shown that Freud's account was grossly distorted. First let me show that it is untrue to hold, as Freud later insisted, that his patients told him imaginary seduction stores. In the course of attempting to allay suspicions that his patients may have willfully deceived him, Freud said of their attitude towards the seductions that 'whilst calling these infantile experiences into consciousness they still try to withhold belief by emphasising the fact that they had no feeling of recollecting these scenes.' So before Freud discovered that the seductions were imaginary, he was describing them as experiences which his patients had no feeling of recollecting. After he had discovered that the seductions had not occurred, he described them as 'the deceptive memories of hysterics concerning their childhood.' How can these two accounts be reconciled?

Freud urged against the view that the seduction stories were fabrications the fact that 'patients assure me emphatically of their unbelief.' This implies that not only were they not recollecting the seductions, but that they were not even convinced that the seductions happened. And how is this to be reconciled with the active role Freud later assigned to his patients in phrases like 'hysterics trace back their symptoms to fictitious traumas' or 'patients ascribe their symptoms to passive sexual experiences in early childhood'? Was it not Freud himself who did the tracing and the ascribing?

There is another reason for holding that Freud unconsciously fabricated the patients' confessions. In his retrospective accounts, Freud tells us that the patients' delusions of seduction usually pertained to parents. But, in the original seduction papers themselves, the cast-list includes nursemaids, governesses, domestic servants, teachers, tutors, older children and even brothers—but no parents. The claim that it is the parents who are the seducers is not only *not* made in the original seduction papers, it is inconsistent with them. Freud there says that in seven of the cases it was brothers who were the seducers, and, since brothers are as identifiable as parents, the motive for this discrepancy can hardly be discretion.

Incidentally, even if the seduction beliefs of Freud's patients had uniformly pertained to the cross-sex parent it is not obvious why this is a natural transformation of infantile fantasies about seducing the cross-sex parent. Freud is very unforthcoming as to why this should be so. He merely asserts that the seduction memories are less wounding to the patient than the acknowledgement of his own incestuous infantile inclinations. But is the thought that you were sexually used by your mother really less disagreeable than the thought that you once desired her? I have not found anyone who felt so, though I am struck by the way in which people who gabble happily about the Oedipus complex are mildly affronted if you attempt to introduce a degree of particularity into the discussion. And since the imputed fantasies are unconscious in any case, why isn't that sufficient protection against self-reproach? Why the additional precaution of inverting them and giving the parents the active role actually take by the child? You mustn't even ask.

Still, so far I have merely shown that Freud's patients did not relate stories of seduction, and not that Freud did. My reasons for maintaining this are largely circumstantial. First, there is the matter of Freud's tremendous confidence in his diagnostic powers, combined with a most unpsychological reluctance to credit the power of suggestibility. This is what he said in his book on hysteria, published in 1895, a year before the three seduction theory papers: 'We need not be afraid of telling the patient what we think his next thought is going to be. It will do no harm.'

One bit of evidence that it was Freud's practice to communicate his seduction suspicions to his patients comes from the analysis of one of his own dreams. In the dream, Freud reproaches a patient for not accepting his explanation as to why she was ill and blames the persistence of her illness on this refusal. In his associations to this item, Freud says that the reproach in the dream was probably just a repetition of a reproach he had made his patient in waking life. Freud goes on to add: 'It was my view at this time that my task was fulfilled when I had informed the patient of the hidden meaning of his symptoms.' But this dream was the dream of Irma's injection, and since we know the exact date of that dream we can state that Irma was one of Freud's original batch of presumably seduced patients. Is it rash to infer that the 'hidden meaning of the symptoms' about which Freud made it a practice to inform his patients at that time was a sexual seduction in infancy? You may think this a bit thin. So let me see if I can do better. During the period when Freud thought he was receiving daily confirmation of his seduction hypothesis, a patient confessed that when she was a young girl she had been the victim of a sexual assault by her father. 'Naturally,' Freud wrote to the correspondent to whom he related the incident, 'she did not find it incredible when I told her that similar and worse things must have happened to her in infancy.'

One of the questions that the seduction story presents us with is this: how did Freud come by the discovery that the seduction theory was false? Once again Freud has a ready answer, and once again it is completely untrue. When Freud first publically admitted the seduction error, nine years later, he explained it as follows: 'I did not then know that persons who remain normal may have had the same experiences in their childhood.' But he did know. In the original papers he wrote: 'We have heard and acknowledged that there are many people who have a very clear recollection of infantile sexual experiences and yet do not suffer from hysteria.' Why this discrepancy?

In this account, Freud is explaining his discovery of the seduction error in terms of his realisation that—as he put it—'persons who remain normal may have had the same experiences in childhood.' This makes it sound as if the seduction error consisted only in the rashness of Freud's extrapolating to hysterics in general, and not in his attributing false histories of seductions to his own patients. The measure of Freud's inability to come to terms with the seduction error is to be found in the earlier portion of the sentence I quoted, which says, astonishingly, of the seductions: 'I cannot admit that I exaggerated their frequency or their importance.' It had taken Freud nine years to bring himself to publically admit the seduction error and when it came to the point he funked it.

How then had Freud convinced himself of the reality of the seductions? In his own words, 'by letting the symptoms tell the tale.' Far from basing his conviction on the patients' testimony, Freud argued that, just as a physician can explain how a physical injury has been caused without any information from the injured person, so in hysteria the analyst can penetrate from the symptoms to their causes—without the testimony of the patient.

Why should Freud have gone to such lengths to conceal from himself the real basis of his confidence in the reality of the infantile seductions? For a perfectly understandable reason. Freud could not bring himself to recognise the reasoning by which he had persuaded himself of the authenticity of the seductions, because it was the same sort of reasoning which, for the rest of his career, he was to employ in his reconstruction of infantile fantasy life and of the content of the unconscious in general. This emerges clearly in one of the original seduction papers in which Freud urges against scepticism concerning the seduction the fact that 'patients appeared to live through it with all the appropriate emotions.'

Let me sum up, Freud did not fall into the seduction error through believing his patients' stories; he did not fall into it through ignorance of the fact that persons sexually molested in infancy may, nevertheless, not succumb to neurosis; he did not fall into it through underestimating the frequency of seduction in the general population. Freud fell into the seduction error through the use of a procedure which to this day remains the basis of the psychoanalytic reconstruction of infantile life: the attribution to patients of certain infantile experiences because they appear to the analyst to be living 'through them with all the appropriate emotions'.

The lesson Freud ought to have learned from the discovery that the infantile seductions which he believed to be the specific causes of the psychoneurosis were often fictitious, was not that infantile fantasy life is as important in the genesis of neurotic illness as actual infantile events, but that his own method of eliciting from patients their infantile histories, and more important still, his method of interpreting these elicitations, was an unreliable one, which leads to mistaken reconstructions that deceive not only the physician but the patient himself. But instead of modifying his procedure so as to lessen the risk of mistaken inferences, Freud merely made the inferences themselves so indeterminate that the validity of his methods could never again be placed in jeopardy. Freud, like the Emperor in the story, dealt with bad news by having the bearer executed.

There is an aphorism of Nietzsche's which Freud quoted on several occasions to illustrate the affinity between Nietzsche's thought and his own: '"I did this," says my memory. "I cannot have done this," says my pride, and remains inexorable. In the end memory yields.' On several occasions in after years, Freud attempted to reconstruct the considerations which had led him to assert first that a sexual seduction and then that incestuous fantasy lay at the root of every psychoneurosis. In this talk I have tried to show that whenever he made this attempt Freud's pride would not yield, and it was memory that lost.

8

From Freud's 'Scientific Fairy Tale' to Masson's Politically Correct One

There seems to have been a slight decline in the number of people willing to clap their hands and say they believe in the Oedipus complex. However that may be, Jeffrey Masson, Sanskrit scholar, psychoanalyst, and ex-project director of the Freud Archives is no longer to be counted among them. Masson's book advances a discreditable explanation of Freud's abandonment of the seduction theory and its replacement by the Oedipus complex. In it he achieves the remarkable feat of concocting an account no less tendentious and unreliable than Freud's own. Masson thinks Freud accepted the seduction theory because it was forced on him by the evidence, then rejected it out of timidity. In fact Freud accepted a dubious theory because he was anxious to bring himself to the attention of the medical world and he abandoned it from belated circumspection.

It has long been apparent to a few free and discerning spirits that Freud's account of his transition from the thesis that at the root of every psychoneurosis was the patient's memory of sexual abuse in infancy to the view that it was rather to be found in their infantile incestuous fantasizing is a farrago, in spite of its being re-perpetrated with minor variations in supposedly authoritative and scholarly works such as those of Ronald Clark and Frank Sulloway.

Masson's book does have the merit of addressing anew three questions which have hitherto been answered with gross inadequacy. Why did Freud embrace the seduction theory? Why did he give it up? And why did he replace it with conflicts over incestuous wishes? But the account Masson gives both of what Freud believed and as to why he stopped believing it is a distorted one.

This review of Jeffrey Masson, *The Assault on Truth: Freud's Suppression of the Seduction Theory* (London: Faber, 1984) first appeared in the *Times Literary Supplement* (6 July 1984), and is reprinted by permission.

Masson devotes an entire chapter to horrendous accounts of the torture and sexual abuse of children during the period Freud spent at Charcot's clinic: 'In all likelihood Paris provided Freud with experiences and evidence on which he built his thesis, in 1896, that real sexual traumas in childhood lay at the very heart of neurotic illness.' Masson goes to pointless lengths to establish the topicality of the theme of child abuse during the period Freud spent at the Salpêtrière in order to support his claim that Freud, alerted by the experience, was all the more ready to credit his patients' *a priori* implausible accounts of having been sexually abused in early childhood. Pointless because the phenomenon Masson so assiduously documents is not that to which Freud's seduction theory assigns pathogenic potency. The pathogenic agent in Freud's seduction theory is not pain, terror, or physical injury but precocious sexual arousal. Children may be starved, beaten, or tortured but providing they have not been simultaneously sexually stimulated the experience can have no neurotic aftermath.

Masson is also mistaken in holding that Freud based his conviction of the reality of the seductions on stories recalled and recounted by his patients in the course of analysis, though here he is the victim of Freud's retrospective confabulatory or mendacious accounts rather than his own tendentiousness. Even Freud's contemporaneous accounts are incoherent. Although when he wishes to strengthen his case for the reality of the seductions Freud suggests that the patients themselves recalled and recounted them, when he is concerned that he might appear naively oblivious of the possibility that they were hysterical fabrications we get this: 'Whilst calling these infantile experiences into consciousness they still try . . . to withhold belief by emphasising that they have no feeling of recollecting these scenes . . . patients assure me . . . emphatically of their unbelief . . .' (Incidentally, would an honourable man have represented this state of affairs by speaking of 'statements made by patients in which they ascribed their symptoms to passive sexual experiences in early childhood' as Freud did in 1914?)

Freud's reconstructions were not based on confessions but on his own theoretical requirements and/or intuitions. He believed in the genuineness of the seductions not because his patients remembered and related them but because, in his view, they were re-enacting them. Another consideration which reinforced his belief in their reality was the discovery of his own paedophilic impulses. In a letter to Fliess he reports a dream of sex-play with his nine-year-old daughter (not his niece, as Jones states in the *Life*).

Masson insists that Freud gave up the seduction theory 'not for theoretical or clinical reasons but because of a personal failure of moral courage.' But Freud's dereliction in moral courage showed itself not in what he abandoned but in what he insisted on retaining: the boast that he could reconstruct by psychoanalytic method, dream interpretation in particular, the lost years of childhood. Masson's repeated assertions that Freud dismissed his patients' seduction stories as lies make one wonder as to his grasp of Freud's argument. Freud did not accuse his patients of lying, and it was more than charity that stopped him, for had he done so he would simultaneously have undermined the claim that in 'remembering' infantile seductions his patients were reproducing in distorted form their infantile experience of incestuous fantasizing. The Oedipus complex both explains the adult seduction memories and is rendered plausible by them. For Freud to have cast doubt on the sincerity of his patients' conviction that they had been seduced would have been as fatal to the Oedipus complex as to the seduction theory.

Why then *did* Freud decide that most of the eighteen seductions he had originally reported had not taken place? Although he said that it was 'through contradiction under definitely ascertainable circumstances' it is difficult to construct a plausible scenario along these lines.

'Your daughter, Sir, has alluded to some striking peculiarities in your sexual character. I wonder whether, in the interests of science, you would care to authenticate and perhaps enlarge on them.' It can't often have happened this way. And, in any case, what would a denial prove? You might as a result of inquiries be able to absolve a particular seducer because the seduction story involved inconsistency or anachronism, but how would it enable you to decide that there had been no seduction at all? Freud was perfectly familiar with the fact that an apparent memory may contain both veridical and non-veridical elements. I suspect that his 'contradiction in definitely ascertainable circumstance' belongs with Cyril Burt's series of identical twins.

Freud gave up the seduction theory because he realized that the theme of seduction had been introduced into the material of the analytic sessions by his own preconceptions. His problem was how to disengage from the theory without at the same time conceding the unreliability of psychoanalytic method. He had to find an account of his error from which it followed that 'not the analysis but the patient must in some way bear the responsibility', as he was to put it twenty years later in the *Introductory Lectures*. There may also be something to the view that Freud discovered the Oedipus complex in the course of his own self-analysis and then superimposed it on his clinical data. This would explain how it came about that a clinical practice, the staple of which was women suffering the aftermath of infantile involvement with their fathers, should suggest to Freud a Greek myth about a man who married his mother. (Poor women. Not even their troubles are allowed to have their own names.) The way in which Freud gets from his male patients' 'memories' of false seductions to their true incestuous fantasies is not much less gratuitous. He reported not a single 'memory' of maternal seduction, yet we are asked to believe that infantile incestuous desire for their mothers lay at the root of his male patients' adult seduction memories.

Masson's chapter on the Emma Eckstein episode is interesting but irrelevant. In it we learn that Freud misdiagnosed a patient's post-operative nasal haemorrhaging as hysterical in character when it was due to some gauze having been left in the wound. The connection is supposed to be that rather than admit that Emma was suffering the aftermath of infantile seduction Freud assigned her bleeding to a hysterical mechanism. 'If Emma Eckstein's (bleeding) had nothing to do with the world then her earlier accounts of seduction would be fantasies too.' Even if Masson had better grounds than he offers for Emma Eckstein's having been sexually abused this would in no way have precluded Freud's proffering hysterical conversion accounts of her symptoms. The issues are completely unrelated. The explanatory mode which Freud deployed in accounting for Emma's haemorrhaging ('due to wishes. She bled out of longing') did not need any ulterior motivation. Three years before the Eckstein episode Freud was paying tribute to the uncanny power of the hysterics' unconscious to produce objective physical changes in their bodies. Freud was given to such fatuities, whose appeal is blatant and intrinsic (see Frau Tumler's account of her uterine bleeding in Thomas Mann's *The Black Swan*).

Masson concludes with the following moral: 'By shifting the emphasis from the actual world of sadness, misery, and cruelty to an internal stage on which actors performed invented dramas for an invisible audience of their creation Freud began the trend away from the real world . . .' Isn't Masson just as guilty of deflecting attention from the sadness, misery and cruelty of the real world to his own *News of the World* conception of it? Does he go through life with no apprehensions other than the prospect of being raped or mugged? Why should he think it is otherwise with children?

Masson's child-abuse theory of neurosis is parasitic, for whatever plausibility it possesses, on the assumption that there is no alternative to the self-indulgent, surrealist projections of the Freudians and Kleinians but his own obsession with child rape. But there is another tradition of concern with the hazards of child life, one which neither indulges in unassessable speculation nor restricts the sources of sadness to overt brutality—that of Ian Suttie and John Bowlby.

Masson is correct as to the gratuitousness of Freud's retreat from the determinable circumstances of his patients' childhoods but mistaken as to its significance. Freud did not invoke infantile incestuous fantasies so that he might escape from his commitment to the 'unpopular' seduction theory but in order to cling to his baseless diagnostic pretensions.

There is an understandable reluctance to credit the extent of Freud's opportunism, so it will be some time before we stop hearing of 'Freud, the indefatigable seeker after truth'. (Although some of his more sophisticated admirers are already preparing an alternative niche—'Freud, justified perjurer in a noble cause'. Those who believe neither in Freud's integrity nor in the nobility of his cause can console themselves for the short-term futility of their attempts to set the record straight with a reflection from the Master himself: The voice of reason is soft but it is insistent.

9

Psychoanalysis, Pseudoscience, and Testability

Karl Popper says psychoanalysis is a pseudoscience; others deny this. What is Popper's conception of pseudoscience and why does he hold Freud's psychoanalysis to be an example of one? What would it take to show that Freud's theory is pseudoscientific?

Popper has characterized his demarcation theses as 'bold simplifications', and it is in this spirit that I will treat them and advance my own counters to them. Here is my 'bold simplification' of the substantive issue: when the *bona fide* empirical status of psychoanalysis is rejected, that is, when it is declared a pseudoscience, what is under discussion is not a theory but a practice. (Since a practice implies practitioners, a certain indeterminacy necessarily characterizes such a claim). My 'bold' *exegetical* simplification is that this is Popper's view as well.

I will argue that, though Popper is correct to say that psychoanalysis is pseudoscientific and correct to say that it is unfalsifiable, he is mistaken to suggest that it is pseudoscientific *because* it is unfalsifiable. There are empirical theses which are neither falsifiable nor pseudoscientific, and others which are both. When Freud advances unfalsifiable theses he is being protoscientific. It is when he insists that he has confirmed (not just instantiated) them that he is being pseudoscientific.

There are three main ambiguities about falsifiability as a criterion of demarcation between science and pseudoscience: (1) whether the mere possession of falsifiers is a sufficient condition of scientific as opposed to pseudoscientific status, or whether more is required; (2) whether the lack of falsifiers is a sufficient condition of pseudoscientific status, or whether such utterances are non-scientific, or proto-scientific rather than pseudoscientific;

This first appeared in A. Musgrave and G. Currie, eds., *Karl Popper and the Human Sciences* (Kluwer, 1985) and is reprinted with kind permission of Kluwer Academic Publishers.

(3) whether we are being enjoined to capitulate to apparent discrepancies between the theory's observational entailments and reality, or merely to search assiduously for such discrepancies and note them. Popper is sometimes ambiguous as to all of these but I shall argue that his considered view is, in each case, the latter.[1]

Does Popper hold that a pseudoscience must be unfalsifiable, that is, is the lack of falsifiers a necessary condition of pseudoscientific status? Adolf Grünbaum is foremost among those who have insisted on construing Popper' s criterion for demarcating science from pseudoscience as formal falsifiability, that is, the mere possession of falsifiers. In 'Is Freudian Psychoanalytic Theory Pseudo-Scientific by Karl Popper's Criterion of Demarcation?' (1979*b*, p. 131) Grünbaum says: 'according to [Popper's] criterion, the hallmark of the scientific status of a theory is that empirical findings which would refute it are logically possible.' In 'Is Falsifiability the Touchstone of Scientific Rationality?' (1976) Grünbaum repeats this characterization: 'According to Popper's falsification criterion, falsifiability is sufficient for scientific status' (p. 223). 'For Popper the mere falsifiability of a hypothesis suffices for according scientific status to it' (p. 228). It is clear from what Grünbaum says elsewhere, and from the requirements of his argument, that the term 'scientific' in these remarks is being used as antithetical to 'pseudo-scientific'. In the concluding paragraph of his 'Is Freudian Psychoanalytic Theory Pseudo-Scientific by Karl Popper's Criterion of Demarcation?' he writes: 'Cioffi (1970) has proposed to modify Popper's criterion along the following lines: A theory's refutability is quite insufficient for its scientificality. Even if its claims "are eminently refutable", Cioffi tells us, the theory's pseudoscientificality can be assured by its advocates' wilful employment "of methodological procedures that are calculated to lessen the uncovering of potentially falsifying evidence."' I will attempt to show that the thesis Grünbaum attributes to me is not a modification of Popper's demarcation criterion but that it *is* Popper's demarcation criterion.

Here are the reasons for believing that Popper holds that a theory which is formally falsifiable may, nevertheless, be pseudo-scientific. On p. 81 of the *Logic of Scientific Discovery* (1968*a*) Popper lists four devices 'for attaining, for any chosen axiomatic system . . . its correspondence with reality', the third of which he describes in the following terms: '. . . we may adopt a sceptical attitude as to the reliability of the experimenter whose observations which threaten our system, we may exclude from science on the ground that they are insufficiently supported, unscientific, or not objective, or even on the ground that the experimenter was a liar. (This is the sort of attitude which the physicist may sometimes quite rightly adopt towards alleged occult phenomena).' On the next page he refers to psychoanalysis. (Remarks with similar import occur in Popper's replies in the Schilpp volume. At one point he speaks of 'one vast class of immunizing strategies—those that blame the observation for not presenting the true state of affairs.' (1974, p. 1005). At another he says, 'we can always deny the objectivity, or even the existence of refuting observations' (p. 983), along with an allusion to 'people who refuse to look through Galileo's telescope.')

On p. 82 of the *Logic of Scientific Discovery* he says: 'It is impossible to decide by analysing its logical form, whether a system of statements . . . is a refutable system . . . Only with reference to the methods applied to a theoretical system is it at all possible to ask whether we are dealing with . . . an empirical theory.'

In the paper 'What is Dialectic?' (1969, p. 313) Popper says: '. . . it is most characteristic of the scientific method that scientists will spare no pains to test and criticize the theory in question.' This sentiment is incorporated in 'Remarks on the Problems of Demarcation and Rationality' (Lakatos and Musgrave, 1968, p. 94), where it is supplemented: 'What characterizes the scientific approach is a highly critical attitude towards our theories rather than a formal criterion of refutability; only in the light of such a critical attitude and the corresponding critical methodology approach do "refutable" theories retain their refutability.'

In the autobiographical section of the Schilpp volume Popper writes: 'What impressed me most was Einstein's own clear statement that he would regard his theory as untenable if it should fail in certain tests . . . This, I felt, was the true scientific attitude, utterly different from the dogmatic attitude which constantly claimed to find "verification" for its favourite theories. The scientific attitude was the critical attitude which did not look for verification but for crucial tests . . .' (1974, p. 29).

Moreover, since the 'Oedipus effect' (a self-verifying prediction) is defined in terms of the prevention of conflict with falsifying observations (Popper, 1969, p. 38), it can only be raised as an objection to theories which are formally capable of conflicting with such observations, that is, which are 'P-scientific', as Grünbaum tendentiously dubs them, so that 'P-scientific' can hardly be the antithesis of pseudoscientific. (That it is the notion of spurious confirmations rather than of unfalsifiability with which Popper is working is indicated, too, by the epigraph from Trollope's *Phineas Finn* which introduces *Conjectures and Refutations*.)

I conclude that Grünbaum is quite mistaken to assign to Popper the view that formal falsifiability is sufficient to rebut a charge of pseudoscience. If I may venture a diagnosis of Grünbaum's error, it is that he fails to notice that Popper is working with two antitheses: one, between nonscientific (or proto-scientific, or metaphysical) assertions which are to be distinguished from scientific ones on the score of their falsifiability and another, between pseudoscientific and non-pseudoscientific assertions where the relevant consideration is the conditions under which claims to have confirmed the theory are issued.

Grünbaum's claim that the inductivist criterion of scientific status is more stringent than Popper's is based on the same misunderstanding. Popper and the inductivists are giving different answers to the question, 'under what circumstances is a positive instance of a universal generalization to be considered supportive of the truth of that generalization?' Grünbaum intermittently confuses this question with the quite distinct question, 'under what conditions is a putatively positive instance of a phenomenon to be considered a genuinely positive instance?'

Now it is quite clear that when Popper says that positive instances of white swans are not capable of supporting the universalization that all swans are white he is not speaking of spurious positive instances but of genuine ones. The difference does not lie where Grünbaum locates it but rather in this: if we consider a universalization which it has not been possible to subject to attempted falsification, but of which there are genuine positive instances and, *a fortiori*, no negative ones, then Popper's inductivist must assign some probability value to it while Popper would not. That is, Popper's question is: what measure of support should we permit genuinely positive instances to afford a universal hypothesis with respect to them under circumstances in which it is not possible to distinguish apparently negative instances from genuinely negative ones? Popper's answer to this question is, 'None'. And whether or not he is correct, it is with respect to *this* question that Grünbaum ought to have drawn the contrast between Popper's falsificationism and the inductivist position, and not with respect to the non-methodological (formal) issue, 'what makes an assertion a candidate for scientific status or assessment?', where the distinctiveness of Popper's position lies rather in his refusal to accord such status to uncircumscribed singular existentials as contrasted with the inductivist's willingness to do so.[2]

1. Is Unfalsifiability a Sufficient Condition of Pseudoscientific Status?

Though it is important to make Popper's distinction between theories which are instantiable but not falsifiable and those which are both, it might be better not to make it by calling the non-falsifiable ones 'pseudoscientific'. Nor does Popper always do so. Sometimes he refers to them as 'non-scientific', or 'metaphysical'.

> Psychoanalysis . . . is an interesting psychological metaphysics (and no doubt there is some truth in it, as there is so often in metaphysical ideas), but it was never a science. There are lots of people who may be Freudian or Adlerian cases: Freud himself was clearly a Freudian case and Adler an Adlerian case. But what prevents their theories from being scientific in the sense here described is very simply that they do not exclude any physically possible human behaviour. Whatever any body may do is, in principle, explicable in Freudian or Adlerian

terms. Adler's break with Freud was more Adlerian than Freudian, but Freud never looked on it as a refutation of his theory . . . *the theory was compatible with everything that could happen—even without any special immunization treatment.* (Schilpp, 1974, p. 985)

Even in this predominantly formalist passage Popper slips in nonformalist considerations, for example, the remark that Freud would not consider the occurrence of Adlerian cases as falsifying his theory. But on a formalist interpretation of Popper's remark what choice would Freud have? He would not even be able to conceive of what an Adlerian counter-example might be. If 'Adler's break with Freud was more Adlerian than Freudian' then it cannot be the case that the theory was *a priori* 'compatible with everything that could happen.'

I construe this apparent discrepancy in Popper's characterization to imply that what is pseudoscientific about psychoanalytic theory is not its unfalsifiability, *not* the theory's 'compatibility with everything that could happen' but the pretense (or the illusion) that this is not the case. And in the passage of his autobiography (Schilpp, 1974, p. 29) where Einstein figures as the paradigmatic scientist because of his expressed willingness to abandon his theory if it conflicted with observations, the antithetical 'dogmatic attitude' is characterized *not* as that of entertaining unfalsifiable theories but as 'constantly claiming to find "verification" for its favourite theories', which is a very different thing.

There are further remarks of Popper's which imply that it is not mere formal unfalsifiability which is his ground for considering a theory *pseudo-* as opposed to merely *non-*scientific. When Popper is illustrating the behaviour typical of pseudoscientists it is often not their dogged invocation of auxiliary hypotheses to evade falsification he is complaining of but something else: their treatment of putative falsifiers, not merely as non-disconfirmatory, but as positively confirmatory, on the strength of their ability to suggest ways of reconciling the apparent falsifier with the theory.

His complaint is not that they evade falsification but that they arbitrarily identify apparent counter-instances as positive ones.[3] For example, the famous Adler anecdote: '. . . as to Adler, I was much impressed by a personal experience. Once, in 1919, I reported to him a case which did not seem to be particularly Adlerian, but which he found no difficulty whatever in analysing in terms of his theory of inferiority feelings, although he had not seen the child. Slightly shocked, I asked him how he could be sure of all this. "Because of my thousandfold experience", he replied. Whereupon I could not help saying: "And with this new case, I suppose, your experience is now even thousand-and-one fold."' Note that Popper is not merely objecting to Adler's facility in turning the force of a putatively negative instance but to treating his ability to do this as transforming it into a positive one: 'And with this new case, I suppose, your experience has become thousand-and-one-fold' (Popper, 1969, p. 35).

The distinctiveness of this objection emerges even more clearly in the next paragraph: 'What I had in mind was that his previous observations may not have been much sounder than this new one: that each had been interpreted in the light of "previous experience" and at the same time, counted as additional confirmation. What, I asked myself, did it confirm? No more than the possibility of interpreting a case in the light of the theory.'

Popper is not merely objecting to the possibility of interpreting a case in the light of the theory (he even observes elsewhere that this is true of any theory), nor even just to the refusal to capitulate to a putative falsifier, but to this 'counting as additional confirmation'. There is no necessity for the rejection of falsification to be accompanied by the treatment of the apparent counter-instance as further evidence in favour of the theory. Instances which are not blatantly positive could be treated as *sub judice,* as Freud, in a rare moment of restraint, initially treated the relation of the war neuroses to his libido theory. Why should Adler have modified his theory on the basis of an apparently disconfirmatory report by Popper? But he could reasonably have been required to refrain from treating Popper's counterexample as confirmatory merely because he was able to account for it within the terms of his theory.

When Popper makes unfalsifiability the basis of a judgement that a theory is pseudoscientific it is usually in the context of a discussion of support. For example, when he asserts the pseudoscientific status of 'psychoanalysis itself' it follows the remark that 'real support can only be obtained from observations undertaken as tests (by "attempted refutations").' Popper points out that the availability of the notion of ambivalence to account for apparently discrepant behaviour would prevent a given instance from functioning as a falsifier. But the mere availability of the notion of ambivalence to account for apparent falsifications (and the same is true of contamination —'the Oedipus effect'—and resistance as well) does not suffice to make the theory which contains it pseudo-scientific, for the theory may only contain the notion because the world contains the fact. However, where this is so no claim can be advanced that the theory has survived testing.

Having recognized the asymmetry between instantiation and falsification we can say that the scientist is someone who would not be content with this state of affairs rather than, as the formal criterion suggests, that he should take no interest in it *qua* scientist.

2. Is Psychoanalytic Theory Testable?

Grünbaum roundly contradicts Popper's claim that psychoanalytic theory is unfalsifiable. He does not pause to ask which theses Popper might have had in mind. Not even Popper's circumscription of his claim to 'psychoanalysis itself', an expression which Popper never clarifies, moves Grünbaum to recognize the need for elucidation before proceeding to the pleasure of contradiction. His argument might be paraphrased thus: 'There is a body of theses advanced by Freud. Popper has characterized these theses as unfalsifiable. But among these theses is one which states that in their childhood, hysterics were sodomized by adults. The statement that a child has been sodomized by an adult has observational implications; therefore Popper was mistaken to say that psychoanalytic hypotheses are unfalsifiable.' This is like maintaining the empirical status of Christology on the grounds of the falsifiability of 'suffered under Pontius Pilate.'

Is it too much to ask for a level of discrimination which recognizes that a body of theses might be conceptually miscellaneous and that some might be testable and others not? There are distinctively psychoanalytic theses which do answer to Popper's characterization of them as unfalsifiable.[4] The impression created by Grünbaum that the belief that there are untestable psychoanalytic theses is an idiosyncrasy of Popper's, due to his failure to undertake elementary exegesis, can be dissipated by considering instances of psychoanalytic discourse which have been characterized as untestable by non-Popperian commentators.

Consider an example given by William Alston: 'We find Freud saying things like:

> At the very beginning all the libido is accumulated in the id, while the ego is still in process of formation or far from robust. Part of this libido is sent out by the id into erotic object-cathexes, whereupon the ego, now growing stronger, attempts to obtain possession of the object libido and to force itself upon the id as a love-object. *(The Ego and the Id)*

It is clear that this cannot be construed literally. The ego and the id are not different persons . . . We can picture each as a cartoonist's model in which all personality functions but one have atrophied. This gives us a picture, but we still don't know what to do with it. We don't know how to test the statement, when to say that this attraction has taken place, what role it might have in the formation of neuroses, etc. . . . Until such jobs are done, we are merely amusing ourselves with fables.' (1964, pp. 441–42)

There is another kind of psychoanalytic utterance which poses problems of testability. This time not because of its figurative character but because of the motivational complexity of the situations with which it deals. The problems posed by the notion of infantile oedipal impulses are quite different from those which arise in connection with the relation of the ego to the id. This is illustrated by the remarks of Sybille Escalona, a psychoanalytic researcher, on the reasons for the unfalsifiability of some of Freud's developmental theses:

> Suppose one wished to investigate the psychoanalytic idea that, at about the ages of three and four, little boys characteristically experience hostile and aggressive feelings towards their parents and more specifically their fathers, and that these

hostile feelings are based on the wish to possess the mother and replace the father in the family constellation. Suppose also that you create an experimental situation which would activate the child's feeling towards his parents. For instance, the father might exert his authority by sending the child off to his own room when the child wants to remain with the parents. If, to substantiate the core of the oedipal hypothesis, the child were required to display frank anger against his father, or frank possessiveness towards his mother, things would be reasonably simple. However, no one would seriously believe that oedipal conflicts are at work only when the child obligingly acts out both his wish and his anger at the obstacle to wish-fulfilment. Instead, we assume that the child tends to defend himself against becoming aware of—or openly reflecting—aggression because it engenders anxiety. Thus, if the child gives daddy a goodnight hug and insists that he, rather than mummy, tuck him in, this behaviour may also confirm our original hypothesis. His desire to have the father put him to bed rather than the mother could be the result of a fearful state, i.e. as long as the father is with him the little boy can be sure the father is not doing anything to harm him. On the other hand, or also simultaneously, it may be an act of aggression towards the father in that it separates him from the mother for the time being. Or yet again, it may be because the little boy fears that if mother puts him to bed her seductive powers will prove too much for him; he will then express his possessive love for the mother and try to take his father's place, and the omniscient father will punish him for it. The example could be spun out indefinitely, and it is safe to say that there is nothing our little experimental subject could possibly do, from withdrawal, to sudden intense interest in phantasy play, to asking for a cake, that cannot be regarded in the light of the assumption that he is reacting to an oedipal conflict situation. This being so, it is self-evident that nothing the little boy can do will confirm the original hypothesis, since the hypothesis would still be applicable if he had done the opposite instead . . . Psychoanalytic theory is greatly in need of validation, yet it is the kind of theory incapable of validation by available methods and which require different methods of validation from those now known to us. (Escalona, 1952, pp. 11–41)

In his paper 'How Scientific is Psychoanalysis?' (1977, p. 251) Grünbaum writes, 'despite attempts by some Freudians to immunize the developmental theory against P-falsification, logically that theory as such is falsifiable.' It would have been helpful if Grünbaum had given examples of the 'attempts by some Freudians to immunize the developmental theory against P-falsification' that he had in mind. I do not believe that there have been any such attempts not anticipated by Freud himself in expositions of the 'theory-as-such'. Freud's followers were no freer with the notion of the 'sexual constitution' than Freud himself was. And what is the sexual constitution but our old friend 'hereditary degeneracy' about whose explanatory pretensions Freud himself was so scathing at the outset of his career. And Freud's 'sexual constitution' is even more contemptible. It is tendentious as well as empty, for we are never told how contributions made to its developments by the *sexual* constitution of the child is to be distinguished from that of its *general* constitution. At this point in his expositions Freud invariably invokes a 'quantitative factor' whose operation is only to be discerned *post hoc*.

Grünbaum has the makings of a reply to these arguments for the unfalsifiability of certain psychoanalytic theses: his distinction between psychoanalytic theory 'in itself' and the response of its defenders to actual or hypothetical falsification reports.

Consider Grünbaum's contrast between the 'theory-in-itself' and the tenacity of its defenders: 'Popper' s indictment of psychoanalysis as intrinsically not being P-falsifiable has unwarrantedly derived plausibility from his failure to allow for the following distinction: the (revocable) falsifiability of the theory-as-such in the context of its semantic anchorage is a logical property of the theory itself, whereas the tenacious unwillingness of the majority of its defenders to accept adverse evidence as refuting is an all too human property of those advocates. Thus lack of methodological honesty on the part of the defenders, and even on the part of its originator, does not necessarily render the theory itself unfalsifiable.' (1979*b*, pp. 137–38).

It isn't clear why Grünbaum lays such emphasis on this point. It would only matter if, from the fact that the 'theory in itself' was falsifiable, it followed that it could not therefore be pseudoscientific. But it doesn't. Otherwise we would not speak of astrology, or theories of racial superiority, as pseudoscientific since they are manifestly falsifiable, and for many of us have been falsified, without this fact inhibiting us from continuing to describe them as pseudoscientific.

On one natural construction of Grünbaum's expression, 'the theory in itself', even Popper's paradigm of a falsifiable thesis would not be such since 'all swans are white' is manifestly empirical, and is not made less so by the refusal of some zoologists to accept that it had been falsified by the existence of black swan-like creatures in Australia. We can get round this by regarding the classification of Australian black 'swans' as non-swans as an elucidation rather than an emendation of the original thesis, but this makes the expression, 'the theory in itself', much more problematic than Grünbaum shows any sign of recognizing. For if we say that 'the theory-in-itself' is to be taken as encompassing the original statement of the theory, plus restatements of it in the face of falsification, what shall we call the theory without such restatements? Grünbaum's criteria lead to inconsistent conclusions. The theory-in-itself is both falsifiable, since it was not divested of its natural implications, and unfalsifiable, since it was.

Freud often puzzles us, not by putting forward claims without falsifiers, but by putting forward other claims as well whose natural force is to cancel the falsifiers of the more straightforward ones. For example, only the sexual instincts are libidinal, but the self-preservative instincts are libidinal too; social feelings are disguises for sexual ones, but social feelings are de-sexualized derivatives of feelings that were once sexual and are not themselves sexual.

How temporally proximate to the main text must elucidations be to warrant the judgement that they belong to the theory-in-itself? And must they be individuated biographically so that only the author of the original theory may modify, and thus imperil, the scientific standing of the theory?

When Grünbaum writes, 'despite attempts by some Freudians to immunize the developmental theory against P-falsification, logically that theory as such is falsifiable' (1977, p. 251), it is not clear what kind of immunization is intended. If it is the kind which Popper refers to as 'blaming the observations for not representing the true state of affairs', then Grünbaum's remark, though possibly true, is pointless in a discussion of the pseudoscientific status of a theory as contrasted with a discussion of whether it has potential falsifiers. Moreover, much of the immunization of Freud's developmental theory is not a matter of merely rejecting reported falsifications, but one of emending the content of Freud's developmental claims so as to lower the testability of the theory.

Consider, for example, the following account by Brill, Freud's American translator, of what is meant by the term 'sexual' in Freud's claim that only sexual vicissitudes can bring about a neurosis: 'A child may suffer from a *sexual* disturbance if he is neglected by a parent, or maltreated by someone in authority over him. The loss of a parent may make the child nervous: it is a disturbance in the latter's love life.' (1948*b*, p. 49). Nor was this extension of the term 'sexual' confined to infantile life. Elsewhere Brill wrote: 'Some time ago a young woman consulted me, because, as she said, she was extremely nervous; she declared that she suffered from insomnia, that her appetite was poor, and that she entertained peculiar thoughts. When asked what she meant by peculiar thoughts, she replied that she simply could not stomach her mother, who was constantly "getting in her way". Whenever, for instance, she wished to do something, however trifling, her mother stood in the way. There was nothing of love or sex as we commonly understand these terms, so that to one who is not accustomed to our viewpoint it would have shown nothing wrong sexually. But as there is a very vital and intimate relation between child and parent, there was really a disturbance in the love life of this young woman. So you see how different our conception of sex is from that ordinarily held.' (1948*a*, pp. 28–29)

If Brill is correct in his account of Freud's notion of sexuality it is no wonder that, as Richard Wollheim puts it, 'he uncovered its hidden variety, he demonstrated its utter pervasiveness.' The only question is what, given this extension of the scope of the term 'sexual', there could have been left to 'demonstrate' and 'uncover'. Now, how is it to be determined whether Brill's enlarged conception of sexuality is part of Freud's theory, or whether we are to dismiss Brill's remarks as just another specimen of the 'epistemological excesses of Freud's disciples'?

Grünbaum's distinction between the theory-in-itself and the unwonted tenacity of its adherents, even where we can make it with confidence, is of very limited relevance. Consider Rex Mottram, a character in Evelyn Waugh's novel *Brideshead Revisited*, who wants to marry a Catholic girl and is receiving instruction to that end. His Jesuit instructor, who suspects his good faith, relates the following exchange: 'I asked him: "Supposing the Pope saw a cloud and said, 'It's going to rain', would that be bound to happen?" "Oh yes, Father." "But supposing it didn't?" He thought for a moment and said, "I suppose it would be sort of raining spiritually, only we were too sinful to see it.",' It isn't clear which immunising tactic Rex Mottram was employing: whether he was saying, 'When the Pope says it will rain, it rains; the reports that it didn't are erroneous,' which is equivalent to Freud's argument from resistance, or 'When the Pope says it will rain, it rains in an extended sense of rainfall which captures the essence of the original in a way in which the idea that it didn't rain because it didn't vulgarly rain doesn't,' which is equivalent to Freud's extension of the notion of libido. But let us suppose Mottram had not qualified the claim that it rained with the word 'spiritually', and had unequivocally asserted that it rained and that reports that it hadn't rained were erroneous. We would then have a case where it would be appropriate to remonstrate, as Grünbaum does with Popper, with someone who inferred a formal deficiency in rainfall statements because they were open to the stratagem employed by Rex Mottram. If someone were to argue from Rex Mottram's defence of the Pope's infallibility (or rather his misconception of this) that there was something intrinsically defective about rainfall statements, then a reminder of the distinction between rainfall-statements-in-themselves and the behaviour of those who have asserted them would be pertinent. The situation with Freud's libido theory is very different. We do not have clear cut falsifiers coped with by blatantly *ad hoc* hypotheses but rather a highly indeterminate thesis with highly indeterminate accompanying, or belated, qualifications.

What can be meant by 'the theory-in-itself' where the theory in question is replete with jargon and neologism, for example, terms like libido, narcissistic libido, ego-libido and self-preservative libido? Freud's response to apparent falsifiers of his libido theory, like the influence of the Kaiser's withered arm on his martial propensities, or of the pathogenic role of injuries to self-esteem and of the dangers encountered in warfare, can't be distinguished from 'the theory-in-itself' for they tell us what is meant by expressions like 'narcissism' and how it is distinguished from 'egoism', i.e. how libido differs from interest.

Grünbaum gives as a further example of the falsifiability of psychoanalytic theory the view that phobias represent the displacement of repressed sexual fears. Grünbaum thinks this has been refuted by the success of behaviour therapists in curing phobias by de-sensitization techniques. Grünbaum is under the illusion that Freud did not acknowledge that neurotic symptoms could be successfully cured without resort to psychoanalytic therapy. Freud explicitly states in the 28th of the *Introductory Lectures* that hypnotic suggestion may succeed in effecting permanent cures ('at times everything fell out as one could wish; one obtained complete and lasting success with little difficulty'). So Grünbaum's falsifiers were not falsifiers for Freud. Nor for Ernest Jones. Jones said of the war neuroses, 'I see no reason whatever why a psychoanalysis should be undertaken in the majority of the cases for they can be cured in much shorter ways' (1923, p. 593).

How is it to be determined whether in the light of these facts we are to revise our conception of Freud's 'theory-in-itself' or whether we are to consider the 'theory-in-itself' falsified and treat Freud and Jones as guilty of wanton tenacity? If the grounds being given for the judgement that a theory is pseudoscientific is the behaviour of its advocates, then the issue is of a kind to make the logical status of the 'theory-in-itself' irrelevant. On the other hand, if the behaviour of its advocates is introduced into a discussion of the logical features of the theory, then it is likely that it is their elucidations and emendations of the theory when confronted by falsifiers which is being adduced, and this does bear on the empirical content of the theory and cannot be put aside by an allusion to the 'scientificality' of the 'theory-in-itself'.

3. Must Unfalsifiable Theses Be Pseudoscientific?

Escalona's account of the Oedipus complex shows that Grünbaum is mistaken to deny that Freud's developmental theses are untestable. But what follows from this untestability? Not, I would argue, that they are pseudoscientific. A situation such as Escalona envisages regarding Oedipal feelings may actually prevail. Things may be as Freud says but difficult to detect. If we are sceptical about this, and wish to dissuade others from wasting resources searching for them, we ought to indicate this otherwise than by calling such speculation pseudoscientific. It would deserve this epithet only if the speculation were accompanied (as it is in Freud and many Freudians) by the implication that it had been confirmed, indeed confirmed so fully that discreditable psychological motives had to be invoked to explain why there were those who were still recalcitrant, for example, by Jacob Arlow: 'The existence of the relationships which give the characteristic quality to the Oedipal phase is not a matter of conjecture or reconstruction. It is a matter of observation. Why these observations were not made before Freud is another problem pertinent to the resistance to psychoanalytic findings' (Arlow, 1960, p. 209). Charles Brenner advances the same argument in his article on psychoanalysis in the *Encyclopaedia of the Social Sciences*.

Since Popper concedes the genuineness of the phenomenon of ambivalence (and presumably of resistance as well) it is unlikely that he is demanding that these concepts be expunged from the theory. What then is the psycho-analytic investigator, on Popper's view, to do? The answer is, I think, to refrain from issuing failed disconfirmation reports which, under the circum-stances, would be a form of perjury. What the situation calls for is not the abandonment of the theory, for example, of the Oedipus complex, but the candid admission that we are not as yet in a position to distinguish genuine from spurious negative instances. If Freud had been consistently and can-didly non-falsificationist there would be no occasion to upset the literati by calling him a pseudoscientist.

What is, I think, an appropriate response to this feature of some psycho-analytic theses is provided by Roland Dalbiez in his book on Freud: 'Sooner or later we are induced to wonder whether besides instances in which the existence of a sexual activity in the child may be diagnosed from clinical signs there are not other instances of "unapparent" sexual activity, which can only be reached by means of psychoanalytic interpretation. It seems to us more likely that this question must be answered in the affirmative. But then a new question arises. If besides instances of apparent sexual activity, there are instances of unapparent sexual activity, are there still further instances of children without any psychosexual activity at all, whether apparent or "unap-parent"? Here we must merely confess our complete inability to settle the question one way or another . . . the absence of exact sexual manifestations in childhood seemed to us as normal as their presence . . . but it is quite clear that improvement of the psychoanalytic methods of exploration may . . . enable us to demonstrate the presence of a genuine sexual activity which clinical "macroscopic" investigation failed to reveal. We cannot foretell the future of science' (Dalbiez, 1941, p. 255). Dalbiez sees that the Freudian concept of infantile psychosexuality is unfalsifiable but does not conclude that it is pseudoscientific on that account.

A less indulgent attitude than Dalbiez's and one closer to Popper's is that expressed by R.S. Woodworth seventy years ago: '. . . the doctrine of Freud suffers the disability that it apparently cannot be put to a crucial test; for whichever way the test came out, the Freudian would find in the result a confirmation of his views. For example, a dream is always the expression of a repressed wish; but if a particular dream that is brought forward seems not to be the expression of a wish, it can be regarded as expressing the wish that the Freudian doctrine be not confirmed, or as expressing a subtle and sub-conscious opposition of the patient to the operator. Or again the open expression of sexual interest by a young child is clear evidence in favour of "infantile sexuality", while the absence of such expression is evidence of "repression". It is somewhat disconcerting to find that what is ostensibly a psychological hypothesis to be tested is in reality a faith to be embraced or rejected' (1913, p. 930).

There is no question of demonstrating Woodworth to be mistaken in the attitude he takes up but it is worth pointing out that the unfalsifiability of a psychoanalytic thesis may sometimes be due to a situation's being rich in possibilities rather than to the theory being rich in excuses. What the situation calls for is not a hard and fast rule but what Duhem calls 'good sense'— and, he might have added, good faith.

The difficulty in demonstrating, for example, that Freud's invocation of a wish to prove him wrong in order to account for 'counter-wish' dreams supports the description of him as a pseudoscientist does not lie in doubt about the independent testability of such an auxiliary hypothesis but in doubt as to whether he employs it to justify his treating the apparently negative instance as a positive one instead of resting content to leave the matter *sub judice* in the absence of further evidence. Consider the following specimen of psychoanalytic discourse: 'Delusions of grandeur . . . are initiated by a withdrawal of libido from external objects which give rise to a pathological increase of narcissistic libido. The now excessive charges of libido in the ego stimulate feelings of grandiosity which may reach delusional intensity. This finding was subsequently corroborated by investigation of the traumatic neuroses of war' (Glover, 1956, p. 54). Isn't a difference made to the epistemic character of this specimen of discourse by that last sentence? It matters less whether we say that the exposition was merely non-scientific until we come to the remark reporting corroboration, and only then became pseudoscientific, or that, at that point, one kind of pseudoscience became another kind of pseudoscience, than that the distinction be recognized.

In many discussions of the pseudoscientific character of psychoanalysis the relevant distinction is not between falsifiable and non-falsifiable theories but between those which mislead expectation and those which merely underdetermine it. It makes all the difference whether the content of a thesis was diminished *post hoc,* or whether it was candidly meagre from the outset. If it were indeed the case that 'psychoanalysis itself' was unfalsifiable 'from the start', this is a less discreditable state of affairs than obtains with regard to those components of Freud's theory of which this is not true.

Granted that a theory has been shown to contain qualifications which cancel or diminish its contents, why is this of any interest? Doesn't it only seem so because it is conflated with another question which is of paramount importance—whether the theory owes the impression of having been repeatedly confirmed to our overlooking the self-cancelling qualifications which are responsible for its resistance to falsification? That it is this which matters can be shown by asking what interest these self-cancelling qualifications would have if the tests that the theory survived did not involve them. For example, if the claims as to the reconstructive powers of psychoanalytic dream interpretation were not based on the invocation of ancestral memories to account for apparently erroneous reconstructions, would it matter that the notion of phylogenetic inheritance was a part of psychoanalytic 'theory-in-itself' and rendered erroneous reconstructions irrefutable? The question then becomes whether Freud was a pseudo-falsificationist with respect to his developmental theses, whether he issued what, in the light of the character of his concepts and methods, were spurious and unwarranted confirmation (in the sense of failed attempts at falsification) claims? There are reasons for thinking so. For example, 'My surprising discoveries as to the sexuality of children were made in the first instance through the analysis of adults. But later (from about 1908 onwards) it became possible to confirm them in the most satisfactory way and in every detail by direct observations upon children' (Freud, 1925, p. 70). If Escalona's account is correct Freud was perjuring himself.

What are Grünbaum's own criteria of pseudoscience? In several papers devoted to the subject it is remarkable that he should leave us in doubt as to his answer to this question. In an intellectual culture prolific in irrationalities Grünbaum can think of only two examples of pseudoscience, fatalism and Hartmann's version of metapsychology (NB: not Freud's). He ignores Popper's own examples of astrology and the racial theory of history. He can't be oblivious to the deficiencies of a formalist reply (lack of P-falsifiability). On the other hand, it isn't certain that we are to equate Grünbaum's lack of 'I-scientificality' with pseudoscience, since he himself speaks of theories which fail blatantly to meet his standards of 'I-scientificality' ('I' for Inductive), not as pseudoscientific but only as 'gratuitous' and 'lacking in scientific credibility'. But if we can take these idioms as equivalent to 'pseudoscientific' it is possible to arrive at a piquant conclusion: Freudian psychoanalysis is pseudoscientific by Adolph Grünbaum's own criterion of demarcation. He himself only avoids this conclusion through gross inconsistency. The expressions 'gratuitous' and 'lacking in scientific credibility' occur in his discussion of Erich Fromm's denial that research into psychotherapeutic efficacy, which has uncovered a tie-score effect between psychoanalytic and other modes of therapy, undermines the claims of psychoanalysis to be the treatment of choice for neuroses. Fromm's claim is stigmatized as 'gratuitous' because of his failure to provide evidence for the greater severity of the neurotic conditions of those treated by psychoanalysis. But if a thesis is 'gratuitous and lacking in scientific credibility' because of the failure of its advocates to take up the burden of proof then Grünbaum would have to say no less of Freud's developmental theory, since the advocates of the Freudian account of the infantile pathogenesis of the neuroses, when anticipating counter-examples, invoke a constitutional factor to account for neurotic outcomes of apparently non-pathogenic infancies without supplying independent evidence for the possession of such infantile constitutions, even acknowledging that the identification of such constitutions is not possible in our present state of knowledge.

Grünbaum has a second line of argument against Popper in addition to the denial of the unfalsifiability of psychoanalytic theory, though he doesn't always clearly distinguish it. He gives several examples of what he takes to be Freud's modifying his view in the face of contradictory evidence, of which the seduction theory episode and the case of the Rat Man are the most prominent. None of his examples support his thesis. This is what he says about the seduction episode: 'I am simply astonished that Popper did not see fit to try to deal with some of the hypotheses actually invoked by Freud to furnish explanations such as his famous infantile seduction theory of hysteria. I cannot help wondering, for example, whether Popper knew the following: Freud had hoped to make his reputation by solving the riddle of hysteria, but in 1897 he was painfully driven by unfavourable evidence to abandon his strongly cherished aetiological hypothesis' (1979*b*, p. 135).

Why does Grünbaum think that the seduction episode overthrows Popper's view of Freud as a dogmatist? In part because he is ill-informed as to the circumstances under which the seduction episode was embraced and then abandoned, and in part because, he asks the wrong questions.

Here is how the seduction error struck another psychoanalyst (from a work which gets into Grünbaum's bibliography but seems to have made little impression on the way): 'A striking example of the essential irrefutability of psychoanalytic doctrine is afforded by Freud's handling of his discovery that his patients confabulated infantile memories, in itself strong evidence for the influencing value of his techniques. As he was quick to see, "this discovery . . . serves either to discredit the analysis or to discredit the patients upon whose testimony the analysis, as well as the whole understanding of neurosis is built." This is a bleak predicament indeed, from which Freud extricates himself by a *tour de force*. He points out that "these fantasies possess psychological reality in contrast to physical reality" and "in the realm of neurosis the psychological reality is the determining factor." Therefore, the fact that these infantile experiences were fantasies rather than actualities, far from refuting his experiences, actually *confirms* them' (Frank, 1961). Why did this view not goad Grünbaum into a degree of self-consciousness as to the conclusiveness with which Freud's response to the seduction error illustrates his willingness to 'abandon a strongly cherished aetiological hypothesis'?

The question to be asked concerning the seduction theory is not just whether Freud manifested a willingness to consider evidence that hysterics need not have been sodomized as infants, nor even whether he was willing to consider evidence that those patients whom he had decided had been sodomized had not, after all, been sodomized, but whether he was willing to consider that he was in error in claiming that to the analyst, equipped with Freud's techniques of interpretation, the infantile past of the patient can be reconstructed through an analysis of his dreams, associations and behaviour during the analytic hour.

Grünbaum even misapplies Popper's criterion of *formal* falsifiability, for it entails asking not merely whether the seduction theory was falsifiable, but also the degree to which its successor theory was. Whether or not Freud's post-seduction infantile-sexual pathogenesis is falsifiable may be disputable but that it has less empirical content than the parent theory is not. It is universal where the parent theory was particular (and so is less testable epidemiologically).[5] It has less determinate observational implications than the seduction theory (hidden fantasies for public events). And it was deprived of prophylactic implications. Whereas had the seduction theory been correct parents had only to keep a watchful eye on their children, or control their own paedophilic impulses, for the neuroses to have been eliminated in one generation, psychoanalytic pronouncements on the prophylactic implications of Freud's post-seduction developmental theory are evasive and incoherent.

Grünbaum's argument is defective in another respect. For it is obvious that the capitulation to falsification reports can only reflect favourably on the integrity of the theorist where the refusal to capitulate would not undermine his credibility. But what choice had Freud? He could not say in the case of the seduction theory what his followers have said in the case of his theories of infantile sexual fantasy, that it took years of training to tell whether a child is being sodomized.

Grünbaum says both that Freud's patients had non-veridical memories of infantile seduction and that Freud based his seduction theory on these memories. Although this is Freud's own (later) account of the matter, it is false. There are several remarks in the original seduction papers with which it is inconsistent of which this is one:

> . . . whilst calling these infantile experiences into consciousness they experience the most violent sensations, of which they are ashamed and which they endeavour to hide, and they still try, even after going through them again in so convincing a fashion, to withhold belief by emphasizing the fact that they have no feeling of recollecting these scenes as they had in the case of other forgotten material.
>
> Now this last attitude on their part seems absolutely decisive. Why should patients assure me so emphatically of their unbelief, if from any motive they had invented the very things that they wish me to discredit? (1896, p. 204).

What this passage shows is that Freud based his conviction that his patients had been seduced not on his uncritically crediting their narratives of infantile seduction but on their behaviour being, in his judgement, 'consistent with no other assumption'. The motive for Freud's distortion is transparently clear from Jones's account of the episode: '[Freud] found that several of the seduction stories were simply untrue, there had been no seduction. But he held fast to the fact that *the patient had told him these stories* . . . with the result that he discovered the importance of infantile fantasy life in the genesis of the neuroses' (1939, p. 111; my italics).

Grünbaum's account of Freud's *abandonment* of the seduction error is also erroneous. He tells us that one of Freud's 'explicit reasons' for abandoning the seduction theory was his discovery of the unexpectedly high incidence of hysteria which, since seduction was only a necessary condition of hysteria, would have involved him in postulating a 'preposterously high' incidence of child-seduction. But since Freud tells us that he discovered that some of his imputed seductions could not have occurred, that is, not all 18 of his patients had been seduced, he could not have abandoned the seduction theory 'for several explicit reasons', as Grünbaum asserts, since the discovery that some of the 18 had not been seduced rendered any additional reasons otiose.

As for the error of mistakenly attributing seductions to several of his patients, this is Grünbaum's account of how the hypothesized seductions were (erroneously) 'confirmed': 'The mentioned *prima facie* confirmations of the postulated seduction episodes had been furnished by the seemingly vivid and presumably repressed memories that Freud had been able to elicit from his hysterical patients in the course of their analysis.' In the same paragraph Grünbaum speaks of the 'subjective certainty felt by his adult patients in the reality of purported memories going back to childhood' (1979*b*, pp. 135–36). And we are referred to the letter in which Freud repudiated the seduction theory.

The passage I quoted is difficult to reconcile with Grünbaum's claim that Freud was the recipient of false seduction reminiscences, or that patients felt 'subjective certainty' as to non-veridical infantile seductions. His mistake may spring from reliance on secondary sources for his account of the seduction episode. (The seduction papers themselves do not figure in his bibliography.) The mistake is a serious one for it prevents Grünbaum from realizing that Freud's response to the seduction error, far from illustrating his willingness to abandon the erroneous theory, provides some of the strongest evidence of his inability to take up a critical attitude towards his own convictions; an inability which caused him to give a tendentiously distorted account of how he came to make the seduction error and thus relieved him of the painful necessity of confronting the real implications of his mistake.

4. Does the Rat Man Case Illustrate a 'Testing Strategy'?

As a further counter-example to Popper's 'indictment of Freud' Grünbaum refers us to a paper by Clark Glymour which advances the argument that Freud's response to the facts of the case history of the Rat Man demonstrates that in his aetiological speculations and investigations Freud was pursuing 'a testing strategy': 'The best available evidence concerning the actual life history of his "Rat Man", Paul Lorenz, had refuted his prior hypothesis as to the specifics of the sexual aetiology which he had postulated for adult obsessional neuroses (cf. Glymour, 1974, pp. 299–304)'. There was no 'prior hypothesis as to the specifics of the sexual aetiology . . . for adult obsessional neuroses'; and, if there had been, 'the best available evidence concerning the actual life history' of the Rat Man could not have refuted it; and if it had, and Freud had responded as Glymour describes, it would not have illustrated Grünbaum's claim that Freud manifested a readiness to abandon his theses if they conflicted with the evidence.

It would be difficult for any infantile life to contradict the views Freud held about the aetiology of the neuroses after his abandoning the seduction theory, and even more difficult to discover whether it, in fact, had. This is Freud's first post-seduction statement of the infantile events which predispose to neurotic disorders: 'Their real aetiology is to be found in experiences during childhood, and again exclusively, too, in those impressions which have to do with sexual matters' (1898, p. 242). It is difficult to see how the Rat Man's case history, or any case history for that matter, would reveal that the patient's infancy contained no 'impressions which have to do with sexual matters'.

In a paper of 1905 ('My Views on Sexuality in the Etiology of Neuroses') Freud said of the neuroses, 'these maladies are observed to ensue after the most commonplace emotional, or even somatic, disturbances and a . . . specific aetiology in the form of a particular infantile experience is not forthcoming' (1905a, p. 281). In the *Three Essays on the Theory of Sexuality*, also 1905, Freud says: 'Of the various factors which interfere with development, first and foremost, we must name the innate variety of sexual constitutions, upon which it is probable that the principal weight falls.' (The summary to *Three Essays on the Theory of Sexuality*, paragraph entitled 'Constitution and Heredity'). In the seventh paragraph of this Summary he says, 'it was not possible to say what amount of sexual activity can occur in childhood without being described as abnormal or detrimental to further developments.'

Glymour maintains that Freud introduced infantile sexual fantasies into the aetiology of the neuroses because he failed to find in the infantile life of the Rat Man the sexual events to whose pathogenic potency he was up till then committed: '. . . before (the Rat Man case) there is no statement of the view that sexual fantasies formed in childhood or subsequently, having no real basis in fact, may themselves serve in place of sexual experiences as aetiological factors.' (1974, p. 303); 'increasingly after 1909, Freud thought fantasies themselves, even when derived from no real sexual experience, could serve as aetiological factors' (1974, p. 302).

The distinction between fantasies 'derived from real sexual experiences' and fantasies not so derived needs to be more clearly drawn before we can say with any confidence that only after a certain date did Freud replace or supplement one with the other. In the Dora case (1900) a pathogenic role is assigned to fantasies derived from her experience of thumb-sucking and of the sight of a cow's udder. If these are not sexual experiences in Glymour's sense, and Dora's fantasies 'derived from no real sexual experiences' then the Dora case is a counter-example to his chronological claim; if, on the other hand, they do qualify as sexual experiences then Freud could not have found that there were no experiences of this character in the Rat Man's childhood, or in any other. In any case, how could Freud discover that the infantile sexual fantasies of the patient 'derived from no real sexual experience' when Freud considered that even babies being suckled and washed occasion sexual experiences (1905a, pp. 136–37)?

Even had Freud held the view of infantile sexual pathogenesis that Glymour attributes to him, that sexual intimidation was a necessary condition of obsessional neuroses, the facts in the case of the Rat Man could not have compelled him to modify them and substitute fantasies for events as aetiological factors. Glymour gives the following reasons for believing that 'the clinical evidence in the Rat Man case tested views Freud held': 'That the inferred castigation for sexual misbehaviour was not revealed by the most reliable means—the memory of an adult observer—is presumably evidence that something was wrong with Freud's account of the role of psychosexual development in the aetiology of the neuroses' (1974, p. 301).

The germ from which Glymour's argument seems to have grown is the footnote in the case history of the Rat Man in which Freud records his disappointment at learning that the offence for which the Rat Man had been beaten was not connected with onanism, as Freud had conjectured. Though the Rat Man *had* been beaten, enquiries Freud asked him to make of his mother revealed that it had not been for a sexual offence. Instead of insisting that the mother was mistaken, Freud graciously condescends to leave the matter open and Glymour credits him with a falsificationist methodology on the strength of it.

In asserting that the Rat Man had been punished by his father for masturbating, Freud was not evincing his commitment to a previously stated law linking a specific infantile history with the symptom picture presented by the Rat Man. In the first place, because he was committed to no such law and in the second, because the 'non-theoretical state of affairs, namely, the patient's having been punished by his father for masturbation' was not *inferred* by Freud. He was only *repeating* his patient's story of having been beaten, and *adding* the suggestion that it had been for a sexual offence. The passage from the case history, to the effect that Freud had anticipated the beating episode, which Glymour quotes, was doctored (or whatever euphemism Freudians prefer) after Freud had discovered that the Rat Man had been 'castigated' as a child. If Glymour had read the 'Original Record' with a modicum of care he would have discovered that the original version of the passage he quotes contains no allusion to Freud's anticipation of a 'castigation' suffered by the Rat Man, which was then confirmed by family tradition, thus furnishing evidence of Freud's uncanny prescience. Freud merely conjectures, erroneously as it turns out, that the Rat Man had been *warned* as to his masturbatory practices and 'perhaps' threatened with castration.

This is what Freud says in the published case history:

> Starting from these indications and from other data of a similar kind I ventured to put forward a construction to the effect that when he was a child of under six he had been guilty of some sexual misdemeanour connected with onanism and had been soundly castigated for it by his father. This punishment, according to my hypothesis, had, it was true, put an end to his onanism, but on the other hand it had left behind an ineradicable grudge against his father and had established him for all time in his role of an interferer with the patient's sexual enjoyment. (1909, p. 342)

This is what he says in the notes he made at the time:

> I could not restrain myself here from constructing the material at our disposal into an event: how before the age of six he had been in the habit of masturbating and how his father had forbidden it, using as a threat the phrase, 'it would be the death of you' and perhaps also threatening to cut off his penis. (1909, p. 263)

Notice the 'perhaps'. Freud did not even feel himself aetiologically committed to castration *threats,* much less the castigation for sexual misbehaviour which Glymour attributes to him.

Not only does the failure of the Rat Man's interrogation of his mother to confirm Freud's conjecture not conflict with 'Freud's account of the role of psychosexual development in the aetiology of the neuroses', it does not even provide a test of Glymour's own misconception of this. It merely rendered less plausible one *particular* reconstruction that Freud had ventured in the course of the treatment. Why should Freud's disappointment over the reconstruction of one particular episode have compelled him to abandon his view that the Rat Man had been sexually intimidated? How do the facts recorded in the footnote show that the Rat Man had not been sexually intimidated by his father on some other occasion? In fact we know that he was later beaten for bedwetting (which Freud held to be a surrogate sexual activity). Freud's insistence that the Rat Man was only beaten once, which Glymour repeats, is a slip (Original Record, 1909, p. 384).[6]

Even supposing Freud had held the views that Glymour attributes to him and that the facts in the Rat Man case had contradicted those views, would Freud's behaving as Glymour describes and invoking the pathogenic power of sexual fantasy exemplify a testing strategy? Of what must we be persuaded if we are to concede that Freud's introduction of aetiological factors, which lie in the fantasy life of the child and not in publicly observable circumstances, manifests the willingness to abandon theses inconsistent with the evidence with which Grünbaum and Glymour credit him? How are we to distinguish between Freud's successor thesis to the seduction theory and that of the Christian Scientist who evokes Malicious Animal Magnetism to account for the fact that even Christian Scientists succumb to illness, or the astrologer who explains his faulty forecasts by invoking the influence of the sky-pattern at conception to supplement that at birth? Presumably we do not wish to say that these, too, were evincing their loyalty to a testing strategy and their willingness to abandon theories incompatible with the evidence. In order for us to acknowledge a difference between these cases and Freud's we would need to be persuaded that in Freud's case there is some hope of discovering both what the fantasy life of the child is, with sufficient determinacy to distinguish between rival accounts of its nature, and also how to distinguish its influence on the character of the child from those of other eligible determinants. At present we can do neither of these. Whether this may have been among Freud's reasons for adopting the fantasy theory we will, on this occasion, leave to heaven. If any one can be said to have employed 'a testing strategy' with respect to Freud's infantile sexual vicissitude theory it is those erstwhile Freudians (from Ian Suttie to John Bowlby) who, on failing to find differentiating sexual vicissitudes in the infantile pasts of their patients (as Freud himself had), instead of abandoning the search for personality-malforming influences in the overt life of the child and retreating to fantasy, sought for it in the interpersonal vicissitudes of child-life and ceased demanding that these be sexual. It may redound to Mary Baker Eddy's credit that she abandoned homeopathy on discovering the operation of a placebo effect but does it redound to her credit that she replaced it with Christian Science?

Grünbaum is inconsistent in invoking Glymour's paper to confute Popper since its argument moreover violates the requirement he employs elsewhere, for example, his treatment of the claim that in spite of the lower remission rate for psychoanalytically treated patients psychoanalysis may, nevertheless, be more effective since its patients may be sicker. Grünbaum demands independent evidence that this is the case and since it is not forthcoming stigmatises the claim as 'gratuitous and devoid of scientific credibility'. If the same considerations were applied to the invocation of the pathogenic role of infantile fantasies the same conclusion would follow, for where is the independent evidence that those who later succumb to neuroses are characterised by any distinctiveness in their infantile sexual fantasies. In fact Freud conceded that there was none.

Grünbaum has also argued that 'the conjecture of the sexual aetiology of phobias makes some predictions that are "risky" by Popper's standards', for example, that a non-psychoanalytic method of removing phobic symptoms would result in symptom-substitution. 'But contrary to this psychoanalytic prediction a 1978 report from the Institute of Psychiatry at the University of London concludes: in the overwhelming number of cases the reduction or elimination of a circumscribed fear is not followed by untoward effects. So much for Popper' (1979*a*, p. 514). This is a strange argument. If it is meant to demonstrate that the psychoanalytic theory of phobias has observable implications it would be sufficient to state these and point out their risky character without documenting the actual occurrence of the falsifying observations. That is, we wouldn't find it necessary, in order to demonstrate the falsifiability of 'all swans are white', to supply evidence of the existence of black swans. And so Grünbaum may be making a different point but one which leaves the argument equally strange: the willingness in practice of some investigators to consider the psychoanalytic theory of phobias falsified by certain observations demonstrates the non-pseudoscientific character of the theory. But for this argument to bear on the *bona fide* non-pseudoscientific character of psychoanalytic theory, the willingness in question ought to be on the part of those who hold the theory not, as in the case with Rachman, those who are among its severest critics.

In any case does capitulation to counter-examples suffice to establish the *bona fides* of either a theory or an investigator? An eminent contemporary astrologer reports in the introduction to his book that he had attempted to confirm a time-honoured astrological thesis and failed. 'In making lists of persons with two bodies in good aspect and of other persons with the same bodies in bad aspect we could find no difference in fortune.' Is this sufficient to show either that astrology is scientific, or that he himself is a *bona fide* scientist? It can show neither. It is not the status of the general claims alone which is pertinent to a discussion of the suspicion of pseudoscience but of the reporting practices with respect to particular existential claims as well. The mistake of assuming otherwise is made by Grünbaum when he argues that Freud's theory of melancholia is in good order since it is falsified by the existence of endogenous non-reactive depressions. It does not settle the matter to show that there are exceptions to Freud's explanation of melancholia, or even that they are conceded to be exceptions. What needs to be shown is that the identification of positive instances of the thesis meets acceptable standards.

A theorist may manifest a readiness to abandon his general claims in the face of apparent falsification and still be a pseudoscientist. Since Grünbaum examines only Freud's general claims he is precluded from dealing with the central issue.

5. Can Therapeutic Effects Be Used to Monitor the Truth of Interpretations?

Grünbaum takes exception to the following remarks of Popper's:

> ... how much headway has been made in investigating the question of the extent to which the (conscious or unconscious) expectations and theories held by the

analyst influence the 'clinical responses' of the patient? (I say nothing of the conscious attempts to influence the patient by proposing interpretations to him, etc.). Years ago, I introduced the term 'oedipus effect' to describe the influence of a theory, or expectation, or prediction, upon the event which it predicts or de scribes: it will be remembered that the causal chain leading to Oedipus' patricide was started by the oracle's prediction of this event. This is a characteristic and recurrent theme of such myths, but one which seems to have failed to attract the interest of the analysts; perhaps not quite accidentally. (1969, p. 38)

Whereas 'some recognized analysts have dealt with troublesome considerations in a puzzlingly inconsistent and even evasive manner', Grünbaum thinks Freud did not, and Popper is charged with 'compounding his exegetical felony' (of suggesting that Freudians had not taken proper account of the contamination issue), by hinting that 'analysts are evasive or even repressing an uncomfortable challenge.' Grünbaum rebuts this presumed slander by invoking 'Freud's Tally Argument of 1917' which, though it may be 'unsatisfactory', absolves Freud from the charge of 'having offered a mere *ipse dixit*.'

This is Grünbaum's statement of the tally argument: 'Only psychoanalytic interpretations that "tally with what is real" in the patient can mediate veridical insight and such insight in turn, is causally necessary for the successful alleviation of the patient's neurosis.' (1979*a*, p. 467). This statement of the tally argument is from the *Introductory Lectures* of 1916–17, but Freud was implicitly relying on it a quarter of a century earlier in the *Studies on Hysteria*. Since the seduction error intervened between this work and Freud's restatement of the tally argument in 1917 why shouldn't Popper be surprised at Freud's assertion of the harmlessness of suggestion? In any case how could Freud advance a therapeutic argument for veridicality when once he had the seduction error behind him and thus knew that he could achieve effects without veridicality?

There are reasons for thinking that Freud himself was not entirely convinced by the tally argument. He sometimes implied its invalidity. In 1910 he wrote: '. . . I need not rebut the objection that the way in which we practise the method today obscures its testimony to the correctness of our hypothesis; you will not forget that this evidence is to be found elsewhere and that a therapeutic procedure cannot be performed in the same way as a theoretical investigation' (1910, p. 287).

So Freud did not always invoke the tally argument to support the validity of his method. Instead he appealed to the fact that psychotics express thoughts and wishes of a similar character to those he uncovered by interpreting symptoms. Though this might, if one were inclined to generosity, be taken as evidence that neurotics harbour the same wishes that are explicitly expressed by psychotics how could it show that it is these wishes which are responsible for the neurotic symptomatology Freud invoked them to explain? How would a psychotic's direct expression of incestuous wishes assuage our doubts as to whether the bedtime ritual girl's transactions with her pillow and bolster was an expression of her wish to be penetrated by her father? How does the fact that a female psychotic expresses blatant deflo-ration fantasies help to show that Freud was correct in assigning an hysteri-cal patient's headache to this source?

Freud also seems anxious, to the point of prevarication, to deny that he held his convictions as to the sexual source of neuroses before the material which confirmed them was forthcoming. If Freud thought the operation of suggestion 'epistemically innocuous', as Grünbaum maintains, why did he so often deny (untruthfully) that he had held his convictions as to the sources of neurotic illness *before* he received the patient's confirmation of them? In 'The Question of Lay Analysis' he wrote: 'The analyst never entices his patient on to the ground of sex. He does not say to him in advance: "We shall be dealing with the intimacies of your sexual life!" He allows him to begin what he has to say wherever he pleases, and quietly waits until the patient himself touches on sexual things. I used always to warn my pupils: "Our opponents have told us that we shall come upon cases in which the factor of sex plays no part. Let us be careful not to introduce it into our analyses and so spoil our chance of finding such a case." But so far none of us has had that good fortune' (1925, pp. 118–19). And yet in the very paper on dream interpretation, to Popper's comments on which Grünbaum objects, Freud speaks of patients who 'reproduce the forgotten experience of their childhood only after one has constructed them from their symp-toms, associations and other signs and has propounded these constructions to them . . . unless one interprets, constructs and propounds one never obtains access to what is repressed in them' (1923, p. 142).

Here is another illustration of Freud's tendency to back away from the tally argument and inadvertent testimony to the force he really attributed to Popper's Oedipus effect—Freud's false retrospective accounts of the state of his theory at the time he undertook the analyses which led him into the seduction error. In the autobiographical sketch of 1925 he wrote: 'It would have been difficult to guess from the *Studien über Hysterie* what an impor-tance sexuality has in the aetiology of the neuroses' (1925, p. 39). And yet in the preface to that very book Freud and Breuer wrote: 'Sexuality plays the principal role in the pathogenesis of hysteria as a source of psychic traumas, and as a motive of "defence" and of the repression of ideas from conscious-ness' (1895, p. xxx). And in one of the seduction papers themselves Freud refers to the *Studies in Hysteria* in terms which acknowledge his prior com-mitment to a sexual aetiology in that work: 'In earlier publications Breuer and I have already expressed the opinion that the symptoms of hysteria can be understood only by tracing them back to traumatic experiences and that these psychical traumas are related to the patient's sexual life' (1896, p. 156).

It becomes a mystery why, if Freud really believed the tally argument rendered the operation of suggestion 'epistemically innocuous', he should have gone to such lengths (whether consciously or not) to deprive the suggestibility argument of force by rewriting the oracle's prophecies.

It is a measure of Grünbaum's obsequiousness where Freud is concerned that he can consider something as natural as the suspicion that Freud was behaving evasively in his dealings with the suggestion argument as a slander. The feeblest of rationalizations counts in Grünbaum's eyes as 'facing the problem of suggestion'.

6. Conclusion

I have given my reasons for believing that it is a mistake to maintain that 'Popper's own criterion of demarcation does not entitle him to indict psychoanalysis as unscientific . . .' (Grünbaum, 1976, p. 216). I am not sure whether 'falsifiability is the touchstone of scientific rationality', but what Grünbaum calls Popper's indictment of Freud does not depend on its being so.

The idea that the mere possession of potential falsifiers shows that a theory is not pseudoscientific, which Grünbaum mistakenly assigns to Popper, and sometimes seems to hold himself, is wrong. Grünbaum's idea that whether a theory has falsifiers can always be determined independently of the behaviour of its advocates is also wrong; and so is his idea that the empirical content of a theory can be determined by consulting its critics.

Grünbaum's most fundamental (non-exegetical) error is that, when he has succeeded in demonstrating that a thesis is formally falsifiable and thus scientific in a sense antithetical to non-scientific or metaphysical, he thinks he has shown that it is scientific in the sense in which the term is antithetical to pseudoscientific. Grünbaum slides from 'the tenacity of its adherents cannot show that a theory is unfalsifiable' to 'the tenacity of its adherents cannot show that a theory is pseudoscientific', from which it would follow that one of the standard uses of the term 'pseudoscientific' is a solecism.

Furthermore, what Freud presents us with is not merely a theory but copious specimens of his explanatory practice, and these are just as capable of providing an indictment of psychoanalysis as a pseudoscience as the wanton rejection of falsifications of its general claims. Grünbaum, who fails to address himself to the justice or otherwise of the complaint that its singular instantiation reports are unwarranted, is disqualified from making a substantial contribution to the discussion.

Once we recognize that Karl Popper's criterion of demarcation is not merely formal falsifiability but 'severe attempts at refutation', we will give an affirmative answer to Grünbaum's question: Freudian psychoanalytic theory *is* pseudoscientific by Karl Popper's criterion of demarcation.

NOTES

1. There is another ambiguity worth mentioning: whether an auxiliary hypothesis, introduced to save a theory from falsification, must, if it is not to count as *ad hoc*, merely entail *entertainable* (conceivable) falsifiers, or whether these must be *ascertainable* as well. (This is akin to Carnap's distinction between testability and confirmability). Popper speaks at one point of the 'at the time untestable' character of *ad hoc* hypotheses. This sounds like an objection to their lack of ascertainable, rather than of entertainable, falsifiers. One of Popper's expositors seems to equate falsifiability with the possession of ascertainable and not merely entertainable observation statements. When J.O. Wisdom states that had there been no moon, or no planet Mercury, Einstein's general theory would have been less falsifiable, it is not the notion of entertainable falsifiers that he is employing but that of ascertainable ones, since the logical implications of Einstein's theory would have been the same even had there been no moon and no planet Mercury. That is, if the day before the solar eclipse of 1919 the moon had exploded, or gone off into space, Einstein's theory would have become less testable but not less confirmable, or, in my terms, it would have had fewer ascertainable falsifiers but no fewer entertainable ones. The issuance of confirmation reports where theories lack ascertainable falsifiers is as disreputable as it would be had they lacked entertainable ones.

2. In 'Is Falsifiability the Touchstone of Scientific Rationality?' (1976, p. 228) Grünbaum says, 'For Popper the mere falsifiability of a hypothesis suffices for according scientific status to it, but the inductivist may be prepared to grant it no more than potential scientific status in virtue of its inductive supportability.' But the sense of 'scientific status' in which Popper allows it is not the same as the sense in which the inductivist denies it. For Popper the demonstration that a thesis has falsifiers may be a defence against its characterization as metaphysics but not against its characterization as pseudoscience. (My objections to Grünbaum's dealings with the relative stringency of inductivist and falsificationist criteria of pseudoscience is completely independent of the cogency or otherwise of his defence of inductivism.) There is even some doubt whether formal falsifiability is considered by Popper to be inconsistent with the metaphysical ('non-scientific') status of a speculation. At one point he gives the 'readiness to look out for tests' as distinguishing science not merely from pseudoscience but 'especially from pre-scientific myths and metaphysics'. Aristarchus is said not to qualify as a scientist yet his cosmic heliocentrism is said to be false and his local heliocentrism to have been confirmed by Kepler, which seems inconsistent with either lacking falsifiers.

3. This is the weakest of my exegetical reconstructions of Popper. Though he does concede that a certain degree of dogmatism is required for science to advance, and that there are occasions when the rejection of putative falsifications is justified (1968*a*, p. 81), he also sometimes speaks as if the resort to *ad hoc* hypotheses is sufficient to brand someone a pseudoscientist. Whichever view we assign him on this issue it would not affect his adverse account of psychoanalysis since, though unequivocal refutations of its theories are not common and so their tenacity can be justified, this could not extenuate the unwarranted and spurious confirmation reports which are a staple of the literature and which is the alternative basis of Popper's indictment of it. Even if Popper does sometimes suggest that unfalsifiable theses are on that

account alone pseudoscientific, he is then using 'pseudoscientific' in a different sense than that in which he employs it when he complains about incessant and unwarranted confirmation reports ('the stream of verifications'). Here is another remark which shows Popper objecting neither to the unfalsifiability of a theorist's claims, nor to his refusal to capitulate to apparent falsifications but to his reporting practices: 'The most characteristic element in the situation seemed to be the incessant stream of confirmations, of observations which verified the theory in question; and this was a point constantly emphasized by their adherents . . . The Freudian analysts emphasized that their theories were daily, nay, hourly verified by their "clinical observations".'

4. From time to time Freud himself conceded the untestability of his dream theory. In the *New Introductory Lectures* chapter on dreams he said that though every dream was meaningful not every dream could be interpreted. In the *Outline* he said, 'It is often hard to detect the unconscious motive force and its wish-fulfilment but we may assume it is always there' (1904*a*, p. 33).

5. Freud invoked a constitutional factor to explain why universal features of infantile life, like incestuous fantasies, should nevertheless only sometimes be pathogenic but objected to the emptiness of this explanation when invoked by others. In his *Mental Hygiene* review of *The Problem of Anxiety* Rank chides Freud for his inconsistently failing to concede that the constitutional factor might just as readily be invoked to meet Freud's own objections to Rank's birth trauma theory (Rank, 1927, pp. 185–88).

6. This is Freud's account of the second beating in the 'Original Record': 'when he was a little boy (age uncertain, perhaps five or six) he was lying between his father and mother and wetted the bed, upon which his father beat him and turned him out' (1909, p. 384).

Glymour commits another exegetical error: 'Freud was already committed to the primacy of masturbation as a form of sexual gratification in infancy and early childhood and as an aetiological factor in neurosis. Indeed he repeats this commitment in the very same section of the case study in which the previous quotation was taken.' Glymour then quotes in support: 'Infantile masturbation reaches a kind of climax, as a rule, between the ages of three and four or five, and it is the clearest expression of a child's sexual constitution, in which the aetiology of subsequent neuroses must be sought' (1909, p. 202). On this occasion Glymour is the victim of a genuine ambiguity in Freud's text rather than his own tendentiousness. It is clear from the German version that it is to the sexual constitution and not masturbation that we are to look for the etiology of subsequent neuroses. If avoiding this ambiguity were the only consideration the translation ought to run: 'Masturbation . . . is after all the plainest expression of the sexual constitution of the child, to which constitution we must look for the aetiology of the neuroses.' ('Aber die Onanie der Pubertätsjahre ist in Wirklichkeit nichts anderes als die Auffrischung der bisher stets vernachlässigten Onanie der Kinderjahre, welche zumeist in den Jahren von 3 bis 4 oder 5 eine Art von Höhepunkt erreicht, und diese ist allerdings der deutlichste Ausdruck der sexuellen Konstitution des Kindes, in welcher auch wir die Aetiologie der späteren Neurosen suchen' (1909, pp 423–24).

REFERENCES

Alston, W.P. 1964. The Elucidation of Religious Statements, in W.R. Reese and E. Freeman, eds., *Process and Divinity: The Hartshorne Festschrift.* La Salle: Open Court.

Arlow, J. 1960. Psychoanalysis and Scientific Method, in S. Hook, ed., *Psychoanalysis, Scientific Method and Philosophy.* New York: Grove Press.

Brill, A. 1948*a*. *Basic Principles of Psychoanalysis.* New York: Washington Square Press.

———. 1948*b*. *Lectures on Psychoanalytic Psychiatry.* New York: Vintage.

Carter, C. 1954. *An Encyclopedia of Psychoanalytic Astrology.* London: Theosophical Publishing House.

Dalbiez, R. 1941. *Psychoanalytic Method and the Doctrine of Freud.* London: Longmans.

Eddy, M.B. 1875. *Science and Health.* Boston: Allison V. Stewart.

Escalona, S. 1952. Problems in Psychoanalytic Research. *International Journal of Psychoanalysis* 33:11–21.

Frank, J. 1961. *Persuasion and Healing.* London and Baltimore: Johns Hopkins Press.

Freud S. 1896. The Aetiology of Hysteria, in *Collected Papers,* Volume 1. London: The Hogarth Press and the Institute of Psycho-analysis, 1924.

———. 1898. Sexuality in the Aetiology of Neuroses, in *Collected Papers,* Volume 1. 1924.

———. 1900. *The Interpretation of Dreams.* London: Allen and Unwin, 1954.

———. 1904*a*. On Psychotherapy, in *Collected Papers,* Volume 1. 1924.

———. 1904*b*. Freud's Psychoanalytic Method, in *Collected Papers,* Volume 1. 1924.

———. 1905*a*. My Views on the Part Played by Sexuality in the Aetiology of the Neuroses, *Collected Papers,* Volume 1. 1924.

———. 1905*b*. *Three Essays on the Theory of Sexuality.* New York: Basic Books, 1963.

———. 1909*a*. Notes upon a Case of Obsessional Neurosis, *Standard Edition,* Volume 10. London: Hogarth Press, 1953–66.

———. 1909*b*. Bemerkungen Ober einen Fall von Zwangneurose, *Gesammelte Werke,* Band 7. Franfurt am Main, 1972.

———. 1910. The Future of Psychoanalytic Psychotherapy, *Collected Papers,* Volume 2. 1924.

———. 1916. *Introductory Lectures on Psycho-analysis.* London: Hogarth Press.

———. 1923. Remarks on the Theory and Practice of Dream Interpretation, in *Collected Papers,* Volume 5, 1950.

———. 1924. The Question of Lay Analysis, in *Two Short Accounts of Psychoanalysis.* London: Penguin, 1962.

———. 1925. *An Autobiographical Study.* London: Hogarth Press, 1950.

———. 1933. *New Introductory Lectures.* London: Hogarth Press, 1949.

Freud S. and Breuer, J. 1895. *Studies in Hysteria.* New York, 1966.

Glover, E. 1956. *Freud on Jung.* New York: Norton.

Glymour, C. 1974. Freud, Kepler, and the Clinical Evidence, in R. Wollheim, ed., *Freud: A Collection of Critical Essays.* New York: Anchor Books.

Grünbaum, A. 1976. Is Falsifiability the Touchstone of Scientific Rationality? in R.S. Cohen et. al., eds., *Boston Studies in the Philosophy of Science,* Volume 39. Dordrecht: D. Reidel.

———. 1977. How Scientific is Psychoanalysis?, in R. Stern et. al., eds., Science and Psychotherapy. New York: Haven.

———. 1979*a.* Epistemological Liabilities of the Clinical Appraisal of Psychoanalytic Theory. *Psychoanalysis and Contemporary Thought,* Volume 2, number 2.

———. 1979*b.* Is Freudian Psychoanalytic Theory Pseudo-Scientific by Karl Popper's Criterion of Demarcation? *American Philosophical Quarterly* 16: 131–41.

Jones, E. 1923. War Shock and Freud's Theory of the Neuroses, in *Papers on Psychoanalysis.* London: Balliere, Tindall, and Cox, 1950.

———. 1930. Sigmund Freud, *Proceedings of the Royal Society of Medicine* 33:11–15.

Popper, K.R. 1963. *Conjectures and Refutations.* London: Routledge.

———. 1968*a. The Logic of Scientific Discovery.* Fifth edition (revised). London: Hutchinson.

———. 1968b. Remarks on the Problems of Demarcation and of Rationality, in I. Lakatos and A. Musgrave, eds., *Problems in the Philosophy of Science.* Amsterdam: North-Holland and Kegan Paul, pp. 88–102.

———. 1974. Replies to My Critics, in P.A. Schilpp, ed., *The Philosophy of Karl Popper,* Book II. La Salle: Open Court.

Rank, O. 1927. Review of Freud, *Inhibitions, Symptoms, and Anxiety. Mental Hygiene* 11: 181–88.

10

'Exegetical Myth-Making' in Grünbaum's Indictment of Popper and Exoneration of Freud

Adolf Grünbaum believes himself to have shown that contrary to Popper's characterization of him as a dogmatist, Freud was 'hospitable to refutation', 'responsive to adverse findings', and 'alert to the need for safeguarding the falsifiability of [his] interpretations and/or reconstructions of the patient's past' (1984, p. 273). Popper was particularly guilty of exegetical myth-making' in charging Freud and his followers with evasiveness in dealing with the objection that the apparent confirmation of their theories was due to their own prepossessions in conjunction with the compliance of the Patient (the Oedipus effect). In fact Freud 'carefully', 'brilliantly', 'squarely', 'unflaggingly', 'unswervingly' (though ultimately unsuccessfully) 'faced up' to the problem of suggestion.

I

In 'Is Freudian Psychoanalytic Theory Pseudo-Scientific by Karl Popper's Criterion of Demarcation?' (1979*a*) Grünbaum asserts that Freud's 'repeated modifications of his theories were (as a rule) clearly motivated by evidence'. He illustrates this claim by citing Freud's 'modification' of the seduction theory. Was the abandonment of the seduction theory and its replacement by infantile incestuous fantasies 'clearly motivated by evidence'? Let us take these questions separately.

Why did Freud abandon the seduction theory? This is *one* of Grünbaum's accounts:

> The incidence of hysteria was unexpectedly high, but sexual molestation in child-
> hood was causally quite insufficient to generate hysteria. Hence if actual child-

---

This first appeared in Crispin Wright and Peter Clark, eds., *Psychoanalysis and Theories of the Mind* (Blackwell, 1988), and is reprinted by permission.

hood seductions were causally necessary for hysteria as Freud had hypothesized, then the required incidence of perverted acts against children was preposterously high, even in the face of the attempted concealment of these transgressions by the guilty adults. And this over-taxed Freud's own belief in his seduction etiology. (1979a, p. 135)

Was the 'incidence of perverted acts against children' required by Freud's theory 'preposterously high'? In the first place the presence of adult seducers among Freud's cases was adventitious and not required by the seduction theory. In seven of Freud's first 13 cases the seducer was another child. If Freud's seduction theory were adequately glossed as sexual victimization by an adult paedophile then the required incidence might be plausibly maintained to be 'preposterously high'.

But though Grünbaum thinks of the seduction theory as a theory of child rape (perhaps influenced by Jeffrey's Masson's misrepresentations), he is wrong to do so. Freud's seduction theory is not a theory of child rape, not even in the broadest sense of sexual relations between an adult and a child. Though adults figured in an unspecified number of his patients' seduction histories, this was not necessitated by Freud's account of the source of the pathogenic power of sexual arousal in childhood which lies quite simply in its precocity. The question is not 'What are the chances of getting through childhood without being at the receiving end of the attentions of an adult pervert?' but 'What are the chances of avoiding "doctor and nurse" games and kindred forms of sex play with other children?' If Grünbaum thinks that even so understood the incidence of acts required by the seduction theory was 'preposterously high' then either he is extrapolating from a particularly chaste and protected childhood milieu, or I lived in a particularly depraved one, for I can see nothing 'preposterous' about the assumption that such occurrences are common enough to account for the presumed incidence of hysteria.

Furthermore, Grünbaum's thesis that Freud discovered the acts required by the seduction theory to be 'preposterously high' contradicts the account Freud himself gives in *Three Essays on Sexuality* (his first public disavowal of the seduction theory), where he denies that he had exaggerated the frequency of seduction. The reason he then goes on to give, that he abandoned seductions because he discovered that healthy people may also have undergone experiences of infantile seduction, is both untrue and incoherent. Untrue in that he could not have *discovered* this since he explicitly alludes to it in the seduction papers themselves, and incoherent in that even had he discovered it it would have provided him with no grounds for abandoning his seduction aetiology since this only committed him to the necessary and not the sufficient condition of adult neuroses. In other words, for a case to overthrow Freud's seduction aetiology it would have had to consist of a neurotic who had *not* been seduced, and not just a non-neurotic who had.

He repeats this spurious argument in 'My Views on the Role of Sexuality in the Neuroses' (1906*a*): 'Investigation into the mental life of normal persons yielded the unexpected discovery that their infantile history in regard to sexual matters was not necessarily different in essentials from that of the neurotic and that seduction in particular had played the same part in it' (Freud 1924, p. 279). How could the fact that non-neurotics may also have been seduced in infancy have been an 'unexpected discovery' when in one of the seduction papers themselves he went out of his way to insist on it?—'We have heard and acknowledged that there are many people who have a very clear recollection of infantile sexual experiences and yet do not suffer from hysteria' (1924, p. 207). 'It is easy enough to find people who remember scenes of sexual seduction and abuse in their childhood but yet have never suffered from hysteria' (1924, p. 203).

But Grünbaum has an alternative account as to why Freud abandoned the seduction theory, one which does not depend on intuitive assessments of the incidence of seductions: he refers to 'adverse evidence [Freud] himself had uncovered', i.e. Freud simply came across a neurotic who had not been seduced in infancy. Freud himself gives countenance to this view in one of his belated accounts of the theory and its desertion when he speaks of 'contradiction in definitely ascertainable circumstances' (1924, p. 299). But a proper conception of Freud's seduction theory poses difficulties for this account as well. In 'Heredity and Aetiology' Freud describes the pathogenic agent in hysteria as a 'passive sexual experience undergone with indifference or with a slight degree of disgust or fright' (1924, p. 152) and this does raise the question of how he could be sure that an adult neurotic had not as a child had a 'passive sexual experience undergone with indifference'.

Grünbaum may have got the impression that seductions have a blatancy which makes Freud's claim to have discovered 'contradiction in definitely ascertainable circumstances' credible from Freud's reference to 'grave sexual injuries, some of them absolutely appalling' (1924, p. 157). But nothing in Freud's theory of the pathogenic effect of seduction commits him to brutal assaults such as we can easily credit might be discovered not to have taken place.

The 'grave sexual injuries' remark does, however, raise problems as to the credibility of Grünbaum's thesis that the alteration in Freud's views were 'clearly motivated by evidence' if it is construed to comprise Freud's seduction *reconstructions* and their later retraction. For it means that we are to imagine Freud, having originally decided that his patients had suffered grave sexual injuries, later deciding that this was a mistake. This raises doubts as to the empirical character of either the procedure which led him to assert the occurrence of 'grave sexual injuries' in the first place or to deny them in the second. We must distinguish between Freud's *aetiological* error and his *reconstructive* error when speaking of the 'seduction debacle'. There is a difference between failing to find any evidence of infantile seduction in new patients and deciding that many of his 18 patients whose seductions in infancy he was confident enough to have reported as confirmation of the seduction theory had not after all been seduced. Of Freud's ostensibly seduced patients how many did he change his mind about? He never gave a precise figure but he did say that the majority had not after all been seduced, which means at least ten errors. Now we can credit that with extraordinary luck and extraordinary pertinacity Freud might have confirmed his suspicions that he was mistaken in two or three cases; but in ten? Let me confide my nasty suspicions; we need not rack our brains to attempt to reconstruct how Freud could possibly discover that the reported brutal assaults of ten or more of his patients were 'contradicted under definitely ascertainable circumstances' because there may have been no such discoveries. Freud did not falsify his reconstructions. He merely withdrew from them. Why? Well, consider the alternative. Although there would have been no logical contradiction in Freud's maintaining both that the seduction theory was mistaken *and* that his own reconstructions were nevertheless sound, it would have strained their credulity excessively to ask his colleagues to believe that *by chance* 100 percent of his clientele had been seduced in early childhood.[1]

We can't be sure why Freud abandoned the seduction theory but only that his own account makes no sense. My own guess is that the major difference between 1896 and 1897 is not that in the interval Freud discovered the seductions had not always occurred but that he discovered how to do without them. To whatever theoretical reasons Freud had for clinging to infantile sexuality and therefore retreating to 'psychic reality' must be added the advantageous elusiveness and malleability of that 'psychic reality' itself.

In his book Grünbaum supplements his earlier account as to why Freud dropped the seduction theory with the suggestion (contained in the Fliess letter) that the disappointment of his therapeutic hopes may have caused Freud to doubt the correctness of his aetiology. That his therapeutic achievements were often incomplete was acknowledged by Freud in the

---

1. I would like to correct a mistaken argument on this point employed in a previous paper (Chapter 9 above). I there argued that seductions are so blatantly observable that the acknowledgement of counter-instances was not evidence of any notable degree of 'hospitality to refutation'. Whereas I still think that capitulation to counter-instances is equivocal evidence of an investigator's probity where the phenomena are blatant or easily replicable, I was wrong to think seductions an example of this. I only thought so because I confused the event, seduction, with the indirect evidence for the event, testimony and memory. I confused the relative ease with which someone witnessing a putative seduction could discriminate it from mere horseplay (what one might call its intrinsic observability) with the trouble he would have in determining whether an act of unconscious incestuous fantasizing was taking place. But of course this is a gross *non sequitur* since what is at issue is the relative accessibility of the evidence for these and not their intrinsic observability.

seduction papers themselves and so need not have been felt by him to be inconsistent with the seduction aetiology. In any case he had never placed much weight on therapeutic success as the source of his aetiological conviction: 'Without wishing to lay special stress on the fact I will add that in a number of cases the therapeutic test also speaks for the genuine nature of the infantile scenes. . . . The aetiological pretensions of the infantile scenes rest . . . above all on the evidence of the associative and logical connections between these scenes and the hysterical symptoms' (1924, p. 206). Furthermore, though therapeutic failure might prompt Freud to suspect the pathogenic *influence* of seductions in childhood it could not, of itself bring their *historicity* into question.

Grünbaum is able to confer a semblance of plausibility on his thesis that the seduction episode illustrates Freud's hospitality to refutation by choosing a formulation which enables him to place the emphasis on what Freud abandoned rather than on what he retained.

Freud himself characterized his seduction phase in terms which permit us to pose more pointed questions about his transition from seduction to incestuous and polymorphous perversity than Grünbaum's. In his first extended account of the post-seduction aetiology Freud said: 'I consider it worth emphasizing that, in spite of all the changes in them, my views concerning the aetiology of the neuroses have never caused me to disavow or abandon two points of view: namely, the importance of sexuality and of infantilism' (1924, p. 280).

What grounds had Freud for not abandoning these more general views? He was able to retain both sexuality and infancy while abandoning seduction by persuading himself that the infantile seduction scenes he found in his 18 consecutive patients, when they were not authentic, were distorted recollections of infantile incestuous fantasizing. But it was not only a substantive thesis as to the infantile determinants of psychoneuroses that this manoeuvre enabled Freud to retain but also, and more essentially, the authenticity of his novel diagnostic and reconstructive methods. As Ernest Jones put it, 'In finding that these seductions had in most cases not taken place he could only conclude that his method was fallible or that there was some other explanation' (Jones, 1957). The question Grünbaum does not address is what justification Freud had for not concluding 'that his method was fallible' rather than 'that there was some other explanation'.

Why should the belief that s/he had been sexually abused by a parent be less distressing to a patient than the memory of having sexually desired one? And why, since the fabricated memory of seduction was as unconscious as the genuine incestuous fantasy it replaced, was there any point to subjecting the latter to distortion in the first place?

There is reason to think that Freud himself came to find his account of adult seduction convictions as distortions of infantile incestuous fantasies unconvincing because twenty years after the desertion of the seduction theory he suggested that the seduction reminiscences were not illusory after all. Only they were authentic reminiscences of episodes in the life, not of the patient, but of a prehistoric ancestor at a time when paternal paedophile attacks on children were a reality ('in the pre-history of the human family' (Freud, 1963, pp. 323–24).) Ug-a-wug, it seems, was a paedophile. (Strange that Alley Oop never mentions it.) In any case, male cross-sex seduction memories require maternal paedophiles. Was this, too, a reality in the 'pre-history of the human family'? Did Mrs Ug-a-wug share her mate's kinks?

The alternative to the view that the seduction ideation Freud found to underlie his patients' symptoms was a self-protective distortion of their infantile incestuous fantasies is that Freud's *a priori* conviction that the neuroses had sexual sources led him both to influence his patients' productions and to place tendentious constructions upon them. Freud mentions the possibility only to dismiss it with the assurance that he had undertaken the treatment of the seduction patients without any such prepossessions.

In his autobiographical study Freud says of his discovery of the pathogenic influence of sexual life: 'I had begun my investigation of neurotics quite unsuspectingly' (1935, p. 41) and refers his readers to the book he had published with Breuer in 1895. 'It would have been difficult to guess from the *Studien uber Hysterie* what an importance sexuality had in the aetiology of the neuroses' (1935, p. 39). Freud had issued the same reassurance in the lectures delivered in America in 1909, where he said of the development of his view that 'the predominant significance [in neurotic disorders] must be assigned to disturbances in erotic life'; that 'far from this position having been postulated theoretically, at the time of the publication of the *Studies on Hysteria* I had not yet adopted it' (Freud, 1962, p. 69).

Would anyone have suspected from these utterances that what Freud had said of the pathogenic role of sexuality in the Preface to the *Studies on Hysteria* was that 'sexuality seems to play a principal part in the psychogenesis of hysteria' (Freud and Breuer, 1966, p. xxx), or that in the body of the book he wrote, 'the determining causes which lead to the acquisition of neuroses . . . [are] to be looked for in sexual factors' and described himself as submitting his cases 'to a deliberate and searching investigation of their sexual foundations'? (1966, p. 305). Even earlier (at the beginning of 1894) he had expressed the view that 'the source of the incompatible ideas which are submitted to defence is solely and exclusively sexual life' (S.E. [1897], 111, p. 225). Even if we construe Freud's disavowals of sexual expectations to refer specifically to infantile seductions rather than the general pathogenic influence of sexual life, they are untrue. In a letter to Fliess in 1895 he speaks of a patient 'giving me what I waited for, "infantile abuse"' (1985, p. 149). And in a draft sent to Fliess, dated 1892, he cites as one of the aetiological factors in neuroses 'sexual traumas dating back before the age of understanding' (1985, p. 33). And yet in his autobiography Freud says of the role of sexual factors in neuroses, 'I was not prepared for this conclusion and my expectations played no part in it' (1935, p. 41). Was it not Freud's memories rather than those of his patients that had undergone self-protective distortion?

So much for the state of Freud's convictions on the role of sexuality in the aetiology of the neuroses while he was treating the seduction patients. A related question rises. Did he tell his patients of these convictions? Did his patients' seduction material sometimes emerge only after Freud had told them of his suspicions? There are reasons for thinking so. In the *Studies on Hysteria* (1895) he dismissed the danger of suggestion: 'We need not be afraid of telling the patient what his next thought connection is going to be. It will do no harm' (Freud and Breuer, 1966, p. 341). In the same work he says of a patient, 'I assured her that she would see something that was directly related to the causes of her condition in her childhood.' In one of the seduction papers themselves Freud says of his patients' response to the seduction scene, 'They are generally indignant if we tell them something of the sort is now coming to light' (1924, p. 199); and in another, 'The mental image of the premature sexual experience is recalled only when most energetic pressure is exerted by the analytic procedure against strong resistance' (1924, p. 150).

Even if Grünbaum was unfamiliar with these pronouncements of Freud he ought not to have accepted Freud's account of the seduction error since it is apparent from the seduction papers themselves, without any familiarity with Freud's other statements on the subject, that his denial that his expectations of a seduction aetiology anticipated his patients' confirmation of it is quite impossible. For example, how had Freud so cleverly managed to synchronize his treatment of the first 13 seduction patients as not to permit the conclusion he had arrived at concerning any one of them to affect his anticipations with respect to any of the others? Furthermore, we know that Freud followed up his report on these 13 in which he had committed himself to the indispensability of infantile seduction with a report on five more. Could he have approached them too without anticipation, as he claims?

There are still other considerations internal to the seduction papers themselves that are inconsistent with Freud's denials that his conviction that his patients had undergone infantile seductions anticipated their own. In the last of them, 'The Aetiology of Hysteria', Freud argued that it was not sufficient that an occurrence be found which had been repressed and had coincided with the beginning of the illness. In order to be a satisfactory explanation the trauma must meet two other requirements. First, it must have traumatic force. Thus, an occasion on which a patient had bitten into a rotten apple would not be a satisfactory explanation of his nausea even if he had repressed it and his neurosis had dated from it, for it was not severe enough for the neurosis to be attributed to it.

Freud's second requirement of an adequate trauma was that it have what he called 'determining quality'. Even though the patient's memory efforts terminated in the recovery of an experience which did have traumatic force, like a railway accident, this too was unsatisfactory as an explanation since it did not explain why the patient was suffering from nausea rather than an hysterical paralysis, say. The railway accident lacked 'determining quality'.

Let me quote Freud's own words: 'When the scene first revealed does not satisfy our requirements, we say to the patient that his experience does not explain anything, but that there must be hidden behind it an earlier and more significant experience' (1924, p. 189).

Now Freud tells us that a common presenting complaint of his hysterical patients was painful genital sensations. But if you begin with a patient among whose presenting symptoms are painful sensations in the region of the genitals, painful sensations while defecating, say, and you further insist that the originating trauma must have determining quality, how can it be a matter for astonishment that the infantile trauma turns out to involve penetration of the rectal area? In any case Freud is explicit that before arriving at the infantile seduction he had already invariably uncovered a pubescent sexual trauma (1924, p. 194). He construed this to mean either that hysterics were so constituted as to respond pathologically to sexual life or that they had suffered a still earlier trauma related associatively to the pubescent one and capable of supplying its explanatory deficiencies.

Once Freud laid down the determining requirement, the sexual character of the traumas was a foregone conclusion, and Freud must have known this; so he couldn't have been surprised at the character of these traumas. Why then does he insist that he was? Because, I suggest, of his need to undercut the objection that the patient's production of seduction material was due to Freud's own anticipations of it.

A particularly deplorable instance of Grünbaum's 'exegetical myth-making' is his claim that 'the prima facie confirmations of the postulated seduction episodes had been furnished by the seemingly vivid and presumably repressed memories that Freud had been able to elicit from his hysterical patients in the course of analysis'. Grünbaum goes on to refer to 'the subjective certainty felt by his adult patients in the reality of purported memories going back to childhood'. I have given my reasons elsewhere for doubting that Freud's patients generally had seduction memories of which they were subjectively certain (chapter 7 above). ('Patients assure me emphatically of their unbelief'; 'They have no feeling of recollecting these scenes' [Freud, 1924, p. 199].) But Grünbaum's more important error is in claiming that it was his patient's 'subjective certainty' that formed Freud's grounds for his belief in the reality of the seductions. Though this is Freud's later account, in the seduction papers themselves he is adamant that this is not the case ('I would charge myself with blameworthy credulity if I did not offer more convincing proof'). Nor is this 'more convincing proof' Grünbaum's highly touted Tally Argument. It is what Grünbaum himself describes as 'the consilience of extra-clinical inductions'.

It was to such 'consilience' that Freud appealed in the seduction papers. In the last of them he wrote: 'Just as when putting together children's puzzles we finally, after many attempts, become absolutely certain which piece belongs to the gap not yet filled . . . so the content of the infantile scenes proves to be an inevitable completion of the associative logical structure of the neuroses' (1924, pp. 200–01). What Grünbaum's account mischievously obscures is that it was this very mode of reasoning, or at least Freud's uncritical confidence in it, which led to what he refers to as the 'seduction debacle'. And yet a quarter of a century later Freud was still at it. In 'Remarks on the Theory and Practice of Dream Interpretation' (1923) he wrote: 'What makes [the analyst] certain in the end is precisely the complication of the problem before him, which is like the solution of a jigsaw puzzle' (1950, p. 142).

Freud made a tendentiously inadequate response to his realization that many of his reconstructions of his patient's infantile sexual life were erroneous. His dealings with the possibility that this was due to a combination of the contaminating effect of his own prior convictions and the looseness of his criteria for determining the correctness of his reconstructions was uncandid. His failure to modify these accordingly meant that his grounds for assigning his patients a history of polymorphous, perverse and incestuous fantasizing were as dubious as his grounds for assigning them histories of infantile seductions had been. Grünbaum's laudatory account of Freud's response to the seduction error performs a serious disservice in allowing this point to be lost. Contrary to Grünbaum's assertions the abandonment of the seduction theory is equivocal evidence that Freud was 'clearly motivated by evidence'. His replacement of it with the incestuous fantasy theory is unequivocal evidence that he was not.

II

Grünbaum holds that one of the 'episodes of significant theory modification that eloquently attests to Freud's responsiveness to *adverse* clinical and even extra-clinical findings' is 'the lesson that Freud learned from the failure of the Rat Man case to bear out his etiological retrodiction' (Grünbaum 1984, p. 281). What Grünbaum means by Freud's 'etiological retrodiction' is that Freud said that the Rat Man had been beaten by his father for masturbating but it turned out that he hadn't. The 'significant theory modification' (the 'lesson') is Freud's supposed consequent supplementation of public events like beatings with private events like fantasies in the aetiology of the neuroses. Grünbaum misdescribes Freud's post-seduction aetiology and misdescribes the Rat Man case itself but, even had he done neither, the supplementation of public events by fantasies would not constitute evidence of a creditable reponsiveness to 'adverse findings'.

Clark Glymour (on whose papers Grünbaum draws) says of Freud's speculation that the Rat Man had been beaten for sexual misbehaviour, 'Freud makes it sound as though the construction was but a conjecture peculiar to this case and not required required by psychoanalytic theory. But that is not correct' (Glymour, 1974, p. 299). It *is* correct and nothing Glymour goes on to say shows otherwise. Grünbaum follows Glymour in confounding a particular reconstruction with a generic aetiology. What Grünbaum calls Freud's aetiological retrodiction in the case of the Rat Man was not 'based on' his 'specific etiology for obsessions'. He had none. Freud's claim to have anticipated that the Rat Man was beaten in childhood is contradicted by the account given in the Original Record of the case.[2] The fact that the Rat Man had not been beaten for a sexual offence could not in any case have had any adverse bearing on Freud's post-seduction aetiology. Grünbaum writes: 'Freud had postulated that premature sexual activity, such as excessive masturbation, subject to severe repression is the specific cause of obsessional neurosis' (1984, p. 281). Not so. This is Grünbaum's account of the concept of specific causation: 'by claiming that P is a specific pathogen of N, he was asserting not only that P is causally necessary for N but also that P is never, or hardly ever, on etiological factor in pathogenesis of any other pathologically distinct syndrome'. And yet, whereas Grünbaum tells us that Freud's postseduction theory held excessive masturbation to be the specific cause of obsessional neuroses, Glymour, whom he invokes in support, takes it to be the specific cause of hysteria (1974, p. 302). It cannot have been the specific cause of both. In fact it was the specific cause of neither. In his first extended account of his post-seduction aetiology Freud writes, 'A specific aetiology in the form of particular infantile experiences is not forthcoming' (1924, p. 281).

The proffering of premature sexual activity as a specific cause of the obsessional neuroses occurs for the first time in the Rat Man case itself and is contradicted by the cases of Dora and of Little Hans, both of whom are said by Freud to have been sexually precocious, as well as by the statement

---

2. This is what Freud says in the published case history: 'Starting from these indications and from other data of a similar kind I ventured to put forward a construction to the effect that when he was a child of under six he had been guilty of some sexual misdemeanour connected with onanism and had been soundly castigated for it by his father' (S.E., 1909, X, p. 342). This is what he says in the notes he made at the time: 'I could not restrain myself here from constructing the material at our disposal into an event: how before the age of six he had been in the habit of masturbating and how his father had forbidden it, using as a threat the phrase, "It would be the death of you" and perhaps also threatening to cut off his penis' (S.E., 1909, X, p. 263).

in the *Three Essays on Sexuality* that sexual precocity is a characteristic of neuroses generally (section in the 'Summary' headed 'Precocity').

Freud had no independent criteria for either 'premature sexual activity such as excessive masturbation' nor for 'severe repression'. The fact that someone had fallen ill as an adult was adequate grounds for the retrospective attribution of either. What was excessive for one child might be tolerable for another, and what was optimal for one child might be pathogenic for another. In the 1905 edition of the *Three Essays on Sexuality* Freud wrote: 'It was not possible to say what amount of sexual activity can occur in childhood without it being described as abnormal or detrimental to later development' (1965, p. 139).

Thus the case of the Rat Man could not have refuted Freud's postseduction aetiology because even if his childhood had been without abnormal sexual traumas this was fully consistent with the role allotted in Freud's theory to the constitutional factor which was capable of rendering traumas otiose. (This is not to say that Freud's post-seduction theory was without empirical content but only that it was not testable by single case studies but only by large-scale epidemiological inquiry. Freud was committed to there being a lesser incidence of sexual intimidation, such as castration threats, among non-neurotics but he was not committed, as Grünbaum thinks, to any particular neurotic, e.g. the Rat Man, having been sexually intimidated.)

Furthermore, in implying that Freud's discovery that the Rat Man had not been beaten for a sexual offence would have left him bereft of eligible pathogens, thus forcing him to fall back on fantasies, Grünbaum is misrepresenting the contents of the Rat Man case itself, which is replete with eligible pathogens. How could the 'lesson' that infantile sexual fantasies would do as well as infantile sexual experience as a pathogenic agent be learned from a case history which in fact records infantile sexual experiences ?[3]

Let us suppose that Freud *had* held that sexual intimidation in early childhood was a necessary condition of adult neuroses and that the only eligible candidate for such intimidation in the Rat Man's childhood had been his father beating him. Why should Freud's response to the discovery that the beating was not an instance of sexual intimidation by supplementing sexual intimidation with fears of sexual intimidation as factors in the aetiology of the neuroses be held to illustrate responsiveness to adverse evidence? Ought we not to reserve that expression for the admission that the Rat Man's neurotic disposition may have been brought about by castigation

---

3. To complicate matters further Freud forgot that the Rat Man had been beaten on another occasion, and for bedwetting, which Freud held to be a substitute for nocturnal emissions. So the Rat Man was after all beaten for a sexual offence, the same one Freud himself had been berated for (see the dream of Count Thun in the *Interpretation of Dreams*). This extenuates Freud's error but not Grünbaum's (unless he has similarly poignant revelations to make).

which was *not* construed as sexually intimidating? There is something disingenuous in Grünbaum's invoking as 'telling evidence' of Popper's 'exegetical oversight' an account of Freud's procedure which makes it illustrative of just those practices that Popper was concerned to reprobate.

The introduction of infantile fantasies as pathogenic factors meant that though Freud's reconstructions might still be imperilled by independent inquiry if they contained allusions to public states of affairs, his aetiology was, nevertheless, proof against refutation since the child's propensity to pathogenic fantasizing was freed from environing circumstance.

One of Grünbaum's more original discoveries is that Freud was a good falsificationist, always 'alert to the need for safeguarding the falsifiability of the analyst's reconstructions of the patient's past' (1984, p. 237). This is both false and misleading. Misleading because, whatever the formal position with respect to extra-clinical events, it was Freud's practice to validate his reconstructions of the patient's past intra-clinically. False, because when Freud does deal with external evidence he often manifests no alertness to safeguarding anything but his own reconstructive pretensions.

In *The Psychoanalytic Movement* Ernest Gellner writes: 'Freud rather revealingly repudiated the relevance of historical reconstructions of the public event on the ground that by invoking independent witnesses it imposed an external judge on the process of analysis' (1985, p. 183). The passage that Gellner had in mind occurs in a footnote to the second chapter of the case history of the Wolf Man: 'It may be tempting to take the easy course of filling up the gaps in a patient's memory by making inquiries from the older members of his family; but I cannot advise too strongly against such a technique. Any stories that may be told by relatives in reply to inquiries and requests are at the mercy of every critical misgiving that can come into play. One invariably regrets having made oneself dependent upon such information . . . confidence in the analysis is shaken and a court of appeal is set up over it' (Freud, 1925, p. 482).

I put the same construction as Gellner on these remarks in 'Freud and the Idea of a Pseudo-Science'. Grünbaum argued that any implication of evasiveness is neutralized by a sentence I 'tendentiously omitted'— 'Information of this kind may as a rule be employed as absolutely authentic material.' Since the information Freud is referring to in this sentence is 'stories about his childhood which the patient was told' *before* the analysis and these were just those external facts from which Freud had least to fear as he could ascertain them before he advanced his reconstructions, I do not think the self-protective interpretation of Freud's remark is necessarily undermined. However, Grünbaum has another argument:

> But does Freud here reject all use of independent external evidence as to the historical veracity of his clinical reconstructions of a patient's infancy after the completion of the analysis? It would seem not. What Freud does renounce here is the

questioning of senior relatives, conducted by the analyst, to fill up the gaps in the patient's memory as a procedural technique for making progress in the analysis. This renunciation does not preclude his willingness to test his clinical reconstructions by means of independent external evidence once the analysis has been completed. Indeed he displayed this kind of willingness in his retrospective external evaluation of his clinical findings in the Rat Man case (1979*b*, p. 86).

Grünbaum then goes on to cite Freud's withdrawal of his original conjecture as to why the Rat Man was beaten.

There are times when Grünbaum goes through Freud's text like a sleepwalker. For of course it is not the case that Freud waited until after the analysis was completed before making inquiries as to the circumstances under which the Rat Man was beaten. He even wove the information provided by the patient's mother (that he had bitten someone) into his solution of 'the great obsessive fear'. So Freud had no hesitation in using information from the very sources he condemns in his Wolf Man remarks. Doesn't this entitle us to suspect a degree of opportunism in the advice he there gives?

In the case history of the Rat Man Freud has no scruples about inciting the patient to make 'pointed enquiries' of his mother as to the beating episode and of incorporating the reply (that it was for biting someone) into his interpretations, using it to bolster his view that the Rat Man identified himself with rats since he and they both bit and both were persecuted for it. 'It is seldom that we are in the fortunate position of being able, as in the present instance, to establish the facts upon which these tales of the individual's prehistoric past are based, by recourse to the unimpeachable testimony of a grown-up person' (Freud, 1925, p. 344). What had happened to transform 'the unimpeachable testimony of a grown-up person' of 1909 into 'stories that . . . are at the mercy of every critical misgiving' of 1915? Until Grünbaum can bring himself to address such questions he ought to attempt to control his compulsion to issue ill-considered testimonials to Freud's 'responsiveness to adverse evidence'.

III

Grünbaum calls Popper's observation that suggestibility 'seems to have failed to attract the attention of analysts, perhaps not accidentally', 'incredibly uninformed and grossly unfair' (1984, p. 282). Grünbaum insists on glossing Popper's remark to mean that Freud and his followers never raised and discussed the problem of suggestion. This would be 'incredibly uninformed' and for that very reason it is incredible. I know of no one who has ever taken Popper to mean anything other than that Freud and his followers never took proper account of the influence of suggestion on their patients' productions, however infelicitously he may have put it.

Fortunately, Grünbaum advances arguments which do not depend on his pedantic construal of Popper's remark. He argues that Freud did more than merely discuss the problem of suggestion. He 'brilliantly', 'unswervingly' faced up to it even if he failed to resolve it. How did Freud, on Grünbaum's view, 'face up' to suggestibility? Via the Tally Argument. 'Freud's 1917 Tally Argument was a brilliant effort to come to grips with the full dimensions of the challenge of epistemic contamination by adulterated clinical response' (1984, p. 283). What is the Tally Argument? Grünbaum derives the expression from the *Standard Edition* translation of a sentence in *Introductory Lecture* 28: '[the neurotic's] conflicts will only be successfully solved and his resistances overcome if the anticipatory ideas he is given tally with what is real in him' (S.E., 1917, XVI, p. 452). Grünbaum makes three errors in his dealing with Freud's Tally Argument: he gratuitously concedes Freud's entitlement to therapeutic superiority; he gives therapeutic superiority justificatory powers it does not possess; and he overstates Freud's dependence on and commitment to its justificatory status.

Grünbaum has not sufficiently emancipated himself from the bad historiographic habits of psychoanalytic commentators. He speaks of Freud's having dealt 'brilliantly' with objections to his theories but shows no knowledge of these objections except through Freud's account of them. For example he denies that Freud's reply to the charge of suggestibility was a mere *ipse dixit*. While it may not have been so with respect to the question Freud set himself, it was with respect to the question he was asked. The objection Freud had to meet (from Aschaffenburg, Kraeplin and Janet among others) was that he could not use therapeutic efficacy to support his infantile sexual aetiology since other therapists had treated neuroses as successfully without holding such an aetiology. What Grünbaum calls Freud's necessary condition thesis (NCT) amounts to the claim 'Only my therapy really works, your results are either ephemeral or superficial'. (In 1904 he wrote: 'The analytic method of psychotherapy is the one that penetrates most deeply and carries farthest' [1924, p. 252].) What grounds had Freud for the assumption that his therapy refreshed the parts Aschaffenburg, Ziehen, Prince, Sidis, Janet, et al. could not reach?

The question Freud set himself in *Lecture* 28 was how to distinguish the rationale of psychoanalytic therapy from that of suggestion therapies since both exploit the physician's ascendancy over the patient. That is, Freud assumes a critic who concedes the efficacy of his methods but objects that they amount to disguised versions of suggestive therapy. Having assumed both the efficacy of his therapeutic efforts and their superiority to those of rival practitioners, Freud addresses himself to the question of how, given the admitted role that the physician's relation to the patients plays in the treatment, he can be sure that either his acquiescence in Freud's aetiological and dynamic proposals, or his production of material apparently confirmatory of them is not due to his compliance rather than the truth of Freud's interpretations and/or reconstructions. Freud's reply is an account of how the rationale and procedure of psychoanalysis differ from those of suggestive therapies and an assertion that the efficacy of psychoanalytic therapy depends on the veridicality of the account of himself that the patient comes to accept. Grünbaum thinks that Freud was entitled to advance this argument until sometime in the mid-twenties when he was compelled to acknowledge the reality of spontaneous remission and so lost his grounds for maintaining that psychoanalytic treatment was a *sine qua non* of recovery from neurosis. But Freud had never been in a position to claim that psychoanalytic treatment (i.e. treatment in which an essential component was the anamnesis of the content of Freud's infantile sexual aetiology of the neuroses) was a *sine qua non* of therapeutic efficacy and even less that veridical anamnesis was.

The question Grünbaum evades is how Freud could *ever* have employed the Tally Argument with any credibility or conviction when it committed him to an assertion that it was manifest he was in no position to make, viz., that he had examined the outcomes of other therapeutic methods and found them inferior to his own.

It is likely that the ephemerality of the results of hypnotic suggestion was a familiar fact. In any case there was nothing implausible about Freud's claim to have employed suggestion with generally disappointing results. What Freud could not plausibly claim was that he had had patients who had anamnesed or abreacted, e.g., Adlerian pathogenic episodes, and had shown only short-term remission of their illness in consequence. But the situation is worse for Grünbaum's thesis than even these considerations bring out. Not only could Freud have no grounds for believing his NCT (necessary condition thesis) true; he had reason for believing it false.

For the Tally Argument to have any force Freud would not only have had to accompany it with reasons for doubting the efficacy of rival therapies but also with a retraction of his own claims to therapeutic achievements before adopting the 'Oedipal' view of neurotic difficulties. He would have had to explain away the 'countless successes' remark of the 1898 paper 'Sexuality in the Aetiology of the Neuroses' (Freud, 1924, p. 244). The least that such a claim would imply is that Freud was able to compare the post-analytic condition of his 'seduction' patients with that of his 'Oedipal' patients and found that the condition of the latter was much more satisfactory. But Freud never made such a claim and if he had would have raised some awkward questions as to what opportunity he had to make the comparison and how he went about it.

Grünbaum says of Freud's seduction patients: 'Clearly the NCT would have been strongly disconfirmed if there had been cases of patients who had been genuinely cured after being given pseudo-insight by their analyses into episodes of sexual abuse that had presumably never occurred in their childhood' (1984, p. 159). This remark indicates some degree of confusion on

Grünbaum's part. The NCT is meant 'to constitute cogent evidence for the specific etiologies of the psychoneuroses'. But since the core of Freud's 'specific etiologies of the psychoneuroses' was the Oedipus complex, i.e., the repression of incestuous longings for the cross-sex parent, the fact that the episodes of sexual abuse had not occurred is completely irrelevant to the disconfirmatory status of genuine cure among the patients of the 1896 papers. For even those who *had* been sexually abused and thus had been given *veridical* insight would, nevertheless, not have anamnesed/abreacted their incestuous desires and castratory fears and thus would have attained their neuroses-free status without benefit of the theory on whose behalf the NCT was advanced. That is, if any single one of Freud's 18 'seduction' patients had been genuinely relieved of their neuroses then Freud would have had reason to doubt that his therapeutic efficacy could be enlisted in support of his Oedipal aetiology.

But even if the assumption of differential therapeutic efficacy was granted Freud, this could still not meet scepticism as to his aetiological claims. The differential therapeutic efficacy of psychoanalysis might have been due to a feature not present in other therapies and yet not related to the veridicality of Freud's theory of pathogenesis. As the psychoanalyst J.C. Flugel conceded in 1924, the argument over the relevance of therapeutic efficacy ended in deadlock because it could not be shown that even if psychoanalysis was more effective this was not because 'psychoanalytic suggestion was more effective than suggestion of a simple and more direct kind' (Flugel, 1924, p. 51).

In 1959 Ernst Nagel wrote: 'The changes in various symptoms which the patient exhibits as the interview progresses do not constitute evidence for an interpretation unless it can be shown that such changes are not produced by some combination of factors for which the whole interview is responsible' (Nagel 1959, pp. 51–52). These considerations were as available to Freud in 1917 as to Nagel forty years later. How then could Freud have believed that with the Tally Argument he had rendered suggestion 'epistemically innocuous'? Stuart Sutherland's accusation, which Grünbaum quotes (1984, p. 172), that Freud was 'taking for granted the very point he is trying to prove' is perfectly just and Grünbaum's exposition leaves us perplexed as to why he thinks otherwise.

So infatuated is Grünbaum with the notion that he has discovered in the Tally Argument something momentous and hitherto overlooked that the most obvious objections escape him. If we state Freud's NCT as 'No one can recover from a neurosis who doesn't anamnese the content of my infantile aetiology' then every time Freud makes a change in this aetiology he either has falsified his NCT anew or has to revise his notion of what constitutes recovery from neurosis; neither a very persuasive proceeding.

The arguments I have hitherto advanced for the feebleness of the Tally Argument are also to a lesser extent reasons for denying that Freud depended on it. But Freud's behaviour in relation to contamination objections provides more direct evidence for thinking that he had little confidence in the Tally Argument.

Grünbaum attributes to Freud 'a sovereign patronizing serenity' (1984, p. 170) towards sceptical arguments based on suggestibility, and he attributes this serenity to Freud's conviction that the distinctive therapeutic efficacy of psychoanalysis rendered suggestibility 'epistemically innocuous'. But the evidence is that the suggestibility argument, rather than meeting with a 'patronizing serenity' goaded Freud into lying. He more often met the suggestibility objection by unveracious accounts of psychoanalytic procedure than by invoking his therapeutic results, which indicates that he did not have much confidence in the Tally Argument. This is what he said in 'The Question of Lay Analysis': 'The analyst never entices his patient on to the ground of sex. He does not say to him in advance: "We shall be dealing with the intimacies of your sexual life!" He allows him to begin what he has to say wherever he pleases, and quietly awaits until the patient himself touches on sexual things. I used always to warn my pupils: "Our opponents have told us that we come upon cases in which the factor of sex plays no part. Let us be careful not to introduce it into our analyses and so spoil our chance of finding such a case"' (1962, pp. 118–19). This is what he said in the 1898 paper 'Sexuality and the Aetiology of the Neurosis' (the one in which he should have announced his desertion of the seduction aetiology but did not): 'an experienced physician does not meet his patients unprepared, and as a rule asks of them not elucidation but merely confirmation of his surmises . . . in the very description of their symptoms, which they volunteer too readily, they will usually have acquainted him with the sexual factors hidden behind' (1924, p. 224). On the same page: 'It would be a great advantage if patients could know the extent to which physicians will henceforth be able to interpret their neurotic ailments with certainty, and to infer from them the sexual aetiology at work.' I think it fair to infer from these remarks that Freud had no inhibitions about informing his patients of the importance he attached to their sexual lives.

The paper whose solution to the problem of patient compliance Grünbaum charges Popper with misrepresenting ('gross unfairness') is 'Remarks on The Theory and Practice of Dream-Interpretation' (S.E., 1923, XIX). This is how Freud deals in it with the suggestibility problem:

> Is it possible, then that confirmatory dreams are really the result of suggestion, that they are compliant dreams? . . . I recall a discussion which I was led into with a patient (who asked) whether his narcissistic wish to be cured might not have caused him to produce these dreams, since, after all, I had held out to him a prospect of recovery if he were able to accept my constructions. I could only

reply that I had not yet come across any such mechanism of dream-formation. (Freud, 1950, pp. 143–44)

But Freud had come across such a mechanism. As early as 1897 he had invoked it to account for a dream of erotic play with his nine-year-old daughter which he attributed to his wish to produce evidence supporting the theory of paternal seduction. And had he forgotten 'counter-wish dreams'? If a patient was capable of producing a dream in order that it might appear to contradict Freud's theories, why should not another patient produce one in order to confirm them?

In this same paper this is the account Freud gives of how he met a patient's objections that his dreams may have been influenced in a manner which deprived them of evidential value: 'He recollected some dreams which he had had before starting analysis and indeed before he had known anything about it; and the analysis of these dreams, which were free from all suspicion of suggestion, led to the same interpretations as the later ones' (1950, p. 144). But since dream interpretation depends on the patient's associations to his dream, how can the 'analysis of these dreams' have been 'free from all suspicion of suggestion'? Do not the lengths to which Freud is willing to go to undermine suggestibility objections suggest that 'sovereign patronizing serenity' is not the *mot juste*? In the same 1923 paper, Freud says: 'On the mechanism of dream formation itself, on the dream-work in the strict sense of the word, one can never exercise any influence; of that one may be quite sure' (Freud, 1950, p. 142). Ten years earlier, in 'Dream Interpretation in Psychoanalysis' (1912) he had said 'The more the patient has learnt of the method of dream interpretation the more obscure do his later dreams become . . . All the acquired knowledge serves as a warning to the dream-work' (1924, p. 310).

Even if Freud was as scrupulous about not prompting his patients to produce theoretically congenial material as he maintained, this would not have met the compliance argument. As early as 1906 Aschaffenburg explained the apparent confirmation Freud was receiving from his patients as due to their prior familiarity with his views (1906, p. 1796). Freud never addresses this obvious objection but instead merely issues repeated (and untruthful) denials that his views anticipated his patients' confirmation of them. A reminiscence from Freud himself supports Aschaffenburg's conjecture. As an illustration of the misrepresentation from which he suffered early in his career he once recalled an occasion at the turn of the century when it was reported to him that a young girl suffering from hysteria, when asked why she didn't consult Freud, remarked, 'What for? He will only ask me if I have ever wanted to sleep with my father' (S.E., 1895, II, p. 236). Freud denies indignantly that he ever asked patients anything of the kind. But the interesting and relevant point is that as early as 1900 it was a matter of common knowledge in the circles from which Freud drew his patients that he believed the source of neurotic difficulties to lie in incestuous wishes. Another illustration of the justice of Aschaffenburg's conjecture and of Freud's unwillingness or inability to grasp its pertinence is to be found in the Rat Man case history. The Rat Man, Paul Lorenz, volunteers a sexual revelation and Freud comments: 'I then got him to agree that I had not led him to the subject either of his childhood or of sex, but that he had raised them both of his own free will' (1925, p. 320). Yet some pages earlier, in his account of the first session, which Paul began by retailing his masturbatory history, Freud says: 'When I asked him what it was that made him lay such stress upon his telling me of his sex life, he replied that that was what he knew about my theories' (1925, p. 297). In such circumstances Freud's repeated assurances that he did not himself introduce the topic of sexuality into the analysis were, at best, disingenuous.

At the period during which Grünbaum holds that Freud believed himself in possession of an absolute reply to skeptics by reason of his unmatched therapeutic achievements Freud shows many signs of believing neither in the cogency of the Tally Argument nor in his dependence on it. The most the Tally Argument could do is to justify, for a time at least, Freud's non-capitulation to the argument from comparable therapeutic efficacy by insisting on subtle though as yet undemonstrated differences between his therapeutic outcomes and that of his rivals; it could not justify Freud's claims to have repeatedly confirmed his aetiological and dynamic theses. But there were arguments that could and Freud availed himself of them. One was the extra-clinical validation of *a priori* implausible claims about childhood initially based on analytic experience.

Grünbaum says at one point that if challenged as to the grounds for this theory of infantile sexuality Freud 'would' have appealed to his Tally Argument. Not so. We know what he 'would' appeal to because we know what he did appeal to: direct observation.

This is how he dealt with the issue in 'The Question of Lay Analysis':

> 'Now tell me, though, what certainty can you offer for your analytic findings on the sexual life of children? Is your conviction based solely on points of agreement with mythology and history?'
>
> Oh, by no means. It is based on *direct observation*. What happened was this. We had begun by inferring the content of sexual childhood from the analysis of adults—that is to say, some twenty or forty years later. Afterwards, we undertook *analysis on children themselves* and it was no small triumph when we were thus able to confirm in them everything that we had been able to divine, in spite of the extent to which it had been overlaid and distorted in the interval . . . we have become quite generally convinced from the direct analytic examination of children that we were right in our interpretation of what adults told us about their childhood. (Freud, 1962, p. 127)

Freud used the same argument from direct observation in the 1910 edition of the *Three Essays on Sexuality*, in 'The History of the Psychoanalytic

Movement' (1914) and in the *Autobiographical Study*, to stop before the date at which Grünbaum says Freud abandoned the appeal to therapeutic superiority, after which such remarks could be explained as Grünbaum (mistakenly) explains the appeals to consilience after 1926, as a fall-back position.

The most succinct statement of the principal grounds for Freud's conviction as to the veridicality of his aetiological and dynamic theses occurs in 'The History of the Psychoanalytic Movement' (1914) where Freud says that the test of the correctness of his hypotheses is that a 'neurosis must become intelligible'.

He responded to Adler's objection that 'the nervous character was the cause of the neurosis rather than its result' not by invoking his therapeutic achievements but by declaring that if Adler abandoned sexuality he would not be 'in a position to account for a single detail of symptom formation or a single dream' (1963, p. 331).

The single most crucial inference in Freud's career was made without the benefit of the Tally Argument. This was his response to the charge that the apparent confirmation his '1896' patients provided for the seduction aetiology was due to the operation of suggestibility by assigning them infantile incestuous fantasies whose subjection to self-protective distortion led to their emergence as 'memories' of seduction, and thus misled him. Freud was precluded from invoking the Tally Argument in these cases since where the analysis was successful it was so in spite of the falsity of Freud's reconstructions, and where it was not there was nothing to appeal to.

It escapes Grünbaum's comment, if not his notice, that in the very lecture from which he extracts the Tally Argument it is advanced along with others which render it, if not entirely otiose, at least merely supplementary.

> a great many of the detailed findings of analysis, which would otherwise be suspected of being produced by suggestion, are confirmed from other, irreproachable sources. We have unimpeachable witnesses on these points, namely dements and paranoiacs, who are of course quite above any suspicion of being influenced by suggestion. All that these patients relate in the way of phantasies and translations of symbols, which have penetrated through into their consciousness, corresponds faithfully with the results of our investigations into the unconscious of transference neurotics, thus confirming the objective truth of the interpretations made by us which are so often doubted. (Freud, 1963, p. 394)

In 'The History of Psychoanalytic Movement' (1914) Freud devotes a paragraph to 'the most irrefragable proof that the source of the propelling forces of neurosis lies in the sexual life'; it is an argument that 'has never received anything approaching the attention it merits, for if it had there would have been no choice but acceptance. In my own conviction of the truth it remains beside and above the more specific results of analytic work the decisive factor' (1924, p. 293). If Freud were here referring to the Tally Argument then Grünbaum would have a formidable case. But he wasn't; he was talking about the transference. Another indication that Freud did not think of therapeutic effectiveness as his guarantor of veridicality is a rather cold-blooded remark in a letter to Jung concerning a patient who was reluctant to continue her analysis with Freud: 'Of course she is right. Because she is beyond any possibility of therapy, but it is still her duty to sacrifice herself to science' (1974, pp. 473–74).

Another reason for holding that Freud did not rely on therapeutic effects (the Tally Argument) is that he professes himself ignorant of things he would on this assumption be expected to know, and professes to know things of which dependence on the Tally Argument would leave him ignorant. An example of the first of these is the psychology of women. The editors of the *Standard Edition* bring together Freud's various pronouncements on the limits of his knowledge of feminine psychology and comment:

> From early days Freud made complaints of the obscurity enveloping the sexual life of women. Thus, near the beginning of his *Three Essays on the Theory of Sexuality* (1905*d*), he wrote that the sexual life of men 'alone has become accessible to research. That of women . . . is still veiled in an impenetrable obscurity.' (S.E., VII, p. 151) Similarly, in his discussion of the sexual theories of children (1908*c*), he wrote: 'In consequence of unfavourable circumstances, both of an external and an internal nature, the following observations apply chiefly to the sexual development of one sex only—that is, of males' (*ibid.*, p. 9, p. 211). Again, very much later, in his pamphlet on lay analysis (1926*e*): 'We know less about the sexual life of little girls than of boys. But we need not feel ashamed of this distinction; after all, the sexual life of adult women is a "dark continent" for psychology.'(*ibid.*, p. 20, p. 212) (S.E., 1925, XIX, p. 241)

Why did Freud feel that feminine psychology was a 'dark continent' to the analyst? Grünbaum's reply would have to be that he had had less therapeutic success with women. But there is no reason for thinking so and Grünbaum offers none. A plethora of illustrations that Freud's confidence in the correctness of his interpretations and reconstructions was independent of their therapeutic effects is to be found in the case histories. Freud often expresses confidence as to the correctness of an interpretation where there is no question of therapeutic effect, e.g., Dora's playing with her reticule, her pseudo-appendicitis, her limp, etc. Such examples seem more typical than those where it is therapeutic effectiveness to which he appeals. (It is arguable that even in these cases Freud's conviction that his interpretations were therapeutically effective was based on their thematic affinity with the symptom content which remitted.) Freud's allusions to the Wolf Man case after it became apparent that he was once more deranged are untouched by any trace of uncertainty or tentativeness as to the correctness of his original account.

One is curious as to how Grünbaum will deal with Freud's complacency once his therapeutic pessimism precluded his appealing to the Tally

Argument. He cites a consilience argument put forward in 1937 and explains that, since Freud no longer felt he could fall back on the Tally Argument, he now had to resort to considerations of consilience. But considerations of consilience had been, since the jigsaw puzzle analogy of 1896, the principal basis adduced by Freud in support of his reconstructions. In 'An Infantile Neurosis' (the Wolf Man) Freud once again advances considerations of coherence and circumstantiality as the justification for his aetiological conviction. He says of the charge that the theoretically congenial sexual episodes of infancy were the products of the patient's compliance:

> An analyst who hears this reproach will comfort himself by recalling how gradually the construction which he is supposed to have originated came about and when all is said and done how independently of the physician's incentive many points in its development proceed; how after a certain phase in the treatment everything seemed to converge upon it, and how later, in the synthesis, the most various and remarkable results radiated from it; how not only the large problems but the smallest peculiarities in the history of the case were cleared up by this single assumption. And he will disclaim the possession of the amount of ingenuity necessary for the concoction of an occurrence which can fulfill these demands. But even this plea will be without effect upon an adversary who has not experienced the analysis himself. On the one side there will be a charge of refined self-deception, and on the other obtuseness of judgement; it will be impossible to arrive at a decision. (1925, p. 525)

How can it be 'impossible to arrive at a decision' if Freud has the Tally Argument at his disposal?

Grünbaum says at one point that NCT is meant to 'constitute cogent evidence for [Freud's] general theory of psychosexual development'. But so conceived the Tally Argument is particularly feeble. Freud can hardly have thought it a reasonable reply to skeptics as to the generality of his putative discoveries that unless neurotics came to accept them they remained ill. An argument which could only salvage Freud's psychopathology would have been of little polemical use to Freud and, in fact, reliance on it would have actively weakened his claims for his general psychology because it would have displayed doubt as to the cogency of nontherapeutic considerations. Since one of the standard objections to Freud was that he was wantonly extrapolating from the mental functioning of neurotics to that of humanity at large, he must show no doubts, such as excessive reliance on therapeutic success would indicate, as to the cogency of arguments not confined to psychopathology. But even within psychopathology therapeutic outcome did not play the role Grünbaum assigns it. Does Grünbaum think that Freud intended the Tally Argument as a vindication of his own interpretations/reconstructions exclusively or was it meant to extend to his followers as well? It is natural to assume that Freud would not intend the entire edifice of psychoanalytic psychopathology to rest on *his* therapeutic achievements alone.

We would thus expect to find that Freudians other than himself appealed to therapeutic superiority to undermine suggestibility and contamination doubts, for example, Jones, Pfister, Brill, Schwab, Putnam, Hitschmann, Eder, Forsyth, Mitchell, Frink, James Glover, Flugel, to confine the list to those who have left us records of their replies to objections to psychoanalytic claims before the date Grünbaum sets for abandonment of the Tally Argument. Did they meet scepticism by an appeal to their therapeutic achievements? Grünbaum doesn't say and appears neither to know nor to know that he needs to know.

Conclusion

At one point Grünbaum raises the question of Freud's 'intellectual hospitality to refutation by others' and resolves it in Freud's favour on the basis of a phrase in a letter to Fliess: 'refutations . . . will be welcomed' (Grünbaum, 1984, p.188). Popper is once again chastised for exegetical malpractice in overlooking it. But the following remark of 1914 from a public source, i.e. one available to Grünbaum for a much longer period than the Fliess letters have been available to Popper, needs to be put alongside Grünbaum's *trouvaille* before a conclusion can be drawn:

> Many a one is tormented by the need to account for the lack of sympathy or the repudiation expressed by his contemporaries and feels their attitude painfully as a contradiction of his own secure conviction. There was no need for me to feel so; for psychoanalytical principles enable me to understand this attitude in my contemporaries and to see it as a necessary consequence of fundamental analytic premises. If it was true that the associated connections I had discovered were kept from the knowledge of patients by inward resistances of an affective kind, then these resistances would be bound to appear in the healthy also, as soon as, from some external source, they became confronted with what is repressed. It was not surprising that they should be able to justify on intellectual grounds this rejection of my ideas though it was actually affective in nature. The same thing happened just as often in patients . . . the only difference was that with patients one was in a position to bring pressure to bear on them. (1924, p. 306)

Either Grünbaum has once again been sleepwalking his way through Freud's text or he thinks these remarks consistent with 'intellectual hospitality to refutation by others'.

When one considers the extent to which Grünbaum leans on Popper's Oedipus effect to undermine Freud's claims, the emphasis he places on Popper's deficiencies begins to look like an instance of the narcissism of small differences. His real objection to Popper amounts to one of anachronism. Popper's accusation of evasiveness with respect to the suggestibility objection only applies to Freud after 1926. In fact it is Grünbaum who is guilty of anachronism. The Tally Argument was not killed by Freud's discovery of spontaneous remission between 1923 and 1926. It was stillborn.

Citizen Kane in the Orson Welles film responded to refutation in what we would all concur was a non-exemplary fashion. On the eve of the election in which he is running for governor he prepares two headlines, 'Kane Elected' and 'Fraud at the Polls'. Grünbaum thinks it libelous to suggest that Freud characteristically behaved in this fashion. I think it pusillanimous to deny that he did. In attempting a demonstration of his claim that Freud was 'clearly motivated by evidence' and 'alert to the need for safeguarding the falsifiability of his reconstructions and interpretations', and that he dealt 'brilliantly' and 'unswervingly' with the contamination issue, Grünbaum has only succeeded in illustrating how prophetic were Wittgenstein's words of almost half a century ago: 'It will be a long time before we lose our subservience'.

REFERENCES

Aschaffenburg, G. 1906. Die Beziehungen des sexuellen Leben zur Entstehung von Nerven- und Geisteskrankenheit. *Munchener medizinische Wochenschrift,* LIII, 1793–798.

Flugel J.C. 1924. Critical Discussion. *British Journal of Medical Psychology,* 51.

Freud, S. 1924. *Collected Papers,* vol. 1. Hogarth Press.

———. 1925. *Collected Papers,* vol. 3. Hogarth Press.

———. 1935. *An Autobiographical Study.* Hogarth Press.

———. 1950. *Collected Papers,*vol. 5. Hogarth Press.

———. 1962. *Two Short Accounts of Psychoanalysis.* Penguin.

———. 1963. *A General Introduction to Psychoanalysis.* Simon and Schuster.

———. 1965. *Three Essays on the Theory of Sexuality.* Avon Books.

———. 1974. *The Freud–Jung Letters,* ed., William McGuire. Hogarth Press and Routledge.

———. 1985. *The Complete Letters of Sigmund Freud to Wilhelm Fliess.* The Belknap Press of Harvard University Press.

Freud, S., and Breuer, J. 1966. *Studies on Hysteria.* Avon Books.

Gellner, E. 1985. *The Psychoanalytic Movement.* Paladin Books.

Glymour, C. 1974. Freud, Kepler and Clinical Evidence, in R. Wollheim, ed., *Freud: A Collection of Critical Essays.* Anchor Books.

Grünbaum, A. 1979a. Is Freudian Psychoanalytic Theory Pseudo-scientific by Karl Popper's Criterion of Demarcation? *American Philosophical Quarterly,* 16, 131–41.

———. 1979b. The Role of Psychological Explanations of the Rejection or Acceptance of Scientific Theories. *Transactions of the New York Academy of Science,* vol. 37.

———. 1984. *The Foundations of Psychoanalysis: A Philosophical Critique.* University of California Press.

Jones, E. 1957. *Sigmund Freud: Life and Work,* vol. 3. Hogarth Press.

Masson, J.M. 1984. *The Assault on Truth: Freud's Suppression of the Seduction Theory.* Faber.

Nagel, E. 1959. Methodological Issues in Freudian Theory, in S. Hook, ed., *Psycho-Analysis, Scientific Method, and Philosophy.* New York University Press.

11

Explanation and Biography:
A Conversation

DAVID ELLIS: I've heard you complain frequently that there is an infatuation in our culture with genetic explanations—tracing the peculiarities of adult behaviour back to very early childhood—and that this has a great deal to do with the influence of Freud.

FRANK CIOFFI: That's right. When Aubrey says, 'Who loses his maidenhead with a bare-legged wench will never run after silk stockings', he illustrates how much a part of folk psychology the notion of the formative potency of early experience is. But the use that Freudianising biographers have made of infancy often seems largely gratuitous. Can you think of many persuasive instances? How much would we lose if we declared a moratorium on the invocation of infantile vicissitudes? Somebody once brought Churchill's toilet training into an account of why as Chancellor of the Exchequer he put us back on the gold standard. Would we miss that? And would we be disadvantaged if we were precluded from explaining Martin Luther's attack on the Virgin Mary in terms of his childhood resentment of his mother? Ashley Montagu imputes a tender loving mother to the 'Elephant Man' because he thinks that only thus can we account for the anomaly of someone who had been so badly treated and exploited nevertheless having such a gentle nature. Merrick himself of course attributed his hideous appearance to the fact that when his mother was pregnant, she went to the zoo and was frightened by an elephant. Is there really so much to choose between these two ways of reasoning?

This is David Ellis's condensed account of our many hours of conversation on the topic of biography in general and literary biography in particular. It first appeared in David Ellis, ed., *Imitating Art* (Pluto Press, 1993) and is reprinted by permission.

ELLIS: I don't see a method is discredited because it has foolish practitioners. But if the tendency to go back to early childhood has, as you say, always been part of our culture1 why are you inclined to blame Freud so much?

CIOFFI: Because he transforms the intuitions of folk psychology into dogma, For example, Freud thought he could account for the development of the Kaiser's bellicose nature in terms of his mother's response to the deformed and useless arm he incurred during childbirth—she being the kind of woman who insisted on physical perfection in her offspring. The difficulty I find with this is that the Kaiser didn't stop having this rejecting mother when he had passed through the stage which Freud insists is the critical one. In fact he went on having her till he was 40. Now how can the influence her rejection exerted in his post-infantile years be segregated from that of the Oedipal phase itself? We are to imagine (implausibly) that if the Kaiser had incurred his injury after the age of seven, the outcome must have been strikingly different or, as implausibly, that if medical intervention had set the matter right after the infantile years, thus altering his mothers attitude, it would have been too late to make a difference. This might be so but how can it be known to be so?

ELLIS: What about a case that you know has a special interest for me? Everyone assumes that the unusual closeness of D.H. Lawrence's early relationship with his mother is responsible for many of the difficulties he had in later life with women. Isn't this an entirely convincing and legitimate causal link?

CIOFFI: I don't deny the legitimacy of invoking Lawrence's early relation with his mother and claiming that it made a contribution to his later difficulties with women, but I would like to see a greater awareness of how speculative causal claims are in cases like this. You have to remember that Lawrence did not just have an intensely possessive mother during his Freudian years; he had one while he was courting 'Miriam' too. Is it reasonable to discount the possible sufficiency of this for some cultural baggage about the pre-potency of infancy? Of course it is *possible* that if Lawrence's mother had died when he was seven it would have made no difference to his sexual life but I sometimes wonder whether we wouldn't benefit if, for a while at least, we adopted the changeling thesis and treated our subjects as if they had all been reborn aged ten or so. How much would we lose? Something, certainly, but wouldn't it be compensated for by the amount of junk we could jettison? I agree that there is nothing like a primal scene or horrific castration fantasy to jazz a narrative up; but I am speaking of truth rather than entertainment.

The application of Freud-inspired accounts of the influence of childhood on the lives of historical and cultural figures has become as mechanical as brick-laying. Langer and Waite on Hitler; Erikson on Luther; Manuel on Newton; Edel on James; Mack on T.E. Lawrence; Storr on Churchill; Holbrook on Plath—all of them attempt to link specific features of their subject's childhood to their adult achievements, vulnerabilities and propensities. How can we determine whether the connections they see are really there? Anthony Storr tells us that Churchill's ambition developed as a response to deprivation of parental love in childhood, but do we really know enough about human character to assign Churchill's ambition to this source? In fact, had Churchill been cosseted in childhood Freud could have enlisted him among those whose peculiar self-reliance and unshakable optimism was attributable to having been the apple of their mothers' eyes. Why is there more reason to think that Churchill's ambition was conditioned by his mother's treatment of him than that his baldness was? In any case, Storr gives us an account of Churchill's schooldays and the humiliation they entailed which could itself explain any element of over-compensation and corner-cutting in his later strivings.

ELLIS: What's perhaps unusual in Lawrence's case is that he himself blames his mother for a lot of his difficulties—not only by implication in *Sons and Lovers* but more directly in texts like *Fantasia of the Unconscious*. Doesn't that make a difference?

CIOFFI: That would depend on quite what he is blaming her for, and what his grounds were. I can't stress enough the precariousness of generalisation in these matters. People may well be authoritative about those aspects of their make-up which were the topic of persistent self-communings and choice-determining ruminations. Prosper Merimée's austere reserve was traced to an occasion in childhood when he wept at a reproach and was cruelly mocked as a consequence. I can imagine grounds which would make this explanation credible but they would be grounds accessible to Merimée alone. The occasion was public and so was its putative upshot: Merimée's self-presentational strategies and mannerisms; but the grounds for believing the one an influence on the other are constituted by Merimée's reminiscences and these he alone had direct access to. Proust's narrator imputes the 'fatal decline of his will' to his parents' indulgent behaviour towards him on a particular evening in his childhood. If we doubt his epistemic authority here, it is because we are not told enough about how he arrived at this conclusion. One of the more baleful effects of Freud's influence is that it makes us over-ready to credit influences of this kind, dating from early life, without the support of the subject's anamneses [reminiscences] as if we had knowledge of reliable connections akin to that between infantile mumps and sterility; yet at the same time we are invited to be dismissive of those whose only grounds for an explanation are the subject's memory-based convictions.

The Australian writer Russell Braddon never lost the hatred for the Japanese he developed during his experiences as a prisoner of war. What are our grounds for crediting the connection between his mistreatment and his animosity except his own say-so? We have no generalisation to fall back on. And yet in this case scepticism seems wanton. Would anyone argue that since Laurens van der Post was also mistreated in captivity but doesn't bear a grudge, Braddon might be rationalising his annoyance that his Sony Walkman keeps breaking down?

John Stuart Mill says that he grew up 'in the absence of love and the presence of fear' and that this had many unfortunate effects on his moral growth. What are we to say of this remark of Mill's? Even if we allow ourselves to be persuaded that though Mill may be authoritative with respect to his dismal childhood he is not authoritative with respect to its causal repercussions—the fact, for example, that he fell into deep depression when he was about 20—can it be denied that a biographer who had set himself the task of discussing Mill's character as well as his achievements and was ignorant of Mill's own view of the role of his childhood would be at a profound disadvantage?

ELLIS: That can't be denied, but the question is presumably just *how far* we can trust Mill's and Lawrence's explanations of themselves.

CIOFFI: There is no general answer: it all depends on the individual case. But what I want to insist on is the importance of trying to recover what people said not only about but also to themselves. Eric Homburger has conveyed well what many people expect of biography: 'Biography seeks to convey the feel of an individual's experience, to see the world as a single person saw it.' 'Have you ever thought what a world his eyes opened on?' Ruskin asks of Giorgione and proceeds to tell us. This recovery of the inner self is not just an end in itself but brings other benefits. When a biographer has reconstituted the history of his subject's internal soliloquy[1]—Lawrence's 'spectral self that haunts our thoughts'; the 'themes on which the mind plays its variations' (in Santayana's phrase); 'the stories that we are always telling ourselves about things' (in Proust's); 'the sort of thing he likes to think about' (in Chesterton's)—he will be well on his way to resolving many of the behavioural puzzles that his subject presents. Sartre speaks of the 'taste which a man necessarily possesses for himself—the savour of his existence'. That secret savour will have many enigmatic manifestations which do not remain enigmatic once it is known. Behaviour is sometimes ambiguous in a way which only an account of what an older generation of mind philosophers described as the subject's 'presentational continuum' can rectify.

ELLIS: Apart from the immense problem of recovering this 'presentational continuum', I still can't help feeling that its usefulness as an explanatory device is severely limited by its unreliability. I mean, people are capable of telling themselves all manner of weird things.

CIOFFI: Look, there are two objections to basing explanations on the subject's internal soliloquy: its fallibility and its dispensability. My thesis is that it is not often fallible and it is frequently indispensable. Take the fallibility issue which you raise. Could Charles Atlas have been wrong as to the role played by his having been a 'skinny, 90-pound weakling' in his embarking on the regimen whereby he became 'the strongest man in the world'? I mean, could not his native narcissism have been sufficient even without the humiliation of having sand kicked in his face? I want to say that it is not enough that we can imagine one without the other. We have to be able to say what grounds there could here be for over-ruling the agent's account. General fallibility is not sufficient ground for rejecting the agent's self-exploratory efforts.

As for dispensability, my inclination is to say that the absence of any internal soliloquy which incorporated wincing reminiscences of that scene on the beach, resolutions that it would never occur again etcetera, would deprive the connection of its cogency.

ELLIS: But putting aside the question of a person's authority with respect to the influence of the remote past on his present inclinations, what about the current motives for his behaviour? Might not they be unconscious and play no part in his 'internal soliloquy'?

CIOFFI: In his essay on literary biography Ellmann raises the question of the significance of Johnson's request to be beaten by Mrs Thrale. If we were as privy to Johnson's mind as we are to our own, would there be a problem left? Now, a Freudian might object—couldn't Johnson's conscious therapeutic or prophylactic rationale for wanting to be beaten be the rationalisation for a masochistic one? Yes, but if the masochistic payoff were nevertheless present to consciousness would that not resolve the issue?—and if it wasn't I am not sure that there is an issue left to be resolved. I mean, if the payoff is as unconscious as the stratagem adopted in its service we may no longer know what we are talking about, even if this fact is hidden from many by the linguistic habits of several generations of intellectuals naturalised in chatter about the unconscious. I want to steer clear of the more profound philosophical issue which arises here and which involves the relation between our ability to settle a question and our ability to understand it, partly because I haven't been able to arrive at a consistent view; but I still want to insist that it is almost as difficult to get Freudianising philosophers to see that not every statement about mental states qualified by the term 'unconscious' makes sense, as it once was to get their predecessors to admit that any do.

One distinct reason for the pertinence of the internal soliloquy is that it is crucial to our conception of someone to know whether, when there is a discrepancy between what he says and what is the case, this is due to mistaken conviction or mendacity. We can't distinguish between lies and errors without assumptions as to the internal soliloquy.

At one period Freud approved the giving of cocaine by injection. Ten years later he denied ever having done this. Are we to impute to him a liar's internal soliloquy or not? I don't know. But what could have a greater bearing on our conception of him than whether he made a conscious decision to lie or merely found himself repeatedly amnesic for what might damage his interests if acknowledged?

ELLIS: I'd like to move on to the question of what in a life we feel calls out for explanation. We've agreed before that we can't simply say that biographers need to deal with anything that strikes them as abnormal because people's notions of normality don't always coincide. I seem to remember that when one of Charlie Chaplin's wives sued him for divorce she accused him of several strange sexual practices and that when he was challenged about them he said, 'But doesn't everyone do that?' We think we are more or less like others and then discover that in certain areas we're not. Another thing we agreed is that our appreciation of biographers is partly dependent on having a similar sense to theirs of what is self-evident and what needs explaining.

CIOFFI: That's quite right. It's a matter of what strikes both the biographer and his reader as an authentic narrative gap. Let me explain what I mean. When Watson learns from an old medical acquaintance that a student at Barts called Sherlock Holmes has found some digs in Baker Street which are too dear for him and is looking for someone to share them with, he expresses an interest since he is looking for a place to live himself. They begin discussing whether Holmes's odd character might not preclude a satisfactory arrangement and Watson is initially appalled at being told that among Holmes's eccentricities is that of beating the cadavers in the dissecting room. This creates what I call a narrative or explanatory gap for Watson ('Beating the cadavers!') which his friend proceeds to bridge by informing him that Holmes beats the corpses in order to determine how far bruises may be produced after death. The scientific rationale! Watson is pacified and so are we. So here is an exemplary explanatory episode—puzzlement succeeded by the information which dissipates it. Isn't this all a biographer can reasonably aspire to?

ELLIS: I suppose so. We have some alarmingly eccentric behaviour which the explanation then allows us to enter into a comprehensible scheme of things. Yet I can imagine situations in which the pressure to force an episode into some preferred explanatory scheme is distorting.

CIOFFI: I certainly can think of examples where the manner in which a narrative gap has been closed or narrowed could well be judged gratuitous. Ernest Jones traces Freud's Lamarckism to 'the indelible mark left on his mind when he learned as a child that God visits the iniquity of the fathers on the children, yea even to the third and fourth generation'. But when a man whose discourse is largely constituted of reconstructions of the psychic life of infancy adopts a position according to which those reconstructions can never be shown to be wrong since, if the situations they involve are not found in the infancy of the patient they were to be found in the infancy of his ancestors, it seems unnecessary to seek for its sources in any 'indelible mark' made in his childhood.

ELLIS: You mean Freud's adoption of Lamarckism was self-evidently convenient? Not everyone would agree with that.

CIOFFI: Of course not. Though most people would find it gratuitous to invoke Freudian symbolism to explain why we store wine in containers instead of hanging it from hooks, it might be difficult to get consensus on matters less blatant. But we are not condemned to total relativism. Though someone might feel the rationale that satisfied Watson an insufficient reason for mistreating a corpse, can we imagine many people feeling that Holmes's behaviour was perfectly natural and did not therefore require rationalisation? (Why shouldn't he beat a cadaver if it amuses him?') There is considerable consensus as to when a story legitimately requires supplementation, if not as to the kind of supplementation required.

ELLIS: It seems to me that you are inclined to feel biographers go in search of obscure, psycho-dynamic explanations when whatever puzzles them can be clarified by access to the subject's own reflections.

CIOFFI: Well I do feel that unconscious motives are often resorted to prematurely. Leon Edel interprets an entry in James's notebooks psychoanalytically to show that marriage was unconsciously associated with the idea of death for James and thus explains his remaining single. Before proceeding to a search for unconscious determinants shouldn't we ask how James felt about women?—whether he was aroused by the thought of making love to them, etcetera. If we decide that the answer is a resounding 'yes' then, unless he had apprehensions that he might not be able to put his wishes into effect, his remaining unmarried *is* a problem that needs resolving. But not getting married isn't quite like running to Canada to escape the draft—it's more like not volunteering—and the absence of a strong desire for what marriage (or cohabitation) most notably brings would be a sufficient reason for abstention.

Or take the question of how Freud came to hold the deluded belief that the main component of feminine psychology is penis envy. Even those who agree that this—and not how Freud discovered penis envy—is the relevant question are divided by judgements as to when it is justifiable to introduce the personal make-up of the subject in accounting for erroneous beliefs. Actually, most commentators who are sceptical about penis envy do invoke Freud's patriarchal view of women, but though this is not implausible it still falls short of explaining how he came to see them as mutilated males and sullen and envious in consequence, and overlooks a less personal source of the tenacity with which Freud clung to penis envy. He was committed to it willy-nilly (or maybe I had better say *nolens volens*) because of the demands of other components of his theory. According to these, boys were induced to inhibit their incestuous inclinations because they feared castration if they didn't; and it was by replacing their desire for the mother by identification with the father that they became moral beings. How, since women do not possess penises, were they to manage this transition? Because Freud thought that it was only in part that they failed in this aim, he needed an equally anatomical motive to account for such moral sense as women do possess ('Anatomy is destiny'). The little girl, it turns out, gives up her incestuous inclinations towards her mother and directs them towards her father because she blames her mother for her lack of a penis and perhaps hopes that her father has one to spare. If Freud had allowed women to be socialised merely through the threat of the withdrawal of love (which he did from time to time), why not men? Because in that case one of the most distinctive features of his theory—castration anxiety—would have to go. No, patriarchy need not have come into it. Women had to resent not having penises because men had to fear losing them.

ELLIS: One thing that worries me about all this is how we reconcile different kinds of explanation. Take the fact that we know D.H. Lawrence used to hit his wife from time to time. Now for some people that might not be a problem ('Doesn't everyone do that?'), but for those who find it disturbing there are a variety of possible explanations. You might go back, for example, to the domestic violence in his parent's home and talk about the way, after admiring his mother, Lawrence gradually came to take his father as a role-model. You could investigate tuberculosis and see if there is any link between Lawrence's occasional bursts of uncontrolled anger and the fact that he was often ill. These are two broadly determinist avenues of enquiry. But you could also talk about the conscious decision which Lawrence took, and which Frieda helped him to take, to abandon repression—let it all hang out. Or then again you could take each documented incident of domestic violence in turn and try to show the specific determinants of each.

CIOFFI: You mean that Frieda was provocative? When she asked Ernest Jones to provide her with refuge because Lawrence was intending to kill her didn't he say that he was surprised Lawrence hadn't done it years ago?

ELLIS: I think he did. But what I find difficult is how these different explanations relate to each other. It is the problem Sartre raises when he is talking about Ludwig's life of Kaiser Wilhelm in the *Carnets de la Drole de Guerre*. He goes through a series of possible 'causes' of the First World War —economic, political, psychological (the Kaiser's withered arm)—and then points out that although they all seem legitimate in their own right, Raymond Aron has made a powerful case for the impossibility of ever combining them with each other.

CIOFFI: I think Aron was right. They're not commensurate. If in physics you have a number of forces acting on a body to make it move in a certain direction, you can usually compute them in the same terms, calculate how differently the body will move if one of the forces is removed, and so on. It is one of the conditions of working in the humanities that you can't do that kind of thing.

ELLIS: What then is the use of accumulating a heterogeneous pile of possible determinants and, if they are incommensurate, isn't one consequence that there are insufficient controls against a person pursuing one line of enquiry self-indulgently? I mean that the awareness that there is not and could never be a total explanation might make someone less anxious than he ought to be about the likely truth of his own speculations. Isn't it precisely one of your chief criticisms of Freud, for example, that he allows himself too much discretion?

CIOFFI: I think that there are standards which apply, or should apply, in humanistic thinking but they are much harder to define than they are in science. You're right, though, about the discretion Freud allowed himself. In Trevelyan's *Life of Macaulay* there is an account of how Macaulay met in India a clergyman who said he could prove Napoleon was the Beast of the Apocalypse. This was because if you write Napoleon Bonaparte in Arabic and leave out only two letters it will give you 666. Macaulay tells him he must be wrong because he has discovered that the House of Commons is the Beast: 'There are 658 members of the House: and these, with their chief officers—the three clerks, the Sergeant and his deputy, the Chaplain, the doorkeeper, and the librarian—make 666.' Freud is often like this man who had given numerical values to the letters in Napoleon's name. The only way to counter him when he is absurd—and he is of course by no means always absurd—is through reductios like Macaulay's: impugning the plausibility of a certain level of cogency by finding instances where a similar level leads to unacceptable conclusions. Remember that when Emil Ludwig had his conversation about biography with Freud, Freud chided him for his failure to take account of the influence of his subject's childhood. For example, for overlooking the influence over Napoleon of the fact that he had an elder brother whom he both loved and hated called Joseph which accounted for his marrying a woman called Josephine and for his going to Egypt. In a letter to Thomas Mann the ill-considered invasion of Russia is interpreted as Napoleon's attempt to punish himself for divorcing Josephine/Joseph. How do you deal with cases like that which are so common in the Freudian literature?

ELLIS: I've no idea, but then I've no idea either what biographers are supposed to do if philosophers can't show them how to combine various determinants into a single explanatory structure.

CIOFFI: Well, they can try to do what their most gifted and judicious predecessors have done. There are models.

ELLIS: You mean like Johnson's account of how, when he was living with Temple, Swift would visit his mother once a year.

> He travelled on foot, unless some violence of weather drove him into a wagon, and at night he would go to a penny lodging, where he purchased clean sheets for sixpence. This practice Lord Orrery imputes to his innate love of grossness and vulgarity: some may ascribe it to his desire of surveying human life through all its varieties; and others, perhaps with equal probability, to a passion which seems to have been deep fixed in his heart—the love of a shilling.

I like this immensely. Here is a genuine narrative gap or puzzle (penny inns were not presumably 'normal' for a person in Swift's position). Johnson offers three explanations but makes it clear in his syntax that his own money is on the third.

CIOFFI: Yes, it is very good and very characteristic. But doesn't a case like this illustrate our ambivalence in that we feel the biographer should tell us quite *why* Swift was so mean at the same time that we know it would be presumptuous to do so, or at least that most attempts at this order of explanation have been dismal?

ELLIS: You don't think much of the explanatory prospects of biographical research, do you?

CIOFFI: It isn't just that the prospects of learning something that will illuminate the character of the subject are so slim as that a lot of what passes for explanation is so unsatisfactory and its real rationale is often disguised.

Edmund Wilson invoked Ben Jonson's excretory training to account for several features of his work as well as of his make-up. He thinks that we are not shown Mosca squandering Volpone's gold as we ought to be (and as we are in Stefan Zweig's adaptation of the play) because of Jonson's habit of infantile retention; and he sees in Jonson's explosions of rage substitutes for the explosive expulsion of faeces. Of course it may be that, in cases like this, what fails to work as explanation is nevertheless effective as simile; but why then should it appear in a biographical work?

ELLIS: That you feel it might work in any fashion is a comfort given that, in the population as a whole, millions of hours must be spent each year in reading biographies. I take it that their popularity partly derives from an assumption that discovering more about the lives of artists or writers (for example) deepens our appreciation of their work, and that you believe this assumption to be false?

CIOFFI: Not quite. I can think of three possibilities. The first is when information produces no aspect change—at most an intellectual judgement of incongruity. The Christian fundamentalism of the creator of *Beano*'s Desperate Dan is piquant but I don't think that it has much influence over our perceptions any more than learning of Schrödinger's obsessive pursuit of pubescent girls affects our attitude to matrix mechanics.

The second is where there is 'veridicality-independent' aspect change—the change provoked by information so continuous with latent, unformulated impressions that it fails to reverse when the information is discredited. John Berger says that when we learn that 'Wheatfield with Crows' was the last canvas Van Gogh painted before his suicide it 'changes the image'. But suppose it is true, as has been maintained, that Van Gogh did not intend his self-inflicted wound to be fatal but that Dr Gachet bungled the treatment, would 'Wheatfield with Crows' look any different? I don't deny that Berger's story may change the image but I do deny that its doing so need depend on its historicity.

And then there is the case in which the biographer can take some comfort: 'veridicality-dependent' aspect change—where the aspect changes only so long as we credit what we have been told. This would supply literary biography with a strong critical rationale. How common is it? Though I have reread several of Joyce's early works since reading Ellman's biography I can't say I have noticed any striking difference in my response. Of course at points I was reminded of things Ellman told me but that's not what we are talking about, is it? These points were not aspect-transforming in the way that Wittgenstein's 'smiler' is transformed when we switch from thinking of him as observing children at play to imagining him looking down on the sufferings of an enemy.

ELLIS: Isn't your scepticism here associated with Wittgenstein's complaint that when something has made a deep impression on us—a book or painting for example—we are inclined to want further information about its origins, when what we should really be doing is clarifying what we feel.

CIOFFI: Or attempting to evoke what we feel. As I was beginning to suggest before, isn't it significant how often what is introduced as an influence turns up later as a simile or metaphor? A notorious example is that story of the young Flaubert, 'son and brother of eminent doctors', peering in through the window of the dissecting room where his father was performing postmortems. This is often used to account for some feature or other of Flaubert's work to which a term like clinical can be applied—the feature which Sainte-Beuve was referring to when he described Flaubert as 'holding the pen as others hold the scalpel' or when he said that Flaubert got under Madame Bovary's skin as his father got under that of his cadavers. In LeMot's famous cartoon, Flaubert is dressed as a doctor and Madame Bovary is stretched out before him on the dissecting table. When we subtract what we get from this cartoon from what we get from discursive attempts to relate Flaubert's experience of postmortems to the procedures and qualities of his fiction, what have we left of value? Isn't the historicity of the account otiose?

Zola was able to say of one of his own novels that he made of people 'the analytic study that surgeons make of corpses' without the benefit of familial medical connections. When Flaubert wanted to know how a tenotomy was performed or what the effects of taking strychnine were he didn't consult his memories of childhood in the precincts of the Hotel Dieu. He looked the information up in medical textbooks. Is it to be thought that unless he had spent his childhood on hospital grounds he would not have done that? Something else is going on here—picking out whatever in a writer's life is most congruent with our sense of his work. This has the form of empirical conjecture but it is really more like Reynold's painting a portrait of what Johnson must have looked like as a baby. Something similar can be said of Walter Benjamin's connecting Proust's asthma with the impression made by his sentences. I once heard someone argue for a particularly intimate connection between the physician and the novelist evidenced by the fact that several writers have had medical educations—Maugham, Chekhov, etcetera. But when Proust, Flaubert, Hemingway, Sinclair Lewis and John O'Hara were all added to the list of those whose medical background manifested itself in the medical ethos with which their work is imbued, not because they themselves were doctors but because their fathers were, the line between what is seriously offered as a causal explanation and what is merely being used as metaphor seems to me to have been crossed.

ELLIS: What was supposed to be the consequence of the medical ethos in which these writers grew up?

CIOFFI: Well, I remember the critic referring to 'a realism which seemed to lay bare the anatomy of life' and adding: 'O'Hara went with his doctor father on his rounds and I *cannot* doubt that it was from this privileged period that his protean and voyeuristic talent developed.' I can.

Explanations like these seem to have less to do with advancing reasonably supported solutions to behavioural conundrums than with the compulsion to make anything we learn of someone equally expressive of them—the monistic pathos.

The fundamental irrelevance of empirical enquiry in such cases is hidden from us by the fortuitous gratification it affords. Proust describes this impulse to prolong an agreeable experience by whatever means when he discusses the feeling of turning the last page of a novel that has absorbed us: 'One would have wanted so much to have more information on all these characters, to learn something about their lives, to devote ours to things that might not be entirely foreign to the love they had inspired in us.' Sometimes this impulse finds its consummation in the reading of biographies.

ELLIS: But then when we go off to read a biography of Proust and find that he tortured rats.

CIOFFI: If we are disappointed by learning such things we discover that one of our real motives for going to the biography has been to prolong our transactions with what we find engaging about its subject, not for information. But I wouldn't, of course, want to deny that people also read biographies out of a desire to see the eminent laid low.

ELLIS: I think Johnson says somewhere that it comforts us to learn that the eminent experience many of the same difficulties we do. To want to lessen our sense of isolation with this form of 'human interest' doesn't seem to me so unworthy, especially now that modern novelists are less inclined to provide it.

CIOFFI: It's not unworthy at all. But if you really wanted to account for the popularity of biographies you would have to decide at the outset what kind of biographies you were talking about. As a concept, 'biography' is too epistemologically diverse. There would have to he a lot of preliminary ground-clearing before you could begin to say anything plausible.

ELLIS: Since we may have been wandering the grounds rather than systematically clearing them, do you think you could sum up your main points?

CIOFFI: I think I have been saying three things. The first is that where we agree that an account of a life seems discontinuous it is arbitrary to invoke the influence of the earliest phases of that life. There are often shorter and more plausible ways of restoring continuity. The second is that we tend to be too dismissive of the illumination which can be produced by discovering the view that the subject himself took of the matters which we find perplexing.

Although his own view may mask the real determinants, we can't assume this but ought to demand independent evidence rather than simply appealing to the general fallibility of all self-deliverances. The third and perhaps most contentious point is that we often frequent biography under a misapprehension as to our own motives. What we often really want is to get a better grasp of our relation to the subject or his creations, to resolve the puzzle of their power over us or to prolong our transactions with those aspects we found beguiling.

Kenneth Clark says of Freud's account of Leonardo's painting of the 'Virgin with her Mother and the Christchild' that, even if false, 'it does convey the mood of the picture'. If that's the case, why not be more straightforward and practise or frequent a mode of biographical discourse whose avowed aim is felicitous evocation?

ELLIS: But if that's the way it is, why do we need the internal soliloquy?

CIOFFI: Because it isn't always that way.

NOTE

1. It has to be said that the suggestions of the term 'internal soliloquy' are sometime infelicitous. When I frown there is no psychic event accompanying the physical one manifested in the action of the orbiculars or whatever the relevant muscles are—there is just a modification of facial expression in a certain setting—certain surroundings as Wittgenstein puts it. If you are told to frown so that the muscles activated can be inspected, what makes it a pseudo-frown is not the absence of the usual mental accompaniment but the different surroundings. Of course, not all philosophers find this account compelling. Nevertheless—one more go. Isn't seeing what someone did sometimes knowing what he thought and felt? Can I imagine someone who is playing tennis having the internal soliloquy of someone playing chess so that when he delivers an ace he imagines himself checkmating? And yet. . . There is a remark of Carlyle's which Froude was so struck with that he put it on the first page of his biography: 'The world will never know my life even if it should write

and read a hundred biographies of me. The main facts are known and are likely to be known to myself alone of all created men.'

But the reservations mentioned above crowd in on us. There is something artificial about describing the biographer's task as that of intuiting the internal soliloquy of his subject since for many purposes an account of his activities suffices. If you have ever lived for long periods in a dormitory or a barracks there is much you can say about the characters of those who shared it with you even if you weren't among their confidants.

Ortega writes, 'We must get over the error which makes us think that a man's life takes place inside himself and that consequently it can be reduced to pure psychology . . . to live is to be outside oneself—to realise oneself—the vital programme which each one of us irredeemably is overpowers environment to lodge itself there'. I suppose we could call a novel such an enlodgement. It is possible to regard the creations of artists as more perfectly themselves than anything they do outside their creative lives, which I think was Proust's view.

12

Through the Psychoanalytoscope: Bouveresse on Wittgenstein's Freud

Jacques Bouveresse has attempted the arduous and risky task not only of constructing and assessing Wittgenstein's scattered, largely unflattering remarks on Freud but of relating them to current issues in Freud studies. The result is a valuable exercise in itself but I am not sure that this strategy was the best one for expounding and assessing Wittgenstein's views in all their idiosyncratic splendour. Though Bouveresse says much that is illuminating, several important ambiguities are left unresolved and one major misgiving is unallayed.

It is on Freud rather than Wittgenstein that Bouveresse makes his most astute comments, though there are lapses. How can he take seriously Jeffrey Masson's thesis that Freud substituted the Oedipus complex for the seduction theory out of a timid hope that it would be 'more acceptable to the scientific community'? Is it credible that having upset his colleagues by introducing the unseemly topic of paedophilia into the etiology of the neuroses Freud then attempted to placate them by announcing that he had misconstrued his data and that the real trouble was that they all lusted after their mothers?

Though Wittgenstein speaks of Freud's 'scientific achievement' and describes himself as a 'disciple', he also tells us that 'psychoanalysis is a foul and dangerous practice' and that Freud 'performed a disservice' in providing models for asinine explanations of neurotic symptoms. He says that Freud 'discovered phenomena and connections not previously known', and yet that psychoanalytic interpretations are 'not matters of discovery but of persuasion'.

This review of Jacques Bouveresse, *Wittgenstein Reads Freud: The Myth of the Unconscious* (Princeton: Princeton University Press, 1995) first appeared in *The London Review of Books,* Vol. 18, No. 2 (25 January 1996), and is reprinted by permission.

In addition to apparent inconsistencies Wittgenstein's remarks display notable omissions. Bouveresse justly observes that though 'the crucial question' is 'whether Freud employed appropriate methods to justify his causal assertions', Wittgenstein is perfunctory in his discussion of these. Consider the most notable division among Freud's critics on this issue. On the one side, it is maintained, most vociferously by Adolf Grünbaum, that only 'controlled enquiry' is capable of conferring credibility on Freud's causal claims; on the other, that though this is to be excessively rigoristic, a radical rejection of Freud's distinctive etiological and dynamic theses does not require it—the telling objection to Freud is not that he is pseudoscientific but that he is pseudo-hermeneutic.

The most surprising feature of Wittgenstein's remarks is that he seems to take the side of the more scientistic of Freud's critics. In his dismissal of grounds other than the scientific ones for causal imputations he can sound like Grünbaum, as when he denies that motive explanations based on the subject's say-so can have causal status since 'a cause is found experimentally.' But what experiment could show that the Count of Monte-Cristo's motive for hounding his former persecutors was vengeance and not idle malice, or that Shylock, in plotting the death of Antonio, wasn't just indulging in a general animus against Christians? I would like Bouveresse to have done more to show how the distinctive sense in which Wittgenstein sometimes employs the term 'cause' qualifies his apparent scientism.

Freud several times compares his procedure in identifying the origin of a neurotic condition to the solving of a jigsaw puzzle. 'If one succeeds in arranging the confused heap of fragments, each of which bears upon it an unintelligible piece of drawing, so that the picture acquires a meaning, so that there is no gap anywhere in the design and the whole fits together . . . then one knows that one his solved the puzzle.' Bouveresse's objection that such a procedure necessarily falls short of demonstration is inadequate. Consider the case of Miss Havisham in *Great Expectations,* whose manifold eccentricities include wearing a wedding dress and only one white shoe. When we learn that this is how she was attired at an emotionally disturbing moment years earlier, do we not consider that a case has been made, without the benefit of controlled enquiry, for the existence of a causal connection between her trauma and her eccentricities? The right objection to Freud's etiological claims is not that 'jigsaw-solving' of the Miss Havisham kind falls short of demonstration but that Freud's explanations regularly fall woefully short of the Miss Havisham standard in spite of a tendentious insistence that they meet it.

Bouveresse calls the confusion between reasons and causes 'the philosophical confusion *par excellence*'. The problem is that much that Wittgenstein has to say about this treacherous antithesis is only peripherally related to his claim that Freud confused them. Clues as to what Wittgenstein meant are provided by his remark that Freud's book on jokes was 'a good book for looking for philosophical mistakes because one can ask how far what he says is a hypothesis and how far just a good way of representing a fact'. What Wittgenstein generally means by 'cause', when commenting on Freud, is any factor in an explanation whose influence is only to be determined by empirical enquiry; this can include reasons and thus puts these in confusing opposition to what, in other contexts, Wittgenstein also calls 'reasons' but denies are cause since they are what the subject himself gives and are thus not based on empirical grounds.

Freud is accused of confusing reason and cause because he produces accounts whose acceptability is independent of inductive support, as if they were corollaries of theoretical discoveries and could have an authority not conferred on them by the subject's agreement. For example, the real point of remarks like 'a tendency to economy is the most general feature of joke techniques' lies in their being a good way of representing what it is we find appealing about jokes and not, as Freud intermittently assumes, in their recording his conclusions as to the hidden energic processes underlying the appreciation of jokes. Wittgenstein finds Freud insufficiently aware of this and too intent on 'sounding like science'.

Imagine a world in which people who laughed at jokes did not know what they were laughing at until they observed the unconscious processes hypothesised by Freud. Only when able to peer down a psychoanalytoscope at the joke-mechanism could they pronounce conclusively: 'Just as we thought: a tendency to economy is the most general feature of joke technique.' This is the world Freud intermittently beguiled himself into believing he was living in, and from whose thrall Wittgenstein's admonition—'new regions of the soul have not been found'—proposed to liberate us.

The claim that analysts confound 'good ways of representing a fact' with hypotheses as to hidden processes is not confined to Freud's joke theories. Another example is the defence of his tripartite division of minds into Id, Ego and Superego on the grounds that that is what mental conflict feels like. In his monumental *Freud Evaluated*, Malcom Macmillan refers to 'the psychoanalytic tradition of directly translating subjective impressions into economic terms'. Even Richard Wollheim, who rarely rises above an abject appreciativeness in his dealings with Freud, concedes that Freud 'sometimes treated propositions about energy and its liberation as though they were descriptions of introspectible phenomena'. This equivocation extends beyond the orthodox Freudian formulations. Critics of Kohut and his followers have complained of their oscillation between use of the terms 'fragmented self' and 'disintegrative anxiety' as subjective descriptions of the patients' experiences and as identifying the processes which underlie them.

Wittgenstein was struck by the felicity of Freud's comparison of certain dream images to a rebus. A rebus is a picture representing a word or name—

the cigar at the bottom of the last panel of Segar's Popeye strip is a familiar example. Wittgenstein called the comparison an 'excellent simile'. But the sense in which he thinks dreams are rebus-like puts him in opposition to Freud. For Wittgenstein certain dream images are rebuses because that is how they strike us; but something could strike someone as rebus-like and not be a rebus in Freud's sense because it did not come about in the appropriate way: it wasn't a product of homunculoid dream-workers busily transforming the latent dream thoughts into the manifest dream by condensing, displacing or symbolising. When Wittgenstein speaks of the meaningfulness of a dream he is referring to its manifest property of being redolent of secret significance, a property which it could have even if lacking significance in Freud's sense. But Wittgenstein puzzles us when he implies that Freud's rooting of adult proclivities of various kinds in the vicissitudes of infancy may also be just 'good similes'.

What in Freud's etiological speculations might have moved Wittgenstein to this view? He may have felt it was justified because when Freud invoked certain infantile activities as explanatory of certain adult ones what determined their acceptability was not evidence but merely the felicity of the juxtaposition. Thus Freud was claiming to establish causal relations between states of affairs when in reality he was only putting them 'side by side'.

The reason Wittgenstein is appreciative ('excellent similes'), rather than straightforwardly condemnatory, is that even if our infantile transactions with our mother's nipples, say, are not causally related to the turbulence the sight of breasts provokes in us as adults, they may nevertheless clarify it by making explicit the nascent tactile and buccal delights augured. By contrast, consider the suggestion of an earlier champion of the unconscious, Eduard von Hartmann, that breasts arouse men because of the unconscious prospect of the plentiful nutrition they would afford offspring. The mysterious delectability of breasts as things to be smothered and engulfed by and slobbered over is not illuminated by the assurance that our children would not be stinted of milk. If von Hartmann's speculation fails as a hypothesis it fails completely, since, unlike many of Freud's, its appositeness as simile cannot redeem it.

But can the value of Freud's speculations in general survive their exposure as disguised similes? Could we retain what is valuable in Freud's insistence on the ubiquity of infantile sexual influences if we divest them of their causal status and take him to be saying instead: 'I am only comparing men's attitude towards money with their infantile feelings about faeces'; 'I am only comparing the catamite's gratification at penetration by penises to the child's pleasure in the expulsion of stools'; 'I am only comparing friendship between heterosexual men to love affairs between homosexual men'; and so on? How are we to persuade someone who finds this kind of discourse fatuous that he is wrong? Should we even try?

Bouveresse has an interesting discussion of Wittgenstein's suggestion that the source of our bemusement by psychoanalysis lies in its 'peculiar charm'. Wittgenstein locates one source of this 'charm' in 'the idea of an underworld. A secret cellar. Something hidden. Uncanny.' He doesn't illustrate, but he may be referring to Freud's tendency to populate the unconscious with hidden agents moving in mysterious ways their wonders to perform, like the Numskulls in the *Beano*. Blinky pulling his master's eyelids down like blinds when he doesn't want to see what is going on outside is akin to the eye that 'refuses' to see in Freud's account of psychogenic blindness. This engaging *façon de parler* also crops up in his account of the consolatory power of humour, which he sees as a consequence of 'the superego speaking kindly words of comfort to the intimidated ego'.

Wittgenstein suggests that our obliviousness to the deficiencies of Freud's monotonous invocation of Oedipal origins is due to its having the attraction of mythological accounts: 'it is all the outcome of something that happened long ago . . . giving a sort of tragic pattern to one's life.' (He was anticipated on this point by Svevo's Zeno: 'they have found out what was wrong with me. The diagnosis is just the same as the one that Sophocles drew up long ago for poor Oedipus: I was in love with my mother and wanted to murder my father . . . I listened enraptured. It was a disease that exalted me to a place among the great ones of the earth: a disease so dignified that it could trace its pedigree even to the mythological age.') The term 'myth' has lost much of the pejorative force it had for Wittgenstein. What was once taken as derogatory is now a familiar component of Freudian apologetic. As befits a Teflon culture hero, Freud is rarely permitted to be straightforwardly wrong about anything; whatever turns out to be empirically false is pronounced poetically true. What fails as fact succeeds as parable.

However, what Wittgenstein calls our 'subservience' to Freud—which he predicts we will be long in overcoming—isn't just due to the intrinsic 'charm' of his ideas. Bouveresse himself inadvertently provides an instance which can't be so explained when he tells us that Freud's erroneous seduction theory was based on his patients' claims to have been sexually molested as infants. But if there is one point on which Freud's initial proclamation is definite, it is that it was not based on the claims of his patients; rather, it was based on the hypothesised molestation fitting so neatly the rest of the jigsaw presented by the patient's symptoms, dreams, etc. Why then the singular uniformity with which an account has been propagated that an hour in a library would have exposed as baseless? (It even got by the ultra-scrupulous Janet Malcolm and the legendary fact-checkers at the *New Yorker*, as well as Adolf Grünbaum, where it is accompanied by hubristic protestations at 'exegetical mythmaking' in Freud studies.) I think that the deluding charm in these instances, as in many others, was that of the Freud legend itself.

Grünbaum, Malcolm, and a legion of others erred because they followed Freud's own retrospective, strategically distorted accounts, and were incapable of suspecting that he may have been fabricating. King Richard will lose his hump before Freud his unmerited reputation for candour.

It is a pity that Bouveresse did not avail himself of one of the few specific examples which Wittgenstein gives, and in connection with which he voices his strongest objections to Freud's interpretative procedure, castigating it as 'immensely wrong'. The rebuke was provoked by an interpretation Freud gives of a flowering branch held by the dreamer which she herself associates with the lily spray carried by Gabriel in paintings of the Annunciation but whose meaning Freud insists is genital. Wittgenstein says that in bringing this image into relation with the dreamer's sexual life Freud had 'cheated' her. I don't think that at this point Wittgenstein is saying that the dreamer is being cheated because instead of searching for the true causes of the dream-image Freud insisted on rounding up the usual suspects, but rather, because the ideas whose confluence determined the branch image— an erect phallus, masturbation guilt, etc.—did not coincide with those of which she was already aware in a penumbral, nascent way. I believe that Wittgenstein is objecting to the proffering of objective, pre-existing meanings, however empirically warranted, because he sees them as constituting a violation of the compact between analyst and patient. What was 'immensely wrong' was for Freud to take his patient away from her vague sense of the significance of that which she contemplated—whether her dream or her life—to its diagnostic implications. This view provoked one outraged psychoanalyst to compare Wittgenstein to someone who encourages a victim of cancer to neglect her condition until it is too late.

Though the implied equation between an analyst's interpretative powers and a biopsy report explains why Freudian analysis arouses such profound mistrust, Bouveresse is nevertheless mistaken to say that there is no way other than a dreamer's acquiescence to determine the acceptability of an interpretation. This can be illustrated by the very dream which Wittgenstein discusses. Freud thinks that the camellias which sprouted from the branch show that the dreamer was unconsciously identifying herself with the courtesan-heroine of *La Dame aux camélias*. Let us suppose that the dreamer rejected this interpretation but related that in the dream she was incomprehensibly addressed as 'Madame Valéry', which the analyst recognises as the name of 'la dame aux camélias' in the opera Verdi based on the story. It is this kind of consideration which makes conceivable, if not often feasible, an alternative, objective way of conferring meaning on the dream, independent of the dreamer's agreement.

There are obviously cases where it is morally obligatory to treat a patient's experiences diagnostically and to refuse to assist in the development of their unformulated subjective significance. Shatov (in Dostoevsky's

The Devils) is impatient of Kirilov's rhapsodising about his intense 'moments of harmony' and warns him they may signify epilepsy. Is Shatov cheating Kirilov? Does an analyst stand to his patient's complaints as to the symptoms of an undiagnosed epileptic?

Psychoanalysis has evolved in a direction which gives Wittgenstein's criticism more relevance than it once would have. What would be patiently obscurantist when applied to the paralyses, contractures, convulsions, pains, paraesthesias and anaesthesias which were so common among the presenting symptoms of Freud's first patients is more defensible when applied to the apprehensions, dejections and vague malaises which figure prominently among the complaints of present-day analysands. Unlike the scientific critics of psychoanalysis Wittgenstein is not asking that it live up to its scientific pretensions but that it abandon them. This implies an explanatory nihilism as to the possibility of causal knowledge continuous with that implicit in Montaigne's resignation to his ignorance of the source of his love for La Boétie: 'Because it was him; because it was me.'

Even if we confine the problems addressed by the analyst to the states of mental distress that patients typically complain of—feelings of worthlessness, helplessness, neglect, humiliation, rage—the same antithesis nevertheless arises between 'getting clear' about the distress and discovering its causes, and demands clearheadedness as to which aim we are pursuing.

Bouveresse sees an analogy between the kind of understanding afforded by a psychoanalysis stripped of explanatory pretensions, and that afforded by philosophy as Wittgenstein conceived it. I think it lies in the extent to which the aim of both is facilitated by 'putting into order what we already know without adding anything'. A type of understanding of our past, for example, is conceivable which promises nothing more than an enhanced command of the themes on which our mind plays its variations—a discursive equivalent of time-lapse photography. But there must be more candour as to the limitations of such a project. Wittgenstein reminds us that 'one can learn the truth by thinking as one learns to know a face better by drawing it.' But however rewarding we find this activity we must resist the temptation of thinking that it can tell us why the nose is strong and the chin weak. This mode of exploration of my condition may leave me clearer as to who or what I blame, yet no wiser as to who or what is really to blame.

Even if the idea of an Unconscious, decodable only by a technique for which Freud held the patent, were finally to succumb to scepticism, something somewhat continuous with psychoanalysis as we have known it might still be tenable. The practice could transmute into an autonomous activity divested of explanatory and crudely therapeutic pretensions, disdainful of the grandiosity of the founder and devoted to one object only—the elucidation and articulation of self-feeling. But would an activity so conceived be psychoanalysis? Perhaps we could claim for it what Wittgenstein claimed for his new conception of philosophy—that those involved in it might come to feel: 'That's what I really wanted.'

The real problem this kind of Wittgensteinian self-understanding presents is not the genealogical one of its relation to Freud but rather that of deciding what value is to be placed on an activity which merely focuses the unfocused, thematises the unthematised, propositionalises the unpropositionalised and so forth, if the outcome is not causal knowledge. It is this question which Wittgenstein's criticism of Freud compels us to address.

13

A Final Accounting

Those who are interested in Freud and psychoanalysis will be familiar with questions such as 'Is Freudian psychology pseudoscientific?' 'Is Freudian psychology falsifiable?' 'Is unfalsifiability an adequate criterion of pseudo-science?', and they might naturally suppose that it is these questions of which Erwin has attempted a 'final accounting'. Surprisingly, these questions hardly feature in Erwin's book. Though at the outset Peter Medawar's notorious judgment that psychoanalysis is 'the most stupendous intellectual confidence trick of the twentieth century' is cited, Erwin does not seem to think it is part of his final accounting to say either whether he thinks it justified or, if not, why someone of Medawar's distinction should nevertheless have thought so.

Since theorists as intellectually diverse as Carl Rogers, John Bowlby, and Thomas Szasz have characterized Freudian theory as pseudoscientific one would have thought an account purporting to be final would have addressed the question as to why. But the arresting question of how Freudian theory became, and for so long remained, both institutionally and informally, the standard account of mental functioning and neurotic affliction, routinely transmitted in introductory text books, manuals for nurses and social workers and in reference works from *Pears Cyclopedia,* purchasable at any Woolworth, to the *Encyclopedia of the Social Sciences,* is ignored.

But though ignored by Erwin it has been repeatedly raised by others. Three decades ago Alasdair MacIntyre wrote: 'I know of no other example of a system of unjustified beliefs which has propagated itself so successfully as Freudian theory. How was it done?'[1] The same question was more

This review of Edwin Erwin, *A Final Accounting: Philosophical and Empirical Issues in Freudian Psychology* (Cambridge, Massachusetts: MIT Press, 1996) first appeared in *Philosophy,* Vol. 72, No. 281 (July 1997) and is reprinted by permission.

1. Alasdair MacIntyre, 'Psychoanalysis: The Future of an Illusion', *Against the Self-Images of the Age* (London: Duckworth, 1976), p. 35.

recently posed by Ernest Gellner: 'We are trying to cope with the problem . . . why this system of ideas did not sink . . . why it conquered our language and to some extent our thought.'[2]

Paul Kline responded to the failure of extra-clinical research to substantiate Freud's account of the sources of oral and anal character traits with the injunction that 'The aetiological hypotheses may not be rejected until better techniques of investigation have been devised.'[3] Although Erwin deals extensively with Kline he does not see it as part of his brief to discuss the issues raised by such pronouncements. 'A Final Accounting' is an overweening title for a work so perfunctory in its treatment of such central features of the Freud controversy.

What Erwin has really produced is an assessment of three theses; that Freudian theory is supported, or at least capable of support, by clinical data; that there is experimental evidence in its favour; that the therapy based on the theory is effective.

In the section of his book devoted to the experimental investigation of Freudian theory Erwin devotes several pages to experimental studies purportedly supportive of Freud's theory of the castration complex. The major problem which besets such research is to find an adequate criterion of degrees of castration anxiety. It would then be possible to see whether its relation to other features of the subject's personality were in the direction anticipated by Freudian theory. In one study degrees of castration anxiety were measured by asking subjects to imagine that a child had found its toy elephant broken and to say what was wrong with it. If the answer was that its tail was missing the subject was assigned a high degree of castration anxiety. In another study—held most strongly supportive of the castration complex—subjects were shown a drawing of a dog witnessing another dog about to have his tail cut off and asked to impute degrees of anxiety to it. Those who imputed the higher degree of anxiety were classified as higher in castration anxiety, on the assumption presumably, that the mechanism of projection was responsible for the assignment of high anxiety to the dog. Though Erwin objects to this inference he does not point out that had those who imputed the *least* degree of anxiety to the dog been assigned the highest degree of castration anxiety this would have been equally consonant with psychoanalytic theory and just as explicable via the operation of the mechanism of denial—the mechanism Freud invokes when he explains why some women analysts report they are unable to detect penis envy in their female patients.

---

2. Ernest Gellner, *The Psychoanalytic Movement* (London: Paladin, 1985), p. 162.
3. Paul Kline, *Fact and Fantasy in Freudian Theory* (London: Methuen, 1972), p. 94; 1981, p. 129.

In another study subjects were asked to draw a house, a tree and a person. 'On the assumption that a chimney symbolizes a penis it was predicted that subjects suffering from castration anxiety would omit the chimney when drawing a house' (p. 157). Drawing a tree which had been cut down, or a person as bald or decapitated were also considered evidence of castration anxiety. These features were found to a significantly greater degree in subjects who had recently undergone sterilisation than in those who had undergone surgery for other reasons. This had been cited as strong support for the theory of castration anxiety since sterilisation is equated with castration. Erwin rejects all these studies but he does not remark on their avoidable feebleness. Most of his objections could easily have been anticipated and built into the experiment. For example, his objection that those who imputed a higher degree of anxiety to the mutilation-witnessing dog were merely more generally anxious or that they were more concerned about the mistreatment of animals could have been met if pictures of dogs being mistreated in other ways than having their tails cut off had been included.

The claim that these experiments supply support for Freud's castration complex are so tendentious that all they demonstrate is that there are psychologists who would sooner part with their own penises than with the concept of castration anxiety.

Nevertheless, one of Erwin's criteria of pertinence to Freudian theory is too restrictive He says that even if the high anxiety-imputing subjects were more concerned about the vulnerability of their own genitals this would not support Freudian theory, because this concern would not have been unconscious. But if the more penis-anxious subjects behaved differently in situations held by Freudian theory to be symbolic surrogates for castration than those who, though equally anxious, were less concerned with their phallic fragility this would certainly go some way towards supporting the importance Freud attached to castration anxiety. Suppose we drop projective tests of which Erwin is justifiably suspicious and instead monitored the heart beat and galvanic skin response of subjects exposed to the film clip in which James Bond's genitals were about to be bifurcated by a laser beam. If those whose responses were differentially intense also showed a greater fear of death, or of other things held by Freudians to be castration surrogates, then even though their genital apprehensions were conscious, this would vindicate something quite distinctive in the Freudian view of the springs of action.

Erwin's comments on the studies of anality and its relation to character show the same underestimation of the possibility of more adequate investigation. He distrusts projective tests and yet doesn't see how they can be dispensed with. It does not occur to him to ask why our attitude to an activity which all of us engage in several times a day has to be indirectly measured by projective tests. It should not be too difficult to taxonomize people's modes of toilet hygiene and excretory life generally so that they could be classified along different dimensions (putting aside cultural differences like the use of the left hand etc.).

Erwin's overall conclusion is that not only is there no experimental support for Freudian theory but that there are no prospects that there ever will be. But this is contradicted by his discussion of the research programme of the late Lloyd Silverman, the real moral of which is that more rigorous attempts at replication are required. Silverman maintained that his experiments showed that unconscious stimulation of libidinal and aggressive mental contents can intensify psychopathology. Those experiments which bore most directly on Freudian theory involved the tachistoscopic presentation of pictorial or verbal stimuli designed to intensify unconscious conflicts and consequently increase the particular psychopathology to which Freudian theory annexed them. For example, in the case of homosexuality the Freudian hypothesis tested was that activating conflicts over incestuous wishes would intensify homosexual feelings and reduce heterosexual ones. A stimulus assumed to provoke incestuous ideation—and thus the attendant pathology—was FUCK MOMMY. And so it did. Since it did not have this effect on heterosexuals and no non-incestuous stimulus had a similar effect Silverman concluded that he had provided support for a distinctively Freudian thesis. Similar results were achieved with depression and stuttering. In the case of stuttering, the stimuli involved anal material (GO SHIT) and increased the incidence rate of stuttering (as measured blind by raters who listened to successive samples of speech). Only stimuli related to anal matters (GO SHIT, for example) intensified stuttering. Neither the stimulation of aggressive nor of anal wishes affected homosexual manifestations; only incest-related stimuli did. In general only stimuli which Freudian theory held causative of conflicts which produced a particular pathology influenced that pathology.

Silverman concludes that 'specific relationships are demonstrable between particular libidinal and aggression contents and particular forms of psychopathology.' Erwin disagrees, but some of his reasons are not good. For example, he objects that there is no certainty that the stimulus was truly unconscious. Erwin thinks 'the fatal flaw' in Silverman's procedure is that the subjects may have been aware both of the ostensibly subliminal stimulus and of its anticipated effects. But if the expression FUCK MOMMY intensifies pathology only in homosexuals, or the instruction GO SHIT only affects stutterers but not non-stutterers, would this have no bearing on Freudian theory? We would still have a surprising result accountable most readily on Freudian assumptions. As for the subjects' possible foreknowledge of the effect anticipated by the experimenters, is it likely that they would know that their symptoms would be influenced by exposure to the stimulus for 4 microseconds but not for 10? More to the point is Erwin's objection to Silverman's measures of psychopathology ('the weakest aspect of the programme'). But he concedes that in the case of stuttering, at least, the problem of test validity is 'nonexistent' since the test consisted of the effect of the stimulus on the degree of stutter. Erwin objects instead that 'it is doubtful that an increase in stuttering constitutes an increase in psychopathology', without explaining either why it does not or why it would matter. It is the failure of attempts at replication that undermine Silverman's conclusions and Erwin ought to have confined his objections to that point.

There are two main modes of non-experimental validation for Freud's hypotheses: clinical and extra-clinical. The clinical are the circumstantial coherence of the interpretations—the famous jig-saw justification (which Erwin dubs 'thematic affinity')—and/or their endorsement by the subject, and/or their therapeutic efficacy. The extra-clinical are the corroboration of analytically inferred episodes in a patient's infantile life by contemporary accounts and the independent validation of clinically inspired speculations as to infantile life in general by direct observation of children. Erwin ignores the external validation claim on behalf of psychoanalytic theory and method and he mishandles the clinical validation issue. He says of clinical validation that though 'thematic affinity . . . plays a crucial role in validating Freudian hypotheses . . . it should play no such role.' Erwin makes a momentous error here. Instead of seeking to undermine the claims made on behalf of Freud's particular appeals to 'thematic affinity', Erwin seeks to impugn the entire class of which they are members. But appeals to thematic affinity fail, when they do fail, because of their feebleness and tendentiousness and not their intrinsic epistemic nature.

Erwin's arguments for the necessity of scientific standards irrespective of the area of enquiry will not persuade anyone who is convinced that historical research with all its necessary deficiencies has increased our knowledge of causal relations between events and can see no reason why the same concession cannot be made in the case of psychoanalytic clinical enquiry. If the bulk of psychoanalytic theory is unworthy of credence, as I believe it is, it is not because of the intrinsic objectionability of thematic affinity and like 'unscientific' considerations. It is because it fails to meet the evidential standards generally in use in humanistic disciplines. We can provide good grounds for rejecting Freud's explanatory pretensions without giving so grossly distorted a picture of our epistemic lives as does Erwin.

Let us consider some non-psychoanalytic instances of the warranted appeal to non-scientific types of support. There is a mode of clinical validation which Freud's jigsaw puzzle analogy fits better than the expression 'thematic affinity.' It was more literally and felicitously characterized by William James when he spoke of '. . . transitions which at first sight startle us by their abruptness but which, scrutinized closely, often reveal intermediate links of perfect naturalness and propriety.'[4] When the nervous vicar in the joke introduces Mrs Schlitt as Mrs Pliss we know the route he came just as those familiar with the original version of this joke will know the route I came to this toned-down version. What account can Erwin give of the reasonableness on which he maintains our certitude is based? To take an instance more analogous to that class of Freud's claims which invoke the influence of early life events on adult character consider the case of the eccentric spinster, Miss Havisham, in Dickens's *Great Expectations*. Her dining room contains a mouldering wedding cake and she is garbed in a wedding dress and wears only one white shoe. All the clocks in her home are set at twenty to nine. It seems perfectly reasonable to impute these to the fact that they were circumstances which prevailed years earlier on her wedding day when she was abruptly informed that she had been jilted. What is it that makes it reasonable but Erwin's *bête noir*, thematic affinity? As another example of the manner in which thematic affinity enhances plausibility consider that if all we knew of Miss Havisham was that she was raising a beautiful little girl to break men's hearts we might be unsure whether her motive was personal, or ideological; but, once apprised of the circumstances of the jilting and the manner in which they corresponded to her later eccentricities, the causal relation gains enormous credibility. The question to be raised as to the clinical evidence for Freudian theory is not whether it meets natural science standards but whether it approaches sufficiently close to the Miss Havisham level to be worthy of credence.

Let us consider a notorious example. In the Wolf Man case this is how Freud attempts to dissipate scepticism as to the occurrence and influence of the 'primal scene', (an episode in which the Wolf Man, aged 18 months and sleeping in his parents' bedroom, awoke and saw them having intercourse *'a tergo'*, i.e., doggie fashion): 'The analyst . . . will comfort himself by recalling . . . how after a certain phase in the treatment everything seems to converge on it; and how later in the synthesis, the most varied and remarkable results radiated from it; how not only the largest problems but the smallest peculiarities in the history of the case were cleared up by this single assumption. And he will disclaim the possession of the amount of ingenuity necessary for the concoction of an occurrence which can fulfil these demands.' What considerations are pertinent to our decision as to whether, for example, it is as reasonable to impute the Wolf Man's terror at the image of a wolf in an upright posture to the position adopted by his father during the primal scene as it is to account for Miss Havisham's wearing one white shoe as a spinster to her wearing one white shoe as a bride-to-be. Aren't the

---

4. William James. *The Principles of Psychology* (New York: Dover, 1950), p. 555.

questions which naturally arise, whether the Wolf Man really witnessed his parents having intercourse *a tergo* and how close the affinity is between the putatively explanatory trauma and the 'varied and remarkable results' which Freud traces to it, rather than the issues in the philosophy of explanation discussed by Erwin? What makes Freud's examples of the manner in which the infantile past superimposes itself on later eras smack of tendentiousness is not, as Erwin contends, that they cannot call on our background knowledge of common sense psychology but the dubiousness of the data said to be thematically related, and the tenuousness of the affinity between them.

We want to know, for example, whether Freud has given a plausible account of why the Rat Man is plagued by the thought that unless he pays a debt which he has not incurred his father will undergo a torture in which ravenous rats will be introduced into his rectum. Freud's account—which he claims as another vindication of his emphasis on infantile sexuality—is that the rat torture was a symbolically distorted reactivation of his infantile brooding on an anal solution to the problem of birth and this, coupled with his equation of rats with babies and subjected to the mechanism of reversal, produced the image of rats entering his father's rectum. What makes Freud's claim, that the case of the Rat Man's 'great obsessive fear' illustrates the causal influence of infantile life on the production of symptoms, unacceptable is not its lack of epidemiological support but its utter gratuitousness in the light of the fact that the Rat Man had merely incorporated into his obsessive thoughts an image which had been communicated to him by the same person who misinformed him of the debt only a day earlier. To bring out the difference between my objection and what I regard as Erwin's scientistic one let me state the conditions under which I would regard Freud's claim as to the influence of Rat Man's infantile anal birth fantasies or his obsession worth consideration. If the torture anecdote which was related to him involved ferrets rather than rats, and if the portion of the body involved in the torture had been the face (as in Orwell's *Nineteen Eighty-four*) rather than the rectum but the thought that had plagued the Rat Man had, nevertheless, involved rats rather than ferrets and the rectum rather than the face then Freud's thesis as to the influence of the anal birth fantasies would have the degree of circumstantial support which would undercut the charge of arbitrariness. These considerations seem to me to presuppose no disputable notions about the nature of explanation and remain entirely within the realm of a rational hermeneutics.

The grounds for doubting the genuineness of Freud's interpretative/ reconstructive feats are thus not those raised by Erwin but those raised by Allen Esterson in his discussion of the plausibility of the case histories in his book.[5] When scepticism is expressed as to the warrantability of Freud's clin-

---

5. Allen Esterson, *Seductive Mirage* (Chicago: Open Court, 1993).

ical inferences it is not Erwin's natural science standards of validation that must be invoked but our common sense standards of narrative and explanatory cogency.

Consider the terms in which Paul Meehl expressed his misgivings as to Freud's deployment of the criterion of thematic affinity: 'Freud's jigsaw puzzle analogy does not really fit the psychoanalytic hour because it's simply not true that all of the pieces fit together, or that the criteria of fitting are sufficiently tight to make it analogous even to a clear-cut criminal trial'.[6] Yet Meehl himself, unlike Erwin, upholds the legitimacy of the criterion of fitting ('thematic affinity'). The issue raised by Meehl is the pertinent one but it is ignored by Erwin who mounts, instead, a scientistically inspired attack on the very idea of non-nomothetically supported explanation. The most he will concede is that the nomothetic support is sometimes supplied by background knowledge rather than experiment. But there are copious instances of thematic affinity which do not derive their cogency from background knowledge but from their apparent circumstantiality and it this which must he shown to be illusory if they are to be rejected.

The invocation of a gestalt fit between explicandum and explicans is not an innovation of later generations of analysts. It is Freud's own. In the *Interpretation of Dreams*[7] Freud anticipates the objection that associations might have been produced by the dream without having determined it: 'It may perhaps be doubted whether this memory really had any share in determining the form taken by the content of the dream or whether it was not rather that the process of analysis built up the connection subsequently. But the copious and intertwined associative links warrant our accepting the former alternative'. It is crucial to the criticism of Freud's dream theory, and of Freud's interpretations in general, that 'the copious and intertwined associative links' be shown to be the product of Freud's ingenuity or the sequaciousness of his readers rather than of the data. Erwin fails to do this.

There are reasons for thinking that even in those cases where an appearance of dense circumstantiality appears to be met this may well be specious. Consider what the literary historian, Alistair Fowler, says about the comparable problem of assessing numerological patterns in poetry. Fowler lays down the rule that if the stanza count of a passage is asserted to have an astronomical significance then the stanza counts of complementary passages ought also to have astronomical values and not Pythagorean or Biblical ones. Freud is under no such analogous constraint. In the Dora case history he tells us 'interpretations need not be consistent with one another'[8] And in

6. Paul Meehl, 'Some Methodological Reflections on the Difficulties of Psychoanalytic Research.' *Minnesota Studies in the Philosophy of Science*, Vol. IV (1970), p. 407.

7. Sigmund Freud, *The Interpretation of Dreams* (London: Allen and Unwin, 1954), p. 191.

8. Sigmund Freud, *Collected Papers*, Vol. 3, (London: Hogarth, 1925), p. 65.

the case of the Wolf Man where he gives incompatible interpretations of the Wolf Man's symptoms he notices this himself and comments, 'It was only a logical contradiction—which is not saying much. On the contrary the whole process is characteristic of the way in which the unconscious works.'[9] It is this self-indulgent interpretative license on which Erwin ought to have concentrated.

If we want to know how much credence to place in the particular diagnostic claims advanced by Freud it is no help to be told that they fall short of the standards of the natural sciences. This will be true of the entire class to which they belong and we want to be told how to distinguish the less and more credible among these. Richard Wollheim, among others, is convinced that had the Rat Man's rival in love not been called Richard and thus 'Dick', and thus a homonym of the German word for fat—*dick*—he would not have embarked on his drastic dieting regimen.[10] Is it really sensible to argue that the unacceptability of this is due to its failure to meet the standards of the natural sciences?

What of the possibility of confirmation through the patient's eventual endorsement? Erwin rejects a hermeneutic reading of Freud because, he tells us, Freud advances patently causal claims. Erwin is not the only expositor of Freud to have been confused by Freud's simultaneous dethronement and reinstatement of introspection. He follows Grünbaum's lead without any awareness of how revisionist the thesis that Freud was free of hermeneutic stain is (p. 20). To argue that Freud was straightforwardly, unequivocally, causal is to be almost as selective in reading his texts as are the hermeneuts.

The major embarrassment for a straightforwardly causal construal of Freud, such as Erwin advocates, is the thesis advanced in *Introductory Lecture* 6, but reiterated or implied on numerous occasions elsewhere, that the patient knows the meaning of his dreams, symptoms, etc., only does not know that he knows. Can Freud mean by this that what the patient knows is a *causal hypothesis*? Furthermore, what kind of a causal hypothesis can it be which the patient has to 'look for in himself', as Freud puts it, in words quoted by Grünbaum, and on which he bases so much of his argument as to Freud's rationale of validation. Can what the patient is told to 'look for in himself' be a causal hypothesis? This ambiguity in Freud is something which B.F. Skinner noticed: 'Although it was Freud himself who taught us to doubt the face value of introspection, he appears to have been responsible for the view that another sort of direct experience is required if certain activities of the mental apparatus are to be comprehended'.[11]

---

9. Sigmund Freud, *Collected Papers*, Vol. 3, (London: Hogarth, 1925), p. 557.

10. Richard Wollheim, *Freud* (London: Fontana, 1992), pp. 88–91.

11. B.F Skinner, 'Critique of Psychoanalytic Concept and Theories', *The Validation of Scientific Theories* (New York: Collier, 1959), p. 12.

On p. 98 Erwin urges against the credibility of Freudian theses that 'individuals will accept bogus interpretations'. This ignores a vast class of Freudian interpretations on whose credibility the acceptance of the patient has no bearing. Among the analytic interpretations which the conviction of the patient cannot confirm, even if uncontaminated, are conversion accounts of hysterical symptoms: the repressed thought 'it stabs me to the heart' is converted into a stabbing sensation in the region of the heart; responding to an insult 'one has to swallow' by repressing one's feelings is converted into an hysterical 'aura' in the throat; a reproach that was felt as a 'slap in the face' is converted into a facial neuralgia; the phrases 'not having anything to lean upon' and 'not being able to take a single step forward' bring about a disturbance of walking; anxiety to get on a proper footing with some strangers becomes a pain in the heel; Dora's limp following an abdominal disorder (itself due to a pregnancy fantasy) was expressing/conveying her sense of the illicit character of her pregnancy via an idiom which alludes to taking 'a false step'. The Wolf Man's constipation was a manifestation of a host of fantasies relating to parturitional, rebirth and anal penetration. How could the patient's avowal, even if uninfluenced by the analyst, possibly confirm interpretations such as these? It is clear that the patient's assent is not an appropriate means of determining whether unconscious ideation played a role in the production of such symptoms and so suggestion doesn't come into it.

Erwin makes a good case against the distinctive therapeutic efficacy of psychoanalysis on sound methodological grounds. However, there is something mildly emetic about the sycophantic manner in which he defends Grünbaum against criticisms of his claim that it was Freud's confidence in his therapeutic achievements (the 'Tally Argument') that led him to respond to objections with 'sovereign, patronising serenity.' Erwin merely asserts that Grünbaum is right although critics 'have made some useful points'. We are not told what these 'useful points' are or why he discounts them. Though he purports to give an account of Paul Robinson's survey of criticisms of Grünbaum's 'tally argument' one would never guess from his account that Robinson's conclusion was that 'The Argument was invalid from the start. Grünbaum's painstaking account of its historical rise and fall is disingenuous.'[12] (For a more up-to-date demonstration of how baseless Grünbaum's account of the 'tally argument' is and how lubricious his response to objections see Allen Esterson's 'Grünbaum's Tally Argument.'[13])

---

12. Paul Robinson, *Freud and His Critics,* (Berkeley: University of California Press, 1993), p. 229.
13. Allen Esterson, 'Grünbaum's Tally Argument', *History of the Human Sciences* (February, 1996).

There is another problem connected with clinical validation which Erwin neglects, that of the imponderable, private character of much of the evidence supporting the analyst's assertions. Over and above the sheer mass of material that case reports condense, there is the patient's posture, intonation, facial expression, etc. On at least two occasions Freud himself acknowledges the probative insufficiency of the jigsaw/coherence rationale for crediting his interpretations and reconstructions, and invokes the role of unreproducible nuances of the analytic hour.

In the 1909 case of little Hans he wrote. 'It is a regrettable fact that no account of a psychoanalysis can reproduce the impression received by the analyst as he conducts it, and that a final sense of conviction can never be obtained from reading about it but only from directly experiencing it.'[14] And again in the Wolf Man case history: 'It is well known that no means has been found of in any way introducing into the reproduction of an analysis the sense of conviction which results from the analysis itself. Exhaustive verbatim reports of the proceedings during the hours of analysis would certainly be no help at all.'[15]

How then can Erwin reject the claims of Freudians that non-Freudian alternatives did not articulate with the untransmissible data of the analytic hour as well as Freudian ones but by impugning their judiciousness or disinterestedness? It is a puzzle how Erwin can have overlooked this argument on behalf of Freudian theory when Thomas Nagel, whose case for Freud Erwin believes he has refuted, appealed to it. Nagel invokes on behalf of the analyst's credibility considerations which are not available to non-analysts but depend on 'evidence gathered under the highly unusual conditions of psychoanalytic treatment . . .'[16] Erwin wants to deny that there is support for Freudian theory without being so indecorous as to impugn the testimony of those who claim to have confirmed the theory.

Erwin also seems to confound the grounds for an inference with its validation. Those who defend the intrinsic legitimacy of intraclinical grounds for an inference need not assume that they constitute proof. Though the indentations in a client's walking stick permitted Sherlock Holmes to infer that he was the owner of a dog smaller than a mastiff but larger than a terrier, it was the dog itself which constituted confirmation of this inference. It is striking that Erwin, like Grünbaum, ignores this argument from independent validation. What better reason can there be for belief in the validity of psychoanalytic method than that it enables the analyst to infer infantile episodes which are later independently confirmed, as Freud, James Glover, Robert Waelder, Susan Isaacs, Heinz Hartmann, Jacob Arlow, Charles

---

14. Sigmund Freud, *Collected Papers*, Vol. 3 (London: Hogarth, 1925), p. 245.
15. Sigmund Freud, *Collected Papers*, Vol. 3 (London: Hogarth, 1925), p. 480.
16. T. Nagel, 'Freud's Permanent Revolution'. *New York Review of Books* (May 12, 1994).

Brenner, Hannah Segal, Robert Fliess and others have maintained of their own reconstructions.

The same grounds—direct observation—are given by Freud for considering his clinically based speculations as to infantile sexual life in general confirmed. 'Direct observation has fully confirmed the results arrived at through psychoanalysis.'[17] 'In the beginning my formulations regarding infantile sexuality were founded almost exclusively on the results of analyses in adults, . . . It was therefore a very great triumph when it became possible years later to confirm almost all my inferences by direct observation of children,'.[18] 'My surprising discoveries as to the sexuality of children were made in the first instance through the analysis of adults. But later, from about 1908 onwards, it became possible to confirm them in the most satisfactory way in every detail by direct observation upon children.'[19]

How in the light of these confirmation reports by Freud and others can Erwin state so categorically that the theory is without support? Either Erwin is amnesic for the extra-clinical observational-grounds repeatedly advanced by psychoanalysts for the credibility of psychoanalytic method and theory, or he is too prudent or timorous to admit that he doesn't believe them.

On p. 294 Erwin writes, 'I remain unconvinced by the Popperian argument that it is logically impossible to test Freudian theory.' That this may be an oversimplified account of Popper's views on the relation of testability to Freudian theory we are not permitted to learn, for we are referred not to Popper but to a paper of Grünbaum's on Popper. This is all the more remarkable in that in a 1989 paper on Popper's criterion of testability[20] Grünbaum announced that he had delegated to Erwin the task of dealing with my objections to his view of this.[21] Furthermore, in 1993 Grünbaum announced that Erwin had now discharged this task ('Erwin, 1992, has given a careful defense of my views against Cioffi'.)[22] But neither my objections nor Erwin's 'careful defense' figure in Erwin's bibliography; the latter because it is a figment of Grünbaum's imagination. Had Erwin fallen in with Grünbaum's wishes he might have been driven to concede that Popper's views on testability and its relation to pseudoscience have a complexity and even, perhaps, incoherence, that Grünbaum had not taken account of. What

---

17. Sigmund Freud, *Three Essays on Sexuality* (London: Penguin, 1977), p. 112.
18. Sigmund Freud, 'The Psychoanalytic Movement', *Collected Papers*, Vol. 1 (London: Hogarth, 1924), p. 300.
19. Sigmund Freud, *Autobiographical Study* (London: Hogarth, 1950), p. 70.
20. Adolf Grünbaum, 'The Degeneration of Popper's Theory of Demarcation', in *Freedom and Rationality: Essays in Honor of John Watkins*, Fred D'Agostino and Ian Jarvie, eds., (Boston, Dordrecht: Reidel, 1989).
21. Chapter 9, this volume.
22. A. Grünbaum, *Clinical Validation in the Clinical Theory of Psychoanalysis* (Madison, Connecticut: International Universities Press, 1993), p. 50.

Popper complained of in the most often cited source for his adverse judgment on psychoanalysis, his 1956 lecture 'Conjecture and Refutations', was not just its unfalsifiability but the incessant stream of verifications.

Erwin sees nothing problematic about the notion of testability. The implications of the fact that though both Gellner and Grünbaum distinguish between the theory-in-itself and the behaviour of its advocates, Grünbaum argues that the refusal to capitulate to falsification does not preclude testability and Gellner that acquiescence to falsification does not entail it, pass Erwin by. As well as the intrinsic problems connected with the notion of testability, there are special problems in applying it to Freudian theory. This is because we have no canonical statement of the theory: no agreement on what constitute modifications of the theory rather than *post hoc* elucidations of it, and where it is clear that elucidations are being proffered rather than modifications, we have no way of identifying who is authoritative with respect to these elucidations; or, where the incompatible elucidations both emanate from Freud, which one is to be taken as final. What we have in Freudian theory is a combination of epistemically ambiguous utterances with methodologically suspect practices.

Let me illustrate that there is nothing academic about these concerns by citing Erwin's discussion of the 'Freudian view of the origin of the oral personality.' What is the Freudian view of the origin of the oral personality? Erwin discusses attempts to find evidence for the influence of oral infantile history on adult character but shows no awareness of the way in which the theory which he finds unproblematically testable is qualified by Freud into unconstruability. He even speaks of 'disproof of the Freudian position'. In his final pronouncement on the subject Freud wrote that though 'A child's first erotic object is his mother's breast . . . The phylogenetic foundation has so much the upper hand in all this over accidental personal experience that it makes no difference whether a child has really sucked at the breast or has been brought up on the bottle and never enjoyed the tenderness of a mother's care. This development takes the same path in both cases.'[23] What would constitute a 'disproof' of this 'Freudian position'?

To an acerbic onlooker the Erwin/Grünbaum rationale for assessing the epistemic pretensions of 'Freudian theory' will seem like a disreputable attempt at a plea bargain in which the traditional charge of more candid critics that the theory functioned as a set of non-negotiable dogmas supported by corrupt reporting practices would be dropped in return for admission to the lesser charge of having systematically overestimated the weight of evidence in favour of the theory.

---

23. Sigmund Freud, *Outline of Psychoanalysis* (London: Hogarth, 1949), p. 56.

Index

Abraham, Karl, 106
Adler, Alfred, 17, 24, 215, 259
    'defection' of, 16, 18
    and Freud, differences between, 15,
        16, 18–19, 37, 79, 259
    Popper on, 21, 214
    on sexuality, 15, 16, 94, 259
Alexander, Frank, 162
Alexander, Franz, 66, 167, 168
Alfred, King, 199
Aliquis, 189
Allen, Clifford
    *Modern Discoveries in Medical
        Psychology,* 163
Alston, William, 216
anamnesis, 54–58
Apollo, 190
Appignanesi, Lisa, 20
Aristarchus, 236 n.2
Aristotle
    Metaphysics, 53
    Nicomachean Ethics, 53
Arlow, Jacob, 3, 33, 221, 298
Aron, Raymond, 273
Arsenic and Old Lace, 159
Asch, Solomon, 36, 37
Aschaffenburg, G., 18, 253, 257–58
Atlas, Charles, 269
Aubrey, John, 265
Auden, W.H., 74
Augustine, Saint, 141
Austen, Jane, 98
    Northanger Abbey, 78
    Persuasion, 165

Bailey, Pearce, 176
Baudelaire, Charles, 106
Beatrice, 141
Benjamin, Walter, 276
Berenson, Bernard, 73, 74
Berger, John, 275
Berger, Peter, 26–27
Bergson, Henri, 178, 179
Bettelheim, Bruno, 66, 78
    Uses of Enchantment, 165
biography, issues of, 268, 270–71,
        274–75, 277–78
Bjerre, Paul
    *History and Practice of
        Psychoanalysis,* 173
Bleuler, Eugen, 168
Blum, Harold, 25
Bonaparte, Marie, 108
Bonaparte, Napoléon, 133, 141,
        273–74
Bond, James, 290
Borsch-Jacobsen, Mikkel, 41
Boring, Edwin Garrigues, 85
Bouveresse, Jacques, 280–81, 284–85
    on reasons and causes, confusion
        between, 281–82
Bowlby, John, 208, 231, 288
Braddon, Russell, 268
Brenner, Charles, 22, 221, 299
Breuer, Josef, 1, 20, 40–41, 99 n.12,
        164, 234, 245
Brierly, Marjorie, 162 n.4
Brill, Abraham, 161, 163, 172, 219,
        262

Brown, J.A.C., 162 n.4
Bry, Ilse, 161
Bumke, Oswald, 86
Burgess, Anthony, 40
Burnham, J.C., 162 n.4
Burt, Cyril, 207

Campbell, Roy, 166
Carnap, Rudolf, 236 n.1
Carus, Paul, 178
Cavalcanti, Giovanni, 90
Cavell, Marcia, 26
Chaplin, Charlie, 270
Charcot, Jean-Martin, 40, 206
Chekhov, Anton, 276
Chesterton, G.K., 46, 87 n.199, 181,
    268
Churchill, Winston, 265, 267
Cioffi, Frank, 211
Citizen Kane, 263
Civilization in the United States, 163
Clare, Anthony, 27
Clark, Kenneth, 278
Clark, Ronald, 205
Claudel, Paul, 74
Coleridge, Samuel T., 54
    Kubla Khan, 69–70, 189–190
Crews, Frederick, 25, 32, 75
Critical Dictionary of Psychoanalysis,
    9
Croesus, 8
Crusoe, Robinson, 39

Dalbiez, Roland, 222
Daniel (biblical), 133, 141
Dante Alighieri, 140
    La Vita Nuova, 133
Darwin, Charles, 103, 180
De Morgan, William, 36
Deutsch, Helen, 21
Dewey, John, 149
Dickens, Charles, 32, 70
    Great Expectations, 70, 76, 281,
    293
    Mystery of Edwin Drood, 70
    Our Mutual Friend, 70
Dido, 189

Dora, 107, 137, 151, 158, 185, 188,
    195, 228–29, 260
    and broad sense of 'love', 41
    and Eros, 47
    and fellatio fantasies, 48, 68, 69, 75
    Freud on, 48, 75, 97–98, 154,
    182, 192, 249, 295, 297
    hysterical symptoms of, 68–69,
    97–98
    and metaphor, 61
    questioning Freud's interpretation
    of, 132–33, 193
    Wollheim on, 153, 191
Dostoevsky (Dostoievsky), Fyodor,
    101, 128, 180, 285
    The Devils, 286
dream interpretation (*see also* Freud:
    and dream interpretation)
    different kinds of, 18–19
Dreiser, Theodore, 180
Driesch, Hans Adolf Eduard, 179
Duhem, Pierre Maurice Marie, 223
Dumas, Alexandre, *fils*
    La Dame aux camélias, 139, 183,
    285
Dunlap, Knight, 176

Eagle, Morris, 19
Eckstein, Emma, 208
Eddy, Mary Baker, 117, 231
    Science and Health, 117
Edel, Leon, 267, 271
Edelson, Marshall, 4, 19, 477
Eder, David, 262
Eidelberg, L., 194
Einstein, Albert, 212, 214, 236 n.1
Eissler, Kurt, 3, 4, 76, 86
Eliot, George
    Middlemarch, 77
Ellenberger, Henri, 76
    Discovery of the Unconscious, 161
Ellis, Havelock, 75
Ellmann, Richard, 269, 275
Encyclopaedia of Psychoanalysis, 194
Encyclopaedia of the Social Sciences,
    221, 288
Erdelyi, Matthew, 55

Erikson, Erik, 2, 162 n.4, 191, 265
Erwin, Edwin, 35, 52, 288–300
  critique of, 34, 290, 291, 294–96,
    298–300
  scientism of, 293, 295
Escalona, Sybille, 216, 221, 224
Escher, M.C., 101
Esterson, Allen, 32, 297
  Seductive Mirage, 68, 294

falsification (*see also* Freudian theory:
    and falsifiability)
  and noninstantiation, difference
    between, 5–6
falsification evasion (*see also* Freudian
    theory: and falsification
    evasion)
  and spurious confirmation,
    difference between, 21–22
Fancher, Robert
  Introduction to Psychoanalysis, 29
    n.70
Farrell, B.A., 12, 28, 116, 123, 126,
  191
Farrell, James T., 82
Fenichel, Otto, 79, 81
Ferenczi, Sandor, 19, 50, 95
Ficino, Marsilio, 90
Firth, Sir Charles, 37
Fitzgerald, F. Scott
  The Last Tycoon, 57
  This Side of Paradise, 163
Flaubert, Gustave, 276
Flew, Antony, 182, 183
Fliess, Robert, 299
Fliess, Wilhelm, 72-73
  Freud's communications to, 39, 45,
    72–73, 145, 148, 206,
    243, 245, 262
Flugel, J.C., 22, 52–53, 170, 255, 262
Forrester, John, 4, 20, 36
Forsyth, John, 262
Fowler, Alastair, 137, 295
Frank, J., 225
Frazer, James George, 103–104
Freud, Sigmund
  and allusion, 138–39

on ancestral influence, 125, 217,
    271
animism in, 86, 87, 179
and anti-Semitism, 166
apologetics for, 2–3, 17, 24, 25,
    29, 36, 50, 74, 81–82
  epistemic, 89–90
  substantive, 89
appeal of, 81–83, 84
and argument from resistance,
    81–82, 220
Autobiographical Study, 145, 259
Beyond the Pleasure Principle,
    159
case histories, 3–4 (*see also* under
    specific names)
  inconclusiveness in, 107–108
on castration, fear of, 45, 46, 49,
    51, 230
causes and reasons in, confusion
    between, 281–83
charges against, 1–2
Civilisation and Its Discontents,
    160
clarification/explanation confusion
    in, 60–64
and cocaine, 1, 201, 270
on the constitutional factor, 146–
    47, 250
on delusional jealousy, 13, 120
discrepancies in, 13–14, 43–44, 52,
    112, 122–23, 145,
    147–48, 201–202, 241,
    245, 246–47
as dogmatic, 12, 266
and dream interpretation, 6–7, 52,
    99–100, 125, 138, 187,
    190, 237 n.4, 285, 295
  ambiguity in, 183, 189
  and counterexamples, 100
  inaugurating dream, 201
  and problem of suggestion,
    256–57
  as rebus-like, 282–83
Ego and the Id, 196
and empiricism/evidence, 19–20,
    112, 240, 242, 258 (*see*

also Freud: on observa-
tion, role of)
and etiology (aetiology), 60, 61,
243–44
and therapeutic success,
relation between, 244,
255
and folk psychology, 75–77, 265
on forgetting, function of, 189
hagiography of, 39–41
effect, 41–44
on homosexuality, 12–13, 49, 120,
127
hostile reception, myth of, 161–68
on hysteria, 39–40, 47, 50, 99 n.12
and bodily symptoms, 96–98,
208
and sexual etiology, 144
indeterminate inference in, 126,
128
on infantile sexual life/etiology,
24, 111–13, 121, 125,
128–29, 145–46, 148–49,
150–51, 199–200, 229–
230, 241
elusiveness of, 129–132, 243
and falsifiability, 14, 229
as fantasy, 111, 146, 150,
199, 200, 204, 208, 228,
230, 231, 244–45, 251
as observable, 112, 258, 299
influence of, 265, 267
integrity of, as issue, 32, 34, 208,
224
Interpretation of Dreams, 18, 68,
86, 100, 124, 163, 164,
166, 180, 183, 295
Hannibal/Hasdrubal error, 183
and interpretations, role of, 111–12
Introductory Lectures, 12, 15, 70,
94, 96, 175, 177, 183,
185, 186, 196, 207, 221,
233, 253, 296
on jokes, 63, 282
Lamarckism of, 98, 271
legacy of, 77–79, 81–83
Leonardo, 126

on Leonardo, 106, 126–27, 135,
278
and libido theory, 13, 47, 114,
118–19, 121, 216, 220
objections to, 12, 15, 23, 118–
19, 121
on masturbation, 41–42, 237 n.6,
249
and materialism, 85–87, 179
methodological criticisms of, 175,
204, 207
on neuroses, 7, 101, 228
and anamnesis, relation between,
125–26
and castration, fear of, 45, 46,
230, 272
cures for, 221
and gratification, 155
and illness, 97, 101
incoherences in account of, 145
and perversions, relation
between, 119–20
and role of sexuality, 14–17,
33, 42, 44, 46, 80, 105,
118, 120–21, 129–132,
145–150, 199–200,
244–46, 250, 259
and empiricism/observation,
19–20, 112, 258
and falsifiability, 19–20, 54
and falsification/evasion, 22,
129
and precocity, 241, 249–250
and preconceived views of,
146, 149, 200, 234, 245,
248
psychoanalytic folklore of,
200
and suggestion, problem of,
246–47, 248, 256
New Introductory Lectures, 6, 61,
94, 152, 237 n.4
Nicomachean defense of, 53–54
on observation, role of, 114,
122–24 (*see also* Freud:
and empiricism/evidence)
opposition to, 166–170, 171

Outline, 7, 237 n.4
on penis envy, 272, 289
on phobias, 50, 185
preconceptions in,
problem of, 146, 148–49, 200,
206, 207, 234, 245, 248
preselection of associations in, 110
Problem of Anxiety, 152, 237 n.5
Project for a Scientific Psychology,
143
on psychoanalysis and suggestive
therapies, difference
between, 253–54
on psychology of women, 260,
272, 289
Psychopathology of Everyday Life,
192
revisionist accounts of, 24–25, 26,
27, 29, 33, 50–51, 60,
89, 296
epistemic, 89–90
substantive, 89
and seduction theory, 39, 40, 45,
124, 130, 131, 145–49,
150, 162, 225–26
abandoning of, 14–15, 39, 40,
162, 201, 203, 205, 207,
208, 240–43
contradictions/incoherences in
account of, 201–202, 206,
241, 246–47
errors of, aetiological and recon
structive, 242–43
faulty memory of, 210, 204
Grünbaum on, 2, 225–27
Masson on, 205–208
and patient testimony, role of, 2,
42–43, 199–200, 203,
206, 226
and preconception, role of, 148–
49, 206, 207, 245, 248
and prehistoric ancestors, 225,
227
and response to error, 225, 227
and suggestion, problem of,
175, 202, 240, 246–47,
259

Wollheim on, 145–49
on the 'sexual', 15, 16, 43–44, 46,
47
and Eros, 16, 28, 47
expanded sense of, 15, 16, 47–
49, 150–51, 177, 219
preconceived views of, 200
privileged role of, 24, 44, 94
similes in, 64, 110, 283
status of, 87-88
Studies on Hysteria, 64, 86, 162,
164, 165, 185, 191, 233,
234, 245, 246
sublimation theory, 173
and sublime subtext, 2–3
and suggestion, problem of, 175,
202, 240, 246–47, 248,
253, 256–59
on symbolism, 51–52, 184
on symptoms, 190
and actions, 49–50, 151–52,
188, 191
as discharge-like, 184
and gratification, 193
motives for, 185, 187–88
persistence of, 156
and wishes, relation between,
184, 187, 191, 192–93
and tally argument, 233, 234–35,
248, 253–56, 258,
259–261, 262, 297
and theory, role of, 43–44
and therapeutic efficacy, issue of,
244, 254–55, 259–262
Three Essays on Sexuality, 47, 122,
127, 164, 169, 241, 250,
258, 260
trade-off arguments for, 74–75
on transference, 174
on trauma, requirements for,
246–47
on the unconscious, 7, 94, 95–97,
99, 102, 138, 154, 182,
196
and contradiction in, 136, 296
contradictory account of, 182,
184

and hypnosis, 196–97
as instrumental, 186
and invulnerability to counter-
    example, 102–103
patient relation to, 62–63, 102–
    103, 124, 138, 154–55,
    183, 184, 194–97
as ratiocinative, 184, 186–87
and self-intimation, 183, 184,
    197, 198
somatic effects of, 98
voluntarism of, 50, 189
on wild psychoanalysis, 41, 172
on wishes, 198 (*see also* Freud: on
    symptoms, and wishes)
as causal, 184
and communication, 191
and gratification, 191–92
as providing reasons, 184
Freudian theory (*see also* psycho-
    analysis)
ambiguity in, 8–9, 296
appeal of, 170
and castration anxiety, measuring
    of, 289–290
changes in, motivation for, 19
as dehistoricized, 111, 113
and empiricism, 19–20, 23,
    226
experimental studies of,
    289–291
and falsifiability, 5–9, 14, 20, 23,
    54, 89, 156, 210, 216,
    218, 222, 288
and falsification evasion, 10, 11,
    14, 21–23, 49, 218, 219
and instantiation/confirmation
    distinction, 28–29, 210
as misleading, 8, 9, 15
as mythological, 284
nonexperimental validation for,
    292
and noninstantiation, 5–6, 54
obfuscation in, of truth and
    falsity, 20–21
on the oral personality, origin of,
    300

and patient acceptance, role of,
    297
and pseudoscience, 4, 6, 7, 10,
    18, 23, 24, 39, 140, 221–
    22, 235, 288
recycling in, 38–39, 44, 46–47,
    49, 52
revisionist accounts of, 296
    epistemic, 89–90
    substantive, 89
and spurious confirmation,
    21–22, 89, 221, 224
status of, 288
stonewalling in, 19, 20–21, 38
and testability, 4–8, 49, 137,
    138, 219, 221, 230–31,
    237 n.4, 250, 300
and thematic affinity, 292, 293,
    295
Friedel, Egon, 85
Frink, Horace, 12, 262
Fromm, Erich, 224

Gagnon, John H., 83
Galba, 8
Galileo, 35, 212
Galton, Sir Francis, 76
Gardner, Martin, 134
Gay, Peter, 2
Gellner, Ernest, 22, 289, 300
    The Psychoanalytic Movement, 251
genetic explanations, popularity of,
    265, 266
Gide, André, 180
    La Symphonie Pastorale, 139
Giorgione, 268
Glover, Edward, 19
Glover, James, 262, 298
Glymour, Clark, 4, 227–231, 237 n.6,
    249
Goffman, Erving, 82
Gomperz, Heinrich, 82 n.180
Goncourt brothers, 55
Gorer, Geoffrey, 4
Gould, Stephen Jay, 10, 31 n.73
Grainger, Percy, 56
Green, Aaron, 35

Greenwood, Edward
  Tolstoi: The Comprehensive Vision,
    36–37
Greville, Charles, 55, 166
Groddeck, George, 98
Grünbaum, Adolf, 8, 17, 29 n.70, 52,
    68, 284–85, 296
  critique of, 29 n.70, 34, 51, 70,
    212–13, 217–221,
    224–28, 231–32, 235,
    241–42, 244, 246,
    247–256, 258–263, 298,
    299
  Foundations of Psychoanalysis, 64
  on Freud
    as hospitable to refutation, 240,
      262
    as motivated by evidence, 240,
      242, 248, 251–52, 263
    necessary condition thesis
      (NCT) of, 253, 254–55,
      261
    and the problem of suggestion,
      240, 252–53, 261
  on Freudian theory
    changes in, 19
    exoneration of, 31
    as falsifiable, 15, 217–220, 225,
      251, 300
    in-itself, 218–220, 300
    and tally argument, 233, 248,
      253, 255, 259, 261,
      297
    testability of, 4–5, 6, 7, 15, 23
  on introspective access, 64–66
  on Popper, 6 n.15, 31, 211,
    212–13, 215–16, 218,
    220, 225, 226, 231–33,
    235, 236 n.2, 240, 251,
    252, 256, 262
  on pseudoscience, 224
  scientism of, 17 n.39, 281
  on seduction theory, 2, 225–27,
    240–43, 247–48

Hale, Nathan, 41
Hanaghan, Jonathan, 86

Hans/Herbert, 13–14, 128–29, 136,
    249, 298
Hanslick, Eduard, 76
Hart, Bernard, 18, 19, 175
  *Psychopathology: Its Development
    and Its Place in Medicine,*
    175
Hartmann, Eduard von, 283
Hartmann, Heinz, 298
Hemingway, Ernest, 56, 276
Hitler, Adolf, 11, 40
Hitschmann, Eduard, 262
Holbrook, David, 267
Holmes, Sherlock, 270, 298
Homburger, Eric, 268
homeopathic medicine, 117
Hook, Sidney, 179
Hoover, J. Edgar, 21
Hopkins, James, 49–51
Horney, Karen, 159
Hospers, John, 83
Hossbach memorandum, 11
Hug-Hellmuth, Hermine, 21
Huxley, Aldous, 18, 173
hysteria, pre-Freudian views of, 165
  (*see also* Freud: on
    hysteria)

Inglis, Brian, 117
instantiation and confirmation, differ-
    ence between, 28–29, 30
internal soliloquy, function of, 269,
    270, 278 n.1
*International Encyclopedia of the
    Social Sciences,* 88, 288
Irwin, Edward, 64, 68, 70, 71
Isaacs, Susan, 298
Isserlin, Max, 168

James, Henry, 267, 271
James, William, 10, 54, 67, 198, 292
Janet, Pierre, 172, 253
Jastrow, Joseph, 174
Jelliffe, Smith Ely, 163
John, Saint (biblical), 141
Johnson, Samuel, 25, 164, 269, 276,
    277

Journey to the Western Islands, 35
Life of Pope, 81
Jones, Ernest, 158, 163, 168, 169,
    172, 182, 221, 262, 271,
    273
    on analysis as easy to learn, 38
    on emergence of dissident views,
        17
    on Hans/Herbert, 129
    on imponderable data, 74
    on omnipotence of thoughts in
        Freud, 50, 98
    Papers on Psychoanalysis, 178
    on reception of Freud, 161
    on the seduction stories, 199,
        244
    Sigmund Freud: Life and Work,
        17, 50, 98, 129, 161, 206
Jones, Hugh Lloyd, 9
Jones, Seaborn, 47, 48, 81
    Treatment or Torture, 81
Jonson, Ben, 275
Joyce, James, 275
    Ulysses, 181
Jung, Carl Gustav, 15, 16, 17, 18, 38,
        44, 173, 176, 180, 189
Jupp, James, 13–14

Kaufmann, Walter, 28, 31
Kazin, Alfred, 85, 180
Kepler, Johannes, 236 n.2
Kerr, John, 4
King, A.F.A., 165
King Midas, 190, 192
Kinsey, Alfred Charles, 83
Kohut, Heinz, 282
Kipling, Rudyard, 39
Kline, Paul, 289
Kraeplin, Emile, 162, 253
Krafft-Ebing, Richard, 39, 146,
        162 n.4
Kraus, Karl, 167
Kurzweil, Edith, 40–41
Kuttner, Alfred, 163

Ladd-Franklin, Christine, 167
Lamarck, Jean Baptiste de, 98

Langer, Walter C., 266
Langs, Robert, 65
Laplanche, Jean, 47
    Language of Psychoanalysis, 44
Lawrence, D.H., 163, 181, 265, 267,
        268, 272–73
    The Rainbow, 21
    Sons and Lovers, 267
Lawrence, T.E., 267
Le May, Jack, 79
LeMot, Auguste, 276
Lear, Jonathan, 65
Leonardo da Vinci, 191 (*see also*
        Freud: on Leonardo)
Lewis, Sinclair, 276
libido concept, and testability, 5 (*see
        also* Freud: and libido
        theory)
Lind, James, 116
Lloyd Jones-Tacitus effect, 9, 41
Lombroso, Cesare, 30–31, 31 n.73
Lonigan, Studs, 82
Lorenz, Paul. *See* Rat Man
Lovejoy, Arthur, 91
    Great Chain of Being, 84
Lowell, Percival, 124–25
Ludwig, Emil, 274
    Carnet de la Drole de Guerre, 273
Luhan, Mabel Dodge, 163
Luther, Martin, 265, 266

Macaulay, Thomas Babington, 37,
        133, 141, 273–74
Macauley, Rose, 26
MacIntyre, Alasdair, 183, 288
Mack, John, 267
Macmillan, Malcolm, 19, 32, 68
    Freud Evaluated, 19, 282
Malcolm, Janet, 2, 3, 35, 284–85
Malcolm, Norman, 94
Manicheans, 86
Mann, Thomas, 85, 86, 180, 274
    The Black Swan, 208
    The Magic Mountain, 58, 83, 173
Manuel, Frank E., 267
Martian canals, 124–25
Martin, Michael, 11–12

Masson, Jeffrey M., 205–208, 241, 280
Maugham, William Somerset, 276
McDougall, William, 179
Medawar, Peter, 3, 30, 31, 288
Meehl, Paul, 295
Melbourne, Lord, 166
Mencken, H.L., 163
Mercier, Charles, 167, 169
Merimée, Prosper, 55, 66, 267
Merleau-Ponty, Maurice, 134
Merrick, John, 265
Mill, John Stuart, 54, 268
Milton, John, 190
  Paradise Lost, 69
Mischel, Walter, 83 n.181
Mitchell, S.W., 169, 262
Mitchell, S. Weir, 169
Mitty, Walter, 193
Möbius, Paul, 148
Monroe, Marilyn, 2
Montagu, Ashley, 265
Montaigne, Michel de, 286
Moore, G.E., 103, 105, 107, 113
Morris, Desmond, 60
Moses (biblical), 43
Murray, Gilbert
  Five Stages of Greek Religion, 84

Nagel, Ernst, 255
Nagel, Thomas, 17 n.39, 31, 47, 67, 298
  as apologist, 82
  on Freud's critics, 81–82, 84
  on infantile sexuality, 71, 78
  revisionism of, 29
  on 'rudimentary Freudianism', 73, 80, 90
Nero, 8, 9
Newton, Isaac, 141, 267
  Observations on the Prophecies of Daniel, 133
Nietzsche, Friedrich, 160, 178, 180, 204
Nixon, Richard M., 2

O., Anna, 20, 40–41

Oberndorf, C.P., 167
  History of Psychoanalysis in America, 174
Oedipus complex, 255
  critique of, 44–46, 49
  discovery of, 1, 44, 199, 207
  as replacement for seduction theory, 205, 207, 280
Oedipus legend, 171
  and symbolism, 51, 106
O'Hara, John, 276, 277
Orwell, George, 28, 53, 181
  Nineteen Eighty-Four, 294

Pappenheim, Bertha, 20
Pareto, Vilfredo, 133
Parsons, Elsie Clews, 163
Paul, Saint (biblical), 16, 28
Pears Cyclopedia, 87, 288
penis envy, and revisionism, 27–28, 36, 89 (*see also* Freud: on penis envy)
Percy, Walker, 56
Peters, Richard, 182, 183, 187
Peterson, Frederick, 176
Pfister, Oscar, 16, 262
Pilate, Pontius, 216
Plath, Sylvia, 267
Plato, 16, 28, 47
Poe, Edgar Allan
  Fall of the House of Usher, 78
Pontalis, Jean-Bertrand, 47
  Language of Psychoanalysis, 44
Popper, Karl Raimund, 4–5, 5 n.12, 6 n.15, 116, 236 n.1, 299–300
  on Adler, 21, 214
  Conjectures and Refutations, 212
  demarcation criterion of, 211, 235
  and inductivists, difference between, 213
  Logic of Scientific Discovery, 211–12
  on the nonscientific, 213–14
  psychoanalysis as, 213
  on the Oedipus effect, 212, 215, 233, 234, 240

on problem of suggestion, in
    psychoanalysis, 252
on pseudoscience, 211, 214, 224,
    236 n.3, 299
and ambivalence, 215, 221
psychoanalysis as, 210, 214, 215
as turning falsifiers into confir-
    mations, 214–15
and unfalsifiability, 210–11, 212,
    213, 214, 215, 236–37
    n.2
on scientific method, 212
Post, Laurens van der, 268
Prince, Morton, 12, 253
Proust, Marcel, 58, 267, 268, 276,
    277
pseudoscience
    characteristics of, 115–16, 118
    and falsifiability, 7, 210, 232, 235
    and falsification evasion, 10
    and instantiation/confirmation
        distinction, 30
    and untestability, 6–7
psychoanalysis, 115, 140 (*see also*
        Freudian theory)
    and anamnesis, 55–58
    and apologists, 91
    appeal of, 171
    and causation/clarification
        distinction in, 56–59
    changes in, 27, 91–92
    core claim of, 115
    critique of/objections to, 14, 83–
        84, 88, 172–78
        on symbolism, 176–77
    and disinterestedness, importance
        of, 33–34, 74
    doubts about, 18–19
    fabrication in, 20
    and falsifiability/falsifiers, 23, 223
    and falsification evasion (refutation
        avoidance), 11, 49, 117,
        136
    foundations of, 20, 51–52
    and humanistic evidential standards,
        292
    and imponderable data, 73–74

and instantiation/confirmation
    distinction, 28–29, 30
and introspection, 64–65
legends surrounding, 2–3
and misleading/underdetermining
    distinction, 223
and nuances, role of, 298
and the past, meaning of, 58–59
and pathos
    animistic, 84–85
    metaphysical, 84, 91
and patient-endorsement, 67–69
and penis envy, fate of, 27–28
and plausible deniability, 9, 25, 27
as pseudoscience, 91, 115–16, 223,
    232, 235
reception of, 163, 167, 173, 175–
    78
    as hostile, 166–69, 172, 174
and recycling, 49
and reductios, 72–74
revisionism in, 24–27, 33, 36
schools of, 17
self-deception in, 36-38
and self-knowledge, 66–67
and sexual emphasis, 169–73
    distancing from, 26
and spuriousness, 30–31, 69–72,
    90
status of, 91
and testability/refutability, 49, 116,
    123, 216–17, 223
as testimonial, 32, 74
as uncanny, 95, 101
Ptolemy, 133
Putnam, J.J., 175–76, 262
pyramidologists, 134, 141
Pyrrhus, 8

Quintilian, 86
Quinton, Anthony, 22

Rachman, Stanley, 232
Rado, Sandor, 86
Rank, Otto, 19, 24, 96, 147, 237 n.5
Rapaport, David, 164, 166
Raphael, 73, 74

Rat Man (Paul Lorenz), 54, 137, 138, 182, 225, 227–28, 229–230, 248–49
  Edelson on, 4
  Freud on, 185, 229–230, 248–49, 252, 258, 294
  Glymour on, 4, 227
  'great obsessional fear' of, 72, 252, 294
  Kerr on, 4
  Wollheim on, 157
Reichians, 24
Rembrandt van Rijn, 95
Rhees, Rush, 94
Rifkin, Alfred H., 161
Rivers, Baron William Halse, 18
Riviere, Joan, 38
Robert, Marthe, 162 n.4
Robinson, Carl, 288
Rokitanski, Carl Freiherr von, 74
Ross, T.A., 177
Roudinesco, Elisabeth, 20
'rudimentary Freudianism', 73, 80, 90
Ruskin, John, 268
Rycroft, Charles, 9, 191, 193

Sachs, Bernard, 170, 174
Sachs, David, 29, 51–52
Sachs, Hans, 180
Sade, Marquis de, 159
Sainte-Beuve, Charles Augustin, 77, 276
Santayana, George, 166, 268
Sartre, Jean-Paul, 268, 273
Saussure, Ferdinand de, 79
Schafer, Roy, 59
Scheler, Max, 6
Schimek, Jean, 42–43
Schmidl, Fritz, 70–71, 72
Schopenhauer, Arthur, 178
Schwab, Sidney, 262
Segal, Hannah, 299
Selected Papers in Hysteria, 172
Schrödinger, Erwin, 275
Seldes, Gilbert, 175
  Can Such Things Be?, 174
Selesnick, Sheldon, 167, 168

Shakow, D., 164, 166
Shaw, George Bernard, 91, 178
Sidis, Boris, 169, 176, 253
Sigonious, 133
Silverman, Lloyd, 291–92
Simmel, Georg, 159
Simon, William, 83
Skinner, B.F., 296
Skoda, Henri, 74
Sophocles, 171
Southard, E.E., 167
spurious allusiveness, examples of, 133–34 (*see also* psychoanalysis: and spuriousness)
Stafford-Clark, David
  What Freud Really Said, 162 n.4
Stekel, Wilhelm, 41, 96, 186
Stoddart, W.H.B., 167
Storr, Anthony, 50–51, 75, 267
Strachey, James, 41–42
Strachey, John, 24
Stravinsky, Igor, 163
Sulloway, Frank, 2, 87, 205
Sutherland, Stuart, 255
Suttie, Ian, 208, 231
Svevo, Italo, 171, 284
  Confessions of Zeno, 171
Swift, Jonathan, 274
Szasz, Thomas S., 3, 30, 288

Tacitus, 9
Tacitus effect, 9 (*see also* Lloyd Jones-Tacitus effect)
Tannenbaum, Samuel, 18, 38, 176
Taylor, A.J.P., 11
Temple, Sir William, 274
Tennyson, Alfred Lord
  The Princess, 164
Ternan, Ellen Lawless, 70
Thurstone, L.L., 171
Tolstoi (Tolstoy), Leo
  Anna Karenina, 76, 195–96
  'The Kreuzer Sonata', 76
  War and Peace, 36–37
Trevelyan, Sir George Otto,
  Life and Letters of Lord Macaulay, 273

Trevor-Roper, Hugh, 11
Trollope, Anthony
    Phineas Finn, 212
Tuke, Hack, 165

the unconscious (*see also* Freud: on
        the unconscious)
    in folk psychology, 76–77
    patient relation to, 195
underdetermining and misleading,
        difference between, 7–8
Updike, John, 65, 66

Van Gogh, Vincent, 106, 275
Victoria, Queen, 166
Viereck, G.S., 39
Villaret, Albert
    Medical Dictionary, 144
Voloshinov, Valentin Nikolaevich, 46

Waelder, Robert, 27, 29, 34–35, 38,
        38 n.90, 62, 74, 298
Wagner, Richard
    Die Meistersinger, 76
Waite, Robert G.C., 265
Washington, George, 199
Waugh, Evelyn
    Brideshead Revisited, 220
Webster, Richard, 32
Wells, Frederick Lyman, 18, 19, 176
Welles, Orson, 263
Wheeler, William Morton, 171
White, William Alanson, 167
Whyte, Lancelot Law, 163
Williams, Tom, 38
Wilson, Edmund, 275
Wisdom, John O., 5, 56, 59, 137–38,
        194–96, 236 n.1
Wittels, Fritz, 105
Wittgenstein, Ludwig, 193–94, 263,
        276
    on aesthetics, 103–105
    Blue Book, 101
    Brown Book, 105
    on Freud, 93, 113, 280–81, 287
    appeal of, 94–95, 97, 106, 110,
        114, 284

confusion in, 59, 61, 65, 184, 281–
        82
    on dream interpretation, 99, 100,
        107, 109, 282–83, 285
    on jokes, 282
        as notational, 98, 102
        as pseudo-explanatory, 79, 80
        similes in, 64, 110, 283
    Philosophical Investigations, 104,
        113, 114
    on psychoanalysis, 193, 286
        as aesthetic, 64, 103
        as uncanny, 284
    scientism of, 281
    on the unconscious, 94, 101–102
    Zettel, 99, 113
Wohlgemuth, Adolf, 18, 19, 169–170
Wolf Man, 41, 47, 54, 57, 67, 158,
        182, 293–94
    Eissler on, 4
    Freud on, 32, 48, 68, 75, 124,
        185, 188, 251, 252, 260–
        61, 297, 298
    Gorer on, 4
    primal scene of, 17 n.39, 57, 66,
        293
Wollheim, Richard, 27, 111, 282
    on the constitutional factor, 146
    on the death instinct, 158–59
    on Dora, 153
    on Freud's greatness, 160
    on gratification, 155
    oversights in, 144–45
    on Rat Man, 296
    on repression, 155
    on sadism and masochism, 159
    on seduction theory, 42, 145, 147,
        149
    on sexuality, Freud's extended
        sense of, 47–49, 150,
        219
    infantile, 145, 149
        and neuroses, 144–46, 149
    on symptoms, 151–53, 157, 182,
        184
    on the unconscious, 155, 182
    on wishes, 184, 185, 187, 190–91

Wolpert, Lewis
  Unnatural Nature of Science,
     6 n.15
Woodworth, R.S., 17, 18, 19, 222–23
Wordsworth, William, 64
Wortis, Joseph, 60

Yorke, Clifford, 27
A Young Girl's Diary, 20

Ziehen, Theodor, 253
Zola, Émile, 276